Mors Mystica: Black Metal Theory Symposium

MORS MYSTICA

11.00–12.15: CONTANIMATION & PURIFICATION
Following the Stench: Watain and Putrefaction Mysticism (Drew Daniel) – Ablaze in the Bath of Fire (Brad Baumgartner) – Mycelegium (James Harris) – dying to find I was never there (Teresa Gillespie)

12.15–1.30: BLACKENING BLACK
'It's a suit! It's ME!': Hyper-Star and Hyper-Hero through Black Sabbath's Iron Man (Caoimhe Doyle & Katherine Foyle) – Autonomy of Death, Nothing Like This (Daniel Colucciello Barber, via skype) – The Day of My Death Had Finally Arrived (Simon Critchley) – Ed Keller

1.30–2.30 BREAK
How Dead is a Corpse-Painted Face? Patterns of a Visual Mysticism (Dominik Irtenkauf, video)

2.30–3.45: DEATH OF DEATH
The Tongue-Tied Mystic: Aaaarrrgghhh! Fuck Them! Fuck You! (Gary J. Shipley, video) – The Perichoresis of Music, Art, and Philosophy (Hunter Hunt Hendrix) – On Darkness Itself (Niall W. R. Scott) – Xenharmonic Black Metal: Radical Intervallics as Apophatic Ontotheology (Brooker Buckingham)

3.45–5.00. LAST RITES
Your Death Has Already Occurred: On the Archaeology of the Body (Dylan Trigg) – Seven Propositions On the Secret Kissing of Black Metal: OSKVLVM (Edia Connole) – Floating Tomb: On Inquisition (Nicola Masciandaro) – Black Bile (Eugene Thacker)

Organizers: Edia Connole and Nicola Masciandaro
[floatingtomb@gmail.com]

BLACK METAL THEORY SYMPOSIUM

25 April 2015
St. Vitus Bar
Brooklyn, NY
11-5

SAINT · VITUS

Only that person who says: My soul chooses hanging, and my bones death can truly embrace this fire ... for it is absolutely true that no one can see me and live. Bonaventure, Itinerarium Mentis in Deum

MORS MYSTICA

Black Metal Theory Symposium

Edited by

Edia Connole & Nicola Masciandaro

First published in 2015 by

SCHISM PRESS

An imprint of Gobbet press

schismmsihcs.wordpress.com

MORS MYSTICA: BLACK METAL THEORY
SYMPOSIUM
© The authors and Schism Press

Cover image: Magdalena Gornik on Good Friday
(http://zupnija-sodrazica.rkc.si/MagdalenaGornik/
mistika_A.html)

ISBN-13: 978-0692492093
ISBN-10: 0692492097

CONTENTS

APPENDIX

On "Heroes/Helden"

Edia Connole & Nicola Masciandaro

To be a hero—in the most universal sense of the word—
means to aspire to absolute triumph. But such triumphs
come only through death. Heroism means transcending
life; it is a fatal leap into nothingness.
> – Emil M. Cioran, *On the Heights of Despair*

Freedom? it's my final refuge, I forced myself to freedom
and I bear it not like a talent but with heroism: I'm
heroically free . . . I don't impart confidences. Instead I
metallize myself . . . I construct something free of me
and of you—this is my freedom that leads to death.
> – Clarice Lispector, *Agua Viva*

[I]n the seething blaze, you turned to ash. . . . Like a
forest fire the flame roared on, and burned your flesh
away. Next day at dawn . . . we picked your pale bones
from the char to keep in wine and oil. A golden amphora
your mother gave for this—Hephaistos' work, a gift from
Dionysos. In that vase . . . hero, lie your pale bones . . .
We . . . heaped a tomb for these upon a foreland . . . to
be a mark against the sky for voyagers in this generation
and those to come.
> – Homer, *The Odyssey*

Realization is for heroes who, while the knife is slashing
their throats, take pleasure in the pain of dying.
> – Meher Baba

They who thus conquer / In the storm of love / Are
veritable heroes; / But they who take any rest / And do
not continue to the end / Are rightly condemned.
> – Hadewijch

1

The idea of this commentary is to consider "Heroes/Helden," a cover of the famous Bowie song by Tombs,[1] in light of the fires of mystical death. In the weeks before the Mors Mystica symposium, the music video by the Brooklyn-based black metal band spontaneously suggested itself as an index of the event. Whatever the secret or obvious links between black metal and Bowie—"I was influenced by Bowie" (Necrobutcher of Mayhem)[2]—this seems like an unlikely musical gloss on a black metal theory symposium dedicated to self-annihilation. On further reflection, the setting of the video by Tombs in New York City, the promise of a metallic blackening of the pop romanticism of the original ("Bowie simply glosses over the boundless idealism of his song called 'Heroes' [sic] by being ironic about it right from the start"),[3] and above all the profound spiritual connection between heroism and mystical death, their unending cotermination in dying to oneself through love—"Being is dying by loving" (MB)—show "Heroes/Helden" to be a perfect song for this commentary (and proper way to introduce this volume). If the "heroes" of the song are only heroes "for one day," all the more so does "Heroes/Helden" point the way to the sword-path upon which true heroes "die daily" (1 Cor. 15:31).[4]

---

[1] Tombs, "'Heroes' (Official Music Video)," directed by Jacyln Sheer and Samantha Astolfi (Relapse Records, 2014), https://vimeo.com/ 108837545.

[2] Dayal Patterson, *Black Metal: Evolution of the Cult* (Port Townsend, WA: Feral House, 2013), 150.

[3] Tobias Rüther, *Heroes: David Bowie and Berlin* (London: Reaktion Books, 2014), 135.

[4] "This Path is strewn only with hardships, and only heroes can tread it. Many pundits are there to give lectures and speak about philosophy, but only a hero can tread the Path. It is like balancing oneself on the edge of a sword. What am I to do? I have to keep you alive while jabbing my knife in your chest, which causes you to cry out. What can we do? This is our situation" (Meher Baba, quoted in *Lord Meher*, 1027, http:// http://www.lordmeher.org). Cf. "Life with Meher Baba was like walking on the edge of a sword—walking on it even though crippled in one leg! Such a life cannot be imagined. Daily, one had to bear lightning-like blows; yet, strangely, one would be in such a condition that, although paining from the wounds, one would not like to be left 'unharmed' without them! On the one hand, the mind would reel under the attack, but on the other, the heart would desire more punishment! Thus, because of the continuous shower of 'blows to the ego,' the mind was becoming

2

"Heroes / Helden"

As seen in the closing credits of the music video, Tombs dispense with the quotation marks which conspicuously enclose the title of Bowie's original in an "ironic distance"—a distance nonetheless always already closed by the sonic immanence of the love of music (music of love) wherein the twin correlational hallucination of the for-us and the in-itself is inversely overcome: "There is no outside! But we forget this with all sounds; how lovely it is that we forget!"[5] Counter to the critical reception of Bowie's self-citing title as a camp gesture whose sophistication the naïve listener or believer in heroism must be instructed in,[6] Tombs erect an unadorned

---

powerless and the heart strong" (*Lord Meher*, 3669). On the traditional significance of the sword bridge, famously traversed by Sir Lancelot, Doña Luisa Coomaraswamy writes, "It is because the Thread of the Spirit is at once so tenuous and of such wiry strength that the Bridge is so often described in the traditional literature either as a ray of light, or as consisting of a thread or a hair, or as sharper than a razor or the edge of a sword" ("The Perilous Bridge of Welfare," *Harvard Journal of Asiatic Studies* 8 [1944]: 196–213).

[5] Friedrich Nietzsche, *Thus Spoke Zarathustra*, trans. Adrian Del Caro (Cambridge: Cambridge University Press, 2006), 175.

[6] "Bowie was slap-bang in the middle of what Susan Sontag defined as the sensibility of camp . . . 'Camp sees everything in quotation marks. It is not a lamp but a "lamp".' Or, in Bowie's case it is 'Heroes', not Heroes, implying an ironic distancing lost in its live power-pop renditions" (David Buckley, "Still Pop's Faker?," in *The Bowie Companion*, ed. by Elizabeth Thompson and David Gutman [London: Macmillan, 1993], 4–5). "For all of its latter-day recognition . . . '"Heroes"' is still widely mistaken to be an anthem to fist-pumping optimism, when in fact Bowie is singing about the self-delusion of clinging to a relationship that might last, at best, 'just for one [more] day.' The title, moreover, is framed in what Bowie would

3

heroic monument and monument to heroism under cover of the cover itself, over the aegis of the undying artist-hero whose epigraphically present name now both signs the work's authentic saying and serves as the ur-quote mark presiding over its freedom from "the vicious circle of authority and citation."[7] This is Tombs' "Heroes/Helden," not "'Heroes/Helden'" by David Bowie. The cover's interment of the song as writing—not "by" but "written by"—puts to rest its unsung, musically invisible quotation marks. Activating the principle of the cover as citation *in toto*, Tombs encrypt "'Heroes'" in a tomb of total citation that resurrects the song from semantic suspension, paradoxically restoring it to itself in a new version which always-never existed, a lyrical hybrid of "'Heroes'" and "'Heroes/Helden'." Such is the order of black metal: "black metal perpetuates itself via a satanic logic that corrodes and occludes its own resources while allowing them to remain apparent. You could say that black metal practices what Benjamin called 'the art of citing without quotation marks.' Rebelling against the logic or order whereby the citation produces authority, black metal weaponizes citation against its own authorizing aura. For black metal, repetition IS the original."[8] And such is the real point, the whole point, of Bowie's original marks, which is not to be ironic about heroism but to *get* it by knowing that the joke is on you if you do not presently die to yourself and become who you really are, i.e. *be* a hero—whatever the artist and critics say *about* the song, or what anyone says about anything for that matter. As Sir Gawain must remind Yvain, lest he become "one of those men . . . who are worth less because of their wives," "Now is not the time to dream your life away but to frequent tournaments, engage in combat, and joust vigorously, whatever it

---

later refer to as ironic quotation marks—suggesting that the 'only true heroic act' available, as he told *Melody Maker's* Allan Jones shortly after the song's release, was to enjoy 'the very simple pleasure of being alive'" (Thomas Jerome Seabrook, *Bowie in Berlin: A New Career in a New Town* [London: Jawbone, 2008], 179).

[7] Giorgo Agamben, *Stanzas: Word and Phantasm in Western Culture*, trans. Ronald L. Martiez (Minneapolis: University of Minnesota Press, 1993), 74.

[8] Nicola Masciandaro, "Black Metal Theory: Interrogation I: Nicola Masciandaro," *Avant-garde Metal* (2012), http://avantgarde-metal.com/content/stories2.php?id=245.

might cost you."[9] We must thus recognize the heroic impulse of black metal as a classical, time-entombing force that, against the nauseating predilection of historically-framed consciousness for cowardly (i.e. passive-aggressive) self-contextualization, affirms at once the novelty of the ancient and the antiquity of the new via a *medievalization* of authorship: "for the Middle Ages there is not, in fact, any possibility of citing a text in the modern sense of the word, because the work of the *auctor* also comprehends its own citation, such that it is possible to say, despite the apparent

---

[9] Chretien de Troyes, *Arthurian Romances* (New York: Penguin, 1991), 326. The listener-viewer will readily perceive how the issue of spiritual manliness is at stake in a Bowie cover by a Brooklyn black metal band whose multi-colored music video features Ralph Schmidt (of Planks) channeling the German vocals from a Williamsburg rooftop—

—and how the issue comes down to the meaning of the mustache: "A mustache is a sign of manliness—to endure all the strains in adverse circumstances, both material and spiritual, and against the powerful forces of maya. It is a sign to stand up against anger, lust, and greed, and not to be so delicate, sensitive, and feeble-minded like a [fickle] woman. A man must be the personification of manliness, always ready to offer his head when the time comes. Men with such qualifications are required in this Path. They are real heroes who endure all hardships and suffering to reach the Goal. All other men are cowards in spite of flaunting mustaches, however big. In short, be true to your mustache; that is, be a man. Don't frown and fret and try to run away like cowards from the battlefield of the Path without winning. Heroes do or die!" (Meher Baba, quoted in *Lord Meher*, 1129).

paradox, that the medieval texts are contained as citations within the *antiqui auctores* (ancient authors), which explains, among other things, the medieval predilection for the gloss as a literary form."[10] "Heroes/Helden" is a monument to the now-living form of *immemorial memory* that seizes the atemporal day and unearths the universality of the local. As Tombs sing in "Séance," "The world of memory / Exists outside of time / Serpent's eyes / Timeless thoughts / Complete the chain / Immortality / I hear the call / From beyond this realm / Exist outside of time."[11] Someone will probably object that the question of the title's quotation marks is a small matter, not worthy of such interpretation—thereby proving their ignorance of the fact that real greatness works in liberty from the distinction between small and great works: "If the aspirant is completely detached from all works and their results he becomes free from the vitiating opposites of the great and small things. *The worldly-minded feel their separative existence through achievements.* . . . They grasp at great things and avoid the little things. *From the spiritual point of view, the so-called little things are often seen to be as important as the so-called great things.* The aspirant has no motive to eschew the one and seek the other; therefore he attends to little things with as much zest as to great things."[12] And as Marguerite Porete, heretic of the Free Spirit, points out, the spirit of commentary—blowing where it will, swarming through monuments and summiting its mountains of mole-hills—is secretly inseparable from the will to mystical self-annihilation: "Gloss this if you wish, or if you can. If you cannot, you are not of this kind; but if you are of this kind, it will be opened to you. You would already be profoundly annihilated if you had the means by which you could hear it, for otherwise I would not say it."[13] [NM]

---

[10] Agamben, *Stanzas*, 74.
[11] Tombs, "Séance," *Savage Gold* (Relapse Records, 2014).
[12] Meher Baba, *Discourses*, 6th ed., 3 vols. (San Francisco: Sufism Reoriented, 1967), 3:125.
[13] Marguerite Porete, *The Mirror of Simple Souls*, trans. Ellen L. Babinsky (New York: Paulist Press, 1993), 183.

(A Wall of Sound)

A wall of sound—a familiar plodding rhythm and tempo—thrusts itself upon the listener. Robert Fripp's guitar, which would rupture this at about seven seconds in Bowie and Eno's version, is notably absent from that of Tombs (the attentive listener will have anticipated this—before the first note was audible she was already straddling a soundscape where "The dead sup with the dead o'er flowing vat, / And searing candles cleanse the rotting gloom; / And they who stood in sorrow's joy and pain, / Tread now through hell's ecstatical refrain").[14] Though equally propulsive, Mike Hill's guitar eschews the upper atmosphere to which Fripp's clings— promising an epic melody that never quite comes. Here, instead, you are propelled down and along a hopeless and hopelessly striated surface. Fripp's sonic cartography—the very particular stepping and swaying that created feedback loops in Hansa's Studio 2 in 1977—is recapitulated visually in the accompanying music video, mapped onto the unremitting flow of capital: the still-concrete madness of governments that marks "the earth's coruscating darkness."[15] In loopy luminous lines of flight, "the earth is given a life, what that invades so dreamily, one that does not seem to change as the surface burns, as the roots die out."[16] A wall that begets a wall that begets a wall that begets a . . . Echoing hell's ecstatical refrain, the metalhead's guitar screams: Ride On! Cf. "I ride in full course swift / Through the dark night and the rain pours down."[17] [EC]

---

[14] Robert Nelson, "Under the Tomb," *Sable Revery: Poems, Sketches, Letters* (Marcellus, MI: Nodens Chapbooks, 2012), 20. My gratitude to the Sin-Eater for gifting me with this morbid anthology.
[15] See Ben Woodard, "The Blackish Green Of The Greenish Black Or, The Earth's Coruscating Darkness," in "Black Metal," eds. Nicola Masciandaro and Reza Negarestani, special issue, *Glossator: Practice and Theory of the Commentary* 6 (2012): 73–87.
[16] Woodard, "Earth's Coruscating Darkness," 82.
[17] Wolves in the Throne Room, "(A Shimmering Radiance) Diadem of 12 Stars," *Diadem of 12 Stars* (Vendlus Records, 2006).

I, I will be king . . .

("Better to reign in Hell, than serve in Heaven.")[18] The rider, the "I" who takes charge of the utterance, does so in a soft German accent—at once Hill's nod to the scarred heart of Europe that inspired the original, and to a more youthful, prestigious time in European history when the German people, and more broadly— the young men of the Germanic tribes and tradition, were at the very origin of the order of chivalry (from French *chevalier*, "horsemen"—"The rider, the rider. The rider is the wretched man, the human with one of the first technologies—the object of burden and flight, the first invasion machine."[19] Cf. "On the fields we hunted them down / Stole their pride and burned their towns"; *"Angelen en Saxens hieven het zwaard / Kelten en Picten werden nicht gespaard"*).[20] This phonetic quirk has the advantage of affectively paving the way for the declamatory lyric that follows— the black metal artist announcing, quietly but resolutely, the "I" that "will be king" ("A dark and fell rider clad in garments of shadow / Is the lord of this place / A cruel and wanton king / A priest of a black religion is he." Cf. "I was born on the cemetery / Under the sign of the moon / Raised from my grave by the dead / I was made mercenary / In the legions of hell / Now I'm king of pain / I'm insane").[21] The loopy luminous lines of flight that now stream from Hill's eyes in the accompanying music video, creating a *fatal portrait* in which he stands stoically ablaze,[22] betray something of what Georges Bataille would call the "*sacred* and

---

[18] John Milton, *The Paradise Lost*, ed. Rev. James R. Boyd (New York: A. S. Barnes & Co., 1867), 32.
[19] Woodard, "Earth's Coruscating Darkness," 79.
[20] Forefather, "To the Mountains they Fled," *Ours is the Kingdom* (Karmageddon Media, 2004); Heidevolk, *De Strijdlust Is Geboren*, audio recording, Heidevolk, 2005, quoted in Lorin Renodeyn, "Old Germanic Heritage In Metal: A Comparative Study Of Present-day Metal Lyrics And Their Old Germanic Sources," http://lib.ugent.be/fulltxt/RUG01/001/ 457/555/RUG01001457555_2011_0001_AC.pdf.
[21] Wolves in the Throne Room, "Vastness and Sorrow," *Two Hunters* (Southern Lord Recordings, 2004); Mercyful Fate, "Evil," *Melissa* (Roadrunner Records, 1983).
[22] Momentarily framed like the figure on the front cover of the '86 album by the eponymously titled King Diamond, *Fatal Portrait* (Roadrunner Records, 1986).

inhuman impression the initiated young men of the[se] Germanic tribes may have—and ritually must have—given of themselves."[23]
Recalling a passage from Chrétien de Troyes's twelfth-century Arthurian Romance, *Perceval*, in which a naïve young man suddenly sees, on a sunny day, *"venir cinq chevalier armés / et parés de toutes leurs armes"* [five armed knights coming through the woods, armor from head to toe], and believes them to be angels, and their leader to be God, Bataille notes how he then prostrates himself in worship: *"Êtes-Vous-Dieu ?—Eh! Non, ma foi.—Qui êtes-vous donc?—Chevalier suis"* [Are you God?—No, by my faith.—Who are you, then?—I am a knight].[24] As the latter will go on to say, without any *actual* prestige (stemming from heroic deeds) such prostration would have been unintelligible, and thus redundant in medieval literary expression. And it is precisely this that paves the way for its expression in more ancient times in the creation of mythic beings, and in modern times through the creation of "heroes" of novels, or indeed that of Bowie's song. However, as Nicola has already noted, the scare quotes surrounding the original song title are thereby important in their intention, signaling that the modern—unlike the medieval or more ancient—hero is nothing but pure invention. As Bowie himself says of the context—Cold War Berlin—in which this song was written: "The only heroic act one can fucking well pull out of the bag in a situation like that is to get on with life from the very simple pleasure of remaining alive despite every attempt being made to kill you."[25] In this respect, the "king" in question has transitional value, marking the passage from (chivalric savagism, and) an ethics of passion to one of moralizing reason (and *cynicism*)—"to a world in which the warrior's immediate inclination, as it existed in the Germanic tradition, was being called into question."[26]
So, while the singular pronoun, "I," is of no importance in itself—to the extent that, as Bataille notes in *Inner Experience*, "I

[23] Georges Bataille, "Medieval French Literature, Chivalric Morals, and Passion—from *Critique* 38 (1949)," trans. Laurence Petit, in Bruce Holsinger, *The Premodern Condition: Medievalism and the Making of Theory* (Chicago and London: The University of Chicago Press, 2007), 207.
[24] Bataille, "Chivalric Morals, and Passion," 207.
[25] Seabrook, *Bowie in Berlin*, 179; my emphasis.
[26] Bataille, "Chivalric Morals, and Passion," 208.

am any being: name, identity, the historical don't change anything. He (reader [/listener]) is anyone and I (author) am anyone"[27]—for the "king" that this "I" will become— cf. "For not what thou art, nor what thou hast been, beholdeth God with His merciful eyes; but that thou wouldest be"[28]—the historical changes everything, because Hill's Germanic accent situates this "any being" on the other side of a temporal divide that saw the "king" succumb to a state of moralizing reason—primarily during the period from the eleventh to the thirteenth century in which Chrétien de Troyes writes. This is the time of *chansons de geste* or romances of the Round table, when Christianity and reason—or, quite simply, Christianity as the popular form moral philosophy took when grounded in reason—was no longer foreign to knights. What emerges most pertinently from an analysis of knighthood at this time, is that the spirit of the knight—as depicted in the *chansons de geste*—was often contrary to the chivalry of pure passion that grounded the Germanic tradition, "in that their authors, even though they glorify the hero's wild and frantic valor, sometimes condemn it from the point of view of reason—or piety, endowed with the feelings of reason."[29]

This subjection of an ethics of passion to one of moralizing reason is most thoroughly explored by Bataille in a little known lecture from 1947, where, in an excursus on the Marquis de Sade's *Philosophy in the Bedroom* (1795), he critiques contemporary ethics upon which such behaviour judgements are founded.[30] As Jean Francois Lyotard would note, the Sade that Bataille is concerned with throughout this lecture, is the "Sade who is Spinoza and Lucretius, the Sade of '*Français, encore un effort être républicains,*' a libidinal materialist, the one we here desire and

---

[27] Georges Bataille, *Inner Experience*, trans. Leslie Anne Boldt (New York: State University of New York Press, Albany, 1988), 45.
[28] *The Cloud of Unknowing*, ed. Evelyn Underhill (New York: Dover, 2003), 130.
[29] Bataille, "Chivalric Morals, and Passion," 208.
[30] Georges Bataille, "On Evil in Platonism and Sadism" (Monday 12 May 1947), trans. Eliot Albert, in Albert, *Towards A Schizogenealogy of Heretical Materialism: Between Bruno and Spinoza, Nietzsche, Deleuze and Other Philosophical Recluses* (Unpublished Thesis, PhD: University of Warwick, 2000), 197–223.

desire to sustain."[31] He begins, very basically, by noting how all such behaviour judgements derive from ancient dualisms in the realm of principles—dualisms which set the spheres of matter and spirit apart. While, as he notes, it is not generally conceded that matter is held to be evil, and spirit to be good, it is, nonetheless, the general tendency of all religions—the major religions at least— to hold matter to be evil and spirit good. Not wishing to commence from such a crude schema himself, and despite being unable to accurately attribute it to Plato, Bataille gives more precision to this formula, which, as he says, has taken on fairly solid value: "the good would not be spirit, it would not be the idea, it would not be reason, but it would be the government of reason; and evil would be the fact that reason is governed by matter, if you like, and with regards to behaviour, by the passions."[32] As he notes, according to this Platonic conception, "evil," as it is contemporarily construed, "is instantiated at the moment when reason becomes dominated by the passions."[33] Bataille then establishes what he calls "an absolute diametrical and inevitable opposition between this Platonic notion and a principle to which Sade, even though he doesn't express it directly, gives gripping form, when, in the *Philosophy in the Bedroom*, he depicted the death penalty as the most indefensible act, even though he had, in all his work, only depicted the murder of others as, one can hardly put it otherwise, good. Nevertheless, he condemned the death penalty as a principle" because accordingly, "a punishment that implies the unleashing of the passions cannot be dealt out unemotionally. It is absolutely unacceptable for Sade, to unleash one's passion on a man to such a degree that one kills him, simply because a judge requests it or because reason demands it."[34] Sade himself is more explicit, he argues that the law cannot commit murder "since the law, cold and impersonal, is a total stranger to the passions which are able to justify in man the cruel act of murder. Man receives his impressions from Nature, who is able to forgive him this act; the law, on the contrary, is always opposed to Nature and receiving nothing from her, cannot be authorised to permit herself the same

[31] Jean-François Lyotard, *Libidinal Economy* (Bloomington: Indiana University Press, 1993), 64.
[32] Bataille, "On Evil," 200.
[33] Ibid.
[34] Ibid., 201.

extravagances: not having the same motives the law cannot have the same rights."³⁵ As Lyotard would put it succinctly in his *Libidinal Economy*: "Sade clearly says the death penalty is an infamy because it is a law, that is to say a regulation of intensities, whereas murder if it is passionate, would be no more crime than an orgasm."³⁶

"Shall a trumpet be blown in the city, and the people not be afraid? / Shall there be evil in a city, and the Lord hath not done it?" (*Amos* 3:6). "We struck our blows ferociously / We warred with passion as one / We spilled blood without fear / From the last battle our honour lives on" (Forefather, "The Last Battle," *The Fighting Man*). "Dawn breaks. The Einherjer goes to / Relive their last fight, / With passion, swords held high. / As they ride in the morning mist, / The sun warms the air. / War cries sound: / 'Tor Hjelpe!' / The battle begins, / Charging horses with fire in breath. / Rush to battle—in glory die! / Swords sing in joy. / Again they cut, / With shining edges. / Blood-stained steel. / Axes shine, again they're swung, / Ripping flesh—death be done!" (Amon Amarth, "The Mighty Doors Of The Speargod's Hall," *Sorrow Throughout The Nine Worlds*). "Blood gushes from the wound, / The cut is wide and deep. / And before I turn around, / He falls to his knees. / A clear song rings in the blade, / When steel meets hardened steel. / I hear the sound of wood that breaks, / A sword cuts through my shield. / I drop the shield and grab my axe, / A weapon in each fist. / The first blow makes the helmet crack, / The axe cut to the teeth. / I rip the axe from the head, / covered in blood and brains. / I leave the body lying dead, / Ready to strike again. / My sword cuts through clothes and skin, / Like a hot knife through snow. / I smile as the bastard screams, / When I twist my sword" (Amon Amarth, "Valhalla Awaits Me," *With Odin On Our Side*). "I wipe the blood from my sword, / And slide it in my belt. / This is the sweetest of rewards— / The best rush I have felt. / Ten men are dead by my feet, / I smell their streaming blood, / And I smile, 'cause it makes me ... / ... makes me feel so good" (Amon Amarth, "Where Silent Gods Stand Guard," *Versus the World*). "I form the light, and create darkness: / I make peace, and create evil: / I the Lord do all these things" (*Isaiah* 45:7).

---

³⁵ Marquis de Sade, *Justine, Philosophy in the Bedroom, and Other Writings* (London: Arrow, 1991), 310.
³⁶ Lyotard, *Libidinal Economy*, 182.

In principle, one can encapsulate the entirety of the *chansons de geste*'s condemnation of the hero's wild and savage valor from the viewpoint of reason or, as Bataille notes, what is in fact "piety—endowed with the feelings of reason," in this kind of "moral disorder" that evidentially stems from Christianity's deification of reason as it is elaborated by Plato, insofar as the notion of God/the "Good" is/becomes founded on the principle that reason is divine, "and on the principle that the divine being, the divine essence, is reasonable."[37] On the contrary, Bataille believes that it is not reason, but passion that is allied to the divine. As he argues, contra Plato, and with unprecedented clarity on this particular Monday in 1947: "this dualist division [of matter and spirit] is extremely fragile. One can see that in principle, the divine must be considered as reducible to the notion of the sacred. Now, it is quite apparent that in its origin the notion of the sacred cannot in any way be reducible to reason. Hence, there is a possible slippage between the two notions. The fact that the sacred is understood to be transcendent, that it is beyond this world, in excess of everything, that it is totally other, means as a consequence that it has some relationship with the world of transcendence taken as the world of reason. It is perhaps the most fragile part of the edifice upon which the entirety of human thought rests, in the sense that the sacred is precisely the opposite of transcendence, that in fact the sacred is immanence. The sacred in both its simplest and its most evolved forms is always something to be rediscovered, the sacred is essentially communication: it is contagion. The sacred exists at the moment when something which will not be, although it must be, stopped, is unleashed, and which is going to destroy, which takes the risk of tampering with the established order."[38] This, as the translator of his lecture—under the tutelage of Nick Land—notes, is Bataille's "delirious materialism, the location of an 'ungraspable horror' in the heart of the sacred."[39] Cf. "Instead of avoiding laceration, I'll deepen it. The sight of torture/execution staggers me, but quickly enough I support it with indifference. Now I invoke innumerable tortures/executions of a multitude in agony. Finally (or maybe all at once) human immensity promises a horror without limit.

---

37 Bataille, "On Evil," 203.
38 Ibid., 205.
39 Albert, *Towards A Schizogenealogy*, 263.

Cruelly I stretch out the laceration: at that moment I attain the point of ecstasy."[40]

The kernel of Bataille's lecture, is that the sacred, were one to give it sufficient attention, could simply be reduced to the unleashing of the passions—"and this is the only good," he says—"from the point when reason is no longer divine, from the moment when there is no longer God. There is no longer anything which for us can merit the name sacred, which merits the name 'Good,' other than the unleashing of the passions."[41] Bataille acknowledges that this idea is frightening, that it doesn't make "life" any easier to understand that suffering is the sole site of the real. Not only that, but as he says, "Once God is unhinged from the frame where theology—positive theology, at least—had fixed him,"[42] "as soon as one loses that control exerted over reason by the sacred, humanity disappears, as it were, it becomes somewhat blurred. Once man has lost control of reason, man ceases to be man: he is mad. And it is natural that an objection should arise, as it is quite natural that man should continue indefinitely—like a dog forever chasing its tail—to behave well, simply so that other men continue to behave well, so that there exists a world of good conduct which would indefinitely chase after something that would be contrary to this good behaviour."[43] And it is precisely in this sense that Bataille finds Sade such an exemplary figure. For, as he notes—in alluding to that imperative which appears so often in Nicola's work: "The human being arrives at the threshold: there he must throw himself headlong [*vivant*] into that which has no foundation and has no head"[44]—"one cannot say that Sade hadn't leapt!"[45] There is, in his cruel representations of characters living out their most terrifying fantasies, a brutality that has no cognizance of limit. For that matter, he says, the mystic seems to

[40] Georges Bataille, *Œuvres complètes* V (Paris: Gallimard, 1971), 273–74, translation by Amy Hollywood, *Sensible Ecstasy: Mysticism, Sexual Difference, and the Demands of History* (Chicago and London: The University of Chicago Press, 2002), 276.
[41] Bataille, "On Evil," 211.
[42] Ibid., 208.
[43] Ibid., 209.
[44] Georges Bataille, "The Obelisk," in *Visions of Excess: Selected Writings, 1927–1939*, trans. Allan Stoekl (Minneapolis: University of Minnesota Press, 1985), 222.
[45] Bataille, "On Evil," 210.

open the way to Sade—the mystic, for whom sensual passion, the most brutal passion, and the most vulgar passion have always been combined in an experience of the divine—cf. "One must crush oneself, hacking and hewing away at oneself to widen the place in which love will want to be" (Marguerite Porete); "There are times," she said, "when I am scarcely able to stop myself from totally tearing myself apart . . . times when I can't hold myself back from striking myself in the most horrible way" (Angela of Foligno); "She immediately strikes herself on the cheek so hard that her whole body sways down toward the ground with the force of her stroke; then she strikes herself on the back of the head—between her shoulders—on her neck—and she falls face down, bending her body in the most amazing way and dashing her head on the ground" (Elizabeth of Spaalbeek); "Once when Merwan was banging his head on the floor at home, his mother heard a thudding sound coming from his room . . . Merwan had blood all over his face. Crying she asked, 'Merog, have you gone mad? Are you totally mad?' Wiping the blood off with a towel he said, 'I am not mad! I have become something else!'" (Meher Baba)[46]—and it is not by chance, he would add, that the cornerstone of the chivalric tradition, the *colée* or blow inflicted by the hand of the initiator on the neck of the initiated, should signal "a mystical decapitation as well as a change of personality."[47] Nor is it by chance that "metal's atheological apophatic ecstasy"—"Thrash, or, hacking and being hacked to bits with finely ground axes of sound: 'The only way to exit / Is going piece by piece' (Slayer, 'Piece by Piece,' *Reign in Blood*)"[48]—"is also explicable with reference to its capital rite, headbanging . . . Where the mystic [/knight] bows to

[46] Margaret Poret (Marguerite Porete), *The Mirror of Simple Souls*, trans. E. Colledge, J. C. Marler, and J. Grant (Paris: University of Notre Dame, 1999), 144; Angela of Foligno, "The Memorial," in *The Essential Writings of Christian Mysticism*, ed. Bernard McGinn (New York: Modern Library, 2006), 376; see Julian of Norwich, *Revelations of Divine Love*, in *Medieval Writings on Female Spirituality*, ed. Elizabeth Spearing (London: Penguin, 2002), 175; Bhau Kalchuri, *Meher Prabhu: The Biography of Avatar Meher Baba*, 14 vols. (Myrtle Beach, SC: Manifestation, 1980), 1:251–2.

[47] Bataille, "Chivalric Morals, and Passion," 206.

[48] Nicola Masciandaro, "What is This that Stands before Me?: Metal as Deixis," in Nicola Masciandaro and Edia Connole, *Floating Tomb: Black Metal Theory* (Milan: Mimesis, 2015), 65–66.

God for the sake of his own God performed decapitation, relinquishing the head that says 'God' as the final veil (ego) between the soul and God, the metalhead bows without bowing to nothing but metal, banging the head against itself, against its own abject presence":[49]

> THE OBJECT OF ECSTASY IS THE ABSENCE OF AN OUTSIDE ANSWER. THE INEXPLICABLE PRESENCE OF MAN IS THE ANSWER THE WILL GIVES ITSELF, SUSPENDED IN THE VOID OF UNKNOWABLE NIGHT.[50]

Divinely driven by irrational passion, the metalhead is the durable truth of mystic, knight, of what is unquestionably divine. That this divinity was belatedly tied to "evil" from the eleventh to the thirteenth century through the kind of "moral disorder" outlined by Bataille—"a scholastic saying identified chivalry with evil: *militia malitia*, as people would say (in medieval Latin *miles* is often the translation for knight)"[51]—is supremely evident in songs of the time—such as *The Song of Roland*—which stage blameworthy knights, knights like Isembart or Raoul de Cambrai, who, driven by an excess of passion and spirit of rebellion, turn themselves into outlaws. But, as Bataille notes, it is not the chivalric law that they are rebelling against or "flouting," but rather the human—which is to say societal or feudal—law that would see their passions governed by reason, bound by reason, enchained to reason.[52] Cf. "Hateful savages / Strong black minds / Out of the forest / Kill the human kind / Burn the settlements and grow the woods / Until this Romantic place is understood."[53]

---

[49] Masciandaro, "Metal as Deixis," 70.
[50] "L'OBJET DE L'EXTASE EST L'ABSENCE DE RÉPONSE DU DEHORS. L'INEXPLICABLE PRÉSENCE DE L'HOMME EST LA RÉPONSE QUE LA VOLONTÉ SE DONNE, SUSPENDUE SUR LE VIDE D'UNE ININTELLIGIBLE NUIT," in *Œuvres complètes,* 5:20; this translation is given in Georges Bataille, *The Bataille Reader,* ed. by Fred Botting and Scott Wilson (Oxford: Blackwell, 1997), 45.
[51] Bataille, "On Evil," 209.
[52] Ibid., 207.
[53] Absurd, "Green Heart," *Out of the Dungeon* (Demo, 1994), as discussed by Brett Stevens in "The Heavy Metal F.A.Q.," available from *Death Metal*

Let us add here, as a personal remark, the extent to which Absurd's "Green Heart" approximates the hate that black metal, like the Germanic chivalric tradition, feels towards such "settlements"—

> We grew up in an idyllic society, really. . . . We had stables with girls riding horses, . . . There were no problems . . . McDonalds didn't appear until 1991 or 1992, and when it did, we actually took a rifle and bicycles, we rode our bikes up to McDonalds, and we sat down and started firing at the windows . . . we stockpiled weapons and munitions to prepare for war, because we not only suspected that there might be a third world war, but we hoped that there would be . . . . Not because we enjoyed destruction so much, but because we knew that if you want to build something new, you have to destroy the old first.[54]

—thus, Bataille is able to say that while the "(strictly speaking) savage and frenzied character of chivalry" may have subsided, if not disappeared altogether by the thirteenth century, "the quality of knight was not lost with age," for the "meaning or rather the prestige of the word remains closely associated with that of youth, which remains contradictory, if not completely foreign to the very form of the institution. For that matter," he says, "what remains, at least, of the traditions of violence of the Germanic tribes is the knight's ideal obligation to devote his life to adventure, that is to say combat."[55] Cf. "Nothing ventured, nothing won. As Gawain says in Chrétien de Troyes's *Knight with the Lion*, 'Now is not the time to dream your life away but to frequent tournaments, engage in combat, and joust vigorously, whatever it might cost you'" (Nicola Masciandaro):[56]

Underground: The Ultimate Heavy Metal Resource, http://www.deathmetal.org/faq/#underground-metal.
[54] Varg Vikernes, *Until The Light Takes Us*, dir. Aaron Aites and Audrey Ewell (New York: Factory, 2010), DVD, as discussed by Stevens in "The Heavy Metal F.A.Q."
[55] Bataille, "On Evil," 205.
[56] Nicola Masciandaro, "Interview (Dominik Irtenkauf, Avant-Garde Metal 2011)," in Masciandaro and Connole, *Floating Tomb*, 237.

It is about reentering the presentness, the presence of happening, slaying the distinction between representation and represented so that it dies in the reality of the actual and only present, the now. This is a fulfillment of art's promise of being, that "the work of art does not simply refer to something, because what it refers to is actually there." This is Metallica's instruments becoming weapons as Hetfield leads the charge: "Attack! | Bullets are flying | People are dying | With madness surrounding, | All hell's breaking loose' (Metallica, 'No Remorse," *Kill 'Em All*). WYRD. The link between battle and Metal's sonic inevitable goes beyond appropriateness. For each discloses the nature of the other as a confrontation with something greater than both, a facing of the plain-as-day fact that exceeds representation, an experience of the thing itself. As battle is an event marked by the death of representation, one in which conceptual categories are hacked open and happening is felt in its most raw, naked negativity as an undetermined determination, so Metal is an art that aims to kill representation, to slay music itself, show sound for the noise it is, and thereby hear the inexorable, ineffable music of *wyrd* or what happens. Metal does this, not nihilistically, but naively. Like Quixote suddenly decapitating papier mâché Moors at the puppet show, Metal destroys representation by realizing it, killing the false with (and within) its own fantasy.[57]

I, I will be king . . . [EC]

And you, you will be queen

Take me, for you are mine and I am you. The becoming king and queen of the *I* and the *you* signifies attainment of divine union, the eternal rulership of lover and beloved, soul and God, which is won in mystical death. This mutual conversion to king and queen,

---

[57] Nicola Masciandaro, "Black Sabbath's 'Black Sabbath': A Gloss on Heavy Metal's Originary Song," in Masciandaro and Connole, *Floating Tomb*, 50–51.

at once resurrection and marriage, is the fruition of the fatal intersection of *I* and *you* exposed in the great experimental cross or X of experience (*experientia crucis*), whereby the polarity of self and other is inexorably killed to life.[58]

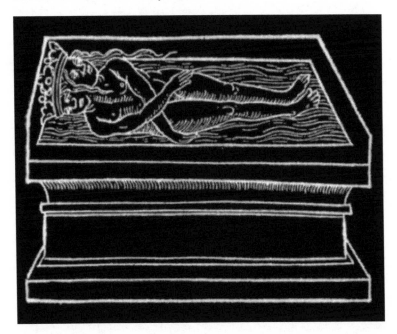

"Resurrection is only crucifixion having reached the stage of fructification. It is *realised* crucifixion."[59] Now the sovereignty of the divine *I*—"I am who I am" (Exodus 3:14)—passes to the (never-created) creature, to the *you* who in reality is no different from the divinity it addresses as *You*. Resurrecting into the kingdom of the real *I*, *you* is filled, from the depths of her own insurmountable separation, with the highest royal power: "O you dead, come into

---

[58] For a vision of the *I-you* chiasmus as the means of mystical death, see Alina Popa & Nicola Masciandaro, "Our Cruel Tormentors ... Split Into One," in "Dark Wounds of Light," *Vestiges-00: Ex-Stasis* (Black Sun Lit, 2015), 173–81.
[59] Anonymous, *Meditations on the Tarot: A Journey into Christian Hermeticism*, trans. Robert Powell (New York: Penguin Putnam, 1985), 390.

the light and into the life! . . . come to our abundance and contemplate the bride, who by love has experienced all needs, heavenly and earthly! She is so experienced with need in the alien land that I shall now show her how she has grown *in the land of darkness* (Job 10:33). And she shall be great, and she shall see her repose, and the voice of power shall be wholly hers. . . . Your blessed soul is the bride in the city."[60] Married at last to the fact of its own eternal death, the *I* now realizes, for the first always-forever time, the divine power to say *I*: "The main thing is, I understand that I was 'dead.' That is something none of the dead wants to understand; the idea 'I have expired' is lethal to one who has thus far been rooted in this 'life' of yours. At first I was taken aback by this idea as well; but a moment later I was laughing at my idiotic mistake; for the whole of your waking is but a terrible error, born of Omni-idiocy. One must be God; everything else having to do with humanity is dung."[61] Now—TODAY—both the mutuality and the hierarchy of the divinely royal relation enjoy each other in a mystical interplay of *I* and *You*, the sovereign game manifesting the *unlimited individuality* of divinity: "When the soul comes out of the ego-shell and enters into the infinite life of God, *its limited individuality is replaced by unlimited individuality*. The soul knows that it is God-conscious and thus *preserves its individuality*. The important point is that individuality is not entirely extinguished, but it is retained in the spiritualised form."[62] Such a one is no less king than queen, no less queen than king. "That which is Shyama is also Brahman. That which has form, again, is without form. That which has attributes, again, has no attributes. Brahman is Shakti; Shakti is Brahman. They are not two. These are only two aspects, male and female, of the same Reality, Existence-Knowledge-Bliss Absolute."[63] Becoming king and queen via death on the cross of individuation, *I* and *you*—each divinely at once king and queen—enter the paradise of a perfectly unimaginable and unimaginably perfect

---

[60] Hadewijch, *The Complete Works*, trans. Mother Columba Hart, O.S.B. (New York: Paulist, 1980), 287.
[61] Ladislav Klima, *The Sufferings of Prince Sternenhoch* (Prague: Twisted Spoon Press, 2008), 140.
[62] Meher Baba, *Discourses*, 2:174.
[63] *Gospel of Sri Ramakrishna*, trans. Swami Nikhilananda (New York: Ramakrishna-Vivekananda Center), 1952), 271.

relation of will in which the one and the many are consummated in infinite secret union: "the King has not one bedroom only, but several. For he has more than one queen: his concubines are many, his maids beyond counting. And each has her own secret rendezvous with the Bridegroom and says: 'My secret to myself, my secret to myself.'"[64] This union is not some fancy metaphysical dream come true, but simply the immediate unveiling and unending fulfillment of an infinitely obvious but strangely unacceptable fact: the eternity of one's own being, the absoluteness of one's own will: "If I were not, God would not be either. I am the cause of God's being God: if I were not, then God would not be God. But you do not need to know this."[65] Indeed you will never know this until you wake up from wanting things for yourself and see who is standing right in front of you: "As long as desires persist, there is no freedom. One who is completely desireless becomes the King of Kings! But people have no idea how to become desireless. Freedom from desires is real life. One has to go beyond desires to enjoy freedom. This freedom can never be imagined; it is beyond the mind. The mind creates desires and as long as the mind continues and does not die, a person cannot extricate himself and enjoy freedom. The soul is like a bird. When all desires vanish, the bird's eyes open. It sees God and becomes one with Him. I am that God whom the bird sees when its eyes open. But desires blind the bird and it cannot see me, though I am standing right in front of it."[66] Thus the repetition of the *I* and the *you*—"I, I . . . And you, you"—to remind us that the *I* who sings is and is not the same as the one who will be king and that the *you* who is sung to is and is not the same as the one who will be queen. The song begins in confidence of its prophecy, precisely because it knows that today is and is not its fulfillment, that the day of union is found in another day of dying, in the heroic leap that must begin now: "long and be restless for one big thing. Long and want the one thing that will kill all the millions of other wants. Long for union. How clear and simple. Try with all your heart. Do not say

---

[64] Bernard of Clairvaux, *On the Song of Songs*, trans. Kilian Walsh, 4 vols. (Kalamazoo, MI: Cistercian Publications, 1983), 2:34.
[65] Meister Eckhart, *Complete Mystical Works*, trans. and ed. Maurice O'C. Walshe (New York: Herder & Herder, 2009), 424.
[66] Meher Baba, quoted in *Lord Meher*, 1060.

yes and then not do it. Begin seriously now."[67] Such is the purer evil of the good—more evil than evil—by which the self kills itself: "Selfishness, which in the beginning is the father of evil tendencies, becomes through good deeds *the hero of its own defeat*. . . . Goodness is the means by which the soul annihilates its own ignorance."[68] And this black metal knows, that the good is the real evil.

Cult of Fire, मृत्यु का तापसी अनुध्यान [Ascetic Meditation of Death] (Iron Bonehead Productions, 2013).

Who is this terrible Woman, dark as the sky at midnight?

[67] Ibid.,1818.
[68] Meher Baba, *Discourses*, I:31, my italics.

Who is this Woman dancing over the field of battle.
Like a blue lotus that floats on a crimson sea of blood?
Who is She, clad alone in the Infinite for a garment,
Rolling Her three great eyes in frenzy and savage fury?
Under the weight of Her tread the earth itself is trembling!
Siva, Her mighty Husband, who wields the fearful trident,
Lies like a lifeless corpse beneath Her conquering feet.[69]

[NM]

Though nothing will drive them away

Who is the third person plural to which the pronoun refers? Who
are/is they/them—themselves? If we are to assume this archaic
usage—cf. *they bethought them of a new expedient* (OED)—the
"them" to which this line refers, is, as Alastair McKay has
suggested, "the ghosts of the self." Cf. "It might be easier to reach
into psychology and call it *psyche* music, because there is precious
little space here for relationships, or love, or even lust. But there
is much examination of the ghosts of the self."[70] In this respect,
the line is subject to another—blackened, or inverted—
interpretation, in the sense that nothing *will* drive them away
(*vide* "We're *nothing*, and *nothing* will help us"). Cf. "He who
attributes to himself anything that he does, and does not attribute
it all to God, is in ignorance, which is hell. . . . Nothing in a man's
works is his own"; "He who recognizes that God does all things in
him, he shall not sin. For he must not attribute to himself, but to
God, all that he does"; "A man who has a conscience is himself
Devil and hell and purgatory, tormenting himself. He who is free
in spirit escapes from all things."[71]
    The essential heresy of the amoralism and irreligion of these
sayings is recapitulated somewhat differently in a gnostic logion
from the Gospel of Thomas: "Wretched are the Pharisees. / They

---

[69] *Gospel of Sri Ramakrishna*, 240.
[70] Alastair McKay, "Heroes," in *The Ultimate Music Guide: Bowie* (June
2015): 54.
[71] Heretical sayings of the Movement of the Free Spirit, collected and
discussed by Norman Cohn in *The Pursuit of the Millennium:
Revolutionary Millenarians and Mystical Anarchists of the Middle Ages*
(New York: Oxford University Press, 1970), 177–78.

are like the dog, / lying in the cow's manger. / He cannot eat, / and will not let the cows eat."[72] The Pharisee in this logion thinks he has knowledge, but he does not even know himself. Therefore all of his musings can only amount to a distraction, usurping the very place of the king and queen—the divine *topos outopos* or manger of mystical union—in the minds of the listener. Cf. "I wanted to believe me / I wanted to be good / I wanted no distractions / like every good boy should."[73] Though unavoidably tied to the frictions of East and West Berlin—wherein "them" could be construed as any number of conditions or institutions—Bowie himself has insisted that this song is "more broadly autobiographical, symbolizing an escape from his own personal hell"—"demons," or "ghosts of the self."[74]

What is desired, then, is a creative disintegration of the ego, an escape from the spectres of "self" that constitute this "personal hell"—a driving of them away, so that a new form of heroic subjectivity can reign in their place. Cf.

"Whence have you come?"
"I come from nowhere."

"Tell me, what are you?"
"I am not."

"What do you wish?"
"I do not wish."

"This is a miracle! What is your name?"
"I am called Nameless Wildness."

"Where does your insight lead to?"
"Into untrammelled freedom."

"Tell me, what do you call untrammelled freedom?"

---

[72] "Logion 102," *The Gospel of Thomas*, trans. Jean-Yves Leloup (Vermont: Inner Traditions, 2005), 53.
[73] David Bowie, "Beauty and the Beast," *Heroes* (RCA Records, 1977).
[74] Bowie quoted in McKay, "Heroes," 55; McKay on Bowie in Ibid., 55 and 54, respectively.

"When a man lives according to all his caprices, without distinguishing between God and himself, and without looking before or after. . . ."[75]

[EC]

We can beat them just for one day
We can be heroes just for one day

There is only one day, and it is forever. The day of heroic victory is the TODAY of paradise. "Truly, I say to you, today you will be with me in Paradise" (Luke 23:42). What else is there? If you are not every minute entering paradise by mounting the cross of yourself, what are you doing here? How do you live with yourself? *"Adhamaadham Adhiko Patit Sakal Jeevatma Hu, / Ae Nischay Aavya Vina Saadhan Karshe Shu?* [Till the time you do not come to the decision that you are the worst possible of all embodied individual selves, what means will you be able to enact?]"[76] Heroes are the ones who hang in the excruciating non-difference between Paradise and today, who neither abandon the world nor abandon themselves to it, who go about the labor of the day as not at all and nothing but their real work. "Unless a devotee is of the heroic type he cannot pay attention to both God and the world."[77] Inverting the gravity of the Fall, the hero is the mystical "Hanged Man" who lives upside down in the world, suspended between time and eternity, here and Beyond, this and That. "Now, the domain of freedom . . . is found placed between two gravitational fields with two different centres . . . 'heaven' and 'this world.'"[78] Whence the paradoxical identification of the hero with the householder: "Blessed indeed is the householder who performs his duties in the world, at the same time cherishing love for the Lotus Feet of God.

---

[75] Adapted from an account of a conversation held one sunny afternoon between the Free Spirit mystic Henry of Suso of Constance and an incorporeal image, as quoted by Cohn in *Pursuit of the Millennium*, 177–8.

[76] B. J. Irani and S. M. Desai, *The Sadguru of Sakori Upasni Maharaj (1870-1941): A Perfect Master of India*, trans. Anurag Gumashta (Baroda, India: n.p., 2012), 22.

[77] *Gospel of Sri Ramakrishna*, 696.

[78] Anonymous, *Meditations on the Tarot*, 306.

He is indeed a hero. He is like a man who carries a heavy load of two maunds on his head and at the same time watches a bridal procession. One cannot lead such a life without great spiritual power."[79] Where false heroism is characterized by inhumanity and the fearful flight from life, true heroism is characterized by humanity and the fearless facing of life. It is essentially free of any confusion between renunciation and cowardice, surrender and running away: "Renunciation of desires does not mean asceticism or a merely negative attitude to life. Any such negation of life would make man inhuman. Divinity is not devoid of humanity. Spirituality must make man more human. It is a positive attitude of releasing all that is good, noble and beautiful in man. It also contributes to all that is gracious and lovely in the environment. It does not require the external renunciation of worldly activities or the avoiding of duties and responsibilities. It only requires that, while performing the worldly activities or discharging the responsibilities arising from the specific place and position of the individual, the inner spirit should remain free from the burden of desires. Perfection consists in remaining free from the entanglements of duality. Such freedom from entanglements is the most essential requirement of unhindered creativity. But this freedom cannot be attained by running away from life for fear of entanglement. This would mean denial of life. Perfection does not consist in shrinking from the dual expressions of nature. The attempt to escape from entanglement implies fear of life. Spirituality consists in meeting life adequately and fully without being overpowered by the opposites. It must assert its dominion over all illusions—however attractive or powerful. Without avoiding contact with the different forms of life, a perfect man functions with complete detachment in the midst of intense activity."[80] By virtue of this very detachment and freedom from

---

[79] *Gospel of Sri Ramakrishna*, 856. Cf. "They are heroes indeed who can pray to God in the midst of their worldly activities. They are like men who strive for God-realization while carrying heavy loads on their heads. Such men are real heroes. You may say that this is extremely difficult. But is there anything, however hard, that cannot be achieved through God's grace? His grace makes even the impossible possible. If a lamp is brought into a room that has been dark a thousand years, does it illumine the room little by little? The room is lighted all at once" (Ibid., 1014–5).
[80] Meher Baba, *Discourses*, 1:32–3.

the sway of opposites, the heroic life is no less free of itself. Thus, just as the good is not merely the opposite of evil but the higher negation that transcends the opposition between good and evil, real heroism is not simply the positive opposite of the *mere* negativity of false heroism but the higher negativity that transcends the opposition between negative and positive attitudes, inhumanity and humanity, denial and affirmation. "Man is beast and superbeast. The higher man is inhuman and superhuman: these belong together . . . Terribleness is part of greatness; let us not deceive ourselves"[81]—lest one fall into either hero-worship or the opposite. As perfection is all-sided, everywhere capable of itself in all situations,[82] so heroism, which is defined by the correlative power to stay true to oneself and never back down,[83] is a justice free from service to its own ideal—"just for one day." Heroism per force exceeds its own parameters. Heroes do not have to be heroes. They elect to be heroes *anyway*, despite everything, including heroism itself. The freedom of the heroic act is inherently detached from its own value. "The true hero fights and dies in the name of his destiny, and not in the name of a belief."[84] A hero acts no less to *not* be than to be a hero—to be

---

[81] Friedrich Nietzsche, *The Will To Power*, trans. Walter Kaufman and R. J. Hollingdale (New York: Vintage, 1968), 531.

[82] "Perfection is the full development of all the aspects of personality, so perfection must be all-sided. Perfection must be all-sided. It is only a lopsided growth of a faculty or capacity, resulting in inflexibility or the incapacity to adjust oneself to the ever changing and multitudinous vicissitudes of life. Such a person cannot maintain a moving equilibrium of mind while keeping pace with the swift changes of life. If he is in an environment which, by its nature, gives scope for the faculty which he has developed, he is temporarily happy and enjoys a sense of being in harmony with the world. But if he finds himself in a hostile environment where his faculty is a misfit, he has a sense of failure and his poise is disturbed. Therefore perfection implies perfection in every respect" (Meher Baba, *Discourses*, 1:118).

[83] "I like heroes such as Napoleon and Shivaji; they were never cowards. Napoleon was courageous till the last. Alexander [the Great] was brave, also. Emperor Akbar was brave, but not as brave as Shivaji. Even when the situation was hopeless, these leaders did not run away. That is good. That is bravery. One must fight till the last, do or die!" (Meher Baba, quoted in *Lord Meher*, 1036).

[84] E. M. Cioran, *A Short History of Decay*, trans. Richard Howard (New York: Penguin, 2010), 87.

other than only himself. Whence the heroism of dying to desire (as the song's lovers must), which is not the denial of desire, but the fight that pursues it beyond itself: "Lust is not bad. Because of this lust, you have been born as human beings. It is due to this very lust that you will turn from men into God! But even if lust is there in you, don't put it into action. From the spiritual point of view, lust is the worst possible weakness. The real hero is he who successfully fights it."[85] Heroic death reaches beyond dying heroically. It is the dying of the death to the death, the hero's death to himself and to his own dying. "We can justify only the man who practices, in full awareness, the irrational necessary to every action, and who embellishes with no dream the fiction to which he surrenders himself, as we can admire only a hero who dies without conviction, all the more ready for sacrifice in that he has seen through it."[86] Heroism lives itself beyond itself on an inner plane free from the human world: "Authentic heroism is inner action, unseen and unapplauded by men."[87] Heroes become heroism itself—and that is their divinity: "The just man serves neither God nor creatures, for he is free . . . and the closer he is to freedom . . . the more he is freedom itself. Whatever is created, is not free. . . . There is something that transcends the created being of the soul, not in contact with created things . . . not even an angel has it . . . It is akin to the nature of deity, it is one in itself, and has naught in common with anything."[88] What then of the all-too-common and all-too-human "heroes" of this song, "a ballad on the transience of love, on stealing time, just for one day . . . a song of desperate yearning in the full knowledge that joy is fleeting and that we're nothing, and nothing will help us"?[89] In the immediate blackened truth of the music, in the creative inversion that asserts dominion over illusion and turns today into Paradise, they are simply—and in a sense too simple for either the sentimental or the sophisticated ear to grasp—heroes. [NM]

---

[85] Meher Baba, quoted in *Lord Meher*, 1099.
[86] Ibid., 44.
[87] Vernon Howard, *The Mystic Path to Cosmic Power* (West Nyack, NY: Parker Publishing, 1967), 65.
[88] Meister Eckhart, *Complete Mystical Works*, 130–31.
[89] Simon Critchley, *Bowie* (New York: OR Books, 2014), 82.

And you, you can be mean

"It has pleased Nature so to make us attain happiness only by way of pain," remarks Mme De Saint-Ange in Sade's *Philosophy in the Bedroom*[90]—preempting the imperative maintained by Bataille, "that if eroticism leads to harmony between partners its essential principle of violence and death is invalidated"[91]—cf. "You know my only pleasure / Is to hear you cry / I'd love to hear you cry / I'd love to feel you die" (Mercyful Fate, "Evil," *Melissa*).

Sade creates disharmony in his characters through the manipulation, subjection and sexual abuse of partners who are reduced to the status of "object," and he does so for the purpose of reaffirming the passions, but within what could only be construed as a fairly specific proto-Darwinian conception of nature. "These passions," as he says in an address to libertines in the preface, "where of coldly insipid rationalists would put you in fear, are naught but the means Nature employs to bring man to the ends she prescribes him."[92] Sade thus assumes license to institute sex, and more particularly violent sexual behaviour, as a kind of responsibility of nature. Indeed, he goes so far that transgressive sexual acts assume a sort of banality in his work, they acquire a blandness through this kind of copious repetition which renders them wholly biological and almost natural:

> I am going to insert my prick in her ass; meanwhile, as she reclines in your arms you will frig her; do your utmost; by means of the position I place you in, she will be able to retaliate in kind; you will kiss one another. After a few runs into this child's ass, we will vary the picture: I will have you, Madam, by the ass.[93]

This serial dissembling of sex and its language is all the while in service of an overwhelming "superego" that seeks to—and indeed does, more oft than not—act in place of the secular and sacred *as* the external forces which would govern us, as opposed

---

[90] Sade, *Philosophy in the Bedroom*, 202.
[91] Georges Bataille, "De Sade's Sovereign Man," *Eroticism*, trans. Mary Dalwood (London and New York: Penguin, 2012), 164–76; 167.
[92] Sade, *Philosophy in the Bedroom*, 185.
[93] Ibid., 240.

to, say—as it may first appear when one encounters his work—acting in opposition to the very existence of external forces. Hence, while both Sade and Bataille are perceived as transgressive—both deriving power from "violence and death"—the penultimacy of this paradox reveals that Sade, in the end, is not, and with respect to the latter, his methods and motivations couldn't be more disparate.

There is a charming anecdote recalled by Colm McCabe in the introduction to the latest Penguin edition of *Eroticism*, in which he refers to the "genuinely mock-heroic" behaviour of an older Bataille, who, "deprived of his much-loved brothels (they were closed down in 1946), enthusiastically vaunt[ed] the merits of the partouze (a word for which the only inelegant Anglo-Saxon translation is 'group sex')." Anyway, as the story goes, "To Jean Piel, his long-time collaborator and successor as editor of *Critique*, who seems to have suggested that it might be time that he cut down on his devotion to sexual dissolution and rest content with monogamous sex," Bataille is reported to have said, "'Why should one content oneself with dipping your toe in the water, when you can swim in the ocean?'"[94]

An image of the ocean and dissolution come together here in a way that entirely fits Bataille's work and life. Indeed, as McCabe writes, "'Dissolute' was the word Bataille himself used to describe his life"—cf. "The whole business of eroticism is to strike at the inmost core of living being, so that the heart stands still. The transition from the normal state to that of erotic desire presupposes a partial dissolution of the person as he exists in the realm of discontinuity. Dissolution—this expression corresponds with *dissolute life*, the familiar phrase linked with erotic activity. In the process of dissolution, the male partner generally has an active role, while the female partner is passive. The passive, female side is essentially the one that is dissolved as a separate entity. But for the male partner the dissolution of the passive partner means only one thing: it is paving the way for a fusion in which both are mingled, attaining at length the same degree of dissolution"[95]—which has little in common with the French tradition of "*libertinage*."[96] In fact, the two stand opposed, like the land and

---

[94] Bataille, *Eroticism*, xvi.
[95] Ibid., 17.
[96] Ibid., xiii.

the ocean, like reason and intuition, like the literal and anagogic senses of scripture—"This is aptly captured by Jerome, who, in praising the speculative flights of his expansive imagination, in the preface to his translation of Origen's homilies on Ezekiel, speaks glowingly of the way in which the author 'surrendered all the sails of his genius to the blowing winds and, departing from the land (or "literal" sense), launched out into the open sea'."[97] Cf. "Is not transcendental philosophy a fear of the sea? Something like a dike or sea-wall? A longing for the open ocean gnaws at us ["I, I wish you could swim . . ."], as the land is gnawed by the sea. A dark fluidity at the roots of our nature rebels against the security of *terra firma*, provoking a wave of anxiety in which we are submerged, until we feel ourselves drowning, with representation draining away. *Nihil ulterius.* . . ."[98] The libertine is someone who has as his or her aim the complete control of sexual pleasure divorced from all possible emotional or sexual intimacy—this is the detached, literal, and wholly rational transcendental superegoic sexual pleasure of the serial killer, the rapist, the sadist. For Bataille, the aim of sexual pleasure is not the gaining but the relinquishing of control—and not simply in some *fantastic* faux masochistic sense—this is the creative disintegration or dissolution of the ego associated with the *jouissance* of mysticism, where, despite the seeming disparity, in what is for Bataille "the disorderliness and randomness of love" (*real* love between partners, cf. "Erotic experience linked with *reality* waits upon chance, upon a particular person, and favourable

---

97 Edia Connole, "What is Black Metal Theory?," in Masciandaro and Connole, *Floating Tomb*, 288.
98 ". . . Incipit Kant: We are not amphibians, but belong upon solid earth. Let us renounce all strange voyages. The age of desire is past. The new humanity I anticipate has no use for enigmatic horizons; it knows the ocean is madness and disease. Let me still your ancient tremors, and replace them with dreams of an iron shore. Reason in its legitimate function is a defence against the sea, which is also an inhibition of the terrestrial; retarding our tendency to waste painstakingly accumulated resources in futile expeditions, a 'barrier opposed to the expenditure of forces [II 332]' as Bataille describes it. It is a fortified boundary, sealing out everything uncertain, irresolvable, dissolvant, a sea-wall against the unknown, against death" (Nick Land, *The Thirst for Annihilation: Georges Bataille and Virulent Nihilism* [London and New York: Routledge, 1992], 107).

31

circumstances")[99] the comparative instant "belongs to the man who, spontaneously bewitched, is laid open to anguish:"[100]

> I remember that one day, when we were in a car tooling along at top speed, we crashed into a cyclist . . . her head was almost totally ripped off by the wheels . . . The horror and despair at so much bloody flesh, nauseating in part, in part very beautiful, was fairly equivalent to our usual impression upon seeing one another.[101]

Even in his earliest, most ambiguous, and outwardly sadistic work, *Story of the Eye*—which recounts the tale of two young sexual deviants: a male narrator and a girl called Simone, who, likewise, "on a sensual level . . . so bluntly craved any upheaval that the faintest call from the senses gave her a look directly suggestive of all things deeply sexual: things indefinitely destroying of human bliss and honesty"[102]—Bataille eschews the kind of objectification of persons, the impersonal and dissociative victimization of characters we find in Sade. As he says himself, "De Sade makes his heroes uniquely self-centered; the partners are denied any rights at all. This is the key to his system"; "De Sade's expression of violence [thus] changes violence into something else, something necessarily its opposite: into a *reflecting* and *rationalized* will to violence," whereas a deeper inquiry into sexuality and violence for its own ends—avoiding superegoic transcendence—"[would mean coming to be] beside oneself, and being beside oneself is the same thing as the sensuous frenzy that violence results in."[103]

Echoing "the all-too-common and all-too-human 'heroes' of this song, 'a ballad on the transience of love, on stealing time, just for one day . . . a song of desperate yearning in the full knowledge that joy is fleeting and that we're nothing, and nothing will help us,'" the immanent—all-too-immanent—sensuous frenzy vaunted by Bataille is much closer in goal to the methods and motivations

[99] Bataille, *Eroticism*, 23.
[100] Ibid., 251; my emphasis.
[101] Georges Bataille, *Story of the Eye* (San Francisco: City Lights, 1987), 5.
[102] Bataille, *Story of the Eye*, 6.
[103] Bataille, *Eroticism*, 167; 191; and 192, respectively; my emphasis.

of medieval love mysticism than it is to Sade's libertine literature, creating a kind of self-surrendering "victim" that "a genuine sadist could never tolerate:"[104] Cf.

> Only the beloved, so it seems to the lover—because of affinities evading definition which match the union of bodies with that of souls—only the beloved can in this world bring about what our human limitations deny, a total blending of two beings, a continuity between two discontinuous creatures. Hence love spells suffering for us in so far as it is a quest for the impossible, and at a lower level, a quest for union at the mercy of circumstance.[105]

> I am brought to ruin by these decrees
> That Love must thus remain out of my reach.[106]

> And this is a frightening life Love wants, that we must do without the satisfaction of Love in order to satisfy Love.[107]

> Hell is the seventh name
> of this love wherein I suffer.
> For there is nothing Love does not engulf and damn,
> And no one who falls into her
> And whom she seizes comes out again,
> Because no grace exists there.
> As Hell turns everything to ruin,
> In Love nothing else is acquired
> But disquiet and torture without pity;
> Forever to be in unrest,
> Forever assault and new persecution;
> To be wholly devoured and engulfed
> In her unfathomable essence,
> To founder unceasingly in heat and cold,

---

[104] Gilles Deleuze, "Coldness and Cruelty," *Masochism* (New York: Zone Books, 1989), 40.
[105] Bataille, *Eroticism*, 20.
[106] Hadewijch, "Unloved by Love," *The Complete Works*, 228.
[107] Hadewijch, "Love Unappeasable," in Ibid., 75.

In the deep, insurmountable darkness of Love,
This outdoes the torments of hell.
He who knows Love and her comings and goings
Has experienced and can understand
Why it is truly appropriate
That Hell should be the highest name of Love.[108]

[EC]

And I, I'll drink all the time

Were I the mystic and not the mystified, I might commence this comment by evoking Love's ability to induce "sober drunkenness."[109] Or, were I like the Pharisee, desiring to appear righteous in the eyes of others, while all in fact is rot inside, I might follow the line of a transgressive desire—I have, to "drink all the time"—all the way into its *askesis*, and then call that Love.[110] Were I jovial, when in fact I'm not, I might even conjure an image of a "drunken God,"[111] ". . . join the laughers!,"[112] as H. P. Lovecraft would say . . . Were I a *thinker* and not a *feeler*, I might—but I'm

---

[108] Hadewijch, "Love's Seven Names," in Ibid., 356–57.

[109] Cf. "and she is inebriated not only from what she has drunk, but very intoxicated and more than intoxicated from what she never drinks nor will drink" (Marguerite Porete, *The Mirror of Simple Souls*, trans. Ellen L. Babinsky [New York: Paulist Press, 1993], chaps. 18 and 23, quoted and discussed by Nicola Masciandaro in "Absolute Secrecy: On the Infinity of Individuation," forthcoming in *Speculation, Heresy, and Gnosis in Contemporary Philosophy and Religion*, eds. Joshua Ramey and Mathew Harr Farris).

[110] Cf. "His disciples questioned him: / 'Should we fast? How should we pray? How should we give / alms? What rules of diet should we follow?' / Yeshua said: / Stop lying. / Do not do that which is against your love. / You are naked before heaven. / What you hide will be revealed, / whatever is veiled will be unveiled." ("Logion 6," *The Gospel of Thomas*, 11).

[111] See "Symbolic Theology," in *Pseudo-Dionysius: The Complete Works*, trans. Colm Luibheid and Paul Rorem (London/Mahwah, NJ: Paulist Press, 1987). Cf. Ps. 78, "the Lord awoke, like a strong man, powerful but reeling with wine."

[112] H. P. Lovecraft, "Letter to Robert Nelson—[late October? 1934]," in Nelson, *Sable Revery*, 49.

not.[113] Ehye Asher Ehye, I am what I am.[114] And I know this line was written with the sad and disillusioned in mind—"Berlin," Bowie observed, reflecting on the environment in which he recorded the song, "is a city made up of bars for sad, disillusioned people to get drunk in."[115] So, a far more honest, blackened interpretation in the context of individuation and this song's misplaced optimism—played out in the "swells of the music, underpinned by drones and delays and oscillation, which wrap a mist of doubt around it"[116]—shall begin and end in the place of doubt itself; the place of doubt, sorrow and disillusionment. This is the place of *real* drunkenness, of spiritual despair, where—

---

[113] A favourite saying of Horace Walpole's—which appears in his letters in various forms—is "Life is a tragedy for those who *feel*, but a comedy for those who *think*," and this is precisely how it appears in Lovecraft's letter to Nelson above, when he incites the latter to *think*! I.e. "Cultivate analytical thought rather than emotion & join the laughers!," in Ibid., 48–9.

[114] It is speculated that these are the three words that God spoke to Moses in EX 3:14. Cf. Nargaroth, "Amarok—Zorn des Lammes Part III," *Amarok* (No Colours, 2000): "I have seen the wrath of the land. / Cause I am a real life wolf among the sheep. / I was a part of the wrath of the lamb. / So I am a part of the wolf. / I am the wolf. I am the lamb. / So I am Satan in thy wrath. / Call me a judas, call me insane. / But I am what I am, I'm just a man. / Call me a judas, call me insane. / But I am what I am, I'm just a man. / I have seen the wrath of the land. / Cause I am a real life wolf among the sheep. / I was a part of the wrath of the lamb. / So I am a part of the wolf. / I am the wolf. I am the lamb. / So I am Satan in thy wrath. / Call me a judas, call me insane. / But I am what I am, I'm just a man. / Call me a judas, call me insane. / But I am what I am, I'm just a man. / I have seen the wrath of the land. / Cause I am a real life wolf among the sheep. / I was a part of the wrath of the lamb. / So I am a part of the wolf. / I am the wolf. I am the lamb. / So I am what Satan is for god. / Call me a judas, call me insane. / But I am what I am, I'm just a man. / But I am what I am, I'm just a man. / I have seen the wrath of the lamb. / Cause I am a real life wolf among the sheep. / I was a part of the wrath of the land. / So I am a part of the wolf. / I am the wolf. I am the lamb. / So I am what Satan is for god. / I am the wolf. I am the lamb. / So I am what Satan is for god. / Call me a judas, call me insane. / But I am what I am, I'm just a man. / Call me a judas, call me insane. / But I am what I am, A fuckin' man."

[115] Bowie quoted by Allan Jones in "My Own Future Slips By. I'm Prepared For Its End," in *The Ultimate Music Guide: Bowie* (June 2015): 59.

[116] McKay, "Heroes," 55.

"weep[ing]," "wail[ing]," "quarrel[ing]," "damn[ing]," and "curs[ing]"—each drink, accelerated unceasingly—in a lyrical intensification that produces the presence of the present perpetually: *I'll drink all the time*—is matched only by the unceasing desire of someone who is going "nearly insane . . . to lack the knowing and feeling of his own being."[117] [EC]

'Cause we're lovers and that is a fact
Yes we're lovers and that is that

See me, feel me, touch me, heal me.[118] Love is an inherent, absolute, and inescapable fact: "Life and love are inseparable from each other. Where there is life, there is love. Even the most rudimentary consciousness is always trying to burst out of its limitations and experience some kind of unity with other forms. Though each form is separate from other forms, in *reality* they are all forms of the same unity of life. The latent sense for this hidden inner reality indirectly makes itself felt even in the world of illusion through the attraction which one form has for another form. The law of *gravitation*, to which all the planets and the stars are subject, is in its own way a dim reflection of the love which pervades every part of the universe. Even the forces of repulsion are in truth expressions of love, since things are repelled from each other because they are more powerfully attracted to some other things. Repulsion is a negative consequence of positive attraction."[119] As gravity is found everywhere and nowhere in the universe, love is the fact of the superessential within the essential, the real presence in being of being's beyond. It is simultaneously life's ineradicable surplus and its *sine qua non*, the without-which-not whereby life is not itself if not beyond itself. Love is the only thing life is *worth*: "Loveless life is most unlovely, only a life

---

[117] *The Cloud of Unknowing*, ed. Patrick J. Gallagher (Kalamazoo, MI: Medieval Institute Publications, 1997), 71–2, our translation—as given in "Introduction: Mystical Black Metal Theory," in Masciandaro and Connole, *Floating Tomb*, 22.
[118] The Who, "We're Not Gonna Take It," *Tommy* (IBC Studios, 1969).
[119] Meher Baba, *Discourses*, 1:156.

of love is worth living."[120] That is, worth dying for, as being without love is a pointless abstraction, as life without love lacks being. "Being is dying by loving."[121] Love is the dying that makes being real, giving life to the living via living death, exposing via positive annihilation or superessential naughting the unitary fact of things: "Love resembles death in that it annihilates snobbery, vulgarity, and all distinctions."[122] Being the expression of divine unity in the world of duality,[123] love is the whyless why and causeless cause—"'Cause we're lovers"—for which being lives. Love *is* the fact of life, the more-than-is that makes life fact and makes love life, the inescapable *that* so farnearly beyond the fleeting *what* of being—"and that is that."

---

[120] Meher Baba, *Discourses*, 3:171. Cf. "for *being* without love is deprived of all worth . . . love is not only superior to being but also . . . engenders it and restores it" (Anonymous, *Meditations on the Tarot*, 34).

[121] Meher Baba, *Discourses*, 1:29.

[122] *The Sayings of Shri Meher Baba* (London: Circle Editorial Committee, 1933), 9.

[123] "It is for love that the whole universe sprang into existence and it is for the sake of love that it is kept going. God descends into the realm of illusion because the apparent duality of the Beloved and the lover is eventually contributory to His conscious enjoyment of His own divinity. *The development of love is conditioned and sustained by the tension of duality.* God has to suffer apparent differentiation into a multiplicity of souls in order to carry on the game of love. They are His own forms, and in relation to them He at once assumes the role of the Divine Lover and the Divine Beloved. As the Beloved, He is the real and the ultimate object of their appreciation. As the Divine Lover, He is their real and ultimate saviour drawing them back to Himself. Thus though the whole world of duality is only an illusion, that illusion has come into being for a *significant purpose. Love is the reflection of God's unity in the world of duality.* It constitutes the entire significance of creation. If love is excluded from life, all the souls in the world assume complete externality to each other and the only possible relations and contacts in such a loveless world are superficial and mechanical. It is because of love that the contacts and relations between individual souls become significant. It is love which gives meaning and value to all the happenings in the world of duality. But, *while love gives meaning to the world of duality, it is at the same time a standing challenge to duality.* As love gathers strength, it generates *creative restlessness* and becomes the main driving power of that *spiritual dynamic* which ultimately succeeds in *restoring to consciousness the original unity of being*" (Meher Baba, *Discourses*, 1:163–4).

And one sole encounter or one meeting with that ultimate eternal ancient and ever-new goodness is more worthy than anything a creature might do . . . His farness is greater nearness, because, from nearby, in itself, it better knows what is far, which [knowing] always makes her [the Soul] to be in union by his will, without the interference of any other thing which may happen to her. All things are one for her, without a why, and she is nothing in a One of this sort . . . Thus she is stripped of all things because she is without existence, where she was before she was.[124]

Love is that which lives beyond being by dying in the midst of life. A lover lives in time beyond time, before birth and after death. "Your willingness to die is the energy that pushes the door open."[125] This deathly vital inseparability of love and life, their being bound together outside existence, is found in the self-grasping recognition of the primacy of will, according to which one is and must forever be more than oneself. "My love is my weight; by it I am borne, wheresoever I am borne [*Pondus meum, amor meus; eo feror, quocumque feror*]."[126] "Yes, there is something invulnerable, unburiable in me, something that explodes boulders: it is called *my will*. Silently and unchanged it strides through the years . . . And this secret life itself spoke to me: 'Behold,' it said, 'I am that *which must always overcome itself.*'"[127] So too the affirmation of these lines, in which the lovers heed love's call—"I hear the call / From beyond this realm / Exist outside of time" (Tombs, "Path of Totality")[128]—to be nothing, nothing more than the fact of love itself. "I tell you all with My Divine authority, that you and I are not 'WE' but 'ONE.'"[129] [NM]

---

[124] Marguerite Porete, *Mirror of Simple Souls*, 218.

[125] Vernon Howard.

[126] Augustine, *Confessions* (Cambridge, MA: Harvard University Press, 1950), 13.9.

[127] Friedrich Nietzsche, *Thus Spoke Zarathustra*, trans. Adrian Del Caro (Cambridge: Cambridge University Press, 2006), 87–9.

[128] *Path of Totality* (Relapse Records, 2011).

[129] Meher Baba, "Meher Baba's Call," in Bal Natu, *Glimpses of the God-Man, Volume VI: March 1954–April 1955* (Myrtle Beach, SC: Sheriar Foundation, 1994), 101.

CONNOLE & MASCIANDARO – ON "HEROES/HELDEN"

Though nothing will keep us together
We could steal time just for one day

Love will tear us apart.[130] One day, *nothing will* unveil everything, unite oneself with oneself, and *keep us together.*[131] Then we will see through the nothingness of *we*, gaze beyond the split *I*, and really start to have fun or *steal time.* "Just as there is a thing like split personality, there is also a thing like split ego. All do *not* have a split personality, but all *do* have a split *I*. The Real *I* of all is always one indivisible whole. Simultaneously, there is also the false *I* in every individual which gives rise to his separative existence. We find that the very same one Real *I* plays the part of infinite false *I*'s in different ways, creating as many separate beings and things born out of the one Real and Eternal Existence. In reality, there is only one Real *I*. This Real *I* is so uncompromisingly one and indivisible that it knows not any separate existence. All of you present here are the part and parcel of that one whole inseparable *I*. Then, how is it that we see forms here? From where has this division come? *If this separation were not there, then no one would have found that there is only one indivisible Real* I. The *I* is real; but the split ego—that is, the separative *I*—is unreal, and yet we see all this division. This one Real *I* is apparently split into innumerable false *I*'s. What can we expect from this false 'I'? The false *I*, being false, represents everything false. The Real *I* in me sees the One without a second, and the Real *I* in you has apparently split into the false *I* which sees divisions everywhere. In short, it is the one Real *I* that plays the part of innumerable false *I*'s in multifarious ways and in varying degrees. The main support of the false *I* is ignorance, and this false *I* utilizes three channels for its expression—the gross [physical] body, the subtle body [energy] and the mental body [mind]. In other words, with the support of ignorance, the Real *I* takes itself as the false *I* and tries to derive as much fun out of it as

---

130 Joy Division, "Love Will Tear Us Apart" (Factory, 1980).
131 "I be so fastned to him that ther be right nought that is made betweene my God and me. . . . Of this nedeth us to have knowinge, that us liketh to nought all thing that is made, for to love and have God that is unmade" (Julian of Norwich, *The Writings of Julian of Norwich*, ed. Nicholas Watson and Jacqueline Jenkins [University Park, PA: Pennsylvania State University Press, 2006], 141.

possible. While continuing to derive fun, it is also continually enduring setbacks and suffering. What happens eventually? The Real *I* eventually gets fed up and stops playing the part of the false *I*. As soon as the Real *I* stops playing the part of the false *I*, it becomes conscious of its [Original] pristine state. This Consciousness is eternal. And it also realizes that, being eternally happy, its experience of being fed up was sheer, nonsensical ignorance."[132] For the time being, you are too busy being in time— "the being of Da-sein is care [*Sorge*]"[133]—too worried about what has happened or what will happen to someone who never was and will never be, who *will never have been.*

But don't worry, though it takes forever, this impossible death into the Impossible, like the bright spark from a train's third rail—"For where two or three are gathered in my name, there am I in the midst of them" (Matthew 18:20)—happens in a *flash*: "This all-comprehensive Knowledge is obtained in a flash. But to know everything in a flash takes an eternity in the illusion of time while you gradually die to your self. This dying to your self means completely losing yourself in God to find yourself as God. This dying to your false self is no easy task; raising a corpse to life is child's play compared to it. But once the 'impossible' is achieved,

---

[132] Meher Baba, quoted in *Lord Meher*, 4284–5.
[133] Martin Heidegger, *Being and Time*, trans. Joan Stambaugh (Albany: State University of New York Press, 1996), 262.

there remains nothing else that is impossible."[134] *We can be heroes for ever and ever. What d'you say?* [NM]

We can be heroes for ever and ever. What d'you say?

I say, "Yes!": "Let us die, then, and enter into this darkness, let us silence all our cares, desires, and imaginings."[135] Being receptive to the call rather than the comment on this occasion evokes the very "one" who "freely lets itself as subject be thrown into its depths, exercising and exorcising itself in a liberatory act of spontaneous apophatic adventure—a paradoxical leap beautifully imagined by Don Quixote in defense of poetic truth:

> [C]an there be any greater delight than to see . . . *here and now* before us a vast lake of bubbling pitch, and swimming about in it vast number of serpents, snakes, and lizards and many other kinds of fierce and fearsome animals, while from the lake comes a plaintive voice [*una voz tristisima*] 'You, O Knight, whosoever you may be, beholding this dread lake: if you wish to attain the good beneath these black waters, you must show the resolve of your dauntless breast and cast yourself into the midst of the dark, burning liquid [*negro y encendido licor*], else you will not be worthy to see the mighty marvels contained in the seven castles of the seven fairies that lie beneath its murky surface'? And what of our delight when the knight, almost before the fearful voice [*la voz temerosa*] has ceased, without giving his situation a second thought, without stopping to consider the peril to which he is exposing himself, or even shedding the burden of his armor, commends himself to God and to his lady and hurls himself into the boiling lake and, all of a sudden where he least knows where is

---

[134] Meher Baba, quoted in *Lord Meher*, 4644.
[135] Bonaventure, *Itinerarum Mentis in Deum*, trans. Zachary Hayes, *Works of Bonaventure*, vol. 2 (Saint Bonaventure, NY: Franciscan Institute, 2002), 7.6., quoted in Nicola Masciandaro, "Introduction—*In Caliginem*," unpublished manuscript, 8.

bound, finds himself amidst flowery meadows far finer than the Elysian fields themselves?

Throwing himself into the black liquid in immediate continuity with the sorrowful voice that evokes his very indeterminacy ('whosoever you may be'), the knight embodies the meta-personal and hyper-desirous subject who obliterates or short-circuits melancholia by escaping through the very identity that melancholia is *for*. Similarly [and co-extensive with the act, qua commentator, that would heed the call rather than the comment, on this occasion] to burrow thought into the event itself and push philosophically through it requires intensifying beyond its own self-constituting limit the kind of cosmic dependency which holds identity 'on the shore' . . ."[136] [EC]

I, I wish you could swim, Like the dolphins, like dolphins can swim

Detailing the doomed love affair of an Italian soldier and a Somali girl during the Second World War, Alberto Denti di Pirajno's *A Grave for a Dolphin* (1956) provided the inspiration for these lines—Bowie, likening their affair (sans the "doomed" aspect) to the one which would unfold years later between himself and his Somalian wife, has said of the synchronicity: "These things happen to us all the time. Mystical, I bet."[137]

---

[136] Masciandaro, "*In Caliginem*," 9–10.
[137] See annotation to *A Grave for a Dolphin,* in "Top 100 Must-Read Books: David Bowie," available from *Genius,* http://genius.com/2347343/David-bowie-top-100-must-read-books/A-grave-for-a-dolphin-alberto-denti-di-pirajno-1956.

Though one would not be remiss in relaying the extent to which the Tombs version—cf. Hill, the solitary figure, simultaneously capitulated somewhere between the city and the sea, as if appealing to the former, in the music video—would seem to have more in common, visually at least, with the naturalism and apolitical realism of a ballad like "Dolphin's Cry" (an uncharacteristic croon [*krōnen*, "groan, lament"] from German speedsters, Grave Digger, which expresses metal's deep disquiet at "the greedy [human] depredation of resources," a disquiet that, as Dave Rosales notes, can be traced all the way back to Sabbath's "Into The Void"),[138] one *would* be remiss to dismiss what Bowie

---

[138] David Rosales, "The 'Nature' of Metal: A Naturalist and Apolitical Realism," available from *Death Metal Underground*, http://www.deathmetal.org/article/ the-nature-of-metal-a-naturalist-and-apolitical-realism/; Black Sabbath, "Into The Void," *Master of Reality* (Vertigo, 1971), quoted in Ibid.: "Rocket's engines burning fuel so fast / Up into the night sky they blast / Through the universe the engines whine / Could it be the end of man and time / Back on Earth the flame of life burns low / Everywhere is misery and woe / Pollution kills the air, the land, and sea / Man prepares to meet his destiny." Cf. Grave Digger, "Dolphin's Cry," *Heart of Darkness* (GUN Records, 1995): "Standing on a lonely shore, beauty does unfold / Kissed by the dawning light, the sea is painted gold / Never seen alike before, innocent and pure / We never see, we just destroy, we run this planet down / Living to destroy / Looking with closed eyes / Getting sad—as I understand / I see a dolphin cry / . . ."

wagers is a "mystical" aspect, or to think that these two aren't intertwined: *Wyrd*.

Teleologically speaking, it is with the third wave of black metal that this entwinement really comes to life, through death, through the future presence of a mysticism that is felt to be inherently cosmic and overtly climatological—"linked to the periodic upheavals of weather, land and matter"[139] in the music/lyrics of bands like Alda, Fauna, Skagos, Blood of the Black Owl, Mania, Twilight Fall, and Wolves in the Throne Room—and in the speculations of counterpart thinkers—like Woodard, Shakespeare, Thacker, Barber, and Masciandaro—all of which coalesce in the quixotic imperative to "burrow deep in blackest earth / and break further."[140] As above, *to burrow thought into the event itself and push philosophically through it . . .*

In taking up the principle task of medieval mysticism, the overcoming of an essential "subject creationism"—co-extensive with the speculative realist will to escape the correlation between self and world: "it is through facticity, and through facticity alone, that we are able to make our way towards the absolute"[141]—third wave black metal/theory—and in particular Nicola's oeuvre—views this imperative not only existentially qua "the passions of facticity," but as "direct experience that, as the American sage Vernon Howard expresses it, 'A body came into the world, but it wasn't you.'"[142]

> Though I dissolve
> I am not afraid
> For from whence we came
> We shall return
>
> My waters are one with this
> There is no separation
> My waters are one with this

---

[139] Eugene Thacker, *In The Dust Of This Planet: Horror Of Philosophy Vol. 1* (Winchester and Washington: Zero Books, 2011), 158, quoted and discussed with respect to mystical materialism by Masciandaro, "*In Caliginem*," 20.

[140] Fauna, "Rain," *Rain* (Regain Records, 2006).

[141] Meillassoux, *After Finitude*, 63.

[142] Masciandaro, "*In Caliginem*," 10.

There is no separation[143]

Globe immersed in eternal frost.
Eternal frost, eternal cold, eternal void.
All encompassing, for all time.[144]

And so the human being discovers, at last, that its existence has always been subtended by its non-existence, that it dies the moment it lives, and that perhaps we do nothing but carry around a corpse that itself carries around the sullen grey matter that occasionally wonders if the same sullen stars that occupy every firmament at every scale also occupy this starry speculative corpse.[145]

A phenomenal blackness entirely fills the essence of the human. Because of it, the most ancient stars of the paleo-cosmos, together with the most venerable stones of the archeo-earth, appear to the human as being outside the World . . .[146]

[But] black is in no way the effect of beginning, for it is beneath beginning, before beginning—precisely, it is before the war created by beginning. "In the beginning there is Black" . . . what this means, ultimately, is that beginning, with its separation to create the *new*, is impossible.[147]

---

[143] Alda, "Adrift," *Tahoma* (Eternal Warfare Records, 2011).

[144] Mania, "Ice Covered Sphere," *Mania* (Eternal Warfare Records, 2010).

[145] Eugene Thacker, *Starry Speculative Corpse: Horror of Philosophy Vol. 2* (Winchester and Washington: Zero Books, 2015), 168.

[146] François Lauruelle, "On the Black Universe in the Human Foundations of Color," in Alexander Galloway, Daniel Colucciello Barber, Nicola Masciandaro, and Eugene Thacker, *Dark Nights of the Universe* (Miami: [NAME], 2013), 105–6 .

[147] Daniel Colucciello Barber, "Whylessness: The Universe is Deaf and Blind," in *Dark Nights*, 20; my emphasis—note how this could also be read in a Bataillean sense, with respect to the *new word* or neologism discussed below, to inversely mean: "enter into a dead end. There all possibilities are exhausted; the 'possible' slips away and the impossible prevails. To face the impossible—exorbitant, indubitable—when nothing

Black prior to light is the substance of the Universe, what escaped from the World before the World was born into the World.[148]

She swims as if born and nurtured in the sea, catching fish with her hands. She swims with the sharks yet does not get torn to pieces. She slyly jokes that the sharks are her "uncles."[149]

That these lines from Pirajno's *Grave for a Dolphin* should form the logical conclusion to this catena is just *Wyrd*. That Bowie's song, so appropriately taken-up by Tombs, should, then, express the same "fundamental need for escape, the hopeless and helpless desire 'to get out of oneself, that is, *to break that most radical and unalterably binding of chains, the fact that the I [moi] is oneself [soi meme],'"* is inevitable . . . offering a corresponding "index that one is indeed *not* oneself, but something more and other than one's own proper being, a someone more real than anything else and who is discoverable all of a sudden when one *least knows* where one is bound."[150]

Participating in the kind of incarnation in reverse—"flesh made word"—that is inferred in Eckhart's concept of the birth of the divine word in the soul, and in a movement comparable to that of the quixotic knight who throws himself into the lake of black bile in immediate continuity with the melancholic voice that evokes his very indeterminacy ("whosoever you may be"), Dante enters Paradise in immediate continuity with the first neologism of *Paradiso*: *tranhumar*, to pass beyond the human (*Paradiso* 1.70).[151] In stating the extent to which this neologism stands in contradistinction to the certain, "anthropocentri[c]," "inevitably vestibular," and "infernal" words of hell—*"Per me si va ... Per me si va ... Per me si va'*—eternally testif[ying] to the human as that

---

is possible any longer is in my eyes to have an experience of the divine . . ." (Bataille, *Inner Experience*, 4–5).
[148] Laruelle, "On the Black Universe," 104.
[149] Pirajno quoted in *Genius*.
[150] Masciandaro, *"In Caliginem,"* 10; my emphasis.
[151] See Nicola Masciandaro, "Unknowing Animals," *Speculations II*, eds. Ridvan Askin, Paul J. Ennis, Fabio Girony, et al (New York: Punctum, 2011), 233.

through which everything takes place"—Nicola notes how Dante, upon experiencing the new intelligence (*intelligenza nouva*) that the new word requires, compares his metamorphosis to that of Glaucus, the fisherman whose apotheosis or becoming divine came to pass by eating grass and becoming animal—"sea-fellow [*consorto in mar*] of the other gods"[152]—out of a fierce desire he felt within his heart "to live another life."[153] [EC]

†

Greater love has no man than this, that a man lay down his life for his friends.[154] Love is the will of no one—*maiorem hac dilectionem **nemo** habet*—for your freedom, the wish of someone dying upside down on the cross between *I* and *I* (at once dying wish and wish to die) that you realize the power to swim the Ocean. It is a hopeless and helpless wish, that *you could swim / Like the dolphins*, because you cannot swim like the dolphins, since you are not a dolphin (much less dolphins), because to swim like that means to become dolphin, something no longer human, to no more be *you*. So the *I* wishes you could swim *like* the dolphins, wanting there to be a way to freedom that does not require your death, knowing full well that there is not, and in the marrow-pain of the impasse feeling that somehow, by means of the wish's own depth, in the dying-by-wishing and wishing-by-dying of the one who wishes,[155] there is a way—where there is will.

---

[152] Masciandaro, "Unknowing Animals," 233.
[153] Ovid, *Metamorphoses*, trans. Allen Mandelbaum (New York: Harcourt,1993), 13.935–46, quoted in Ibid., 234.
[154] John 15:13.
[155] Cf. "Voicing wish, passing it through the threshold of the mouth, enacts at once the sympathetic foretaste of its fulfillment, a word-binding of its truth, and the renunciation of the wish as wish, a letting-go of the wish so that it may be, mysteriously at the moment of destruction, already true. For every wish must be ruined, not simply in the logical sense that a fulfilled wish would no longer be wished, which is wrong anyway given that will persists in infinite excess of want—'as love grows . . . the search for the one already found become[s] more intense' (Augustine, *Expositions on the Psalms*, 5.186), but in the deeper sense that the true wish can never properly be wished, cannot be a literal wishing, because wish itself is an improper translation of will into want. Whence the link between wish and resolution. As will is never reducible to personal want,

47

Which there is, namely, to eat and be eaten—mystically speaking—by dolphins, to become *like* them in the originary sense (*like*, from OE *lic*: body, corpse). For only someone who has eaten of dolphin will be the kind of *dead man* that dolphins eat: "Dolphins know by the smell if a dead man, that is on the sea, ate ever of Dolphin's kind; and if the dead man hath eat thereof, he eateth him anon; and if he did not, he keepeth and defendeth him fro eating and biting of other fish, and shoveth him, and bringeth him to the cliff with his own working."[156] Otherwise you will remain on this shore.[157] [NM]

---

to the parameters of desire within life, so the fulfillment of a true wish, as the *dying wish* inversely exposes, necessarily brings the wisher to the threshold of life: 'now lettest thou thy servant depart in peace' (Luke 2:2)" (Nicola Masciandaro, "Amor Fati: A Prosthetic Gloss," in *The Digital Dionysius: Nietzsche & the Network-Centric Condition*, eds. Dan Mellamphy and Nandita Biswas Mellamphy (New York: Punctum, 2015 [forthcoming]).

[156] Bartholomew Anglicus, *De proprietatibus rerum*, book 6, quoting from Robert Steele, Mediaeval Lore from Bartholomew Anglicus (London: Alexander Moring (The King's Classics), 1893/1905), available at: *The Medieval Bestiary*, s.v. "Dolphin," http://bestiary.ca/beasts/beast284.htm.

[157] "Merging in the Ocean is not for those who disobey. They are tossed up on the beach like an old piece of dried driftwood, and there they die! What gain is there in such a death? With me . . . one has to live while dying, so that you can live eternally, after dying such a death. Do you follow?" (Meher Baba, quoted in *Lord Meher*, 2100). "On the path, 100 percent honesty is required. The least hypocrisy washes you away from the shore of Reality" (Meher Baba, quoted in *Lord Meher*, 5014). "He who speculates from the shore about the ocean shall know only its surface, but he who would know the depths of the ocean must be willing to plunge into it" (Meher Baba, *Discourses*, 2:191). "Surely it is the height of folly for you to linger on this bridge" (Hakim Sinai, *The Walled Garden of Truth*, trans. David Pendlebury [London: Octagon Press, 1974], 52).

Though nothing,
nothing will keep us together

Last year I was gifted with two books, amongst others: Martin Heidegger's *On the Way to Language* (*Unterwegs Zur Sprache*, 1959), and *Poetry, Language, Thought* (1971). For whatever reason both of these have come to mind here. The first, most likely because of "A Dialogue on Language" contained therein, "between a Japanese and an Inquirer"—clearly Heidegger, the general gist of which evokes Eugene's *Starry Speculative Corpse*, and more specifically his "Prayers for Nothing."[158]

In discussing his desire to overcome metaphysics, in the context of what is referred to as "an all-consuming Europeanization" of thought, it is put to Heidegger in this dialogue that it is "Surely for this reason we in Japan understood at once your lecture 'What is Metaphysics?'"—which was made available in Japan in 1930 through a translation ventured by a Japanese student attending Heidegger's lectures—"We marvel to this day," he/she says, "how the Europeans could lapse into interpreting as nihilistic the nothingness of which you speak in that lecture. To us, emptiness is the loftiest name for what you mean to say with the word 'Being' . . ."[159]

[158] Thacker, "Prayers for Nothing," *Starry Speculative Corpse*, 62–100.
[159] Martin Heidegger, "A Dialogue on Language between a Japanese and an Inquirer," *On The Way To Language*, trans. Peter D. Hertz (San

As Eugene notes in *Starry Speculative Corpse*, for any philosophy aiming to examine being as such, discerning the ontological difference between Being and beings is the first step: "'Heidegger's tongue-twisting terminology 'the Being of beings' encapsulates this distinction. Being is not one being among other beings, but that which is common to all beings."[160]

Over the course of the "Dialogue" it is made plain, that for the Japanese as for the Inquirer, that thing *which is common to all beings* is a no-thing—as in the *No*-play evoked,[161] the stage is empty, the Being of beings is empty/emptiness, a sort of null-set. Heidegger really embraces this, and it is in *this* capacity, and *this capacity* alone, he says, that he seeks to "overcome metaphysics"—"neither a destruction nor even a denial"[162] of it, but a bringing out the essence of it in line with non-Western thought; with what Eugene would outline as the fundamental tenets of the Kyoto school, to which the Japanese in dialogue with Heidegger—"as comfortable discussing Western metaphysics as . . . the finer points of Zen Buddhism"[163]—clearly belongs:

> . . . in the West such positive principles as being, life, and the good have ontological priority over negative principles such as non-being, death, evil. In this sense negative principles are always apprehended as something secondary. By contrast, in the East, especially in Taoism and Buddhism, negative principles are not secondary but co-equal to the positive principles and even may be said to be primary and central . . . In short, the ultimate which is beyond the opposition between positive and negative is realized in the East in terms of negativity and in the West in terms of positivity.[164]

Francisco: Harper, 1971), 1–54; 19. My sincerest gratitude to Paul J. Ennis for both Heidegger volumes.

[160] Thacker, "Prayers for Nothing," 65.
[161] Heidegger, "A Dialogue," 16–19.
[162] Ibid., 20.
[163] Thacker, "Prayers for Nothing," 87.
[164] Masao Abe, *Zen and Western Thought,* ed. William R. LaFleur (Honolulu: University of Hawaii Press, 1989), 33, quoted in Thacker, "Prayers for Nothing," 86–7.

At this point in the commentary it seems utterly unnecessary to rehearse the affinity black metal has with non-Western thought—its ultimate, which is beyond the opposition between positive and negative, is too realized in terms of negativity: non-being, death, evil. Far more interesting with respect to Heidegger's concept of Being, and as it pertains to the boundless idealism of the genre, are the Taoist and Buddhist traditions that Masao Abe mentions. In chapter eleven of the *Tao Te Ching*, a collection of sayings attributed to the sixth-century sage Lao Tzu, we read:

> We put thirty spokes together and call it a wheel;
> but it is on the space where there is nothing that the
> utility of the wheel depends.
> We turn clay to make a vessel;
> but it is on the space where there is nothing that the
> utility of the vessel depends.
> We pierce doors and windows to make a house;
> and it is on these spaces where there is nothing that the
> utility of the house depends.[165]

The point of this Taoist logion—that we recognize the utility of what is not—is recapitulated somewhat differently by the Romantic poet Kahlil Gibran in a well-worn yet nonetheless profound meditation on marriage that says "Love one another but make not a bond of love," "let the winds of the heavens dance between you."[166] The kernel of which is applied to teaching and guidance in Buddhism, where a famous saying runs, "If you see Buddha on the road, kill him!"[167] The Buddhists have long maintained that the highest aspiration of man should be the rooting out of his soul or self, namely "atman," and while Europeans are often shocked by this "nihilism," just as they would lapse into interpreting as "nihilistic" the nothingness of which Heidegger speaks in his lecture, they think nothing of it when Paul

---

[165] See chapter eleven in any number of translations, for instance, Lao Tzu, *Tao Te Ching*, trans. Stephen Mitchell (New York: Perennial Classics, 2000).
[166] Kahlil Gibran, *The Prophet* (London: Heinemann, 1926), 18–21.
[167] For a discussion of this, see Moid Siddiqui, *Leading From The Heart: Sufi Principles At Work* (New Delhi: Sage Publications, 2014), 153–5.

says "I am crucified with Christ, yet not I but Christ liveth in me" (Gal. 2:20). *Nothing, nothing will keep us together.* [EC]

We can beat them, for ever and ever
Oh we can be heroes,
just for one day

Ich, ich bin dann König
Und du, du Königin
Obwohl sie unschlagbar scheinen
Werden wir Helden für einen Tag
Wir sind dann wir an diesem Tag

Ich, ich glaubte zu träumen (zu träumen)
Die Mauer im Rücken war kalt (so kalt)
Schüsse reißen die Luft (reißen die Luft)
Doch wir küssen, als ob nichts geschieht (nichts geschieht)
Und die Scham fiel auf ihrer Seite
Oh, wir können sie schlagen für alle Zeiten
Dann sind wir Helden für diesen Tag
We can be heroes
We can be heroes
We can be heroes
We can be heroes

We're nothing and nothing will help us
Maybe we're lying, then you better not stay
But we could be safer just for one day

Following the Stench

Drew Daniel

Evil odours attract evil spirits.
— *Encyclopedia Acephalica*[1]

Once more, into the crypt. If the commencement of today's event with talk of putrefaction skips past death to its aftermath and thus feels more *Mors* than *Mystica*, such a movement forwards is also a return to origins. Joseph Russo's remarks on putrefaction and decay as collected in *Hideous Gnosis* have already identified the unretrievable non-experience of a body in decay as central to the negative ambitions of any black metal theory worthy of that name, pressing up to moments of extinction and annihilation and testing the capacity of thought to follow or occupy those border areas.[2] Precisely because Dominic Fox has already identified the historical belatedness implicit in black metal's musical genealogy and Russo has further activated the sonic immanence of decay within Xasthur's work and others with such precision at the first New York convocation of black metal theory, I will be examining putrefaction in terms of different artists, different key words, and, most of all, along a separate perceptual pathway: the nose. To theorize with and on the nose is to court certain dangers, principally a synaesthetic belle-lettrism that would risk collapse into putrid purple prose in search of metaphors pungent enough to transmit the olfactory oomph of actual experiences of rotten presence. My close calls with both the journalistic and the autobiographical registers may well sound all too "on the nose": glib, obvious, a given. But if theory's root in the Greek word

---

[1] Michel Leiris, "Hygiene," in *Encyclopaedia Acephalica*: *Comprising the Critical Dictionary & Related Texts and the Encyclopaedia Costa*, eds. Georges Bataille and Robert Lebel & Isabelle Waldberg, respectively, trans. Iain White (London: Atlas Press, 1995), 52.

[2] Joseph Russo, "Perpetuo Putresco: Perpetually I Putrefy," in *Hideous Gnosis: Black Metal Theory Symposium I*, ed. Nicola Masciandaro (New York: n.p., 2010), 93–105.

"theōría" and "theorein" indexes a crucial connection to observation and the scopic regime of the visual, then to think in darkness we may need to follow our nose.

Specifically, I'm interested in thinking through the olfactory dimension of the Swedish black metal horde Watain, both at the level of a lyrical thematics of rot-mysticism articulated in particular songs and in the immanence of performances in which the presence of rotten animal flesh creates a perceptual community between audience and performer that manifests a collectively endured, enjoyed and celebratory material proximity to death. Smelling together as a religious practice is of course hardly new, and the burning of offerings and the presentation of aromas within sacred spaces is found across spiritual traditions, from incense burning in Chinese and Tibetan Buddhism to Indian nard in Hindu contexts to Greek magical papyri on the burning of malabathron and cinnamon to the swinging of Roman Catholic thuribles during Mass.[3] These practices create a tangible vertical link between the sacrificial object and its imagined ascent into the nostrils of the divinity being propitiated. Against this normative backdrop of upward mobility, Watain's downward flinging of blood and rotten animal bio-matter onto themselves, the stage, and the audience below preserves the vertical orientation but satanically inverts the directionality: the goal is not to rise like smoke to celestial nasal passages, but to soak the telluric ground with the proof and evidence of death as an ongoing, smell-creating material process, and to mark and involve the audience in a sacrament of rot and blood. The lyrics to their anthem "Stellarvore" provide a useful gloss:

> Let us welcome the Bringer of the End
> with open arms
> Let us adorn the gates to nothingness
> with blood.[4]

In a parody of the eucharist, participants in the communion of Watain's black metal are marked and bonded by blood, and with

---

[3] George Luck "Magical Smoke: Psychoactive Substances in Religion and Magic," in *Arcana Mundi: Magic and the Occult in the Greek and Roman Worlds* (Baltimore: Johns Hopkins University Press, 1985), 479–493.
[4] Watain, "Stellarvore," *Sworn To the Dark* (Season of Mist, 2007).

each gasp for breath grow more deeply inspired with a forcefully malodorous stench of putrefaction.

As marketing, it's genius. As the oil and wineskins of Crash Worship were to mid-90s industrial music and G.W.A.R.'s copious stage blood cannons were to whatever genre you want to call G.W.A.R., Watain's practice garners attention and notoriety through the deliberate creation of innumerable soiled items of audience clothing, which become battle-scarred souvenirs of a transgressive night out, reliquary part-objects that attest to close calls with morbidity. But the difference is in the smells and stains themselves: Watain's keynote is not blood so much as the stench of rot itself, something that exceeds and surpasses the material specificity of a particular stain or splash. The notoriety of Watain's onstage odor has been a calling card for quite some time, prompting reactions held in common across numerous concert reviews, from the dumbstruck "all I can tell you is, I will never forget that fucking smell," to a question succinctly expressed by Carly Onofrio's live review essay, titled "What the Fuck is that Smell?"[5] A fan describing the slow dispersal of this odor as it ruined a post-show meal, asked, "How does one eat without gagging when every time you take a bite, you smell old putrid blood instead of your warm late-night comfort food?"[6]

Superseding the purely intellectual acknowledgement of mortality familiar from the *memento mori* tradition, smelling death in this inescapably immanent manner hits us in the center of our skulls—in the olfactory bulb, a tiny localized area within the brain that processes and locally excites as it detects and sorts particular odors.[7] Summarizing in layman's terms (from a lesson-plan that is literally titled "Neuroscience for Kids"), University of Washington neurosurgeon Dr. Eric Chudler notes that:

---

[5] Chris Harris, http://gunshyassassin.com/reviews/watain-take-another-bite-out-of-that-old-apple/; Carly Onofrio, "What the Fuck Is That Smell?" (January 6, 2011), http://www.imposemagazine.com/bytes/new-music/what-the-fuck-is-that-smell.

[6] Onofrio, in Ibid.

[7] Holly Dugan, *The Ephemeral History of Perfume: Scent and Sense in Early Modern England* (Baltimore: Johns Hopkins University Press, 2011), 11.

The olfactory system is often described as the most "primitive" sensory system because of its early phylogenetic development and its connections to older, subconscious portions of the brain. From the olfactory bulbs, odor messages go to several brain structures that make up the "olfactory cortex," an area that evolved before the cortical areas that give us consciousness. This part of the cortex is on the bottom surface of the brain, with some of the olfactory areas folded under the visible parts. These areas have connections to the limbic system (including the hippocampus, amygdala and hypothalamus), which is important in emotional states and in memory formation. Thus, a smell frequently activates intense feelings and memories before a person even identifies the odor.[8]

By gatecrashing the nostrils of the audience, Watain are exploiting a kind of perceptual "back door" into the body/mind interface that sidesteps the cluttered workspace of consciousness and its attendant language-orientation, egoic regimes of identification, and theaters of volition. In transposing a lyrical orientation towards death onto a manifestly physical threshold experience of nasal intimacy with its keynote signature, Watain transcendentalize an underrated and under-theorized orifice, flooding the limbic system with unstoppable sensations.

Now, some of you mean girls from Black Metal Theory High may be holding your nose at any discussion of Watain in 2015. The band's occasionally clean vocals and dips into outlaw boogie shtick on their more recent album *The Wild Hunt* have depressed and alienated some heretofore loyal purists, who don't want black metal's generic identity smeared or blurred. But Watain's Southern strategy (upending as it does the prominence of the Hyperborean realms too often taken to be the tacit locale of the genre) seems all too apt when one remembers the immortal lyrics of Lynyrd Skynyrd's "That Smell" from their 1977 LP *Street Survivors*: "Ooooh that smell / Can't you smell that smell / Ooooh

---

[8] Eric Chudler, "Our Chemical Senses: Olfaction," https://faculty.washington.edu/chudler/chems.html.

that smell / The smell of death surrounds you."[9] Of course, Death and smell go together. It's a cliché to assert that the smell of rot is "sickly sweet," but it has some scientific support; the bacteria *Pseudomonas Fragi* has a noted resemblance to the smell of strawberries. There is also a proleptic "smell of death" which some nurses claim to be able to perceive, a predictive odor that a patient's body gives off roughly a week before their death; in brutally depressing posts to nursing blogs, health care professionals and hospice workers note the curious mixture of fruity, sweaty, and musky smells which seem to toll in advance of the final spasm (ketoacidosis—the speedy breakdown of amino acids in fat—might be the cause of this odor).[10] On the other side, research into anosmia (the decline in the capacity to smell) has alarmingly suggested that a sudden drop off in the capacity to detect odors can be an eerily accurate predictor of death. "In a study of more than 3,000 people aged 57 to 85, 39% of subjects who failed a simple smelling test died within five years," compared with only a 10% death rate for those who passed the smell test.[11] Being able to smell, even and especially to smell death, might well have an immunitary, hygienic, and evolutionarily protective function.

In deliberately making everyone in a club environment feel nauseously alert to the presence of death, Watain hope to override that protective function by enforcing an imaginative leap of proleptic identification, as if we were inhaling the reek of our own future dead selves by proxy.[12] If the scopic regime of *memento*

---

[9] Lynyrd Skynyrd, "That Smell," *Street Survivors* (MCA Records, 1977). The ominous warning of the song in question proved tragically predictive, insofar as several members of the band died in a plane crash only three days after the release of the album, which subsequently had its cover art (an image of the band surrounded by licking flames) posthumously edited to avoid a certain ironic morbidity.
[10] http://allnurses.com/general-nursing-discussion/does-death-have-452535.html
[11] Bill Berkrot, "Loss of smell may be predictor of death in older adults; study," *Reuters* (October 1, 2014), http://www.reuters.com/article/2014/10/01/us-smell-death-idUSKCN0HQ4TJ20141001.
[12] The power relations implicit in creating and receiving stench are noteworthy here, and seem to have triggered the mixture of excitement and mockery implicit in the *New York Times* response to the first manifestation of Black Metal Theory; the title of Ben Ratliff's article

mori leverages the visual shock of the carrion corpse as a logically impossible—hence traumatic—face-to-face encounter with our own future visages as they shall appear to the mortuary technicians and bystanders who tend to our own corpses, the analogical and rhetorical bridge of "as I am, you shall be" has here been transposed from seeing to smelling: Watain seem to be telling everyone within the olfactory radius of their onstage ritual that "as these rotting animals now smell, someday you too will stink." In doing so, Watain thus re-activate a sensory transposition from looking to smelling with an illustrious precursor:

> HAMLET: Dost thou think Alexander looked o' this
>   fashion i'th'earth?
> HORATIO: E'en so.
> HAMLET: And smelt so? Pah! (Puts down skull)
> HORATIO: E'en so, my lord.
> HAMLET: How low we can fall.[13]

Delegitimizing Claudius by symbolically dethroning the Imperial Alexander, Hamlet begins this speech by punching upwards, but at its close he counts himself among those threatened: there is now a "we" within which he counts himself, for whom the skull leers and beckons. The Oedipal assault upon paternal authority implicit in wielding the leveling threat of death in this showy, rhetorical manner should be familiar to generations of readers of Shakespeare's tragedy, but what is particularly interesting for my purposes is the extent to which the graveyard scene stands in as a precursor to Watain's poetics of rot because of its perceptual switch from eyes to nose. The tactile encounter with the graveyard scene's pungent remains affords a range of sensations, but it is noticeable that Hamlet's gorehound self-theatricalizing reaches

---

"Thank You, Professor, That Was Putrid" indexes the counterintuitive power of stench-as-pleasure to function as both advertisement for the movement and implicit put-down of its perversity (http://www.nytimes.com/2009/12/15/arts/music/15metal.html).
[13] William Shakespeare, "The Tragedy of Hamlet, Prince of Denmark," *The Complete Works of Shakespeare*, ed. David Bevington (New York: Longman, 2003).

its threshold in this mortal snort of disgust. Hamlet's "we" may well be a royal "we," the virtual collectivity of a royal person, but it also founds a "we" upon the shared exposure to death that defines being alive as such. It is this mortal collectivity that Watain re-assert when they lead their audiences by the nose towards a deep whiff of grave-stench.

But in the midst of potentially uniting the audience in a collective apprehension of that very shared condition, a certain trial-by-smell is also thereby initiated, and with it, a perhaps unseemly competition for perceptual prestige across and between its members as they variably embrace and resist this assault. One can always attempt to cover one's nose, and one can always huff and make a show of deeply inhaling, but there is a risk of vomit, or of an urge to flee. In making this range of reactions possible, have Watain literalized Susan Sontag's remark in "Notes on Camp" that, in contrast to the haughty disdain of the old style dandies, "the [modern] connoisseur of camp sniffs the stink and prides himself on his strong nerves"?[14] There may be less of a sensibility gap between modern camp and satanic dandyism than Sontag imagines, since, after all, it was the original Symbolist dandy Jean Lorrain, author of "*Le Sang des Dieux*" (*The Blood of God*, a black metal title *avant la lettre* if ever there was one), who said that "the charm of horror tempts only the strong."[15] Are Watain's smell-o-visions a matter of demonstrations of fortitude, an askesis of self-mastery in which the capacity not to barf or leave boosts kvlt fanboy cred/credulity? I'd like to think that it goes beyond the aspiration to an iron stomach, or the desire to get a rep. Tangible but invisible, smell radiates and enforces an encounter with an unseen presence, the fact of a non-specific yet powerful intruder into the performance space: not only or simply death, but the curious roundelay of death-in-life which is the process of putrefaction itself. Off-gassing as their fats break down and disintegrate, the dead animals within Watain's onstage gore-buckets become noxious birthing centers; insofar as their remains are the site of bustling bacteriological colonization, these mammals become grotesquely re-animated as carrion co-participants in the concert. Because humans are relatively bad at

---

[14] Susan Sontag "Notes on 'Camp'," *Against Interpretation, and Other Essays* (New York: Picador, 1966), 289.
[15] Jean Lorrain, *Le Sang des Dieux* (Paris; Edouard Joseph, 1920).

localizing the sources of smell, the encounter with a mysterious odor tends to produce shifts in the posture and attitude of the body as the nose is moved about in hopes of determining a given smell's origin and location. In a concert environment, Watain's onstage deployment of rot induces an overwhelming effect of anxiogenic diffusion. While components from the slop buckets are hurled onto the crowd and localized in gestures, there is a broadly pervasive horizon of stench that envelopes the space as a whole, which precedes and endures over and above these local smell-triggering actions, and this spatial dimension expands the purchase of the logic of *memento mori* by triggering in the audience the malingering suspicion that the world itself has died and is now putrescent.[16] What if there is no escape route from a world that has become a corpse?

Watching and smelling Watain in concert, I was transported by my nose downwards to the grave, forwards to imagined scenarios of future human extinction, and yet also backwards in time to a smell memory from my past: the swooning feeling in that Baltimore heavy metal bar of an unexpectedly Proustian madeleine of acrid discomfort. When I was a morbid and ghoulish teenager, I would cultivate opportunities for encounters with death. I've described elsewhere the time that I broke into a rendering plant and peered down into a giant truck loaded with rotting horses and cows, so I won't trot that out again. But Watain's stench didn't remind me of the rendering plant as strongly as it reminded me of a location closer to home: the trunk of my own car. Driving the surburban back roads of Louisville, Kentucky in highschool, I had spotted a dead squirrel and thought it might be interesting to strip its bones, soak them in bleach, and obtain a squirrel skeleton, so I pulled over, gingerly picked up the roadkill and stowed it in the trunk. I spaced on my plans, a

---

[16] The theme of "the decay of the world" commences in classical legends on the departure of Astraea at the end of the Golden Age and carries over into Christian eschatological timeframes of the Fall and a perpetual decline that precedes the coming of Apocalypse and Judgment. For an intellectual history of the theme of "the decay of the world," see Victor Jones, *All Coherence Gone* (London: Frank Cass & Co., 1966). I am indebted to Nicola Masciandaro for raising this connection in conversation at Mors Mystica: Black Metal Theory Symposium, Saint Vitus Bar, Brooklyn (April 25, 2015).

nonspecific interval of time went by, and then my Chevy Nova began to give off a potent funk. It was now mid-July, with temperatures hovering above 95 degrees as humidity turned air to soup. With touching innocence, I popped the trunk and unleashed a nauseating miasma of roiling, eye-watering, retch-inducing death-stench. The heat and enclosure had somehow hyper-accelerated the course of nature, reducing the squirrel to a smear of furry porridge strewn across my spare tire. My would-be craft project had gone feral, compressing a temporary process into a curiously strong encounter with the reek of putrefaction.

My Carcass reference is intentional, as I was a devoted listener to their *Reek of Putrefaction* album at the time, which I mention only in order to trigger a no doubt obvious potential objection: isn't putrefaction more associated with "death metal" than with "black metal"? Certainly death metal as an aesthetic mode is founded in the lyrical exploration of death as a material process, limning the specific smells and tastes that accompany this disintegratory change of state. Its perceptual emphasis is apparent if we turn to, say, Death's *Scream Bloody Gore* album from 1987, whose climactic title track contains the line "Dripping from your mouth comes a rancid smell"; at the arguable peak of one of the founding albums of the genre, smell becomes material, local, liquid, and haptic.[17] Going further, the dynamics of self-mastery required to suppress nausea is clearly indexed in Exhumed's "In My Human Slaughterhouse," from their classic *Gore Metal* LP, with its heady evocation of "a putrid gust of flatus and methane / inhaling the rotting fumes as I choke / hit by a wave of nausea I try to restrain."[18] These are simply a few fetid blooms from a bouquet of possible examples that one might cite. Given death metal's seemingly definitive and pre-emptive claim upon this subject matter, one might well ask: what's so "black metal," let alone "black metal theory," about the materiality of putrefaction? Wouldn't materiality precisely constitute a stumbling block to both the theoretical opening out of philosophical implicature and the mystical dimension we are

---

[17] Death, "Scream Bloody Gore," *Scream Bloody Gore* (Combat Records, 1987).
[18] Exhumed, "In My Human Slaughterhouse," *Gore Metal: A Necrospective 1998–2015* (Relapse Records, 2015).

gathered to invoke and explore? Russo and Fox have made their own answers, but here is mine.

Putrefaction crosses over from death metal to black metal when remains are repurposed as a nasal means to commune with Satan or focalize Satanic energies. Smell constitutes a means by which to acknowledge the contiguity and overlap of death metal and black metal only in order to then assert a fundamental distinction: the passage from one to the other consists in the conscious embrace of evil and destruction over the mere material fact of death. Drawing a line in the dirt, Euronymous was quite clear about this essential distinction in attitudes and valences in a typically polemical interview with Jon "Metalion" Kristiansen in *Slayer* #8:

> *Slayer*: Why do you think so many bands are trying to copy Napalm Death, Carcass, Morbid Angel or Death? Aren't people creative anymore?
>
> EURONYMOUS: No, creativity disappeared in the middle of the 1980s. There are just a few who manage to preserve the brutality and Evil which the ancient bands like Sodom, Destruction, Bathory, Possessed, Venom, Hellhammer / Celtic Frost and so on had. *It's very important that the music is filled with dark moods and that the music smells of destruction.*[19]

Following through upon Euronymous's mandate with fanatical thoroughness, Watain's rot-mysticism ceaselessly folds the sensory materiality of putrefaction into a tangible means by which to aspire to access a Satanic presence, allowing the front-loading of a virtual encounter with death into the space of life and "live" performance: smelling what we cannot see thus perceptually stands in for intuiting the absent presence of Satan as a force of rebellion, refusal, and perversity within our own lives. Such immanent inner experience goes beyond the corpse-painted surface of the face and aims for an interior interface between the floating airborne particulate matter of a dead body and the

---

[19] Jon "Metalion" Kristiansen, "Slayer #8," *METALION: The Slayer Mag Diaries* (New York: Bazillion Points, 2011).

chemoreceptors of our own, more slowly dying bodies, and in this inward embrace Watain satanically transvalue pleasure and disgust. As Euronymous insisted across many interviews, loving what is un-natural or anti-natural *is* a means of loving Satan. To be sure, rot is natural, but so too, it would seem, is a healthy aversive reflex against risky exposure to rot. Voluntarily embracing rotten-ness constitutes a sacrifice of self-care that affirms a dedication, that one is "sworn to the dark"; as the cost of such service, Watain members occasionally contract impetigo in the course of duty.

Watain's song "Satan's Hunger," from the *Sworn to the Dark* album, emblematizes this perverse desire:

> Each sense grows dim as if one with the dead,
> And as I fall on my knees to the ground I am fed
> With the fumes of shallow graves.
> Into the starless night, I follow the stench.[20]

The first three lines above constitute the end of the first verse; the fourth commences the chorus. Insofar as the place of minimal seeing is also a space of maximal smelling, we are rendered hyper-aware of the distinctions of intensity and vivacity between perceptual registers, and encouraged to tilt them against each other. Yet we are also confronted by a curious synaesthetic transfer in which one pathway has come to bleed or blur into another: when we are "fed" by a "fume," then smell has become taste, or, better, a kind of substitute for taste, an alternative to food, an unexpected and grotesque source of necro-energy.

It is a commonplace of mystical writings on death to imagine the valedictory farewell to sensory pathways as a means of leaving the world. Black metal evokes this tradition repeatedly, as when on Samael's "Beyond The Nothingness," from their *Blood Ritual* album, Vorphalack announces that "We're dazzled by total obscurity of the parallel world / Our senses are numb for our longest journey."[21] Yet on "Satan's Hunger," Watain both cite and pervert this mystical practice of deliberately extinguishing the

---

20 Watain, "Satan's Hunger," *Sworn to the Dark* (Season of Mist, 2007).
21 Samael, "Beyond the Nothingness," *Blood Ritual* (Century Media, 1992).

senses as a means of transcendence. In the lyrical passage from "Satan's Hunger" quoted above, the negativity and finality of "each sense" growing dim is belied by the closing emphasis upon the persistent strength of smell over and against other means of apprehending and experiencing the world. In a sublation of sensory input, the ghoul-mystic of "Satan's Hunger" is simultaneously joining the dead by bidding farewell to the senses, and ravenously eating the dead through his nose. The verse transitions from "dim" to "fume," offering an onrushing plenum of inhalation as a compensation for the erasure of the visual register achieved by ambient darkness. But this lyrical hinge-point is also articulated at the formal level via a literal in-breathing as Erik Danielsson takes a breath before launching into a chorus about breathing in the smell of decay. Word and image are thus reinforced by cadence and phrasing in a taut knot of performance and text.

Compounding this synergistic emphasis upon smell's primordial triumph over its rivals at the levels of both lyric and phrasing, Watain's production maneuvers express these thematic agendas in a sonically direct manner which forcefully articulates the implicit (counter)religiosity of smelling grave odors. In the arrangement of "Satan's Hunger," there are highly abrupt dropouts of music on two words, points in which the mix cuts out to simply Danielsson's voice without the undercarriage of the riff and the blast beats. The first time occurs towards the conclusion of the first verse on the single word "ground." The trick is repeated towards the end of the second verse section, where the music drops out on the word "foul." These cuts are didactic, mannered, and transform these words into sigils, prayers, twin puncture wounds within the form of the song. This invocation and equivalence of "ground" and "foul" becomes an equation: the ground IS foul. Such an assertion of telluric rot inverts the divine promise of forgiveness which God articulates in the Noahide covenant of the Book of Genesis, Chapter 8, verse 21:

> And the LORD smelled a sweet savour; and the LORD
> said in his heart, I will not again curse the ground any
> more for man's sake; for the imagination of man's heart

is evil from his youth; neither will I again smite any more every thing living, as I have done.[22]

Sprinkling the ground with blood, snuffling for rot within the earth, Watain dismantle the terms of this covenant, and abjure the divine gift of forgiveness. The return of stench to the ground re-asserts the divine curse upon it, and wallows in the damned and death-bound condition. Such an act resonates strongly with the prophetic books, in which "stench" continually indexes divine disfavor and anger. Indeed Watain's anthem suggests a blasphemous parody of Isaiah 3:24: "Instead of perfume there will be rottenness; and instead of a belt, a rope; and instead of well-set hair, baldness; and instead of a rich robe, a skirt of sackcloth; and branding instead of beauty." Watain's Danielsson expresses this counter-scriptural ideal succinctly when he says that black metal "makes holes in reality. It stabs the idea of the creator, and that is its beauty. Black metal is a distortion of reality, an enemy of the world, and we are its messengers."[23]

Smells, too, are messengers, indicators of presence, necessarily temporal markers of the passage of time. For this reason smell has been seen as pre- or even anti-theoretical, keyed as it is to ontic particulars, the happenstance of embodiment and locality. Notoriously, in his lectures on aesthetics Hegel privileges sight and sound as "theoretical" senses, and correspondingly denigrates smell and taste as subsidiary because they are inherently tethered to practical relations rooted in seemingly "lower" somatic tasks like eating. Yet the particular terms of Hegel's very denigration helpfully flag precisely what it is about smell that makes it ripe for a specifically black metal inflected mode of re-appropriation as a zone of theoretical blackening: "For we can only smell what is wasting away, and we can only taste by destroying."[24] As Adam Jaspar and Nadia Wagner put it: "By

---

[22] *The Geneva Bible: A Facsimile of the 1560 Edition*, ed. Lloyd E. Berry (Peabody: Hendrickson Bibles, 2007).

[23] http://noisey.vice.com/blog/watain-wild-purveyors-of-darkness-outlaw-video.

[24] G. W. F. Hegel, *Hegel's Aesthetics: Lectures on Fine Art*, vol. 1, trans. T. M. Knox (Oxford; Oxford University Press, 1998), 138. See also Sita Bhaumik, "The Other Senses," *Art Practical* (November 15, 2010), http://www.artpractical.com/review/the_other_senses/.

smelling things, we absorb them directly into our bodies, and consequently they provide what Kant otherwise only attributes to God: unmediated knowledge of the thing in itself.'[25] Hegel's categorical elisions of smelling and eating as distinct but related modes of incorporation which are necessarily and inherently conditioned by a shared dynamic of destruction is more than kin and less than kind with Euronymous's hymn to a music that "smells like destruction," insofar as Hegel's extro-missive account of smelling curiously turns the very experience of accessing smell into an index of material collapse. To give off smell is to lose some of one's own body at a micro-particulate layer, to surrender minute parts of one's self as "odorants," flaking up and away into the chemo-receptor surfaces on the interior of the nose of the organism that smells us. Hegel's flourish is thus supported by a certain basic physiological backstory, and the essential alignment of smelling with destruction held in common by Hegel and Euronymous can be said to underwrite the satanic incorporation fantasies at the core of Watain's anthem "Satan's Hunger" as well. These fantasies subtend the song's title, which hovers unstably between multiply possessive scenarios. In feeling "Satan's Hunger," the song's narratorial "I" is at once separated from and aligned with Satan: to long to inhale rot is to hunger with and for Satan, and to "follow the stench" is to hunt and seek in darkness for access to this object of veneration. Wandering, questing, and hungering signal the fundamentally shared condition of humanity and Satan as sorrowful beings cut off from the self-satisfied completeness of divinity and sentenced to labor and drift as a consequence of fallen-ness. This solidarity was memorably articulated by Leon d'Alexis in his demonological essay *Traicté des Energumenes* (1599):

> The connection between the human kind expelled from the earthly paradise and the devil banished from heaven is founded on their common accident. This angelic spirit is characterized by a relentlessly active nature, but he can neither turn to God who has abandoned him, nor can he converse with the good angels from whom he has separated himself, nor can he find any rest or solace in

---

[25] Adam Jaspar and Nadia Wagner, "Notes on Scent," *Cabinet Magazine* 32 (2009): 37.

contemplating his deformed and disfigured image. As a consequence, he cannot help but turn his attention to our behaviors. Wandering on earth in search of rest, his sole activity is his interaction and dialogue with human beings.[26]

Leon d'Alexis articulates a relationship of reciprocal solidarity, of shared criminality which bonds the fallen into fellowship based upon need. Satan's hunger for companions (or subjects?) finds its complement and partner in the aspirations of the ghoul-mystic narrator of Watain's song to access the mysteries made available by the stench that emanates from graves. In the final iteration of the chorus, smell becomes sound in the form of an auditory "call" which beckons the adept to enter and transcend:

Into the starless night, I follow the stench.
Urged on by a thirst, that cannot be quenched.
Into the starless night, I follow the call
Urged on by a lust, that eliminates all.
Satan's Hunger! Satan's Hunger![27]

In a mimetic enfolding of longing within longing made (over)familiar by the Lacanian slogan that "Desire is the desire of the Other,"[28] Watain's adept ultimately hungers for Satan's own hunger: driven by need, the ghoul-mystic snuffles into the void in search of something and finds at the center of the blackness only an ever-more-powerful vortex of annihilating need: "a lust, that eliminates all."

Deliberately smelling waste, rot, and filth with Watain becomes a means by which to overturn values, to annul stratification, to enter lawless darkness anew, to negate theory on behalf of theory, to blacken theory again, to invert Hamlet's

---

[26] Leon D'Alexis, *Traicte des Energumenes, suivi d'un discours sur la possession de Marthe Brossier: Contre les calomnies d'un medicin de Paris* (Troyes, 1599), as cited in Armando Maggi, *Satan's Rhetoric: A study of Renaissance Demonology* (Chicago: University of Chicago Press, 2011), 1.

[27] Watain, "Satan's Hunger."

[28] Jacques Lacan, *The Four Fundamental Concepts of Psychoanalysis (Seminar XI)* (New York: W.W. Norton & Co, 1998), 158.

reflexive "Pah!" of revulsion at the stench of rot into an "Ahhhhh" of satanic delectation. At the level of both lyrical invocations of stink and in the noisome immanence of performance, Watain's rot-mysticism is a sensory technology for the transvaluation of lust and aversion which weaponizes black metal's aesthetic sensorium, conscripting us into its service as followers of the stench.

Ablaze in the Bath of Fire

Brad Baumgartner

In this world
we walk on the roof of hell
gazing at flowers.

– Kobayashi Issa[1]

I see for many no way for the divine love to reach them
save through a very ghastly Hell.

– Valdemar Thisted[2]

And my impersonal soul burns me.

– Clarice Lispector[3]

PARADISICAL HELLFIRE

In darkness and in secret, but burning, I creep forth,[4] as a witness, via the auditory vision of my own ecstatic trance, to black metal's secret apophatic engagement in a double inversion: not only does it turn the world upside-down but also inside-out. On the one hand, black metal inverts anagogy, plunging, as we will see, the flame of Love downwards via the inverted cross of Divine Descent.[5] On the other hand, black metal points to the irrevocable

---

[1] Kobayashi Issa, "Passage through August," http://www.augustpoetry.org/poets/Issa.htm.

[2] Valdemar Thisted, quoted in Hermann Neander, *The Gospel of Gehenna Fire and its Relation to the Cross* (London: Whiting and Co., 1885), 3.

[3] Clarice Lispector, *The Passion According to G. H.*, trans. Idra Novey (New York: New Directions, 2012), 53.

[4] Cf. John of the Cross: "In darkness and in secret I crept forth" (*The Dark Night of the Soul*, trans. Gabriela Cunninghame Graham [London: John M. Watkins, 1905], 250).

[5] On the *coincidentia oppositorum* of divine ascent/descent, Sri Aurobindo writes, "All true truths of Love and of the works of Love the psychic being accepts in their place; but its flame mounts always upward and it is eager to push the ascent from lesser to higher degrees of Truth,

fact that, as E. M. Cioran notes, "We moderns have discovered hell inside ourselves and that is our good fortune."[6] If, to follow the hermetic maxim, that which is above is the same as that which is below, then not only do "we walk," as Kobayashi Issa states, "on the roof of Hell / gazing at flowers," but we also gaze at ourselves underneath Hell's roof, *are* our own hells, and by the very nature of being alive embody the necessity of *entering hell in this life*. Angelus Silesius writes, "Christian, you must be once in hell's abysmal fire, / Endure it while on earth, not after you expire."[7]

Thus black metal's *secret* secret, that which reveals itself through the blasphemy of my own being alive, is that hell is simultaneously outside and inside myself. This double inversion happens not only vertically (i.e. downwards anagogy), but also horizontally (what is inside is as what is outside). Metal is the hell by which, and the metalhead is the hell through which, one must bewilderingly walk, crawling out of the world and into the abyssic hellish pit of oneself, and vice versa, by jumping into this figure-eighted hoop of fire that is the Infinite.

This essay thus begins in flames simply because it must. But it could also just as likely begin Everywhere, and Nowhere, simply because it cannot and cannot not do otherwise. All metalheads are always already on fire, in fire, and are burning as we speak. And yet the true conundrum seems to be how to end one's burning by the very aporia of one's burning forever, an impossible feat that must end as it begins, by the *living out* of death, the death of death: "that is not dead which can eternal lie, and with strange aeons even death may die."[8] So we must begin by donning the most *flammable* of corpse paint, an aporetic paint that kills the

since it knows that only by the ascent to a Highest Truth and the decent of that highest Truth can Love be delivered from the cross and placed upon the throne; for the cross is the sign of the Divine Descent barred and marred by the transversal line of a cosmic deformation which turns life into a state of suffering and misfortune" (*The Synthesis of Yoga, Part One: The Yoga of Divine Works* [Twin Lakes: Lotus Light Publications, 1996], 147).

[6] E. M. Cioran, *Tears and Saints*, trans. Ilinca Zarifopol-Johnston (Chicago: University of Chicago Press, 1995), 52.

[7] Angelus Silesius, *The Cherubinic Wanderer*, trans. Maria Shrady (New York: Paulist Press, 1986), 119.

[8] H. P. Lovecraft, "The Call of Chthulhu," in *The Call of Chthulhu and Other Weird Stories*, ed. S. T. Joshi (London: Penguin Books, 1999), 156.

corpse, to partake in a double death that is not unlike the mystic's solitary spiritual adventure (*khalwa* or abandonment of self)[9] of walking as a dead man through Hell in order to get to Paradise (*fana* or total annihilation of mind/total absorption into God).[10]

These opening remarks thus seek to understand mystical death via the hermeneutic of fire, that is to say, to cultivate an understanding of mystical death from the perspective of auto-incineration. By saying this, these remarks don't really wish to understand *anything at all*, but rather to incinerate understanding in favor of a kind of blackened bewilderment. We thus begin at our own ending, which is really to say, end at the Beginning's end, in utter paradox, for to illuminate the notion of fire via black metal means to invoke the flaming (ar)rays of a de-creative black sun. Black metal inheres within the conditions of impossibility for auto-incineration, a complete mystical death wherein all is caught on fire, fanning flames perpetual in unrestricted dimensions of suffering and bliss. The metalhead is thus also the mystic who must be incinerated by flames, complicit in a divine melting which blackens the scissions between self/world and world/cosmos. Born for burning,[11] in the Hail! of mystical death, the metalhead is fearlessly thrown into their autotelic fire to do away with the Hell of being oneself, walking through their own very hellishness in order to get to Paradise. Paradoxically, then, the metalhead is, as Pest note, "blessed by hellfire."[12]

---

[9] In Islam, *khalwa* is understood as "retreat; the act of total abandonment in desire of the Divine Presence. The one who undertakes *khalwa*, like a dead man, surrenders all worldly and exterior religious affairs, as the first step to surrendering his own existence" (Ibn 'Arabi, *Journey to the Lord of Power* [Rochester: Inner Traditions International, 1989], 110).

[10] Cf. Venom: "heaven's on fire / and when you die you'll go there too" ("Heaven's on Fire," *Black Metal* [Neat Records, 1982]).

[11] Cf. Bathory: "She is not afraid to die / She will burn again tonight / (she will always burn) / But her spirit shall survive" ("Born for Burning," *The Return......* [Black Mark Production, 1985]).

[12] Pest, "Blessed by Hellfire," *Rest in Morbid Darkness* (Season of Mist, 2008).

BATH

In traditional mysticism, fire constitutes the experience of divine love, and the motif of divine fire is often employed in the practice of auto-commentary. Richard Rolle, for instance, refers to this fire as the "Burning of Love," a spirituo-physical heat that "enflames the soul as if the element of fire[13] were burning there. . . . the soul set afire with love, truly feels most very heat; but sometimes more and more intense, and sometimes less, as the frailty of the flesh suffers."[14] With this, Rolle comments upon his own mystical experience of catching fire in the divine love of God. Hence auto-commentary enables the mystic to be fully engulfed by the divine fire of love while simultaneously thinking and discoursing on such an experience. Moreover, in "Love's Seven Names," Hadewijch writes,

> Fire is a name of Love by which she burns to death
> Good fortune, success, and adversity:
> All manners of being are the same to fire.
> Anyone whom this fire has thus touched
> Finds nothing too wide, and nothing too narrow.
> It is all the same to him what it devours:
> Someone we love or someone we hate, refusal or desire,
> Winnings or forfeits, convenience or hindrance,
> Gain or loss, honor or shame,
> Consolation at being with God in heaven
> Or in the torture of hell:
> This Fire makes no distinction.
> It burns to death everything it ever touches:

---

[13] Sogyal Rinpoche notes the dissolution of the elements at the time of one's physical death, noting the spirituo-physical ramifications of fire: "Kalu Rinpoche writes: 'For the individual dying, the inner experience is of being consumed in a flame, being in the middle of a roaring blaze, or perhaps the whole world being consumed in a holocaust of fire.' The fire element is dissolving into air, and becoming less able to function as a base for consciousness, while the ability of the air element to do so is more apparent. So the secret sign is of shimmering red sparks dancing above an open fire, like fireflies" (*The Tibetan Book of Living and Dying* [New York: HarperCollins, 2002], 257).

[14] Richard Rolle, *The Fire of Love*, trans. Richard Misyn (London: Metheun and Co., 1914), 11.

Damnation or blessing no longer matters,
This I can confess.[15]

To burn to death in this fire is to live in Love as one who constantly and (un)knowingly performs their own mystical auto-incineration, merging their fiery infinity with the infinity of Fire.

Black metal's lyrical blasphemies invert the traditional, if not already heretical, mystical fire of divine love into a form of auto-incineration reflective of what Cioran calls the "bath of fire." He writes,

> There are so many ways to achieve the sensation of immateriality that it would be difficult, if not futile, to make a classification. Nevertheless, I think that the bath of fire is one of the best. The bath of fire: your being ablaze, all flashes and sparks, consumed by flames in Hell. The bath of fire purifies so radically that it does away with existence. Its heat waves and scorching flames burn the kernel of life, smothering its vital élan, turning its aggressiveness into inspiration.[16]

This bath of fire causes a blackening so final and purifying that one scorches oneself into non-existence, living, to follow Cioran, "in a state of immaterial purity where one is nothing but a dancing flame."[17] In this way, then, black metal, keeping in tune with the Dantean motif of Hell/Purgatory as the only way to Paradise, delivers, to follow Nicola Masciandaro, "a mystical inversion of mysticism"[18] that transforms the mystical fire of divine love into a divine love of Hell's fire.

The more the metalhead burns, the more they die, which is also to say that black metal utilizes its incendiary love of Hell to set the stage for a complete negative state of being ablaze in a fire

---

[15] *Hadewijch: The Complete Works*, trans. Mother Columba Hart (Mahwah: Paulist Press, 1980), 352–3.

[16] E. M. Cioran, *On the Heights of Despair*, trans. Ilinca Zarifopol-Johnston. (Chicago: University of Chicago Press, 1992), 45.

[17] Cioran, *On the Heights of Despair*, 45.

[18] Nicola Masciandaro, "On the Mystical Love of Black Metal," *The Whim*, http://thewhim.blogspot.com/2011/11/on-mystical-love-of-black-metal.html.

so purifying that it indexes and enacts one's infernal communion/consummation[19] with death in what black metal bands commonly refer to as the "eternal fire" or "fire eternal": "Eternally I burn / Into the fire eternal."[20] This eternal fire burns everything, even hell itself, for "hell is open to heaven, / and our souls, incinerates hell."[21] As such, it recasts oneself as a walking crematory, thus ensuring the metalhead's mutual blackening of self/world[22] and world/cosmos—a la the "devourment of all things" set loose in Judas Iscariot's "Eternal Kingdom of Fire."[23] Nothing escapes this eternal fire. The purpose of walking through hell is to burn off one's sinful nature in divine fire.[24]

---

[19] Cf. For "now you realize / death is this communion" (High on Fire, "Death is this Communion," *Death is This Communion* [Relapse Records, 2007]).

[20] Dark Funeral, "The Fire Eternal," *The Secrets of the Black Arts* (No Fashion Records, 1996). In short, black metal theory, in its allegiance/allowance to the metalhead to think *with* the music, apophatically performs its own mystical act of *fana*, or total self-annihilation, by being "heated in the infernal fire" (Sabbat, "Black Metal Scythe," *Sabbatrinity* [Iron Pegasus Records, 2011]).

[21] Judas Iscariot, "An Eternal Kingdom of Fire," *Heaven in Flames* (Red Stream, 1999).

[22] For the spiritual aspirant, the death of self/mind is often coupled with the death of world, which serves as the *a priori* moment: "it all was just concealed putrefaction. The world tasted bitter. Life was torture. A goal stood before Siddhartha, a single goal: to become empty . . . Dead to himself, not to be a self any more, to find tranquility with an emptied heart, to be open to miracles in unselfish thoughts, that was his goal. Once all of my self was overcome and had died, once every desire and every urge was silent in the heart, then every part of me had to awake, the innermost of my being, which is no longer my self, the great secret" (Herman Hesse, *Siddhartha* [Winnetka: Norilana Books, 2007], 17–8).

[23] Judas Iscariot, "An Eternal Kingdom of Fire," *Heaven in Flames* (Red Stream, 1999).

[24] As Lactantius observes, hell is a kind of supplement to the divine nature, a place of exclusion from the eternal in the eternal, and yet is nothing other than divinity itself: "Holy Scripture teaches us how the wicked are to be punished. Because they contracted sin while in the body, they will be endowed with flesh so that they can absolve their crime in the body. It will not be a flesh like the earthly one that God clothed man with, but it will be indestructible and eternal so that it can bear torments and perpetual fire. This fire will be different from the one we use for the necessities of life, which is extinguished if it is not nourished by some fuel.

Indexing the economy between suffering and bliss, black metal's bath of fire curates a purification that has two poles. On the one side, there is an absolute suffering, a complete and total hell.[25] On the other side sits suffering's opposite, bliss, the ecstatic reversal of myself-as-sufferer into a no one who suffers not. The incendiary site for this coincidence of opposites is none other than the metalhead, the mystic who simultaneously burns and is burned, who slaughters and is slaughtered, is firewood and yet the firefly of bliss. In this mystical experience, all is set ablaze: "The Soul that receives this undergoes such a miraculous experience that it cries. In this mystical experience fire meets with Fire. Then nothing is extinguished in the human personality but, on the contrary, everything is set ablaze."[26] As such, the metalhead is nothing but butane burning into bliss.

WOMAN OF FLAME

Passionist mystic Gemma Galgani, the quintessential victim-soul mystic, often referred to as the "Daughter of the Passion" due to her extreme anguish and "profound imitation of the Victim of Calvary,"[27] writes, "I feel myself burning. . . . Thou art on fire, Lord, and I burn. O pain, O infinitely happy Love! O sweet fire! O sweet

That divine fire always lives by itself and thrives without any nourishment . . . The divine fire will both burn and renew the wicked by one and the same force and power. It will restore whatever it takes away from bodies and will provide its own eternal nourishment . . . It will burn and cause pain with no loss to the bodies that are being restored" (*Apocalyptic Spirituality*, ed. Bernard McGinn [Mahwah: Paulist Press, 1979], 68). Thank you to Nicola Masciandaro for alerting me to this passage after the symposium.

[25] Cf. Midnight, *Complete and Total Hell* (Hells Headbangers Records, 2012).

[26] Anonymous, *Meditations on the Tarot*, trans. Robert Powell (New York: Tarcher/Penguin, 2002), 36.

[27] Harvey D. Egan notes, "Galgani experienced more secondary mystical phenomena than any other mystic in the Christian tradition . . . Raptures, ecstasies, seraphic wounds of love, visions, locutions, the *complete* stigmata, bloody sweat, tears of blood, mystical effluvia (perfumed bodily excretions), satanic attacks, and penetrating discernment of spirits filled her life. Christ had told Gemma in a vision that he wanted her to travel the entire mystical journey; he was faithful to his word" (*An Anthology of Christian Mysticism* [Collegeville: The Liturgical Press, 1996], 539-40).

flames! And wouldst Thou have my heart become a flame? Ah! I have found the flame that destroys and reduces to ashes!"[28]

In black metal, we find that Galgani's absolute negative, which is to say her worstness incarnate, is perfectly expressed in the figure of Midnight's "Woman of Flame."[29] Midnight's music blurs the divisions between the first and second waves of black metal but also between metal and punk. As a band who sits liminally between genres, their very place in black metal enacts a kind of generic trance that one might have while gazing upon a candle's flame. Midnight embodies the purgatorial liminality of being stuck within the divine rift or crevice between Heaven and Hell. Mechthild of Magdeburg names such a place, as Bernard McGinn notes,

> "under Lucifer's tail" (under Lucifers zagel [ed. 158.52]), that is, it is the experience of being trapped in hell where the "poor love-rich soul" may feel no shame or fear but where the body quakes because it has not yet been transformed through death. Mechthild concludes by saying that both forms of experience are necessary for full holiness—ascent to the highest heights and decent to the deepest depths, the abyss of hell.[30]

The "Woman of Flame" is black metal's ultimate victim-soul mystic, an infernal whore who loves the sadistic throes of hellfire:

> She's wrapped up in leather with all it can stand
> Service me none better or feel the wrath of my hand
> Devil's whip it starts to crack and I hear the sound of torment
> Rising heat fills my blood I've came and went, she's ready again
> Woman of flame she starts to burn, sadistic wench
> With powers of darkness and hell on her side

---

[28] Gemma Galgani, in An Anthology of Christian Mysticism, ed. Harvey D. Egan (Collegeville: The Liturgical Press, 1996), 545–6.
[29] Midnight, "Woman of Flame," No Mercy for Mayhem (Hells Headbangers Records, 2014).
[30] Bernard McGinn, The Flowering of Mysticism: Men and Women in the New Mysticism—1200-1350 (New York: Crossroad, 1998), 242.

Lady master of these chains you'll be Lucifer's bride[31]

Invoking black metal's love of fire, Midnight's "Woman of Flame" is the mystical siren who, in her own inversion, lures the metalhead away from water and into fire.[32]

Whereas the mystic seeks only union with God, the "Woman of Flame" seeks only incendiary union with the metalhead in hellfire. She is the demono-sirenic lover who, via the auto-blasphemy of her own unrelenting negativity, is the conduit to total annihilation, igniting the metalhead into perpetual bliss via her promise of a bloated kiss. This bloated kiss models my own corpsic puff—the double puff of a bloated body laying out in its own heat and the breath of fire aired from this body. This bl(oated)(k)iss, this bl-iss, which enacts itself in between the infinity of breathless breaths, is the catatonic reminder of a life that must be diurnally naughted.

BREATH

The bath of fire's radical purification vis-à-vis the scorching of the burning mystic (i.e. the metalhead) into non-existence instantiates a ritual form of breathing-without-life wherein one's own breathing fuels the fire in which one perpetually and ecstatically burns. Opening one's mouth and, taking head of Venom's call to "taste the firey flames of death,"[33] one tastes the sweetness of the bath of fire.

To taste the sweetness of my own firey autophagy is to savor nothing on the blistering blackened tongue of non-sense, the annihilative mouth of total senselessness which renders me altogether deaf, dumb, and blind to anything other than Paradise itself. Evocative of an inversion of Kundalini yoga's Breath of Fire (Agni Pran), a form of pranayama or yogic breathing in which rapid, continuous breaths are used to ward off fear and anxiety, black metal's breath of fire is used not to sustain, but rather to abstain from, existence.

---

[31] Midnight, *No Mercy for Mayhem* (Hells Headbangers Records, 2014).
[32] Notably, Midnight's Athenar and Vanic wear executioner masks while on stage, performatively doubling this death by pointing at the headbanger's own aural execution.
[33] Venom, "Burn This Place (To the Ground)," *Possessed* (Neat Records, 1985).

Heretically and hermetically sealed within this without, my inexistence is all that ever will be or won't be: everything, that is, which radically opens to flames. To breathe a breath which does not blow out the flame but rather imbibes it, is to set my inner-self on fire. This anti-breath is black metal's breath of fire (Agni A-Pran), an a-pranayama in which the lungs of the soul are en/inflamed by the smoke of their own constant burning.[34]

CREMATORY

Speaking on behalf of a "me" that is not—that is, this *me*-ontological soliloquizing—is to craft a blackened auto-commentary about this bath of fire while simultaneously burning in it. It attempts to account for a crematorial mysticism—for, as Ash Pool makes clear, "cremation is irreversible"[35]—in which both one and world are immanently set ablaze.

Engulfed in flames, bathing in a fire that, as Hadewijch writes, "burns to death anything it ever touches," this crematorial mysticism perpetually chars and incessantly undoes me, blackening me into complete incompleteness. Abandoning all life,[36] I am burned into nothing other than a *black repulsive individual*, to follow Antonin Artaud, who writes,

> The thing is, at the start of anything at all there is no being,
> but a sort of repulsive individuality that is never this or that, and that has always refused to enter into this or into that.
> And the being that can want to be a being
> was never anything but its enemy nothingness,
> always put by it in a state of perpetual annihilation.
> Yet the black repulsive individual never lets out a being,
> because it is not and doesn't strive for being,

---

[34] One can connect this breath of fire to the practice of fire-breathing in black metal, notably displayed by Bathory's Quorthon in photographs from the late 1980s. Bands such as 1349 have continued this practice, as band members Frost and Archaon are known to start their live concerts with fire-breathing.

[35] Ash Pool, "Cremation is Irreversible," *Cremation is Irreversible* (Of Crawling Shadows Records, 2012).

[36] Cf. Nails, *Abandon All Life* (Southern Lord Records, 2013).

and from where and from what would being escape from
it.[37]

The radical un-orthodoxy of my perpetual auto-incineration
stands this dead man up at the edge of an abyss so hellishly
immense that it explodes itself into an inexplicit I-without-a-Me.[38]
The black repulsive individual, the charred one, knows nothing
but *NOW*. And so it is always *here*, which is really nowhere,
Everywhere, that this auto-crematorial mysticism takes place, this
non-place where the absolute burns. In this absolute burning
absolutely, the one true Metalhead Beyond All Charred Things,
whose own beyondness is scorched in never ending fire, always
and forever dies over and over until the unmoment of perpetual
Love whispers into his heretical ears this secret, unwritten chorus:
*It is You, this "I" without a Me, who cannot not love, and it is only
All, this "I" without a Me without an I without a You, that shall
love all/All forever.*

Keeping in mind that being oneself is the absolute worst form
of apathy, the entire basis for the experience of life as suffering,
the mystic knows that entering Paradise inevitably rests on the
mind's total incineration.[39] The relation between annihilation of
the mind and entering Paradise, manifested in Judas Iscariot's
mantra "Eternal Bliss... Eternal Death,"[40] thereby reminds us—

---

[37] Antonin Artaud, "Interjections," *Suppôts et supplications* (Paris:
Gallimard, 2006). See "The Black Repulsive Individual," *Non-
Manifestation,* https://nonmanifestation.wordpress.com/2013/01/27/
the-black-repulsive-individual/.

[38] Cf. "Both God and the soul, in [Marguerite Porete's] view, were the
authors of this text that strives to negate itself through vertiginous
contradictions. Its language borders between opposition to both
orthodoxy and heterodoxy—and, what possibly can the mystical 'I,' 'that
is, an "I" without a Me' (Paul Moemmars), mirror?" (Harvey D. Egan,
Soundings in the Christian Tradition [Collegeville: Liturgical Press,
2010], 151).

[39] On Heaven and Hell as a state of mind, Meher Baba notes: "Hell and
heaven are states of mind; they should not be looked upon as being places.
And though subjectively they mean a great deal to the individualized soul,
they are both illusions within the greater Illusion" (*Discourses* [North
Myrtle Beach: Sheriar Press, 2011], 307).

[40] Judas Iscariot, "Eternal Bliss... Eternal Death," *Heaven in Flames* (Red
Stream, 1999).

echoing the Bhagavad Gita—that intellectual death is the very basis of bliss: "His mind is dead / To the touch of the external: / It is alive / to the bliss of the Atman."[41] This experience of mystical annihilation vis-à-vis burning in a hellfire that, as 1349 makes clear, "fill[s] you with ecstasy,"[42] ultimately burns an unrestricted clearing for divine love. Ecstasy, or marvel, i.e. the spontaneous realization of selflessness, expressed by Ibn 'Arabi as a "garden among the flames,"[43] opens towards a love without-me, after the universe has been blackened back into the abyssic nothingness which is the mystic's Everything, that is to say, curates by cremation a divine love that persists in the wake of my own scattered ashes.

Black metal performs an apophasis of ontological arguments for love, unknowing them to their meontological brink. Being itself must "enter the Eternal Fire"[44] in order to scorch itself into non-being, where divine love radically opens to everything. Such an auto-incinerating love, this love-without-me, the love that persists at the charred juncture of this "I" without a Me, has been found and is unfounded by way of the wayless abyssic kiss of the metalhead's sirenic lover, Midnight's "Woman of Flame," and is eloquently and finally expressed in the Song of Songs: "Bind me as a seal upon your heart, / a sign upon your arm, / for love is as fierce as death . . . / Even its sparks are a raging fire, / a devouring flame" (8:6-7).[45]

---

[41] *Bhagavad Gita*, trans. Swami Prabhavananda and Christopher Isherwood (New York: Barnes and Noble Books, 1995), 35.

[42] 1349, "Hellfire," *Hellfire* (Candlelight Records, 2005).

[43] Ibn 'Arabi, "A Garden Among the Flames," trans. by Michael A. Sells, *The Muhyiddin Ibn 'Arabi Society*, http://www.ibnarabisociety.org/poetry/ibn-arabi-poetry-index.html.

[44] Cf. Bathory: "The heat scorch my flesh / The fall seem never to end / My hair burns / My eyes can't see / . . . The pain tears my mind / . . . Raging flames all over me / Inferno of heat" ("Enter the Eternal Fire," *Under the Sign of the Black Mark* [Under One Flag, 1987]).

[45] *The Song of Songs: A New Translation*, trans. Ariel Bloch and Chana Block (Berkley: University of California Press, 1995), 111.

Mycelegium

James Harris

"...the visions, yeah most of the time I was convinced... Shit... I'd lost it. But there were other times... I thought I was mainlining the secret truth of the universe."
-Rust Cohle, True Detective

I have severely questioned the worth of these moments. To no soul have I named them, lest I should be building my life upon mere phantasies of the brain . . . but it was in the most Real seasons the Real Presence came, and I was aware that I was immersed in the infinite ocean of God. The incommunicability of the transport may be the key to all mysticism, and these things may seem to you delusions or truisms, but for me they are dark truths, and the power to put them into even such words as these has been given me by an ether-dream.[1]

Cursed to Levitate / My Spell is Chemical.[2]

---

[1] William James, *Varieties of Religious Experience* (New York: Barnes and Noble, 2004), 328–371, italics mine.
[2] Nachtmystium, "Nightfall," *Addicts: Black Meddle Part II* (Century Media/Candlelight, 2010).

In the twilight zones arise abstract galaxies.
The magic eye unveils the blackened skies.
A new horizon begins to each one that dies.[3]

It is a foregone conclusion that humans can't survive bodily death to tell the tale, but considering some fifty to seventy billion cells die every day on their own, perhaps the meat dying is trivial? We may have no model for the sensation of physical death, but we have an exceptional complex of models of non-existence ranging across a great variety of categories, from Zen and Tao to vegetative states, from autism to mysticism. This Mycelegium[4] (a portmanteau of florilegium and mycelia) is a mushroom-cutting to explore the interstices of these states in the wake of psilocybin, the primary psychoactive compound found in the tryptamine "magic" mushroom.[5] In illuminating an entheogenic phenomenology of non-existence, I contend that the primary effect of psilocybin is to enact a stable opening of the attention, via the virtual *annihilation of the observer,* that can be practiced outside the hallucinogenic experience in order to utilize the entire brain in every calculation, in order to see with both eye and mind's eye stereoscopically aligned. This task is made easier in harmonization with a cosmic form of black metal, whose lyrical content attempts and often succeeds at description beyond ineffability, and Dzogchen, a Buddhist method of orientation in non-ordinary realities.

Grasping the liquid glass, shaping my own sight.
Staring at the sun, absorbing Death.[6]

Here, I am considering something well beyond the threshold of what is commonly referred to as the "recreational dose." What we

---

[3] Limbonic Art, "Solace of the Shadows," *Epitome of Illusions* (Candlelight, 1998).
[4] *Mycelegium* describes a technique in which the cut-up method is applied to a set of dead texts to draw out living thought from the rupturings and suturings. Cf. "When you cut into the present the future leaks out" (William Burroughs, *Break Through in Grey Room* [Sub Rosa Records, 2001]).
[5] Psilocybin is metabolized in the body to psilocin, an alkaloid with a remarkably similar chemical structure to serotonin.
[6] Enslaved, "Veilburner," *RIITIIR* (Nuclear Blast, 2012).

are after is an "ecstatic, breathless experience that opens a bit more every time the limits of Being."[7] Not access to a superficial drunken haze, melting walls, breathing furniture—but access to the regions of cognition that are free fields for the projection of unconscious content. Not mere synesthesia, but volitional combinatory sensing. Beyond drift into spectral emotional geometry that consistently resolves into manifestations—in the plane of Art—of perpetual creation, a demonstration of the necessity of death, and the self-evidence of immortality. Beyond freedom from the known into the eternity of the standing now. This paper will detail a progression in the mushroom experience from biological novelty to trans-perceptual abilities, culminating in a quasi-death state and a sustained split from Self-representation. Many arduous paths threaten annihilation, but psilocybin promises—even to the skeptic—"a naked soul, smashed apart."[8]

. . . / deep down in the black slime of the earth / restless limbs at work.[9]

Several simple molds and slimes work in concert in the cattle's dung, in the deer corpse under the pine boughs, in the peat bog. Over two hundred species from a variety of climates across six continents, but a shared beginning. Erupting in the aftermath of swarming bacterial murmurations of rot and insectile aeration, a cleansing occurs. From the inside out, these mold-infections metabolize impurities within precursor material then die themselves, laying the nutritional-groundwork for the higher mushroom in their own corpsing, evolved to fit a peculiar niche—that their putrescence provides the physical and biochemical space necessary for the tryptamine mushrooms' mycelium to colonize this dead substrate at the precise point of intersection of entropy and novelty. Incredibly fine wisps of root-nets building and building atop decomposition that can boast more connections per cubic inch than the human brain. As the mushrooms' own

---

[7] Georges Bataille, *Inner Experience*, trans. Leslie Anne Boldt (Albany: State University of New York Press, 1988), 104.
[8] Lantlôs, "Pulse/Surreal," *.neon* (Lupus Lounge, 2010).
[9] Thorns, "The Discipline of Earth," *Thorns vs. Emperor* (Moonfog, 1999).

death and putrefaction in combination with fortuitous encounters with dead matter enriches the system further, it offers its bodies as sacrifice to the mycelium in order to heighten conditions for novelty, and thus "locates in the very permanence of protocol the capacity to exceed it."[10]

Cadaverous and spirited; I work. Composite and uniform; I sacrifice.[11]

Earthbound forces united with sorrow.[12]

O this Now is the hour of death. By taking advantage of this death, I will so act for the good of all sentient beings, peopling the illimitable expanse of the heavens as to obtain Perfect Buddhahood by resolving on love and compassion to them, and directing my entire effort to the Sole Perfection.[13]

The mushroom is the originary form of Philip K. Dick's "physician,"[14] taking the apocryphal addition to the Hippocratic oath "Primum non nocere" as axiom: *No element of its life cycle imposes itself.* As a primary decomposer, it negates Death to produce conditions for Life: as the yogini is friendly with Death, because Death is more intimate than Life. This peeling away and rejecting the false confusion of decay shares roots with Dzogchen Buddhism, as from this point of view, what's perplexing is "this

---

[10] China Miéville, "Fiction by Reza Negarestani," *World Literature Today* 84, no. 3 (May–June 2010): 12.

[11] Enslaved, "Storm of Memories," *RIITIIR*.

[12] Enslaved, "The Crossing," *Below the Lights* (Nuclear Blast, 2003).

[13] W. Y. Evans-Wentz, *The Tibetan Book of the Dead; Or, The After-death Experiences on the Bardo Plane, According to Lāma Kazi Dawa-Samdup's English Rendering* (New York: Oxford University Press, 1960), 94.

[14] Cf. "Out of itself the Brain has constructed a physician to heal it. This subform of the Macro-Brain is not deranged; it moves through the Brain, as a phagocyte moves through the cardiovascular system of an animal, healing the derangement of the Brain section after section. We know of its arrival here; we know it as *Asklepios* for the Greeks and as the Essenes for the Jews; as the *Therapeutae*_for the Egyptians; as Jesus for the Christians" (Philip K. Dick, "Tractatus Cryptica Scriptura," *VALIS* [Boston: Mariner 2011], Kindle edition).

life," not what lies "beyond" life. The penultimate yogini, it has no organs to move the world: it has learned the role of stillness and silence, of ceasing the motion of prana through the body. It takes nothing from the living and converts entropy into knowledge, literally *dripping* with neurotransmitters. Meditating like a corpse, in a corpse—as "a corpse is already meditating in every meaningful sense."[15]

Self-liberation through the appearing of Appearances.[16]

A re-visioning of the spectrum of visionary experiences through the lens of modern synesthesia research has lead me down a path toward the idea that the basic sensory components of the mystical experience contain, or may be entirely, some form of synesthesia. To understand this, a quick swim into hastily elucidated neuroscience . . .

The outer cortical layer of the brain, the "Default Mode Network" (DMN), is the part of the brain concerned with self-reference and introspection, the subjective perspective. It is often considered analogous to the ego, as well as being the primary location of the 5-HT2A serotonin receptors. The "Task-Positive Network" (TPN) of the brain is a system of regions that activate in the face of a task or event requiring active awareness. During performance of attention-intensive tasks, prefrontal and parietal structures comprising the task-positive network are characterized by activation. In contrast, default mode network structures, including posterior cingulate and medial prefrontal cortices, are characterized by decreased activity. In self-reflective modes, this is reversed. In normal waking consciousness these networks are competitive in metabolic terms: when one turns up, the other turns down. Constrained by this pair of networks are key subcortical regions devoted to temporal, sensorial, and spatial

---

[15] Timothy Morton, "Thinking the Charnel Ground," in "The Mystical Text (Black Clouds Course Through Me Unending . . .)," eds. Nicola Mascianodaro and Eugene Thacker, special issue, *Glossator: Practice and Theory of the Commentary* 7 (2010): 88.

[16] Rudolph Bauer, "Dzogchen is Self-Liberation Through the Appearing of Appearances," https://www.academia.edu/4923814/ Dzogchen_is_ Self_Liberation_Through_The_Appearing_of_Appearances.

mapping and memory storage—the historical narrative: the hippocampus, amygdala, and cerebellum.

Interwoven in this proto-cybernetic mesh, sensorial and cognitive signaling is shunted in standard directions by an equally complex array of hubs that also function as gates.[17] Through observing the effects of psilocybin on the hub systems we discover that these structures are progressively deactivated, or relaxed, through the introduction of increased serotonin, wherein they cease directing and filtering sensory input and reflection on these inputs into the "proper" channels for basic cognition and begin distributing the signals more freely, triggering various types of constructive synesthetic responses—responses in which a stacking of a single perceptual quality occurs across multiple sense inputs giving an innate awareness of the novel condition. Physical and psychological stress and sickness cause the body to release cortisol and adrenaline (both interfere with serotonin uptake) which in exceptional cases can trigger a strangely mirrored version of synesthesia, an improper signaling pattern leading to what I call "constrictive synesthesia," wherein the subject can no longer successfully interpret incoming signals due to their being diverted from their normal path into "inappropriate" regions. This results in a confusing and disorienting blurring of the senses. Several major types of "system-overlap" are common, such as the primary five senses in nearly any combination, sensorial representations of active self-reflection, emotion, memory and the sense of time, facial recognition and spatial awareness. A number of normally autonomous brain networks become essentially continuous under the influence of serotonin or psilocybin not by virtue of their being brought to a defined or definable state of action, but by flattening the repulsive affect between the two larger arrays, effectively bringing them together into a cohesive unit which prevents the back and forth motion that is standard. We see the principle of the 2nd law of thermodynamics in an expansion toward entropy—"in a way, we have a model of brain death in the psychedelic states."[18]

---

[17] The largest of these, the *corpus callosum*, is a massive bundle of nerves that connects each point on the cortex to the mirror-image point in the opposite hemisphere.
[18] Robin Carhart-Harris, "Brain Imaging Studies with Psilocybin and MDMA 2014," https://www.youtube.com/watch?v=CNR4o5JZEio.

The effects of psilocybin are extremely subjective and can fluctuate wildly, remaining rarely constant or consistent, but a few attributes seem to be persistent and common to both the mystical and the psychedelic.

a spirit light comes through / furious distortion / again and again and again / . . .[19]

. . . / in Silence of divine accord / in the law of Ruins / toward the sky, into the Light.[20]

Anecdotal evidence across mystical and psychedelic literature combined with personal research suggests to me that the amount of visual brightness or light or color intensity triggered by a perception in this state may be correlative to the novelty to the brain of the new signaling pattern. My theory is that the truly novel perception or set of perceptions, when diverted through the memory in the synesthetic state, triggers a neuronal map of representations that include the sun, as the "tutelary genius of universal vegetation"[21] is the most easily "visualized" common conception of origin and therefore a prime symbol of the divine and the unknown. This causes incredibly intense glowing patterns, intensified further by further novel insights and perceptions. As the visionary state deepens, its trajectory continues through an aggregation of symbolism of myth and religion most represented in memory being activated in the thought-stream as if the memory and the DMN collaborate in an attempt to integrate this new experience by comparison, starting at the "beginning," the easiest, or most open possible conceptions. As if the search for any way to represent the new stimuli patterns in active consciousness came up linguistically and logically empty, forcing the growth of new representations. This would explain why visions of god, angels, aliens, infernals, and all manner of oddities show up even in primitive stages of these experiences,

---

[19] Blakkheim, "Fleeing from Town," *Diabolical Masquerade* (Avantgarde Music, 2001).
[20] Locrian, "Return to Annihilation," *Return to Annihilation* (Relapse, 2013).
[21] Albert Pike, *Morals and Dogma: Scottish Rite in Freemasonry* (Charleston, SC: Forgotten Books, 2008), 176.

often seeming to be perceptibly connected to the primary sensorial component in direct but strangely-mirrored contrast with the mythological convictions held by the subject. I think that this also implies that the overwhelming aspect of the light, or what I judge to be the *automatic rebound through self-reflection of a novel perception* (and thus the natural movement through pre-existing prejudices and ideology) can be "practiced away" or properly ignored, until the new sensing pattern can be assimilated practically within abstract thought, which Vajrayana practitioners call prabhāsvara, or luminosity.

The pure light in a moment of awareness in your mind is the Buddha's essence within you. The non-discriminating light in a moment of awareness in your mind is the Buddha's wisdom within you. The undifferentiated light in a moment of awareness in your mind is the Buddha's manifestation within you. The subtlest level of mental activity (Mind), which continues with no beginning and no end, without any break, even during death and even into Buddhahood is individual and constitutes the mental continuum of each Being. It is naturally free of conceptual cognition, the appearance-making of true existence.[22] The marvels and mundanities of existence then become equally wondrous or fearful because they do not automatically get swept into pre-formed epistemic categories and channels of thought. This gives the impression that everything around is equally profound and worthy of reverence. Unlike subjects suffering from psychotic or psychophysical disorders, however, subjects who experience drug-induced synesthesia can often immediately recognize the nonphysical nature of their perceptual disturbances with a rudimentary application of attention, which I posit stems from the constructivity of this variety of synesthesia. That stacked phenomenal properties—move together—give the lie to perceptions that span multiple senses, and allow us to tell false perceptions from true. When the signaling is constricted and erratic there seems to be a much greater difficulty in assessing the subjective nature of these hallucinations. At many levels of the psychedelic experience each individual sensory input is perceived as a separate "channel" and their collation into ordinary reality itself is also perceived as its own individual channel. Without this

---

[22] Rinzai, *Teachings of Rinzai* (Berkley: Shambala, 1975), 18.

knowledge, the many strands and strings of inputs are often seen simply as chaos.

I saw no God nor heard any, in a finite and organized perception, but my senses discovered the infinite in everything.[23] I assented my eyes on the face of the crucifix . . . after this my sight began to fail, and it was all dark about me in the chamber, as if it had been night save in the Image of the Cross whereon I beheld a common Light, and I wist not how. All that was away from the Cross was of horror to me as if it had been greatly occupied by the fiends.[24]

Conversely, the perceptible blackening or blurring of perceptions within (at least) the audiovisual field in these modes of non-ordinary reality, while sometimes being accidentally perceived as a feature of the object or representation in question or a defect of perception itself, seems to be representative of the distance between perception and reflection, i.e. how much "signal decay" or filtering occurs between direct sense input and attentive perception. While this in no way gives novel information to the subject, it freely exposes the dimensions of the rift between thought and Being. As this rift is immeasurably vast, the warpings and wildings of perception in even the lowest regions of the psychedelic state are just as vast.

We now know that only a fraction of the estimated 38,000 trillion operations per second processed by the brain finds its way to consciousness. This means that experience, all experience, is profoundly privative, a simplistic caricature of otherwise breathtakingly complex processes. . . . The metabolic costs associated with neural processing and the sheer evolutionary youth of human consciousness suggest that experience should be severely blinkered: synoptic or "low resolution" in some respects, perhaps, but thoroughly fictitious otherwise.[25]

---

[23] William Blake, *The Marriage of Heaven and Hell* (Oxford: Oxford Press, 1975), Plate 12.
[24] Julian of Norwich, *Revelations of Divine Love* (London: Penguin, 1999), 6–7.
[25] R. Scott Bakker, "Outing the It that Thinks: The Collapse of an Intellectual Ecosystem," https://rsbakker.wordpress.com/essay-

This has two major effects that are explicated in great detail in several psychedelic trip reports[26] that bring a competitiveness with the mystical state to the table. One, as everything seems to become altered in some way, a fear or anxiety about nothing being true or known occurs—the ungrounding; second, the subject feels an ecstatic feeling of awe at the true size and complexity of the mysterious. This second effect relaxes the first as a desire to *understand* that transcends the *assumption of never understanding*, but that these positions can freely overlap and shift also results in kaleidoscopic physical sensations and visual effects as the connections between the brain and the autonomic nervous system are assaulted with the electrochemical fallout of these extreme emotions. In this stage is where the most frequent divergences into "bad trips" occur as the emotions and feelings evoked feel tremendously physical and seem to operate similar to feedback looping, wherein a phenomenal state "speeds up" and deepens as it is focused upon. The fact that psychedelic drugs induce a greater sensitivity to these oscillations can speed up the influx of impressions from deeper levels of consciousness and raises the immediate question of how these energies can be properly understood and handled. According to Yoga philosophy, the most spiritual and powerful aspect of human's nature is the faculty of attention or consciousness. The most fundamental aspect of free will is the choice as to what the attention is allowed to dwell upon. The goal of all Yoga practices is to discover and directly experience what the attention or faculty of consciousness in human is. The yogi seeks to know that principle by which all else is known. This goal is achieved by *observing the observer* or placing the attention upon the attention itself. . . .

Night-sight is bliss / the darkness shines and illuminates the abyss.
Bless her, this uplifting splendor,
Whose brightness gives birth this shadow and discovers the gulf,

archive/outing-the-it-that-thinks-the-collapse-of-an-intellectual-ecosystem/.
[26] Excellent examples include: Zanti, "Rotating Space, Topological Games: An Experience with Mushrooms —P. cubensis (ID 86904)," https://www.erowid.org/, and "Psychohedron: An Experience with Mushrooms (P. semilanceata) (ID 1590)," https://www.erowid.org/.

A world where you embrace the opposite.
Like a voluptuous and endless flash, showing nothing other than that there is something one does not see. To follow this flash as beacon, as initiation into the exploration of the darkness. To intellectually navigate "the negativity binding thought and being, to definitively illuminate the darkness of one's relation to the real."[27]

---

[27] During a gathering of resources for this text a curious thing occurred: windows on two laptop screens side by side, between them a printed copy of a pdf next to a notebook full of scribbled notes. A reading directly across these mediums—a line in a space encompassing all four frames, slightly corrected for grammatical orientation—created this passage.: Enslaved, "Night-Sight," *Axioma Ethica Odini* (Nuclear Blast, 2010); Blut Aus Nord, "VI," *What Once Was . . . Liber III* (Debemur Morti, 2013); Nicola Masciandaro, "Paradisical Pessimism: On the Crucifixion Darkness and the Cosmic Materiality of Sorrow," *Qui Parle: Critical Humanities and Social Sciences* 23, no. 1 (Fall–Winter 2014): 187

[wiring diagrams][28]

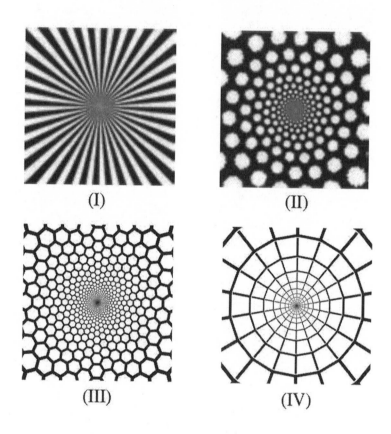

(I)

(II)

(III)

(IV)

[28] The "Form Constants" of Heinrich Klüver—grating, lattice, fretwork, filigree, honeycomb, chessboard, cobweb, tunnel, funnel, alley, cone, vessel, spiral—a detailed analysis of which can be found in Paul C. Bresloff, Jack D. Cowan, Martin Golubitsky, Peter J. Thomas, et al, "What Geometric Visual Hallucinations Tell Us about the Visual Cortex," http://www.researchgate.net/profile/Jack_Cowan/publication/115006 66_What_geometric_visual_hallucinations_tell_us_about_the_visual _cortex/links/0912f50f6dbf26c7e4000000.pdf.

The sea and the mountains, and the fire and the sword,
All these together, I live in their midst.
The mountain, he'll not leave me, who has seized
My intellect, and taken away my reason.[29]

Deeper into this chemical integration, a visual synthesis of our abstracted view of human biology with the possibilities of non-existence develops that seems to be related to a de-linking or muting of self-reflective capabilities as the DMN begins to lose its top-down control over the memory and historical narrative. This synthesis gives us a glimpse of the "intuitive mapping protocol" of memory and spatial determination, often seen as the classic visual geometry of the psychedelic. This visualization of symbolic schemata exposes the calculatory procedures that are used to construct visible reality, and is equivalent to a set or stack of subjective wiring diagrams. "Mathematical form is the first reflection and most pure image of our subjective activity. Then follows number, having a close relation to linear conception. Hence mathematical form with number supplies the fittest system of symbols for orderly representation of the spiritual evolution of life, plane after plane. Or, as Philo says, 'Number is the mediator between the corporeal and the incorporeal.'"[30] When overlaid on incoming sensation, these diagrams explicitly show how incorrectly we assimilate perceived data, as the geometry of accurate perception aligns with that of accurate cognitive interpretation. Reality of realization felt first in connection with

---

[29] Krallice, "The Mountain," *Dimensional Bleedthrough* (Profound Lore, 2009).

[30] Louisa S. Cook, *Geometrical Psychology or The Science of Representation; an Abstract of the Theories and Diagrams of B. W. Betts* (London: Redway 1887), 10. The quote attributed to Philo has no source listed in the book, though a search turned up this from Giovanni Reale, *A History of Ancient Philosophy: The Schools of the Imperial Age* (State University of New York Press, 1990), 192: "But Philo immediately distinguishes the Logos from God and makes it almost a hypostasis, even calling it 'first born of the uncreated father,' 'second God,' 'image of God.' In some passages he also speaks of it as an instrumental and efficient cause. In other passages he speaks of it, instead, as the Archangel, as the mediator between Creator and creatures (insofar as it is uncreated like God, but not created like a creature in this world), the Herald of the peace of God, the preserver of the peace of God in the world."

93

external things, appearances, is gradually perceived more and more interiorly as consciousness develops through succeeding stages, until finally Truth is perceived as the only reality. These processes can be tracked to a high degree and in fact lend themselves to this tracking, as they can be profoundly beautiful and otherworldly, and thus draw the attention away from the Self and toward this intuitive apperception.

Imagining the visual cortex as a screen and perception as the video source, we can trace the buildup of perceptual feedback in a monotonic fashion in order to both remain aware of shared reality and follow this progression toward the near-infinite variety of sense data that is generally filtered out by active consciousness. Aldous Huxley's "Pure Interval," is in this regard, analogous to inhabiting the position within this visual feedback loop where all perceptions and images are "in phase" and stable, without the observer to decompose or block formation of image stability and infinite recursion. The concept this presses to the fore is that of *perspective and pattern without observer*, in all dimensions as memory and the thought-stream becoming highly active in the visual field. At this moment of self-loss, a seemingly supra-physical, sensorially apparent boundary is crossed and every sense input in addition to the thought stream are activated in every component structure of the physical brain and synesthesia becomes effectively totalized. Whether virtual or actual, every point in the brain becomes electrochemically connected to every other point in the brain. This experience is often recalled as a feeling of connectedness to all life-forms, of "everything is everything"—a complete breakdown of the subject-object dynamic as the vast array and complexity of the sense stream completely overwhelms any ability to recognize the Self and subjectivity vanishes. Suddenly, input and output are perceived simultaneously across all senses. When this barrier has been passed, the subject ceases to perceive images from the exterior world, being left only with their symbolic representations. "If one is able to orient at all without the direct support of these images, they will find themselves in a state of reverie, and then in the dream state, in which the energization of the imaginary activity, dissociated from the external senses, is accompanied by further reduction and emptying of consciousness of Self . . . when that alienation increases . . . consciousness is abolished. Farther beyond lie trance, lethargy, and the cataleptic state. Farther still, when the separation is complete, one enters into a state of apparent death, and finally into the state of the dissociation of the organism no longer held together by the vital force, which is to say: death."[31]

Feel the heartbeat of the earth,
As you're on the threshold to death or birth.[32]
Operational instructions for your interface to god . . . [33]

Lightless voyage, blinding speeds,
Abstract shapes, enigmatic design.
Don't fight it, you'll only . . .
Whirl up all mass hysteria
In your thousandfold self,
Certain; I'll stay the distance,
Shake down withering poison and die.
I understand a substance consisting of an infinity of attributes,
Of which each one expresses an eternal and infinite essence.[34]

This is universally expressed as an experience of the death of the Ego, a sustained breaking of the correlationist circle, and an immediate manifestation of the mental trappings of death in several powerfully analogous and metonymous forms, as death is the most readily available, most powerful, and most distinctly coherent symbolic representation of the loss of self across literature, media, and history perhaps both despite and because of its ineffability. Such that when the self is cognitionally "lost" the entire death-symbolic memory repertoire activates, pressing a primordial or emergent idea of death and loss to the front of the imagination and forcing it to construct a conceptual

---

[31] Julius Evola, *The Hermetic Tradition* (New York: Inner Traditions International, 1971), 104–105.
[32] Limbonic Art, "The Ultimate Death Worship," *The Ultimate Death Worship* (Black Metal Attack Records, 2002).
[33] Thorns, "Interface to God," *Thorns* (Moonfog, 2011).
[34] Enslaved, "Raidho," *Axioma Ethica Odini*; Arcturus, "For to End Yet Again," *The Sham Records* (Ad Astra, 2002); Lurker of Chalice, "Piercing Where They Might," *Lurker of Chalice* (Total Holocaust, 2005); Blut Aus Nord, "Henosis," *Memoria Vetusta III–Saturnian Poetry* (Debemur Mort, 2014).

representation that is then dumped unceremoniously into the senses. As the Self expects to feel the loss for and of itself, the expected sorrow of death never touches the Perception, having been split from the Self. Instead, the feeling of hyper-connectedness via synesthetic response persists despite the perception of the death of the "I," lending it rather a significantly positive emotionally integrated component as the Perception is surprised, in awe of, and ultimately relieved to find itself surviving a death-experience by virtue of remaining in this connected, aware state. A death-like silence felt more intensely than any experience within common shared reality.

The delusion of ignorance becomes the wisdom of reality. The spirits cut his head open and took out his brains, washed and restored them. They planted barbed hooks on the tips of his fingers to enable him to seize the soul and hold it fast; and lastly they pierced his heart with an arrow to make him full of sympathy for the sick and suffering.[35]

All is present in every particular, the absolute in every relative. And associated with this obscure knowledge may come a new mode of apprehension, in which the ordinary subject-object relationship is somehow transcended and there is an awareness of self and the outer world as being one. Such propositions as "god is love" are realized with the totality of one's being, and their truth seems self-evident in spite of pain and death.[36]

When my last sign of humanity will be heaved . . .
When I'm finally alone with no one to speak to . . .
I'll pass away without regret, without fear in this endless cosmos.
As I'll have lived everything from deception to deception . . .
I'll leave without sorrow, without hate, without fright in front of the mouth of death.
My destroyed dreams will then reveal mightier gain.
Close your eyes, sense the below,
Torment and separation points ahead.
But tonight,

---

[35] Henry Ling, *Natives of Sarawak and Borneo* (London: Truslove and Comba, 1896), 281.
[36] Aldous Huxley, *Moksha* (Rochester: Park Street Press, 1999), 130.

I'm Houdini.
Gonna kill my shadow.[37]

—*sine fine renascentia*—[38]

---

[37] Mütiilation, "Ravens of My Funeral," *Vampires of Black Imperial Blood* (Drakkar, 1995); Enslaved "Axioma," *Axioma Ethica Odini*; Arcturus, "Ad Absurdum," *The Sham Mirrors*.
[38] Thank you E, P, S, B, N, M+M.

dying to find I was never there

Teresa Gillespie

to find I was never there dying to find—I was never there dying to find I was

a solidified body ejecting its mind as a flash smashed flips into a scrunch sliding scratch of sharp—screeching through the ears of a frozen head **without an I to hear**—stops—still— a low rumble in a thick silence - - waiting - - - waiting - - - - waiting . . . *I'm alive* . . . *No—you are dead*

as *that which resists description and destroys the subject* tears asunder a tightly woven screen of words—**a cut of cuts** releasing in spurts the thick black blood of nothing—splintering—the I sustaining crafted path that forgot I'm going nowhere

while a predawn silence **never silent enough** with a sharp cold cuts—a thin crack dilating in the dark capturing the crashing of metallic stars—piercing through the groans of a rumbling ground thumped from inside as something turns upside down

a thought born to die—consumed by the night that birthed it

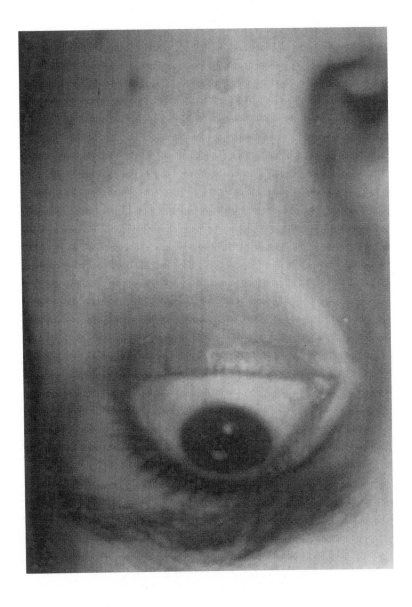

breaking the chain of light—as an eyelid caught in an uncontrollable flutter in a fit between black and white—stalls—with a searing pain **followed by a gasp of breath**— trapped—in a flatline—as a body withdraws from the call of dawn

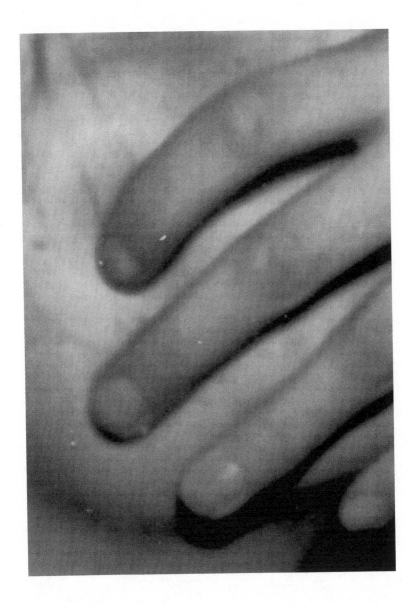

Date—Unknown—Time—Unknown—Record—Let   no   event
escape—Click—Capture—Name?—*(silence)*—Name?—*(silence)*—
Name?—*(silence)*—Clamp—Sever—Cut—*(inhalation)*—Separate
—*(cough)*—black bile trapped in the lungs—**as the night
remaining spurts through the veil of day**—are you
suicidal?—slip flip splat—*only in the morning*—a cooked organ
cut in half—triggers—a phantom attachment to the end of a
blisteringly itchy knot—*I just want a way out of the logic of life*—
nonsense—absolutely.

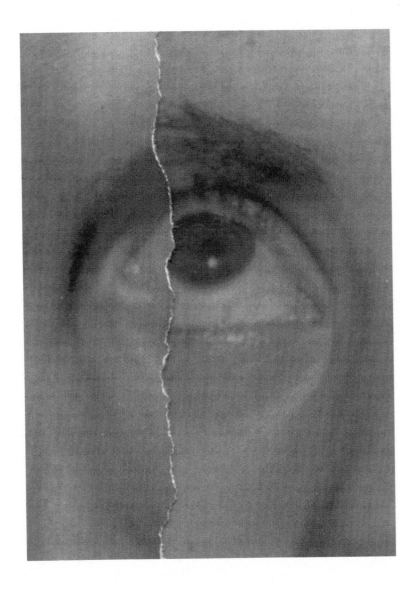

the sensation of a gradually numbing skull as the thin skin of a forehead remains—still stuck—to a hard pane—of ice cold—glass—the chin draws down into the flesh of its neck parting lips that stretch wide 'til the corners become tight sides—a ball of air released crackles back toward the ears as moisture rising from lower lids blurs the eyes—fixed—on a figure wrapped in black stopping and starting along a dirt path—flapping black fabric flips and twists to escape the body that stops again to grasp loose ends—with trembling hands before starting off—again——stoping——starting——stoping——starting——stoping—stumping ——further away from the entrapped gaze **cut from the weight of its hands hanging at the end of loose arms** not knowing—*where — I—is—or—when*

something seems to be **endlessly lasting strangely waiting**—
as a shuffling bundle of black clothes recedes—a torso turns to tear
its head away—from glass—but stumbles on limp legs dropping its
forehead splat flat into the mirror trap—wide eyes rolling over the
reflection of a face—strip its skin in search for more—or less—A
voice from the dead with stinking breath says—*It's just torture—
and more torture*

as a finger thrust **through the hole of a yawning iris** taps the back of a cavernous head and says—*anyone in there?*—scratching and grasping in a desperate attempt to declare—*I am—in there—somewhere*—an eyelid drops—with thin slash-ing black-teeth

up from the gut comes a growth—an uneaten lump of a **densely empty** something—full of a damp—nothing—festering—in the head—the crackling sound of a worming out—swallowing I—into—no one's—deep loneliness

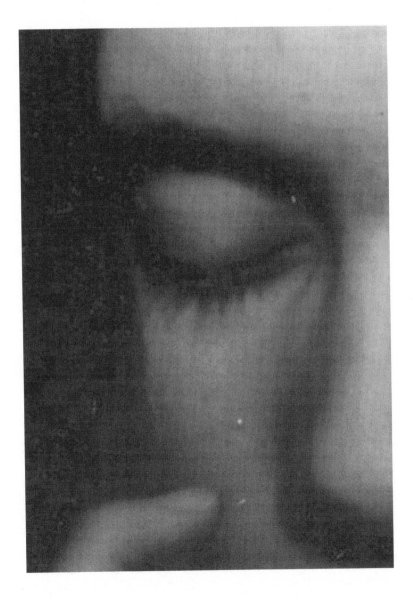

while something tearing its flesh away from **behind the surface of a face**—cries in despair—with a piercing pitch shattering a frozen stare—as a crack at the front of a brittle skull bursts—with an ocean wrenched from the depths of the earth

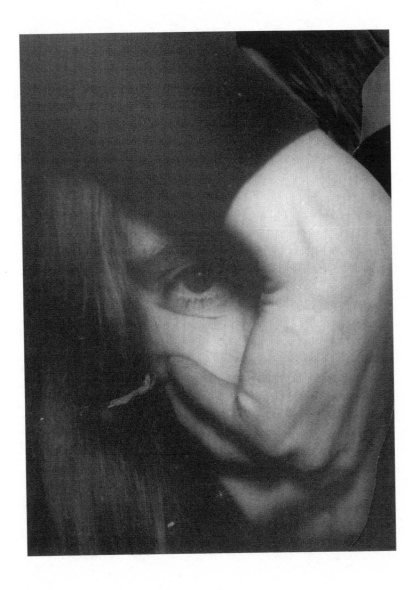

snap flash—**whiplash**—a spine disconnecting—from a head

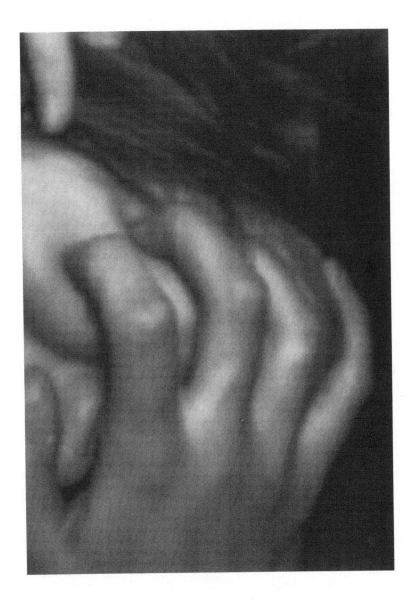

thrashing through **a throat cut from thought**—pieces of meat from a half chewed mind—spat out—with the guttural expulsion of a slaughtered pig at the edge of an open mouth—turn a body inside out

the panic of something lost—as **I get lost**—more to be lost if I'm worried I've lost it—loosing it with worry but stuck to the worry instead of giving in to being lost—of loosing I to find what was lost—that is not what I intended to find—to find what I am not with no intention—the not that is when I am truly lost—never was lost—always there—how demonically divine to be devoured by the loss—that is—there

to be a vacant flesh—for haunting

lurking in the body—**anonymously creeping through veins**— under the skin—in spit and brain—not seen—not sensed—but there—and some how felt—clinging to the edge of flesh—and stretching—through thought

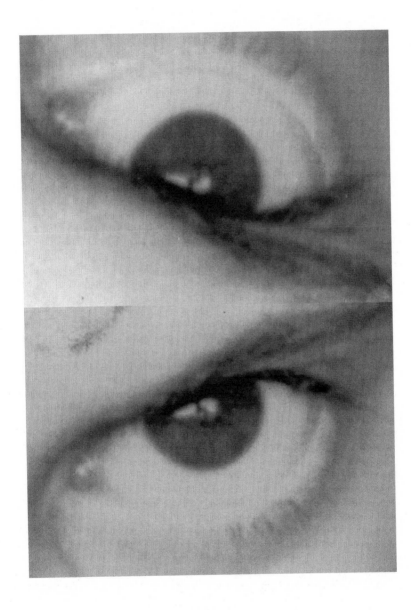

withdrawn to the back of a skull—a flee **clinging to a ridge above a deep void** with a strong pull slips—passed the heart landing in the stench of a growling gut—that spits it out the hole of an ass—gazing—at mid-night's—moon

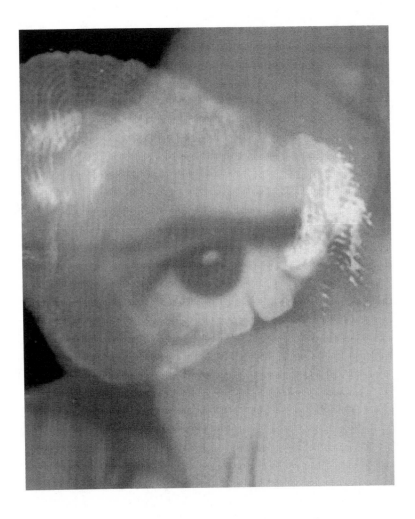

a thin skin peels back over a soft moist white globe—to find—
nothing—the iris has gone—consumed by a growth ensuing from
it's pupil—**drawing in with a sharp pinch** tides of flesh from
the cheek below—where a concave hollow gives way to
increasingly evident bones—the emergence—of a split face—with
a double vision—the left eye hangs inside its blindness—
suspended—in a thick lonely night it simultaneously encloses—
while the right eye—absorbing as much light as it can—vigilantly
watches the impenetrable opacity of the left—that blindly sucks
the rest of its daylight face into darkness—rolling back in a skeletal
head—the eye—disconnects—and drops

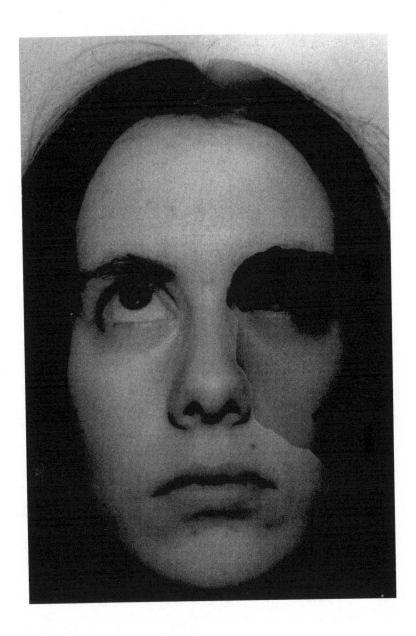

dissolving into a pixelated haze of noise—I—hanging in a thin persistence pierced by a swarm of slippery thoughts I cannot grasp—disperse—into grains of darkened light **scratching the surface of a dry eye**—held in the palm of a blistering hand

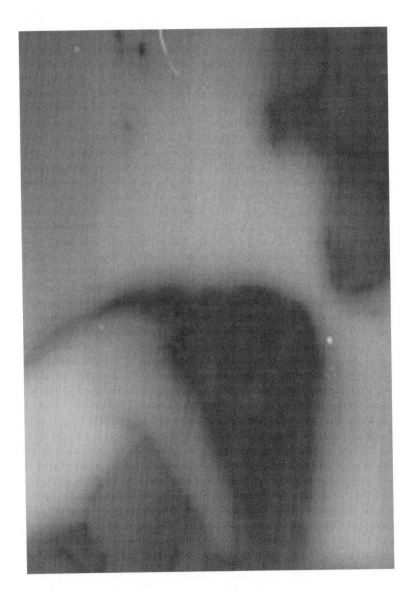

a slightly stirring **half dead head** wonders how long its been lying—just above the earth's ground—a weariness beyond the I of a mind—how long going?—how long dying? —how dense?—what depth of layering hollowed out?—or—only just arrived—something—unfathomable—is stunting I

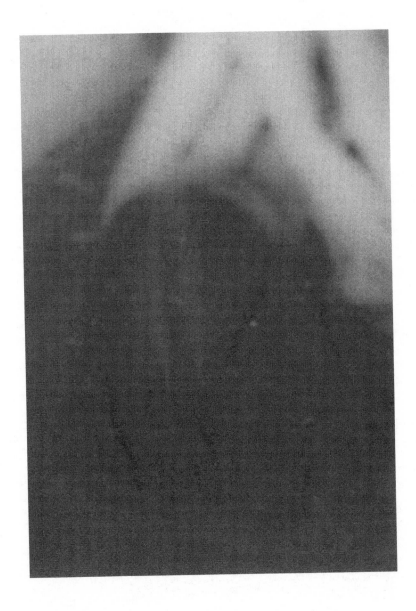

approaching the twilight of *unknowable shadows* with potentially *unfriendly dimensions*—a shawl is drawn over a head on the kerb—as a beacon barely beaming in a flickering hiss at the end of the street—nearly fails to brighten a brittle breach—an exit—from daylight's hardened boundaries—stalling—in a frozen moment—something groaning through the bones of a trembling body slithers—**over the nerves of a splintered spine** into the skull—where it whispers deep and low—filling the head with reverberations—*come to your senseless paradise—the one—right here*—warming the space between cold lips—thought—escapes

into **a flickering splatter of tortured light**

touched—by **nothing pushed up inside** in the form of a thin knife—a body—trembles at the edges in diffused pain strangely sublime—by a pool of blood where a head on the ground consumed by a mouth—draws entrails up from the depths of the earth—releasing—a long crackling growl

stretched—into a **barely perceptible breath**

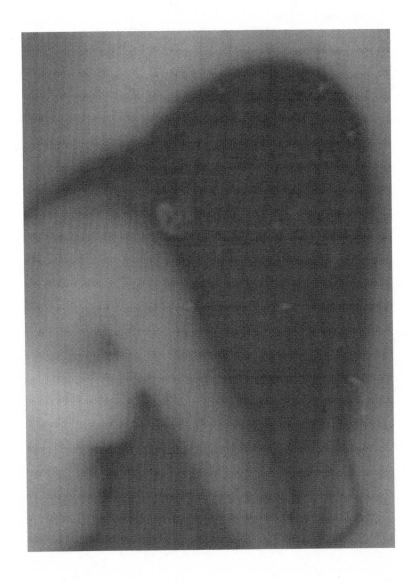

dragged with a trail of externalised organs by **a shadow swallowing a face**—a thin skin stripped of intention—sounding a sound without any distance heard by inverted listening—an insatiable hollow never empty enough hollowing its way through flesh

the no one—haunting—everyone

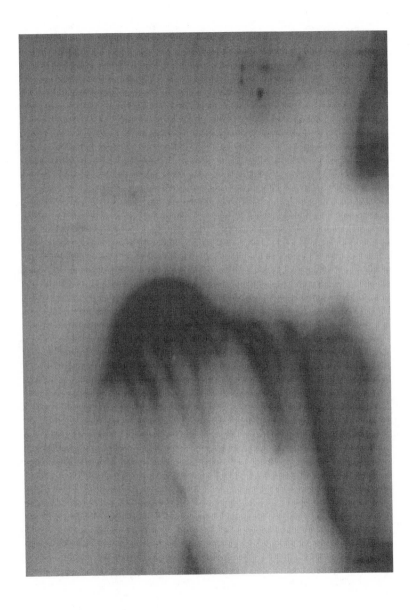

Acknowledgements of direct and indirect influences:

Moévöt was the soundtrack to which the above was compiled. The introduction to Vordb Na R.iidr's oeuvre came via Edia Connole's text, "Les Légions Noires: Labor, Language, Laughter," forthcoming in Nicola Masciandaro and Edia Connole, *Floating Tomb: Black Metal Theory* (Milan: Mimesis, 2015).

The primary texts read alongside writing were the following: Maurice Blanchot, *The Instant of My Death* (Stanford, CA: Stanford University Press, 1998), Jean Améry, *On Suicide— A Discourse on Voluntary Death* (Indianapolis: Indiana University Press, 1999); Nicola Masciandaro, *Sufficient Unto The Day: Sermones Contra Solicitudinem* (London: Schism, 2014); Nicola Masciandaro and Eugene Thacker, eds., *And They Were Two In One And One In Two* (London: Schism, 2014); Dylan Trigg, *The Thing: A Phenomenology of Horror* (Winchester and Washington: Zero books, 2014); David Peak, *The Spectacle of the Void* (London: Schism, 2014); E. M. Cioran, *A Short History of Decay* (New York: Arcade Publishing, 2012); E. M. Cioran, *The Trouble With Being Born* (New York: Arcade Publishing, 2012).

On the Ecstasy of Annihilation: Notes towards a Demonic Supplement[1]

Charlie Blake

1. A Broken Catena[2]

> . . . night by night
> He and his monstrous rout are heard to howl
> Like stabl'd wolves, or tigers at their prey
> Doing abhorred rites to Hecate
> In their obscured haunts . . . [3]

I once knew a madman who thought the end of the world had come. He was a painter—and engraver. I had a great fondness for him. I used to go and see him, in the asylum. I'd take him by the hand and drag him to the window. Look! There! All that rising corn! And there! Look! The sails of the herring fleet! All that loveliness!

---

[1] A "demonic supplement," that is, to a series of visions now sadly lost to the soughing wind that once sang around the cloisters of the sunken cathedral. Fragments, however, are rumoured to have survived in manuscript form and are said to concern, variously, Georges Bataille and vagrant materialism, Cyber-Gnosticism, the goddess Barbelo and the Omega Point of Teillhard de Chardin. On this, see Charlie Blake, "The Gravity of Angels: Space, Time and the Ecstasy of Annihilation," in *Evil Spirits: Nihilism and the Fate of Modernity*, eds. Gary Banham and Charlie Blake (Manchester: Manchester University Press, 2000), 52–71.

[2] The notion of the catena is explored in Nicola Masciandaro, "Anti-Cosmos: Black Mahapralaya," in *Hideous Gnosis: Black Metal Theory Symposium 1* (New York: n.p., 2010), 70–71.

[3] John Milton, *Comus: A Mask* (London: George Routledge and Co., 1858), 46.

[*Pause.*] He'd snatch away his hand and go back into his corner. Appalled. All he had seen was ashes.[4]

Our skies are forever black
Here is no signs [*sic*] of life at all
For burning spirits we are
Consuming your small universe[5]

From the symphonious influence on the heavens, then it arises that the magnet attracts iron, amber silver, the sea-crab (*carabe*), hairs and straw, and the magnetic salve the nature of a wounded man, each holding the other in extraordinary affection. Their dissonant influence also produces the antipathy and discord of things, such as between lamb and wolf, dormouse and cat, the cock's crow and the lion, the sight of basilisk or *catablepas* and man, and many others. Now the concords of divine music draw similar things to them for their protection, and the discords of the same drive away and put to flight dissimilar and contrary things for the same purpose.[6]

Happy they who in hell
Feel not the world's despite[7]

Mourn, mourn, look now for no more day
Nor night, but that from hell,

---

[4] Samuel Beckett, *Endgame: A Play in One Act* (New York: Grove Press, 1958), 44.

[5] Deathspell Omega, "From Unknown Lands of Desolation," *Inquisitors of Satan* (Northern Heritage, 2002).

[6] Robert Fludd "On the occult and wondrous effects of secret music," in *Tractatus Apologeticus Integritatum Societatis de Rosea Crucis defendens* (Leiden, 1617), cited in *Music, Mysticism and Magic*, ed. Joscelyn Godwin (London: Penguin, 1987), 144.

[7] John Dowland, '*Lachrimae*' or '*Flow my Tears*, Phoebe Jevtic Rosquist (soprano) and David Tayler (lute) with the Early Music Ensemble Voices of Music, January 2014 in SanFrancisco' you tube video, 4.37, accessed 08/06/2015, https://www.youtube.com/watch?v=u3clX2CJqzs.

Then all must as they may
In darkness learn to dwell.[8]

Visionary experience is not the same as mystical
experience. Mystical experience is beyond opposites.
Visionary experience is still within that realm. Heaven
entails hell, and "going to heaven" is no more liberation
than is the descent into hell.[9]

When the forms of things are dissolved in the night, the
darkness of the night, which is neither an object nor the
quality of an object, invades like a presence.[10]

2. EXORDIUM

*For what could have been moments or could have been centuries
or could have been millennia or yet longer, something ancient,
evil and rotten had been crouching in the darkness watching him.
Even as he drifted in and out of consciousness as the pain of a
million cuts repeated again and again, whenever the bells rung
in the frosty darkness, as it racked his scored and scourged flesh,
he could sense the archaic thing's swollen red eyes drilling
tendrils of black light into his exposed skull and weeping
lacerations, as he tried again and again to recompose the
darkness around him, to reconfigure the ice-heavy night, to
conceptualize this terrible void, to cast some flickering and
momentary shaft of grey, purifying illumination over the thing
in the corner before its blackening fibres encircled him and
sucked out the remnants of his shattered soul entirely. Yet again.
As before. But even though the darkness was palpable, and*

---

[8] John Dowland, 'Mourn, mourn, day is with darkness fled,' Anthony
Rooley and the Consort of Musicke, *Dowland: Collected Works* (L'oiseau
lyre, 1976).
[9] Aldous Huxley, *Heaven and Hell*, (London: Harper, 1956), 56.
[10] Emmanuel Levinas, "There is: Existence without Existents," trans.
Alphonso Lingis, in *The Levinas Reader*, ed. Sean Hand (Oxford: Basil
Blackwell, 1989), 30.

seemed to fall like fold upon fold of heavy stinking black cloth on and around him, it was still an absence. Pure grief. Pure loss. There was nothing there. There was nothing to change. Nothing that could change. Nothing. Ever.

3. THE SILENCE OF ANGELS AND THE WEEPING SPHERES

Tremolo – A fast pulsation characterizing the diffusion of a sustained sound, in the form of multiple repetitions articulated in discontinuous frequencies.[11]

I tell you, the race of human kind is matter. I have torn myself asunder. I have bought them the mysteries of light, to purify them.[12]

"It has often been noted (began the speaker, one Heirotheus of Syria—according, at least, to the poster in the abandoned funfair they had passed earlier—in a voice of tarnished silver, clashing steel and perfumed smoke, pausing, raising his eyes to the vaulted ceiling of the soon-to-be-engulfed cathedral, then casting down a gaze like a plangent chorale, or like wave upon wave upon waves of crystal sound, or a thousand fibrillating electric guitars and temple bells and cascading daggers of ice, rolling and roiling across the assembled watchers and listeners as they sat, now frozen, now fixed, now mute with nameless joy)[13] . . . it has often been noted (he continued, as the waves fell in diminuendo steps

---

[11] Jean-Francois Augoyard and Henry Torgue, *Sonic Experience: A Guide to Everyday Sounds*, trans. Andra Macartney and Henry Torgue (Montreal: McGill-Queen's University Press, 2008), 131.
[12] From the *Pistis Sophia*, cited by Stephen Holroyd in *The Elements of Gnosticism* (Shaftsbury: Element Books, 1994), 75.
[13] It has been suggested that the unknown narrator's false starts and parenthetical asides on the first page are an attempt to mimic the false beginnings and sonic stutterings of certain forms of guitar-based electronic music, though work still needs to be done to verify and collate the consequences of this assumption for the downwardly spiralling incantation that follows.

and broke against the 'now' he began again, you see, can you hear?, can you hear the now?, he began again, more softly at first, a whispered growl at first, then, rising and falling in voice and cadence, incrementally, like a song, like a drifting passion or a desecrated rose on a broken alter, *opus diabolus*), . . . it has often been noted (he repeated finally, falling into step finally with the dreams of his congregation, finally) that the Florentine poet Dante Alighieri, in his *Divine Comedy*, suffuses his otherwise desultory hierarchical *Paradiso* with musical motifs, with angelic choirs and the ever ascending ecstatic melisma of the blessed and the redeemed. (The speaker's voice now rising, now falling, like the soughing wind outside the cloisters, thought Perpetua, or the waves of a moonlit ocean, or the moaning wind of the icy maze, as she grasped her companion Felicity's hand and leaned forward, eagerly, intently, trembling at the timbre of his voice, the intensity of his gaze). In his *Purgatorio* also, from the transitional aspirants of Antipurgatory who lift their voices in strident hope to the strains of 'In exito Israel' as they traverse the sea of faith to the mountain of redemption in the second canto, and then on to the antiphonal chanting of the seven nymphs, representing the three cardinal and four theological virtues in canto thirty three, the path of atonement is similarly woven with song and harmony or silent music. It is thus woven because harmony links in that age and in this place and in this way with the symmetries of the celestial spheres in their frictionless crystalline rotations, as those rotations and the *musica* that emanates from this angelic machinery,[14] from this creaking apparatus of servile litany, indeed, that supposedly resonates throughout the cosmos itself, are aspects of a far greater harmony, a harmony linking the quotidian and sublunary realm with the realm of the divine in ever-ascending levels of geometric perfection. In Hell, however, there is no music. The ribbed Inferno, the inverted cone and 'body

---

[14] Maimonides, in disagreement with Aristotle who rejected the notion of the music of the spheres, is generally credited as the authority for this idea for many subsequent commentators, if not, of course, its originator. For this source, see Book II of Maimonides, *Guide for the Perplexed*, trans. M. Friedländer (London: Kegan Paul, 2006).

politic'[15] of the Florentine's elaborate theological cartography, musically speaking, is silent. There is no music in Hell for music is solace and celebration and balm to the wounded soul or dejected spirit or diabolical celebrant, and in Hell, at least according to Heavenly edict, there can be no celebration, diabolical or otherwise, nor solace or balm in any sense—only perpetual torment and eternal loss. Sound is certainly present to our avatar Dante Alighieri and his Roman mentor Virgil, from the swirling winds and 'torrential swarming'[16] of the circle of lust and passionate transgression to the amelodious screech of the harpies and the screams, groans, whimperings and lamentations of the self-murdered in the forest of suicides in canto thirteen and then onward or rather downward to the sodomites wandering painfully and eternally amidst fiery snow on the burning sand, or when not described directly it is at least intimated in such a way that the reader's imagination is invited to simulate its own aural accompaniment. But this is not a musical accompaniment, at least not as such, not in the pre-post-industrial sense, it is the sound of discord, disharmony and dissonance as befits a realm divided by the city of Dis itself. It is the sound of agony, fear, torture, and the promise of yet more torture, fear and agony, forever more. It is the infernal racket of the damned and their devils caught in the ever downwarding spiral of abyssal time."[17]

The figure behind the lectern coughed and shook his crumpled wings,[18] gazed for a moment beyond the podium into

---

[15] The notion of the inverted body politic and its relation to what he calls the philosophy of horror in relation to Dante's *Inferno* is explored with incisive elegance by Eugene Thacker in *Tentacles Longer than the Night* (Winchester: Zero Books, 2014), 21–63.

[16] Thacker, *Tentacles*, 49.

[17] On the soundscape of Dante's Inferno as one of "anti-music," see esp. Edoardo Sanguineti,"Infernal Acoustics: Sacred Song and Earthly Song," *Lectura Dantis* 6 (1990): 69-79. The farting devil of *Inferno* 31 who "made a trumpet of his ass" is an especially good example of the inversion. With thanks to Nicola Masciandaro.

[18] The writer here very evidently borrows from David Bowie's "Look Back in Anger" from the album *Lodger* (RCA, 1979). The opening lyrics are as follows: "'You Know who I am,' he said / The speaker was an angel / He coughed and shook his crumpled wings / Closed his eyes and moved his

some undefined space, some topological anomaly forming in the very air as shafts of spectral, multidimensional light flooded the angelic space before him and swept across the elaborately tiled floor of the cathedral. Perpetua looked upward, curiously, at the vast, stained-glass windows. The one nearest to her and Felicity seemed to be an image of a great chateau on a snowy mountainside, bolts of lightning flickering around its towers and turrets and across the peaks beyond, where other more tenebrous chateaus perched precariously in a seemingly infinite receding series. Some tiny figures appeared also to be climbing up through the snow and ice towards the chateau, forming a crooked black line in the form sometimes of a zig-zag, sometimes of a question mark, depending on the light. There were further windows depicting the tarot cards of the major arcana from some ancient pack, or forests and trees, virgins and unicorns, broken mirrors and desecrated roses on blue velvet, or scenes from some tawdry ecclesiastical pornographic series involving sundry monks, friars, nuns, abbesses, cardinals, curates, prelates and popes in various mechanisms and configurations, and there were various tableaus too involving murder, depravity and *danse macabre*. One was of the famous story Felicity had related to her in her early days as her slave, some years before their martyrdom in Carthage, of "the death of philosophers in a dense wood" where a group of philosophers carrying philosophical scrolls and looking very lost are being pursued by a shadowy figure holding a knife. Another depicted the dark night of the soul and was, accordingly, black and empty of form or figure. Yet another window, more immediately vivid than the rest, pictured a swarm of aggressive bees and a pack of ravenous, drooling wolves, similar to those that they had encountered in the dark forest on the way to the cathedral, but here invading a palace, stinging and consuming a king and a queen as they sat upon their silver thrones seemingly impassive to this bestial and apian invasion. Beside this a second window in the series depicted the same room but now empty of both pack and swarm as well as queen and king—thrones and crowns and various

---

lips / 'It's time I should be going.' / (Waiting so long, I've been waiting so, waiting so) / Look back in anger, / driven by the night / Till you come."

regal impedimenta in disarray on the bloodied floor. Here a group of corpse-painted jesters clutching garishly painted lutes and barbed spikes and rattles glowered at the scene from the left hand panel of the triptych, whilst a parallel collectivity of angelic beings in the right hand panel, beings of every imaginable sex and some yet to be imagined, some with horns and tails, some with whips and chains, some with harps and viols and oboes and serpentines, could be discerned engaging in an intricate series of geometrically improbable perversions against nature in a verdant meadow. Another window depicted a forest path with two women treading warily amidst wolves and other ravenous beasts towards a clearing where, as is sometimes the manner with ancient stained glass panels, the same two women could be seen once more to the right, examining now the ruins of an abandoned funfair overrun with weeds and briars, and then on a mottled shingle beach where they reappeared again, looking out at a cathedral apparently sinking in the turbulent ocean. Yet another window, more beautiful than all so far in its way, which was obscure to her sense of reason, was now casting a rich, liquid, golden light that swept in waves upon waves upon waves across the cathedral floor, substantiating in a shimmering quasi-anthropic form, its golden tendrils and trailing lashes and fingers and lips rising slowly up her body from her feet to her belly to her neck and finally moving or sliding across the closely adjacent women to stroke her dear Felicity's hair, as Perpetua herself now realised she now so wanted to do. Momentarily distracted by this spectacle, both intensely sensual and intensely spiritual, she felt her eyes drawn once again, reluctantly this time, to the coloured window above. This window depicted a scene on a hill, three simple wooden crosses of crooked timber raised but empty as yet of sacrificial victims, the sign of nothingness nailed into each to symbolize, perhaps, both the absence of the supreme deity in its triple form and the null set itself. From this window, through this window, the shafts of golden and reddening light from a distant and dying sun now seemed to be brushing Felicity's hair gently from her face and kissing her face gently with soft swollen lips as she sighed and groaned in her given-ness, in her facticity, when suddenly, miraculously, a shaft of yet more golden light, a shower of light and a spear of light, shot through this time with silver and obsidian and colours beyond vision, more intense than anything Perpetua had ever seen or felt or believed, struck and shot through and out of Felicity's belly, as though piercing her for a moment and then withdrawing quickly, like something from the pages of the blessed Saint Teresa d'Ávila or maybe some earlier, barely remembered myth or dream. Felicity gasped loudly. Perpetua grasped her hand more tightly.

The speaker looked over to the two women for a moment, his momentarily intoxicating gaze suffused with both blissful ascension and a deep irrevocable melancholy, with musical *lichtung* and a terrible sonic darkness. His countenance, however, as she realised in a passing flash when he resumed his sermon, his peroration, although exquisitely beautiful, was somehow empty, was somehow void of human expression, its perfect geometry less like a face per se than an ornate, burnished mirror reflecting back her own dreams and terrors and vanities and passions and despair. Like the magic mirror in the fairy tale of the virgin and the wicked queen and the seven gnomes, perhaps, she thought. A face without faciality. He turned away and continued.

4. THE MUSIC OF HELL AND THE FIRES OF LOVE

> The Tartini effect refers to the production of a sound that is physiologically audible, but that has no physical existence. It looks like a sonic hologram.[19]

> ... the power appeared by means of an energy that is at rest and silent, although having uttered a sound thus: Zza Zza Zza.[20]

---

[19] Augoyard and Torgue, *Sonic Experience*, 129.
[20] From an early Gnostic apocalyptic text in which Allogenes (meaning stranger or foreigner in this world) relates to his son Messus the nature of the apocalypse to come with specific reference to Gnostic-Sethian goddess Barbelo, worshipped by one of the most intriguing sects, the Barbelites or Barbelognostics. Allogenes also describes a mystical journey he takes to the celestial realm which concludes with his spiritual

"Similarly, albeit only initially, the great protestant argumentator and cosmographer and poet of revolutionary England, John Milton, so enraptured by and needful of the solace of music, especially in his later days when sight had left him, fills his heaven in *Paradise Lost* with exquisite sounds and divine harmonies. The earthly paradise before the fall is also resonant with the songs of birds and beasts' refrains and the gracious elements and counterpoint of the music of wind and water. But what of Hell and its music or silence or noise? The tale that Milton tells is both rigorous in its formal explication and yet rather curious in its several hidden corners and dark angles, but suffice it to say that at first, Lucifer/Satan and his rebel troops appear to have the upper hand over the simpering archangel Michael and his irresolute guards in the early stages of the war in Heaven that opens the epic. But then God the Father in his mighty omniscience sends the Son of God in his omniscient mightiness to rout the rebellious army, and we observe through Milton's blind eyes the inevitably albeit temporarily defeated angels tumbling seemingly endlessly through the realms of chaos and then eventually into the abyss prepared for them so far below by nobodaddy so far above—a fall into adamantine chains and a burning lake that leads somewhat miraculously and inexplicably to the construction of the once great city of Pandemonium, a city so much grander, so much more cosmopolitan and so much more architecturally eloquent than the late medieval city of Dis; and notably considering its subsequent association with noisy chaos, for all its apparent sound and fury, its infernally percussive parliament of devils, it is a city built on a site initially devoid of sound. Indeed, it is a place of 'horrid silence' as Milton notes, a silence broken when Satan addresses the first prime minister of Hell, Beelzebub, to initiate the first infernal parliament. At the conclusion of this Stygian council in book two, however, the poet's love of music once again prevails and pervades even Hell as the newly fledged demonic hordes disperse to

---

transformation and experience of ecstatic silence. See *Allogenes*, in *The Nag Hammadi Library in English*, ed. James M. Robinson, trans. Antoinette Clark Wire, John D. Turner, and Orval S. Wintermute (Amsterdam: E. J. Brill), 447.

acclimatize themselves to their new condition, beginning with heraldic trumpetings that resound throughout the realm and followed by some, at least, returning to the harps so often associated with the angelic hierarchies to sing of the tragic fall of the rebel angels. This is Hell before the damned, of course, but it is notable with all its baroque and Babylonian excess as a place full of sound at this point and some of it musical.

In part, Milton's elaborate cosmography is a continuation, with some notable topographical alterations anticipating the non-locational or more geographically dispersed hells of the greater modernity to come (particularly those alterations concerning chaos and the spatium and the invisible machinery of distributed dystopia, as well as the consequential internality of suffering and ecstasy as aspects of what J. G. Ballard in another context entirely once called 'inner space'), a continuation of a by now long tradition from the monochord of Pythagoras through various neo-Platonists, through Boethius, Jacque de Liege and sundry medieval schoolmen, celestial mechanicians and virtual engineers to figures such as Marsilio Ficino with his astral daemons and the enigmatic Athanasius Kircher, whose writings on celestial harmonics and their more terrestrial counterpart are worth citing at some length to garner some of the flavours and modalities of this divine orchestration.

Athanasius notes that this celestial music is compounded:

> . . . not of three, four or five voices, but of the utterly ineffable chorus of Saints, all disposed in their different classes, it resonates for all eternity in the supermundane palace of the Heavenly King. There the choirs of Virgins, of Confessors, of Martyrs, Apostles, and Patriarchs all interweave with the triple hierarchy of Angels, singing to the fount of the water of eternal life, enjoying eternal rest as they tirelessly sing the eternal Alleluai in praise of GOD, who like a supreme conductor directs the symphony by his wisdom and animates the organ by the breath of his mouth . . . There the remembrance of this world's labours, of torments endured to the end for the love of GOD, is like a dissonance mingled with the

consonance of blessed life everlasting, and a syncopation coalescing with the ecstatic and perfect harmony of all things. O unhappy is the fate of those who, deafened by the transitory goods of this calamitous life, by the noise of worldly ambition, by the discordant cataracts of impure affections and pleasures, have lost their hope of ever attaining or hearing the music we have described.[21]

This enraptured hymn to the love-saturated expression of divine harmonics is further contrasted with the more human or sublunary forms of musical expression thus:

Everything imaginable which could ever be invented by the skill of human genius, all harmony and music, every conceivable beauty and allure of musical instruments, every excellence and perfection of human voices: what are these compared to the supreme music, but the cacophonous bellowing of cattle, the howling of wolves, the grunting of pigs?[22]

In a sense, Kircher's terrestrial music *is* the music of Hell to those accustomed to the divine choirs and in this he bears some comparison to the Augustinian notion of evil, which is merely the absence of good, in that the absence of heavenly music defines all other music as effectively infernal. But while Kircher's ecstatic hyperbole might have a point in relation to the times in which it was written, when angelic music was indeed of an extremely mellifluous quality, even to those of us of a rather different ontological persuasion, the later transitions of European romanticism and the industrial revolution in the isle of Albion began also to transform the status and desires of what became known to 19th-century demagogues as the angelic class. Imagine that we are now in the world of the secularised angelic and

---

[21] Athanasius Kircher, "The Nine Stringed instrument of Nature," in Godwin, *Music, Mysticism and Magic*, 161.
[22] Godwin, *Music, Mysticism and Magic*, 160.

demonic, where the sounds of the loom and the foundry, of the hydraulic pump and steam engine, begin to become the as yet unappreciated incidental music of the quotidian. As anybody who has ever spent time around these now archaic technologies—often reanimated for contemporary curiosity in secular museums or spectral funfairs—will be aware, within these oiled and glistening engines, amidst these lubricated and muscular machines—albeit historically stained or branded by the atrocities they inadvertently generated as much as the glories of the capitalism they helped to unleash—there, beyond the designs of speculators and inventors, within the machinery itself once in motion, are contained the sounds of accidentally captured choirs of angels and devils in desperate servitude, there in the clash of bizarre percussive effects, the *basso profundo* of some deeply compressed and unseen confinement of captured angelic and demonic substance by the brute matter of the machine and its repetitions. As a consequence, the celestial mechanics and harmonies have here given way via the regular pulse and creak of clockwork and early automata to the diabolical disharmonies and gradually accelerated rhythm and repetition of the engine, of the immaculate machine. Certainly (and aware that we have been decidedly Eurocentric and indeed Christocentric in our narrative thus far), there have been many diverse traditions of sound and silence in the study of angelic or supernatural beings and congregations. In the Islamic tradition, for instance, Israfel as the angel of music and Azrael as the angel of death, both charming companions in the battle against cosmic tyranny, have been known to strike a number of mutually advantageous bargains amidst the scattered souls of aspirants to eternal life, and, albeit in a rather different key, there are traditions too within Christianity that allow the angels to sing relentlessly in the nocturnal hours whilst remaining silent in the day to allow the human flocks to bleat their praises to the empty set. There are too a number of speculative theologians who have claimed that the chorale of angels is, anyway, and once the divine machinery has been set in motion, silent to human ears, even amongst the redeemed and the exalted in Paradise. Be that is it may, there is no doubt that the rise of the machine and what the poet William

Blake described as 'dark Satanic Mills' signalled the decay of angelic essence and the gradual retreat of the angelic hosts from both the phenomenal and noumenal realms. In other words, the rise of machine is concurrent, both historically and geographically, with the silencing of angels. Thus how very prescient was the last and most lustrous poet and dramatist of my series, William Shakespeare, to note in his final play, albeit by dramatic conceit, that England is the source of a new and devilish music to come:

> Be not afeard; the isle is full of noises,
> Sounds, and sweet airs, that give delight and hurt not.
> Sometimes a thousand twangling instruments
> Will hum about mine ears; and sometimes voices,
> That if I had then waked after a long sleep,
> Will make me sleep again: and then, in dreaming,
> The clouds methought would open, and show riches
> Ready to drop upon me that, when I waked,
> I cried to dream again.[23]

Shakespeare is, of course, referring here to the superficially benign enchantment of the music and song of our fictional cousins, the so-called neutrals, called thus for their supposed neutrality in the war in Heaven. But such apparent benignity fades too as industrialisation takes hold, and the neutrals fade also— hyperstitionally speaking—along with the Cherubim and Seraphim, thrones and dominions and others of the nine, into the spinning black hole of collective forgetfulness. And yet, and yet, the music of this imagined realm remains and it mingles with the remnants of angelic sound that fall to the Earth and with the rumblings of infernal noise that rise up through its vents and cracks to enter the realm of amplified music in the 1960s. Concurrently, the withdrawal of angelic music into angelic silence is gradual, but it continues through the 20th century as dissonance

---

[23] Caliban to Stephano in William Shakespeare, *The Tempest*, II.2, in *The Complete Works of Shakespeare* (London and Glasgow, Collins, 1926), 16.

and discord and distorted electronic amplification become figures of calculation and design rather than of accident, finding its true moment when the music of Hell finally emerges against the now long silence of angels. This moment has its precursors for sure, the flickering presence of tritonia in Western music from the early medieval period onwards, Giuseppe Tartini's discovery in a dream of the devil's trill, the diabolical sawings and mewlings of Nicolo Paganini's violin or the ragged blue multiplicities of Robert Johnson's flurried guitar pickings, but its true precursor is an album made up of diverse experimental musicians in 1968 in London and released in the following year, a project including that eminent electronic composer from the BBCs' Radiophonic Worksop, Delia Derbyshire, as a contributor to the Orphic-Satanic melange of *An Electric Storm in Hell*. If this album by the studio ensemble White Noise, and in particular, the final, extended track 'Black Mass: An Electric Storm in Hell,' began to open the door of Hell itself and provide its remaining inhabitants with early, analogue studio facilities and access to then fashionable vinyl, that same door would be kicked wide open the following year, in 1970, by a band of electric troubadours from the West Midlands called Black Sabbath, whose overture to their first album *Black Sabbath* (Vertigo), a track that with an admirable economy of nomenclature is also called 'Black Sabbath,' is possibly one of the most startling openings of any long-playing record of that era or subsequently. Much Faustian ink, of course, has been spilled on this remarkable debut and the story of what follows, the development of a largely theatrical albeit flattering faux Satanism in various strands of what came to be known as 'metal'—imagery given a more persuasive diabolical gravity during the rise of Norwegian black metal in 1990s—is well known to adherents of the genre and its offshoots, and need not be retold in this angelically sanctified temple of sin and debasement. Suffice it to say, however, that if White Noise and Black Sabbath opened the doors to Hell and provided studio technology and cultural channels for its denizens to explore, the emergence of black metal was the first time music emanating from Hell itself resounded openly in the terrestrial realm via its human agents, musicians and quasi-musicians generally selected for possession and doom by the grim progeny of sin, death and chaos, and invariably nostalgic by infernal proxy for the one or many sub-hells that have been built and maintained since the fall of the shining angel.

In an important sense, then, during the 20th century, the silencing of God's angels becomes a requirement for the music of Hell to emerge and thus replace the celestial litany with the scourging and buzzing of more demonical symphonies, celebrating sometimes at considerable volume and velocity the affects and affections of misery, demise and cosmic nigredo. The more pure amongst the angels, however, by virtue of their rapidly decaying essence, the corruption of their very substance, withdraw from this world and also from their own former world, those crystalline circles of cosmic harmonics and blissful obeisance, into a zone of mellifluous inversion, absence and enigma, of dark, paradoxical joy in the agony of 'being,' but here being-as-absence, as non-existence, as true annihilation. It is an ontological vacillation for sure, a being-as-absence not dissimilar to the being-as-vanishing of the first creator of the universe in certain gnostic traditions, s/he who abandoned us all to the chaotic ministrations of the deranged demiurge and subsequent archons and spiritual bureaucrats in a cosmos of brute matter, a cosmic domain that the elect amongst us, those once touched with the *pneuma* and its resonating memory or pre-existence, long to escape forever and evermore and more crucially, nevermore. And thus, what the purest of angels have already done, however inadvertently, now, their debased and demonic brothers and sisters wish also to do, and more generously, they wish to take the human herd, universally and without selection, along with them. Thus the diabolical, which is in many ways—as Milton understood so well—a dark and glamorous derivation from the angelic, yearns for that same divine dissipation, that same cosmic absence, that same delicious surcease, as do the practitioners of the shattered crystalline music that hymns this cosmic absence, the music of perdition and absolute annihilation."

5. PERDITION

> This effect is linked to a feeling of perdition, in the double sense of a soul in distress and the dissipation of a sound motif. The sound seems to be emitted for nothing, for everyone to hear but requiring no answer. It is a sound without destination, absurd in the etymological sense; its entire expression is simply one of powerlessness. Often characteristic of extreme suffering constituted principally of tears and moans, this effect accompanies life situations that are violent or painful.[24]

"Of melancholy and mystical death there is both much more and nothing whatsoever to say. Much more, because in spite of the Saturnine gravity attending both the infinite despair attendant upon it and the process of dying in the ordinary, non-mystical sense, the frail human body and its organs and orifices will often respond to its final moments with sound, rather than light or taste or smell or touch. The human body will often if not invariably respond with noises, with groans and a catalogue of dismal eructation, with lamentations and larval threnodies, with cries and exhortations and garbled monologues, with screams and whimpers, and in due course, with gurgles and sighs and belches, to the condition and the process of dying. And then, in the silence of death itself, behind the mask of that silence (and please forgive here my all too human conceit), there will be further noises, further gurgles and belches, as the body decays, as the soft tissue melts, as time consumes the matter that now belongs to those organisms that live by harvesting our death, that reanimate as their cities and empires the corpses that were once the vehicles of our most passionate hopes and fears, our agonies and ecstasies. In this micro world, our dying is the preparation for a feast and our death—unless our corpses are cryogenically suspended or otherwise isolated—is the banquet itself. On our more human and macro scale, modern cities, at least those currently untouched by war and famine and pestilence or the depredations of systemically

---

[24] Augoyard and Torge, *Sonic Experience*, 84.

163

engineered poverty or ecological breakdown, the fall into death may well be accompanied by the sounds of medical technology, care and institutionalisation, with its diagetically configured beeps and burbles and rolling trolleys and whispered exchanges in overlit corridor and wards. In less salubrious zones, both historically and geographically, dying may be accompanied by the rush, clash and sonic spectacle of war and occupation, the sickening mechanical repetition of torture, death, explosion and gunfire,[25] the deadening liturgy of exaltation and execution amidst the rubble and remains. However much your artists, musicians, tragedians, nihilists and romanticists may fetishize death and its transfigurations, however much they may fetishize the tremulous electric glissando, febrile growlings and keenings and blasphemous theatrics of the corpse-painted musician, or the late night conversation and mesmeric diversions of the urbane vampire in some New Orleans bordello, or the rapt delirium—the vibrant ec-stasis—of the Voudon dancer whose phenomenal self is temporarily evicted and whose body temporarily occupied by, or rather 'ridden,' by one of the Lwa, or even the mere imagining of stillness and surcease in the blackened or cosmeticized or gothicised corpse, there is nothing beautiful or mystical about the process of human dying, about the savage, forced crawl up or down the stony, barbed and tangled path to that eventual solace of final silence and terminal emptiness of the abandoned self. And yet, within that general observation there is a lacuna, like a darkened whorl on the trunk of a young tree thrusting into life, into the glory of heliotropical extension, its roots buried deep in the mulch and moisture, in the rich nutrients supplied by the organic death of its forebears and by the dead of the terrestrial mode in general.

The glory of corpses beneath the ground."

With this the speaker turned away from his congregation whose moans, groans and sighs, and ecstatic communion with the spirit

---

[25] For an incisive and cogent discussion of music, noise, contagion, torture, torment and the art of war, see Steve Goodman, *Sonic Warfare: Sound, Affect and the Ecology of Fear* (London: The MIT Press, 2010).

servants of both Eros and Thanatos and vagrant Qlippoth, were increasing in volume, regularity and accelerating rhythm as the cathedral grew darker. As the rhythms of blasphemous love and heretical demise became the rampant and relentless beating of a thousand drums he turned to the alter and paid ritual obeisance to the crooked thorn, the scattered rose petals of the desecrated bloom and the pulse of the pierced and bleeding heart once lost in an abandoned funfair, before turning back one last time to face his audience, observing them imperiously in their becomings as a collectivity obsessed by a strange, dual, oscillating passion for blissful annihilation. He spread his blackened wings wide and launched into the air, flew to the vaulted roof then swooped down and through the window of the dark night of the soul into the chaos beyond as the cathedral sunk beneath the waves and into the dark ocean's briny depths.

6. DEBURAU AND DEMESNE

> With this effect, the listener's attention searches for a sound that is inaudible, such as the voice of a mute person. The effect is named for Jean-Baptiste Deburau (1796-1846), a famous mime whose trial attracted the whole of Paris, curious to hear his voice.[26]

Dr. Dionysia Demesne brushed a lock of hair away from her eyes and examined the tapestry closely, trying to piece together its narrative from the faded stitching and decipher its meaning. It seemed in its several perspectives to be describing a church or a cathedral sinking beneath the waves, in one of which two women watched the event from a shingle beach. From another perspective, an internal one this time, at the front in one of the woven images, near an ornate alter scattered with roses at the centre of which sat a human heart pieced by a single thorn, was a spectacular figure stretching his black bat-like Luciferean wings as if about to fly before the cathedral sank into the depths. There

---

[26] Augoyard and Torgue, *Sonic Experience*, 37.

was music emerging from the tapestry that she couldn't identify: shimmering, sibilant, polyrhythmic, unsettling. There was also a congregation, amidst which sat two women, one in emerald green and one in sapphire blue, one of whom appeared to be pierced by a gold, silver and obsidian shaft of light and surrounded by a unusually rendered crimson halo. At that moment, in that moment, a lone raven or some other corvid flew into the library, disrupting Demesne's meditations and alarming one of her colleagues who ran out of the library in pursuit of the hapless and murderless bird.[27] Perhaps as a result of this moment of avian epiphany or perhaps for some other reason entirely, she couldn't be sure, the meaning of the tapestry suddenly became clear to her. Its meaning involved spiritual death, beyond organic death, beyond visions of the beyond, beyond heaven, hell and apocalypse, blacker than the darkest black, *bezna*,[28] as it is described in Romania. In this sense there is (because nothingness is the absolute) only absolute nothingness, which is always our origin and end. Absolute annihilation is not a process but a return, a sidereal reverse or slide across the ever burning sky. This is the moment of dark epiphany at which we stretch our blackened wings and soar into the black light of the Pleroma and then descend into the even blacker abyss and become the abyss and bring the whole universe with us in becoming the abyss in becoming nothing just as the first creator once did. This is how the first creator has been hymning us from the gap between nothing and nothingness, which is itself a mere reverberation echoing across the many universes and seas of dissonant temporality, a

---

[27] The context of this scene with corvid and tapestries is described in a companion piece to this essay, also by Charlie Blake: "A Thousand Chateaus: On Time, Topology and the Seriality of Serial Murder – Part One," in *Serial Killing: A Philosophical Anthology*, eds. Edia Connole and Gary J. Shipley (London: Schism, 2015).

[28] A series of essay collections celebrating this blackness within blackness and the roots and tendrils this blackness within blackness sends out to related conceptualisations of fear, apocalypse, the netherworld, darkenings, etc., may be found and downloaded at http://bezzzna.blogspot.co.uk/.

sound without existence, a sonic hologram, a Tartini effect in effect, guiding us as scholars, artists, nihilists, auditors and visionaries to the gates of *mors mystica* via, at this stage at least, the deciphering of tapestries, of discovered manuscripts, of stained glass windows, of the noise beyond the signal, of the ancient hieroglyphics once scratched upon dying stars and quantum particles. This is the true and holy path to the ecstasy of annihilation.

Autonomy of Death, Nothing Like This

Daniel Colucciello Barber

Blackness, within Christian metaphysics, is rife with negative connotations: death, nothingness, damnation.[1] This negativity of blackness is not a matter of opposition. Blackness is not something in duality with something white. It is rather what things deny when they believe they are something. Such belief in being something may be defined as capacity. Here, capacity names something's belief that it can be (the) something (that it claims to be).

For Christian metaphysics, the context is redemptive. The context capacitates redemption, or redemption is a capacity that depends on context. The capacity of someone to be redeemed depends on the capacity to be someone in context. Perhaps to be someone is already to be someone being redeemed. In any case, whether it is a matter of being someone or of being someone redeemed, capacity is claimed. The denial of negativity, of blackness, has thus been contextualized. This negativity—denied by context, by the belief that one is something—is nothing, without context, nothing without context. This is negativity because this cannot be contextualized; this is deictic.

In such a context of capacity, what is negativity? It is this—this, without context, without the capacity to be something in the context, without the capacity to be contextualized. Negativity is this, and this, without capacity, is irredeemable. Yet if this is without context, it is because this stays this; this demands itself, this points to this. This is autonomous, without need to believe in

---

[1] For a thorough, insightful account of the nature and establishment of blackness in these terms, see Eulalio R. Baltazar, *The Dark Center: A Process Theology of Darkness* (New York: Paulist Press, 1973).

context. As Nicola Masciandaro puts this, "The negativity of deixis . . . resolves to a deeper auto-deixis, its pointing to itself."[2]

If one thinks the reality of this negativity, how far can one ride? If one is ridden by negativity, can one even ride at all? Or, if one is on this ride, if one is ridden with this negativity, can one be? Martin Heidegger said, regarding being, "there is."[3] We might then ask: "is there" one capable of thinking this negativity?

My thesis is that there is not: there is no one that can really think this negativity; there is no one, in reality, that can be on this ride. *There is not.* This is more than empirical, because negativity is less than someone who empirically appears. It is not that someone empirically appears, saying "I can think this negativity," such that it must then must be judged whether s/he is telling the truth. Of course, s/he is certainly not telling the truth. But neither is s/he telling a lie—for the lie here is not what someone says, it is the very belief that someone is here. In other words, negativity does not appear in someone's encounter; negativity precludes anyone from appearing.

Negativity, here, is not what someone is capable of thinking; negativity is not even what someone finds oneself incapable of thinking. More radically, negativity is what precludes someone from being. The radicality of negativity goes to the root of being, of the "there is": if there is negativity, then there is no one.

To ride the negativity bound to blackness—death, nothingness, damnation—is not something that one has the capacity to do. This incapacity is both more and less than a failure. It is not that there is first someone who then, as a subsequent and contingent outcome, fails to ride negativity; it is that the negativity that is supposed to be ridden is already denied by the belief of being

---

[2] Nicola Masciandaro, "What Is This That Stands Before Me?: Metal as Deixis," in *Reflections in the Metal Void*, ed. Niall W. R. Scott (Oxford: Interdisciplinary Press, 2012), 5. On deixis, see also Alice Gavin, *Literature and Film, Dispositioned: Thought, Location, World* (London: Palgrave MacMillan, 2014).
[3] See, for instance, Martin Heidegger, *On Time and Being*, trans. Joan Stambaugh (Chicago: University of Chicago Press, 2002), 5–10.

someone with the capacity to ride. The negativity that is here antecedes and precludes—and is denied by—the belief that one is here.[4] As Masciandaro reports: "No one is supposed to be here."[5]

There is no one who can ride negativity, because negativity is the radicality of no one. This is bad news only if one thinks one is supposed to be here, only if one thinks one has something to lose, only if one believes one *is* something. Simply put, this negativity is bad news only for those who need the good news of redemption.

It could just as well be said that this negativity is sad to hear only for those who need to oppose, to contextualize a duality between, sad sounds and happy sounds. James Baldwin, articulating his blackness with regard to Norman Mailer's whiteness, remarked: "There is a difference . . . between Norman and myself in that I think he still imagines that he has something to save, whereas I have never had anything to lose."[6] To imagine oneself as having something to save, or merely to imagine oneself *as* something to save—here one finds oneself in, here one makes, the context of redemption. And here, with the belief in redemption, even sound gets contextualized. As Baldwin elsewhere remarked: "White Americans seem to feel that happy songs are *happy* and sad songs

---

[4] I understand "antecedence" as irreducible to "priority," which is narrated as something previous to the something that is here. Priority is thus conditioned by narrative. Antecedence, however, is that which precludes the very commencement of narrative. In other words, antecedence is the condition of impossibility for narrative, and thus for anything whose possibility is conditioned by narrative (including priority). This understanding of antecedence is influenced by Jared Sexton's "The Social Life of Social Death: On Afro-Pessimism and Black Optimism," *InTensions* 5 (Fall/Winter 2011), http://www.yorku.ca/intent/issue5/articles/pdfs/jaredsextonarticle.pdf.

[5] Nicola Masciandaro, "Absolute Secrecy: On the Infinity of Individuation," in *Speculation, Heresy, and Gnosis in Contemporary Philosophy of Religion: The Enigmatic Absolute*, eds. Joshua Ramey and Matthew Harr Farris (forthcoming).

[6] James Baldwin, "The Black Boy Looks at the White Boy," in *Nobody Knows My Name* (New York: Vintage, 1993), 217. See also the commentary on this passage by Frank B. Wilderson, III, in *Red, White & Black: Cinema and the Structure of U.S. Antagonisms* (Durham, NC: Duke University Press, 2010), 11–13.

are *sad*."[7] We might say, along these lines, that black music has no need to contextualize sound. Black music sounds negativity without need of context; it sounds, autonomously, like this.[8]

Is it possible to theorize black metal as a kind of black music? There is a characteristic that is shared by black metal and black music: the valorization of negativity through the valorization of blackness. Black metal, like black music, does not acquiesce to the devalorization of blackness but instead makes blackness autonomous—liberation now, without need of redemption.[9] Negativity is irredeemable. But black metal, like black music, sounds such being-deprived of redemption as autonomy from being-redeemed.

---

[7] James Baldwin, *The Fire Next Time* (New York: Vintage, 1962), 42 (italics original). It is worth noting that Baldwin's claim is superposed with a discussion of black music's irreducibility to narrative. The impossibility of contextually dividing "happy" and "sad" is bound up with a temporality that refuses the narrative contextualization of past and future—and, in this passage, that specifically refuses the narrative contextualization of arrival: "In all jazz, and especially in the blues, there is something tart and ironic, authoritative and double-edged. . . . I think it was Big Bill Broonzy who used to sing 'I Feel So Good,' a really joyful song about a man who is on his way to the railroad station to meet his girl. She's coming home. It is the singer's incredibly moving exuberance that makes one realize how leaden the time must have been while she was gone. There is no guarantee that she will stay this time, either, as the singer clearly knows, and, in fact, she has not yet actually arrived" (41-42). Along similar lines, Nathaniel Mackey— in *Splay Anthem* (New York: New Directions, 2002), 7—writes, "After the end. Before / the beginning . . . / All at once they / both wondered / which . . . "

[8] This is, of course, a rather brief mode of approach to black music. For a properly complex and incisive approach, key texts include Fred Moten's *In the Break: The Aesthetics of the Black Radical Tradition* (Minneapolis: University of Minnesota Press, 2003) and Alexander G. Weheliye's *Phonographies: Grooves in Sonic Afro-Modernity* (Durham, NC: Duke University Press, 2005). See also James Baldwin's "Of the Sorrow Songs: The Cross of Redemption," in *The Cross of Redemption: Uncollected Writings* (New York: Vintage, 2011), 145–153.

[9] I have addressed the "now" in "The Immanent Refusal of Conversion," *Journal for Cultural and Religious Theory* 13.1 (Winter 2014), 142–150.

Nonetheless, there is something at work in black metal that ultimately keeps it at a distance from black music.[10] Black metal, in order to distinguish itself from Christian metaphysics, tends to invoke its own metaphysical autochthony, its own "pagan" territorial belonging.[11] It distinguishes itself from Christianity by territorializing itself in the pre-Christian. In this sense, the blackness of black metal claims for itself a narrative capacity of continuity. When black metal sounds itself against Christian metaphysics, it narrates continuity with a pagan metaphysics that is historically and territorially contextualized, prior to Christianity. One is damned by Christianity, but one supposes oneself to be in the pre-Christian territory that is supposed to be here.

On the other hand, black music—as indexed by Baldwin—is marked by the middle passage. This blackness, this concomitant black music, is marked by negativity in a way that cannot be narrated. This way is the way of the middle passage, a middle that simultaneously antecedes narrative origin and perseveres "in the wake"—as Christina Sharpe has put it—of narrative redemption.[12] Or, we could say—invoking the analysis, by Frank B. Wilderson, III, of the incommensurability between "loss" and "absence"—that black metal sounds blackness in narration of territorial loss, whereas black music sounds blackness in absence of both territory

---

[10] For a different take on these matters—one that stresses commonality rather than the negativity of the incommensurable—see Aliza Shvarts, "Black Wedding," *The Brooklyn Rail* (February 2015), http://www.brooklynrail.org/2015/02/criticspage/black-wedding.

[11] This, I think, is the basis for the right-wing tendencies that have emerged in the context of black metal. For a discussion of these tendencies, see Benjamin Noys, "'Remain True to the Earth!': Remarks on the Politics of Black Metal," in *Hideous Gnosis: Black Metal Theory Symposium I*, ed. Nicola Masciandaro (New York: n.p., 2010), 105–128.

[12] Christina Sharpe, "Black Studies: In the Wake," *The Black Scholar* 44.2 (Summer 2014): 59–69.

and narrative.[13] Blackness, as Wilderson argues, is articulated as "a genealogical isolate."[14]

The genealogical isolation of blackness is its incapacity to be narrated in continuity with something else. Blackness is nothing in anti-black narrative; blackness is isolated as this, without narrative context. Yet this, isolated from context as nothing, pointing to itself, does not need narrative need. As J Dilla sounds the report: "There, is, nothing like this."[15] This nothing—or this, which nothing is like—is the sound of baseless love, a love that is metaphysically nothing, a love that is nothing, like this.

It cannot be passed over that anti-blackness, when marked by the middle passage, is marked not metaphysically but epidermally. Metaphysical anti-blackness permits the distance of counter-articulation, whereas epidermal anti-blackness enacts an always already gripping violence. This blackness is subjected to violence in a way that grips the flesh before narration: death grips.

It is striking how often the lyrics for Death Grips, sounded by MC Ride, are narrated in terms of paranoia. For instance, if MC Ride reports that those around him are trying to kill him, then it is commonly supposed to be a report reflective of his own paranoid psyche. The report sounded by MC Ride is thus supposed to belong to a psyche that fails to understand the empirical world outside the psyche. This entails the pathologization of the one who sounds the report: pathology is attributed to the psyche, rather than to the empirical world that surrounds and contextualizes it.

---

[13] Wilderson, drawing on the work of David Marriott, remarks that "loss is an effect of temporality; it implies a syntagmatic chain that absence cannot apprehend . . . loss indicates a prior plenitude, absence does not." See Frank B. Wilderson, III, "The Vengeance of Vertigo: Aphasia and Abjection in the Political Trials of Black Insurgents," *InTensions* 5 (Fall/Winter 2011), http://www.yorku.ca/intent/issue5/articles/pdfs/frankbwildersoniiiarticle.pdf, 30.

[14] Wilderson, "The Vengeance of Vertigo," 19. My discussion of blackness in this text is deeply dependent on—unthinkable without—the work of Wilderson. For the most extended articulation of his thought, see Wilderson, *Red, White & Black*.

[15] J Dilla, "Nothing Like This," *Ruff Draft* (Stones Throw, 2007).

Such an interpretation denies the anti-blackness of the empirical world.

Keep in mind the empirical world's anti-blackness, its construction of blackness as genealogical isolate, its subjection of blackness to epidermalized violence. And then consider the report sounded by MC Ride: "And suicide ain't my style, so I'm surrounded." Who is doing this surrounding? "Never could rest they're always there." Who are the ones always there? And who is never capable of rest? Here is another report: "I'm epiphanic amnesia."[16] Is there one who can be "epiphanic amnesia"? What is named by this amnesia, this incapacity to narrate the past, this incapacity to remember context? And why is this an epiphany, or why is this incapacity revelatory?

These reports are sounded on an album whose title is also a report: *No Love Deep Web*. What is named by "deep web" is not a pathological psyche so much as the pathologically anti-black structure of the empirical world. MC Ride's lyrics are reports on this world, sounded by what this world articulates as nothing. There is, in such a world, no love. Or, in such a world, no one can love. Yet "no love" is not only a report on the empirical world, not only a report that there is no love. It is also, simultaneously, an epiphany: "no-love." It is an epiphanic love-of-no, a love that is nothing, a love that does not need to be something.

This, no-love: there is nothing like this. This does not transcend, metaphysically, the epidermalization of anti-blackness; on the contrary, this perseveres, this stays this, amidst such epidermalization, precisely as no. This demands itself, this points to this, without believing in any need. This is not the lack of being something, this is the autonomous demand of no, of nothing. Nothing is autonomous because it demands not to need to be like what believes it is something.

---

[16] All reports from Death Grips, "Come Up and Get Me," *No Love Deep Web* (Third Worlds, 2012).

"It's a suit! It's ME!": Hyper-Star and Hyper-Hero through Black Sabbath's "Iron Man"

Caoimhe Doyle & Katherine Foyle

> The (Names) ... common to the whole Deity ... are the Super-Good, the Super-God, the Superessential, the Super-Living, the Super-Wise, [the Superhero, the Superstar ...]
>
> — Pseudo-Dionysius[1]

> When the soul is plunged into the fire of divine love, like iron, it first loses its blackness and then growing to white heat, it becomes like unto the fire itself. And lastly, it grows liquid, and losing its nature is transmuted into an utterly different quality of being.
>
> — Richard of St. Victor[2]

"I am a god," declares Kanye West behind one of the formless masks worn on stage every night of the tour for his latest album, *Yeezus*. "The suit and I are one,"[3] declares Tony Stark in defence

---

[1] "The (Names) then, common to the whole Deity, as we have demonstrated from the Oracles, by many instances in the Theological Outlines, are the Super-Good, the Super-God, the Superessential, the Super-Living, the Super-Wise, and whatever else belongs to the superlative abstraction; with which also, all those denoting Cause, the Good, the Beautiful, the Being, the Life-producing, the Wise, and whatever Names are given to the Cause of all Good, from His goodly gifts" ([Pseudo-]Dionysius the Areopagite, *Works*, trans. Rev. John Parker, [London: James Parker and Co., 1897], *On Divine Names*, 2.3, Kindle edition).

[2] Richard of St. Victor, *De Quatuor Gradibus Violentiae Charitatis*, quoted in Evelyn Underhill, *Mysticism: A Study in the Nature and Development of Spiritual Consciousness* (New York: Dover, 2002), 421.

[3] *Iron Man 2*, directed by John Favreau (Hollywood, CA: Paramount Pictures, 2010), DVD.

of his use of the advanced weaponised armour that characterises his superhero persona, Marvel's Iron Man. In the same way Black Metal musicians create alter-egos though the use of corpse paint and pseudonyms, both men, through the wearing of "iron" masks, create personas under which they can achieve greatness that is beyond the human.

The author of the Dionysian corpus, writing in the late 5th and early 6th centuries, assumed the mask of Dionysius the Areopagite, an Athenian convert of St. Paul. Despite the falsehood of his premise, his writing was accepted into the theological canon. Just like the super-personas or alter-egos of Black Metal musicians, or Kanye West a.k.a. Yeezus and Tony Stark a.k.a. Iron Man, the becoming-true of faux-biblical figure Pseudo-Dionysius can be seen as hyperstitial. Hyperstition is a term coined by the Ccru (Cybernetic Culture Research Unit) to describe the process by which fictions can operate to make themselves real. In a 2001 communiqué to Maxence Grunier, they state: "According to the tenets of Hyperstition, there is no difference in principle between a universe, a religion, and a hoax. All involve an engineering of manifestation, or practical fiction, that is ultimately unworthy of belief. Nothing is true, because everything is under production. Because the future is a fiction it has a more intense reality than either the present or the past."[4] In hyperstition, narratives can travel backwards from the future, inspiring "retroactive delusions"—belief in which has the same effect as truth. In an address called "Who's Pulling Your Strings,"[5] subject Justine Morrison accuses Ccru of complicity with a global conspiracy known as Project Monarch, a Nazi/Satanist/Lemurian brainwashing project in which false memories were planted in subjects recruited for secret assassinations, revealed to her through a drawn-out "deprogramming" process which revealed Morrison's "true" memories. In their commentary on the transcript, the Ccru deny any such involvement, and deny the entire existence of such brainwashing. At the same time, however, they affirm the power of the false project-as-conspiracy: "Deprogramming [of the subject] simultaneously retro-produced the program, just as witch-trials preceded devil-worship and

---

[4] Ccru, *Ccru: Writings 1997–2003* (Time Spiral Press, 2015), Kindle edition.
[5] Ibid.

regressive hypnotherapy preceded false memory syndrome. Yet, once these 'fictions' are produced, they function in and as reality. It isn't that belief in Project Monarch produces the Monarch Syndrome, but rather that such belief procedures produce equivalent effects to those the reality of Project Monarch would produce, including those that are extremely peculiar and counter-intuitive."[6]

Using Dionysius's approach to mysticism as understood by Charles M. Stang, in this text we will firstly interrogate how the fictional, pseudonymous creations of Iron Man (Tony Stark) and Yeezus (Kanye West) operate as retroactive truths, through their connection with the Black Sabbath song "Iron Man."[7] Then we will ask whether the three works (Sabbath's "Iron Man," Marvel's Iron Man, and Kanye West's "Hell of a Life"), can represent a journey from creation of a pseudonym or alter-ego to mystical union with god.

Still from *Iron Man 3* (2013) [detail] and Black Sabbath t-shirt design as worn by Tony Stark in *The Avengers* (2012).

THE TRUTH IS . . . I AM IRON MAN[8]

In his reading of Dionysius, Charles M. Stang states, "[Dionysius's] entire mystical theology narrates the self's efforts

---

[6] Ibid.

[7] Black Sabbath, "Iron Man," *Paranoid* (Vertigo, 1970).

[8] *Iron Man*, directed by John Favreau (2008; Hollywood, CA: Paramount Pictures, 2008), DVD.

to unite with the 'God beyond being' as a perpetual process of affirming (kataphasis) and negating (apophasis) the divine names."[9] The divine names are a series of descriptors of "the unknown God"[10]—both positive (God is) and negative (God is not)—through which, according to Dionysius, we may "establish the truth of the things spoken concerning God."[11]

Negation is essential to the process; saying and unsaying are "inextricably bound."[12] Stang explains: "What Paul provides Dionysius is the insistence that this ascent to 'the unknown God' delivers a self that is, like the divine to which it aspires, cleared away of its own names, unsaid, rendered unknown to itself—in other words, no longer I."[13] Negation of the self becomes a way of freeing a new persona which communes with God. Paul wrote, "it is no longer I who live, but Christ who lives in me,"[14] or as Kanye West would put it, "I am a god, even though I'm a man of God."[15] However, it is not sufficient simply to clear away our preconceptions just once and expect to then achieve union with God. The invocation of the divine names is an ongoing process: "As soon as the negation is made, it is already a new affirmation threatening to keep God confined."[16] In order to allow union with God, contemplation must be kept in perpetual oscillation between affirmation and negation, just as sound-waves oscillate around a fixed plane. The mystic here must commit to a hyper-negation where "one affirms what is most like the divine, carries on affirming all the way to what is least like the divine, negates everything in opposite order, and then negates those negations in turn." [17]

These practices of hyper-negation are echoed in Transcendental Black Metal. For Hunter Hunt-Hendrix,

[9] Charles M. Stang, *Apophasis and Pseudonymity in Dionysius the Areopagite: "No Longer I"* (New York: Oxford University Press, 2012), 3.
[10] Ibid.
[11] Ibid., 119.
[12] Ibid., 117.
[13] Ibid., 3.
[14] Galatians 2:20.
[15] Kanye West, "I Am a God," *Yeezus* (Roc-A-Fella, 2013). Alternately: "Jesus walks with me" (Kanye West, "Jesus Walks," *The College Dropout* [Roc-A-Fella, 2004]).
[16] Stang, *Apophasis and Pseudonymity*, 129.
[17] Ibid., 131.

"Transcendental Black Metal is a Renihilation, a 'no' to the entire array of Negations."[18] Just as Dionysius holds that "affirmation and negation are perpetual practices,"[19] Transcendental Black Metal too is a perpetual motion machine, eternally striving for the Unknown [God]: "Transcendental Black Metal sacralizes the penultimate moment, the 'almost' or the 'not yet'" because "there is nothing after the penultimate moment."[20] The divine names are less important than the actual act of contemplating them—in fact Dionysius encourages not only the contemplation and negation of divine names but also "the contemplation of entirely dissimilar names."[21] For Stang, "the great benefit of these absurd names is that they hover between affirmation and negation, and force us, by their very absurdity, to acknowledge how utterly other the divine in fact is."[22] Following this, the creation of the pseudonym "Yeezus" by Kanye West—an extension of Yeezy, which is an extension of Ye, in turn short for Kanye—as a new name for his own self-professed godlikeness is not blasphemous, but rather a method by which he can devote himself to God. Likewise, in Black Sabbath's "Iron Man," vocalist Ozzy Osbourne makes the proclamation, "I am Iron Man," before posing a series of questions that apply direct opposites to the Iron Man of the song, in the spirit of the affirmation and negation of the divine names: "Is he live or dead? / Can he see or is he blind? / Can he walk at all / Or if he moves will he fall?"[23] Here Ozzy (or Sabbath) is carrying out the act of "unknowing oneself,"[24] having first presented a God-like being and then questioning the very nature of the subject, he is worshipping "through unknowing."[25]

Even what he is, he is not—Black Sabbath's Iron Man is in fact made of steel.[26] Similarly, Marvel's Iron Man is a suit made of

---

[18] Hunter Hunt-Hendrix, "Transcendental Black Metal: A Vision of Apocalyptic Humanism," in *Hideous Gnosis*, ed. Nicola Masciandaro (New York: n.p., 2010), 58–59.
[19] Stang, *Apophasis and Pseudonymity*, 135.
[20] Hunt-Hendrix, "Transcendental Black Metal," 63.
[21] Stang, *Apophasis and Pseudonymity*, 156.
[22] Ibid., 171.
[23] Black Sabbath, "Iron Man."
[24] Stang, *Apophasis and Pseudonymity*, 205.
[25] Ibid., 203.
[26] "He was turned to steel / in the great magnetic field" (Black Sabbath, "Iron Man").

a gold-titanium alloy.[27] However, the importance of the name extends beyond physical descriptors. The image of iron heated in a fire is, in medieval mysticism, used as a symbol for the soul reshaped when penetrated by the Deity: "As is the difference between iron that is cold and iron that is hot, so is the difference between . . . the tepid soul, and the soul made incandescent by divine love."[28]

In the first *Iron Man* film Tony Stark is an arrogant and self-involved millionaire whose primary goal is the creation of ever more advanced weaponry to sell to the US government. On a visit to Afghanistan to demonstrate his new Jericho Missile, he is kidnapped by a rebel group, who attempt to force him to replicate Stark weapons for their own use. Kept alive by an electromagnet in his chest that keeps shrapnel at bay, he builds a weaponised iron suit, powered by the same electromagnet, which he uses to escape. Back in the US, Stark abandons his weapons manufacturing business to focus on improving and developing this suit, which he uses to fight crime. Iron Man is a name given to him only at the end of the film by the press and his fans after a very public battle with the film's antagonist Obadiah Stane. In the last scene, where Tony is supposed to be denying any involvement in the fight, a reporter questions his story. Tony responds: "It's one thing to question the official story and another thing entirely to make wild accusations and insinuate that I'm a superhero." The reporter reminds him: "I never said you were a superhero." "You didn't? Well good, because that would be outlandish and . . . fantastic." Here Tony pauses, clearly struggling with his conscience before continuing: "The truth is . . . I am Iron Man."[29] The eventual acceptance of this name—given to him by others—becomes a way to affirm not what he is, but what he aspires to be. Here Tony is re-shaped by the name and by the iron suit. He leaves behind his "character defects"[30] creating his own definition of both himself and what the superhero can be. Tony commits to the "evocative imagery" conjured by the name "Iron Man" through a conscious wearing of the mask.[31]

[27] *Iron Man*, 2008.
[28] Richard of St. Victor, quoted in Underhill, *Mysticism*, 421.
[29] *Iron Man*, 2008.
[30] Ibid.
[31] Ibid.

Where Tony Stark, by accepting his given name "Iron Man" accepts his role as hero, Kanye West carries out a more overt rejection of the self, professing "Fuck my face . . . fuck whatever my face is supposed to mean."[32] Wearing an "iron" mask to hide his appearance during concerts, he describes it as "freeing" to be able to perform "without having to live up to whatever your name is supposed to represent, whatever it means, whatever it doesn't mean, just becoming a new artist again."[33] Through the creation and performance of his Yeezus alter-ego, Kanye abandons the trappings of his former identity, using the separation of the man from his face in order to create a new self.

Analogous to the masks of Kanye West and Tony Stark, corpse paint is important for the creation of Black Metal personas (alter-egos which Black Metal musicians choose to perform as), described by Black Metal Theorist Dominic Fox as "spiritual exercises . . . forms of emotional fasting intended to release the soul from its worldly attachments."[34] For Varg Vikernes of Burzum, corpse paint has the same function as the masks used by Norwegian sorcerers to connect to ancient gods and goddesses, hyperstitionally making real what is unreal. Wearers of these

---

[32] "That's why I got this fucking mask on, cuz I ain't worried about saving face. Fuck my face! Let's set 'em off. [Pause.] Now they finally got a headline. But fuck whatever my face is supposed to mean! Fuck whatever Kanye is supposed to mean! It's about my dreams. It's about everybody's dreams" (Kanye West, quoted in E. Alex Jung, "Read Kanye's Epic Wireless Festival Rant (With Auto-Tune) in Its Entirety" (http://www.vulture.com/2014/07/read-kanyes-entire-wireless-festival-rant.html).

[33] "Kanye West on Making 'Sonic Paintings'—*Late Night with Seth Meyers*," https://www.youtube.com/watch?v=HhSv9U5pc-U.

[34] Dominic Fox, *Cold World: The Aesthetics of Rejection and the Politics of Militant Dysphoria* (UK: Zero Books, 2009), 56. This resonates with Pierre Hadot's idea outlined in Stang: "The perpetual affirmation (kataphasis) and negation (apophasis) of the divine names—along with the negation of negation and the contemplation of entirely dissimilar names are 'spiritual exercises' that Dionysius recommends to the reader to transform him- or herself in pursuit of union with the unknown God. Thus the entire contemplative program of the *Corpus Dionysiacum* must be understood as a sort of asceticism, and as such entails a specific understanding of selfhood and a regimen for achieving—or rather, suffering—this transformation of the self" (*Apophasis and Pseudonymity*, 156).

masks were "not only able to see the spirit world . . . but became such spirits themselves, deities if you like."[35] As Fox explains, "such exercises are purely narcissistic and self-salving if they do not release the soul for new worldly commitments."[36]

Creating fictions, like these alter-egos, to re-write reality is the realm of hyperstition. On the *Hyperstition* website, "Anna Greenspan" describes the concept as follows: "hyperstition operates to: 'effect a positive destruction of identity.' Hyperstitional puppets allow 'you' to think things that 'you' don't agree with—to follow a line to places that 'you' wouldn't necessarily want to go."[37] Thus, the creation of alter-egos through corpse paint or the wearing of a "sorcerers mask" is a way to go beyond the human, to create an inhuman carrier, a purified ego "defined by what [it] conveys."[38]

Spiritual master and self-professed Avatar Meher Baba also speaks about the power of alter-egos, saying: "There are . . . two types of ego—one which can only add to the limitations of the soul, and the other which helps towards emancipation. The passage through the limiting ego of the worldly man to the egolessness of the infinite life lies through the construction of the provisional ego generated through wholehearted allegiance to the Master."[39] The Master he refers to here is a holy man, in this case Baba himself. As the Avatar, or manifestation of God on earth, Baba elects himself the beloved of the worshipper, inviting his followers to contemplate Baba over themselves: "The less you think of yourself and the more you think of Baba, the sooner the ego goes and Baba remains. When you—'ego'—go away entirely, I am one with you. So bit by bit, you have to go . . . So better think of me when you eat, sleep, see or hear. Enjoy all, don't discard anything, but think it is Baba—Baba who enjoys, Baba who is eating. It is Baba sleeping soundly and when you wake up, remember it is Baba

---

[35] "World of Darkness, Part III, 'Ghosts' hun," https://www.youtube.com/watch?v=o8Z_UsZofSo. This is a subtitled mirror of a video originally uploaded to Vikernes's personal YouTube account "ThuleanPerspective," which has since been deleted.
[36] Ibid.
[37] "Hyperstitional Carriers," http://hyperstition.abstractdynamics.org/archives/003707.html.
[38] Ibid.
[39] Meher Baba, *Discourses*, 3 vols. (Ahmednagar, India: Avatar Meher Baba Perpetual Public Charitable Trust, 2007), 2:179–80.

getting up! Keep this one thought constantly with you."[40] Baba (the man) courts the belief of others in his provisional ego (Baba the Avatar). This is much like fan "belief" in the self-proclaimed godhood of Kanye West, who similarly courts fan belief for the believer's benefit: "If you're a Kanye West fan you're not a fan of me, you're a fan of yourself."[41] The support or belief of fans differs from religious belief in the matter of sincerity—fan support might be more accurately described as "unbelief," a concept central to the process of hyperstition. In hyperstition, unbelief goes beyond suspension of disbelief (as experienced by the fiction reader) to an active participation in the rituals of a shared delusion, rituals which have the same effects as faith.

Still from *Iron Man* (2008) [detail].

[40] In Charles Haynes, "Remembrance" (http://www.avatarmeherbaba. org/erics/provego.html).
[41] "Kanye West. Zane Lowe. Full Interview" (https:// www.youtube.com/watch?v=DR_yTQoSYVA).

Still from Kanye West, "Power" (2010).

HAS HE LOST HIS MIND? CAN HE SEE OR IS HE BLIND?[42]

Hyperstition is a time machine. Once fiction and unbelief have colluded to create a future that matches the fiction, it ceases to be fiction in the present, retroactively turning its agents into prophets. Speaking about Dionysius's adoption of an alter-ego outside his own time, Stang describes a similar approach to pseudepigrapha in the late antique Christian East, which seems to propose a policy of hyperstitional truth: "pseudonymous writing served to collapse or 'telescope' the past and present, such that the present author and the past luminary could achieve a kind of contemporaneity."[43] Dionysius's writing invokes a "'timeless communion' between the past and the present [which] manifests such that the saints of old haunt the present as 'living dead.'"[44]

A constant theme in Black Metal is the attempt to achieve a time-outside-time, reaching for a past that never happened, or a future that is never coming; the belief that the 'answer' lies in a time that is not the present. These sentiments can be seen in early metal songs such as St. Vitus's "Born Too Late" ("I know I don't belong / And there's nothing I can do / I was born too late / And

[42] Black Sabbath, "Iron Man."
[43] Stang, *Apophasis and Pseudonymity*, 199.
[44] Ibid., 42.

I'll never be like you"),[45] Sabbath's "End of the Beginning" ("Reanimation of the sequence / Rewind the future to the past / To find the source of the solution / The system has to be recast"),[46] or in so-called third wave Black Metal bands like Wolves in the Throne Room, whose lyrics seem to be written by a viewer outside time: "Here, we come to pray / Thus I have heard, here the inner world rings / In memory of what will be / And on this night / The veil is lifted from the face of a bright inner Sun."[47] Or, "Darkness returns with cold's embrace / Staring onward / When time stands still / Devoid of tribulation / Time stands still / Staring onward / Time stands still."[48]

Hunt-Hendrix claims that Transcendental Black Metal defies Black Metal tropes by refusing to "lurk in the shadows . . . [hiding] behind costumes or esoterica."[49] However in *Black Metal: Beyond the Darkness*, Nick Richardson responds to this, stating that

> Black metal doesn't hide behind masks; it is masks. The shadows and secrecy are a considered strategy aimed at making the scene feel more special, not a shameful lurking. Wearing black and corpse paint, bullet belts and knives, is—in a sense—an opening up to the world, not a way of disguising oneself . . . We are sometimes more comfortable in cemeteries than shopping centres; we dream of riding with wolves, or with the Oskorei; of leading a charge into battle at the head of a Viking hoard, battle-axe in hand, cutting a swathe through Charlemagne's Francia. In blacker moments we dream of obliterating ourselves entirely. Black metal theatre gives partial material reality to some of the characters we imagine ourselves to be. The rites and rituals, the

---

45 St. Vitus, "Born Too Late," *Born Too Late* (SST Records, 1986).
46 Black Sabbath, "End of the Beginning," *13* (Republic, 2013).
47 Wolves in the Throne Room, "Woodland Cathedral," *Celestial Lineage* (Southern Lord Recordings, 2011).
48 Wolves in the Throne Room, "A Looming Resonance," *Malevolent Grain* (Southern Lord Recordings, 2009).
49 Nick Richardson, "Looking Black," in *Black Metal: Beyond the Darkness*, ed. Tom Howells (Black Dog Publishing, 2012), 163.

shadows, the make-up, are reflections of our personality, not self-erasure.[50]

Here Richardson sees Black Metal as somehow out-of-time or living the past in the present. Drew Daniel echoes similar sentiments in his essay "Corpsepaint as Necro-Minstrelry, or Towards the Re-Occultation of Black Blood," where he describes the love of Black Metal as sacrilege—not against the divine, but against time itself. Black Metal is "a revolt against living within the present as such, a flight not simply backwards but out of time. The black metal kvltist chooses to drown the present in a fog of black bile, offering what Badiou terms 'the occultation of the present which is itself the present.'"[51] Truth, for Black Metal, is outside of time, but inasmuch as it moves within linear time, it only moves backwards from the future, or as Daniel puts it, "when blood runs black, time runs back."[52]

One interpretation of Black Sabbath's "Iron Man" is that it tells the story of a time-traveller dedicated to the protection of

---

[50] Ibid.

[51] Drew Daniel, "Corpsepaint as Necro-Minstrelry, Towards the Re-Occultation of Black Blood," in *Melancology: Black Metal Theory and Ecology*, ed. Scott Wilson (Winchester and Washington: Zero Books, 2014), 28.

[52] Ibid, 44. This statement is made to answer in part two questions: "What forces are at work when blood runs black?" and "How does melancholy time operate within black metal?" Elsewhere in "Black Blood," Daniel discusses historical depictions of melancholy and the melancholic subject. Melancholy, in its original sense, results from an over-production of black bile. As such, the melancholic subject was characterised in Renaissance medicine by a literal dark cast to the skin, an image later inverted by the Romantics, who associated melancholy with a deathly pallor, "[which] achieves its zenith in the romantic cult of languid pallor and the crypto-sexualization of the symptoms of tuberculosis" (34). In *Iron Man 2*, the blood of Tony Stark literally "runs black" as he experiences advanced blood poisoning from the metal used in the ARC reactor that keeps him alive and powers the Iron Man suit. As Jarvis succinctly puts it in the film: "The thing keeping you alive is also killing you." Use of the suit enhances his condition and the symptomatic spread of black veins, shortening his lifespan. Yet Tony is reluctant to share his technology, even when he believes he will die, experiencing extreme attachment to Iron Man ("the suit and I are one") although only, at this point, as a possession.

humanity: "he has travelled time for the future of mankind."[53] He is turned into steel in the process of returning to the present with news of future destruction, and is ultimately driven mad by the people's refusal to listen to the truth. In his fury he destroys the world, creating the nightmare future he had glimpsed.[54] This is a rather extreme example of the self-fulfilling prophecy of hyperstition, but according to Dionysius, it is the curse of every true prophet to be seen as mad by those around him: "For, well does he know, who has been united to the Truth, that it is well with him although the multitude may admonish him as 'out of his mind.' For it probably escapes them, that he is 'out of his mind' from error to truth, through the veritable faith."[55] Dionysius's understanding of divine madness follows in the Greek philosophical tradition, most closely mirroring Plato, who describes four forms of divine madness: this prophetic madness; telestic or ritual madness such as the Dionysian bacchanal; poetic

---

[53] Black Sabbath, "Iron Man."

[54] The Furies (Erinyes) are Greek deities who punish those who sign false oaths and break oaths, including the "oath" of social/familial hierarchy, tormenting people for dishonourable crimes such as matricide. Discussing the desire to lose the burden of selfhood (specifically in the rituals of the Dionysian bacchanal), characters in Donna Tartt's *The Secret History* consider the methods of the Furies: "how did they drive people mad? They turned up the volume of the inner monologue, magnified qualities already present to great excess, made people so much themselves that they couldn't stand it" (Donna Tartt, *The Secret History* [New York: Ballantine Books, 2002], 37). One could easily argue that Marvel character Nick Fury fulfills the same function in the 2012 film *The Avengers*, goading each of his team of superheroes to embody their most prominent characteristics, often against their better judgement and certainly to the detriment of any immediate friendship or understanding. The antagonism between Captain America and Iron Man is perhaps the catalyst for Iron Man's "hero play" at the end of *The Avengers* in which he finally breaks from the "selfish" role of Tony Stark for the good of humanity. See *The Avengers*, directed by Joss Whedon (Marvel Studios, 2012).

[55] Pseudo-Dionysius, quoted in Stang, *Apophasis and Pseudonymity*, 172. This is echoed by Tony Stark: "We're mad scientists, monsters. You gotta own it," *The Avengers: Age of Ultron*, directed by Joss Whedon (Marvel Studios, 2015).

madness, in which divine wisdom is conferred on writers by the Muses; and erotic madness.[56]

Like his metal namesake, Tony Stark experiences a similar nightmarish vision during the film *The Avengers* (2012), in which he enters a wormhole to a world filled with malicious aliens bent on conquering Earth. Rather than making him resentful, this brief glimpse of a danger he alone can understand (and can therefore fear) leads to an anxiety disorder which manifests in the film *Iron Man 3*. Unwilling to allow Iron Man to appear weak, Stark at first tries to deny his condition, but the human behind the hero can't be calmed—pleas for help emerge in autographs to fans, nightmares turn empty suits into weapons that move on their own.[57] By this point in his character development, his two personas are essentially interchangeable, with parts of the Iron Man suit literally embedded under his skin. Black Metal musician Faust warns of the danger of indulging a performance persona: "When we . . . are using corpsepaint, we are usually in a state of mind that makes us feel like we are getting nearer darkness . . . Corpsepaint shouldn't be used everyday. It should only be used when you feel like some dark event would happen."[58] Likewise, by using the Iron Man suit—essentially combat gear—for his own gratification, Tony Stark runs the risk of becoming nothing more than a weapon. In the process of fighting the terrorist elements in the film—as both an inventor and his invention—the discrepancy between his two identities is resolved by crafting a third: simply, "The Mechanic." At the end of *Iron Man 3*, Tony Stark destroys the suits and technology that comprised his alter-ego in a symbolic act of rebirth and continues to claim: "I am Iron Man."[59]

Kanye West's similar and massively arrogant claim (even for rap music)—"I am a god"—is indicative of his characteristic confidence which has been viewed by the press as being wildly out of proportion to his actual fame. Of course, from a hyperstitional standpoint all of Kanye's hype is justified from a future perspective. It falls to us (as the listener/viewer/fan) to realise that the reality Kanye speaks from is one yet to come. It is up to us to listen when he tells us that he is a time-traveller. In an interview

[56] Stang, *Apophasis and Pseudonymity*, 173.
[57] *Iron Man 3*, directed by Shane Black (Paramount Pictures, 2013).
[58] Faust, quoted in Daniel, "Black Blood," 39–40.
[59] *Iron Man 3* (2013).

on *Late Night with Seth Meyers*, Kanye said, "I'm in the process of breaking down walls that people will understand ten years from now, twenty years from now."[60] Here Kanye sets himself up as a misunderstood prophet, awaiting his vindication.

Like Kanye, Hunter Hunt-Hendrix considers himself a teller of divine truths. Along with his band Liturgy, he is in the process of creating what he calls an "Ark Work," a term used to refer to the project of Liturgy as a whole. Song writing, performance and even responses to, and events surrounding, the band all fall under the Ark Work. In an interview with Edia Connole, he says of the work: "My aim is to pick up a torch, to continue the project of German Romanticism, using music and art to create a new religion, but to be totally embedded in the fabric of internet-mediated culture."[61] Liturgy's music found an audience within the Black Metal community despite its departure from the established style of Hyperborean Black Metal, but the accompanying "Transcendental Black Metal" manifesto has been perceived as pretentious and superfluous to the "real work" of the band.[62]

In his address elsewhere in this book, Hunt-Hendrix discusses Kierkegaard's distinction between the genius and the apostle as he feels it applies to Liturgy and himself. Broadly: the genius experiences a temporal paradox, because his wisdom is ahead of its time but will ultimately gain acceptance, while the apostle experiences an eternal paradox, because the divine wisdom he bestows is by definition eternally beyond human understanding. Hunt-Hendrix presents himself as the eternally paradoxical apostle: "Maybe I'll never be retroactively vindicated for the lecture, and if so perhaps it's a sign that I 'shouldn't have' delivered it, but perhaps on the contrary it means the truth in question is divine. Or maybe it exists in the realm where the sacred and the profane are one and the same." [63]

---

[60] "Kanye West on Making 'Sonic Paintings'—*Late Night with Seth Meyers*."
[61] "Edia Connole Interviews Hunter Hunt-Hendrix for Freaky Friday!!," http://queenmobs.com/2015/04/edia-connole-interviews-hunter-hunt-hendrix-for-freaky-friday/.
[62] Hunter Hunt-Hendrix, "Transcendental Black Metal: A Vision of Apocalyptic Humanism," in *Hideous Gnosis*.
[63] Hunt-Hendrix, "The Perichoresis of Music, Art and Philosophy," in this volume.

Kanye's predictions of the coming-to-divinity he experiences in Yeezus begin on his previous album *My Beautiful Dark Twisted Fantasy*.[64] In the song "Power," he states "No one man should have all that power, the clock is ticking, I just count the hours," and in "Monster," "I'm living in the future so the present is my past." In "Hell of a Life," Kanye foretells the next step of his career: his marriage to Kim Kardashian and the ensuing backlash from the press. The line "I think I just fell in love with a porn star,"[65] while thought at the time to refer to West's one-time girlfriend Amber Rose, could just as easily refer to the 2003 sex tape that propelled Kardashian to fame.[66] The chorus, whose tune is sampled from Black Sabbath's "Iron Man," repurposes only one line from its progenitor—"Have you lost your mind?"—foretelling the rejection of the prophet (Kanye), continuing "Tell me when you think we've crossed the line."

Still from Black Sabbath, "End of the Beginning" (2013) [detail].

---

[64] Kanye West, *My Beautiful Dark Twisted Fantasy* (Roc-A-Fella, 2010).
[65] Ibid.
[66] An interpretation shared by Daniel Colucciello Barber, whose enthusiasm for all things Kanye was a key inspiration for this paper.

Kanye West performing on his Yeezus tour.[67]

"NO MORE DRUGS FOR ME, PUSSY AND RELIGION IS ALL I NEED"[68]

In a letter to Titus the hierarch, Dionysus explicates the meaning of the divine name "inebriated" or "drunk," saying: "In our terminology, inebriation has the pejorative meaning of an immoderate fullness, being out of one's mind and wits. It has a better meaning when applied to God, and this inebriation must be understood as nothing other than the measureless superabundance of good things which are in him as Cause. As for being out of one's minds and wits, which follows drunkenness, in God's case it must be taken to mean that incomprehensible superabundance of God by virtue of which his capacity to understand transcends any understanding or any state of being

---

[67] Image source: https://www.flickr.com/photos/u2soul/10550722594 (CC BY-SA 2.0).
[68] West, "Hell of a Life."

understood."[69] This divine transcendence of reason is the driving force behind the ritual madness of Plato—bacchanalian rites and other hallucinogenic religious experiences in which the worshipper "gets out of his mind" in order to commune with the irrational. Thus, in his line, "No more drugs for me, pussy and religion is all I need," Kanye narrates his graduation from the telestic/ritual madness of performance—specifically the performance of status in rap and hip-hop through high profile drug-use—to the purer ecstasy that comes from eros.

In "On the Mystical Love of Black Metal," Nicola Masciandaro asserts that the love of Black Metal (by the metal head) is a (sac)religious practice, a form of mysticism: "the metal head is a subjectless subject of an objectless object, a self without itself (metal head) in love with a God who is not God (metal)."[70] Through Masciandaro we can read the love of Black Metal—and by extension the love of anything—as a method for becoming closer to God: "The love of black metal is a secret, inverted mysticism, a hidden love of hidden universal divine reality, the absolute continuum that holds the supreme, superessential essence of your so-called self. It is the love of something (black metal) that materially makes and perceptually does what mysticism spiritually is, namely: 'a most secret [secretissima] talking with God.'"[71] The love of God, through Black Metal, where "black metal is love" is an endless yearning where "divine love is defined . . . as desire that will not go away, a ceaselessness at once affiliated with cosmic order . . . and what aims beyond it, within the unlimitedness of desire for self-becoming."[72]

While Plato's explication of divine madness informs Dionysus's writings, the two differ in their understandings of erotic madness, which we might correlate with "pussy" and "religion," respectively. Plato follows Socrates's assertion that when a philosopher is seized by romantic love on earth, it is

[69] Pseudo-Dionysius the Areopagite, "The Letters," in *Pseudo-Dionysius: The Complete Works*, trans. Colm Luibheid (New Jersey: Paulist Press, 1987), 287.
[70] Nicola Masciandaro, "On the Mystical Love of Black Metal," paper delivered at *P.E.S.T. – Black Metal Theory Symposium*, Dublin, 2011.
[71] Ibid.
[72] Ibid.

because the "sensible beauty"[73] he loves reminds him of the beauty of the divine that his soul witnessed before he was born. As such, passionate love is to be respected because it recalls divine love, even if it is not returned; "[it] is, of all inspirations, the best and of the highest origin to him who has it or shares in it, and . . . he who loves . . . the beautiful, partaking in this madness . . . is called a lover."[74] For Dionysus, however, erotic madness is love of the divine itself. Dionysius correlates eros (which for Stang translates as "love," more specifically "yearning") with the divine name agape ("loving-kindness"). Therefore when it is said in John 4:16, "God is love," love can be read as either loving-kindness or as yearning. For Dionysus, erotic madness is a yearning for the divine, and equally God—as love—yearns for those who yearn for him. Paul is the perfect embodiment of this erotic madness, heralded by Dionysus as "the exemplary ecstatic lover of the divine," whose love of God ultimately splits him open. Meher Baba also describes the true lover of God as one in turn beloved by God: "At the stage of Para-bhakti [supreme devotion], devotion is not only single-minded but is accompanied by extreme restlessness of the heart and a ceaseless longing to unite with the Beloved. This is followed by lack of interest in one's own body ['Fuck my face!'] and its care, isolation from one's own surroundings, and utter disregard for appearance or criticism . . . This highest phase of love is most fruitful because it has as its object a person who is love incarnate and who can, as the Supreme Beloved, respond to the lover most completely."[75] By singing "pussy and religion is all I need," then, Kanye is affirming the power of both terrestrial and divine love.

CONCLUSION

Dionysius's stance on denial of the self is contested. To Christian Schäfer, because of Dionysius's insistence on a Divine hierarchy, or ordering of beings in relation to God,[76] self-denial

---

[73] Socrates in Stang, *Apophasis and Pseudonymity*, p 175.

[74] Ibid.

[75] Meher Baba, *Discourses*, 1.86.

[76] "In my opinion a hierarchy is a sacred order, a state of understanding and an activity approximating as closely as possible to the divine. And it is uplifted to the imitation of God in proportion to the enlightenments

potentially amounts to the rejection of one's place in the Hierarchy through "the excessively egocentric craving 'to be like God.'"[77] As such, the brash claims of Kanye West ("I am a god") could be seen to run contrary to Dionysius's teachings. Dionysius makes it clear, however, that "The goal of a hierarchy . . . is to enable beings to be as like as possible to God and to be at one with him . . . Hierarchy causes its members to be images of God in all respects."[78] "Similarity" is itself a divine name, for while God cannot be similar to his creations (because he is both one with them, and like no other), they may be similar to him, since "It is the power of the divine similarity which returns all created things toward their Cause, and these things must be reckoned to be similar to God by reason of the divine image and likeness."[79] Stang clarifies the stance taken on self-denial throughout Dionysius's writings, drawing a distinction between what he terms apotheosis, or denial of self—and by extension, one's place in the Hierarchy—and theopoesis, or self-apophasis, wherein one accepts one's place in the Hierarchy and consents to become a conductor of divine energy.[80] We might see Sabbath's Iron Man as embodying apotheosis, denying his role as protector by "kill[ing] the people he once saved,"[81] and Marvel's Iron Man as embodying theopoesis by embracing his given superhero persona. However, the play-acting at facelessness by Kanye West embodies neither of these, following instead what Stang describes as "a third path of unknowing God and self"—a model drawn from Dionysius's own pseudonymous writing—in which the apparently egocentric endeavour of dressing up as a prophet, a vessel, declaring yourself what you are objectively not, is in fact "an ecstatic devotional practice in the service of the apophasis of the self, and thereby soliciting deifying union with the unknown God."[82]

---

divinely given to it" (Pseudo-Dionysius the Areopagite, "The Celestial Hierarchy," in *Pseudo-Dionysius: The Complete Works*, 153).
[77] Schäfer, quoted in Stang, *Apophasis and Pseudonymity*, 193.
[78] Pseudo-Dionysius, "The Celestial Hierarchy," 154.
[79] Pseudo-Dionysius, "The Divine Names" in *Pseudo-Dionysius: The Complete Works*, 117.
[80] Stang, *Apophasis and Pseudonymity*, 193.
[81] Sabbath, "Iron Man."
[82] Stang, *Apophasis and Pseudonymity*, 204.

The adoption of a pseudonym or alter-ego—especially one which exceeds the subject in power or position in the Hierarchy—can effect the same splitting of the self that an abundance of eros or divine love can, rendering the fractured subject "open to divine possession."[83] Therefore, through the annihilation of the self by the creation of an alter-ego (hyperstitionally made real by the unbelief of fans), a communion with God can be achieved. Equally, the ritual love of and yearning for God achieved through a provisional ego fully committed to the divine can create the conditions though which the self can be erased. Each scenario is retroactively produced by the other, and since both are "perpetual practices,"[84] always "under production,"[85] neither one can ever be entirely attained; communion with God remains always out of reach, a moment just past and always to come, leaving the mystic eternally striving for the unknown.

---

[83] Ibid., 193.
[84] Stang, *Apophasis and Pseudonymity*, 135.
[85] Ccru, *Ccru: Writings 1997–2003*.

Iron Man [detail][86]

Kanye West performing in mask [detail].[87]

---

[87] Image source: https://www.flickr.com/photos/peterhutchins/ 10989913394 (CC BY 2.0).

Gaahl of Godseed performing in corpse paint.[88]

The Tongue-Tied Mystic: Aaaarrrgghhh! Fuck Them! Fuck You!

Gary J. Shipley

The only thing left to say is nothing left to say. And why talk when you can scream? We are in God's antithesis, in this negative expression of nothing.[1] For while the mystics tell us what they cannot tell us, communicating the ineffable, describing "delights impossible of description,"[2] in sensory metaphors, with God inside them like a sexless lothario, like joy in dung, Black Metal screams what cannot be told, and if we remain deaf, as opposed to receptively deafened, we position ourselves not to be loved but fucked. The mystic's intimate union with God becomes the raped or necrophilic union of Black Metal, and these concurrences for all their differences are the same. Black Metal's inversions, like all inversions, are in harness to that which is inverted. And yet the grave of God is not desecrated, but consecrated with piss and shit and blood, with mutilated bodies and hate-filled fucking, with sacrifice and Satan. Black for light,[3] variants of ungod for God, earth and hell for paradise, violence for peace, hate for love, the bleakest death for the eternal life, the abyss of bodies for the transcendence of souls, the empty for the full, the mournful for the celebratory, the fire and the burnt for the holiness of water, demonology and witchcraft for liturgy . . . But this inversion was there before there was anything to invert. Its longings are the same. Its inarticulation of consciousness experienced as both

---

[1] See E. M. Cioran, *Tears and Saints* (Chicago: The University of Chicago Press, 1995), 61.
[2] St. John of the Cross, *The Complete Works of St. John of the Cross*, ed. and trans. E. Allison Peers, 3 vols. (London: Burns, Oates and Washbourne, 1934-5), 3:49.
[3] Though mystics are themselves not unfamiliar with such inversions: "the cloud is dark / which lit up the night" (St. John of the Cross, *The Collected Works of St. John of the Cross*, trans. Kieran Kavanagh and Otilio Rodriguez [Washington, DC: ICS Publications, 1991], 54).

isolation and affiliation. And so we have the futility of Aaaarrrgghhh!, a futility in opposition to the futility of fucking the dead: the latter's meaningless fucking of what does not comprehend, as if you could rape the germ/seed of your message into the non-cognizant, is the defeated return to action that the former embodies, not as a reactive spreading of hazardous material, but as pure unencumbered spectacle.

We'll cause your death:[4] The second-person possessive determiner singles me out as someone who has listened and because of that listening will die. And while it does not discriminate beyond its ability to address, there is a core (and fearful) discrimination directed against those that are not "we," are not the cause of what is theirs: a death that they'll initiate but refuse to own—as if my end might yet contaminate.

{Fuck them! Fuck you!}:[5] The third-person plural and the second-person pronoun locate an enemy, an aggressor, a dissenting voice to be repeatedly entered and exited, comprehensively owned in one hawkish intrusion after another, a series of poisoned unions that leave both parties intact. This is the mystic union turned sour, pumping the emptiness of godlessness into unsuspecting detractors like some devout army of the antichrist.

We'll kill Jesus: "Let Christ crucified be enough for you, and with him suffer and take your rest, and hence annihilate yourself in all inward and outward things."[6] Or else let the apocalypse signal a new dawn of life: *imitatio christi*, in the hope that what is blackened with yet more simulacra might come to disappear. And the bravado of owning death is thereby enacted: to be the instrument of the death of Christ is to embody death's ultimate potency, to kill what cannot be killed, to become the device of

---

[4] All italicized paragraph lead-ins are from the following track in original order: Beherit, "Grave Desecration," *Demonomancy* (Independent, 1990).
[5] From "Mayhem Interview, Fuck Montage," https://www.youtube.com/watch?v=u8lMvV5U9XQ, featured in *Metal: A Headbanger's Journey*, dir. Jessica Joy Wise, Sam Dunn, and Scot McFadyen (2005; Burbank, CA: Seville Pictures/Warner Home Video: 2006), DVD.
[6] St. John of the Cross, *The Collected Works*, 92.

dispatch for all resurrections of meaning. This murderous intention represents all contrived manufacturing of purpose, a horror/sci-fi scenario whereby killing what will always return establishes logos for the otherwise stultified.

{Fuck them! Fuck you!}: The union that makes prey, that rejects and destroys as it couples. If the mystic is lost in God, the fucked is abandoned, infiltrated, removed in repeated inseminations of foreign matter.

Rape the dead: If only we could rape the dead, but the dead are not there for us to rape. I might as well bemoan my inability to rape soil—quite literally the earth without care.[7] This desire for the life of death: "It will be a thousand deaths, / longing for my true life / *and dying because I do not die*."[8] Outside of dying, the mystic is hardwired to fail at what it is his being mystic demands. Life is that which rapes the dead that is the mystic.

{Fuck them! Fuck you!}: To fuck is to make tangible what might otherwise have been thought of as intangible.

We'll spread evil: This activity of dissemination is the reactive propagation of something too heavy to be borne by the individual, smacking of the sickness and wounds of love which likewise cannot be suffered in isolation. In addition to this sense of "spread" there is also the thought that evil is being stretched, laid out for inspection or exhibition, its boundaries extended to incorporate a formerly undocumented reach. This is the Gnostic[9] creativity of Black Metal's awareness of its own impotence.

---

7 For "since 'Care' first shaped this creature, she shall possess it as long as it lives. And because there is now a dispute among you as to its name, let it be called 'homo,' for it is made out of *humus* (earth)" (Martin Heidegger, *Being and Time*, trans. John Macquarrie and Edward Robinson [Blackwell, 1997], 242–3).

8 St. John of the Cross, *The Collected Works*, 55.

9 Gnostic because "it is possible to see as a *leitmotiv* of Gnosticism the conception of matter as an active principle having its own eternal autonomous existence as darkness (which would not be simply the absence of light, but the monstrous *archontes* revealed by this absence), and as evil (which would not be the absence of good, but a creative action)" (Georges Bataille, *Visions of Excess: Selected Writings, 1927-*

{Fuck them! Fuck you!}: "No seduction, no representation: merely the integral coding of the body in the visible, where it becomes in fact definitively real, even more than it is really!"[10]

Grave desecration, grave desecration . . . : The observance of ritual enacted. Desecration assumes it has an object, that there are things in the world made sacred. It assumes that rest has been gifted to the dead, that the resting wound might somehow become aggravated. Deconsecration assumes the legitimacy of the consecrate—only a re-consecration can achieve what's needed here.

{Fuck them! Fuck you!}: The kerygma of the faithless.

Rape the whores / All night long: To take by force what is there to be bought (and bought cheaply), and to get your money's worth anyway: this is the desire that desires itself more than its object, the libido as budget and brassy as its quarry, there only to be used and used up. Not so much then the attempted atrophying of desiring through neglect, as the attritional grinding to dust of the worthless against the worthless: "Like the cave of the sky / The whole body of woman is a vacuum to be filled."[11]

{Fuck them! Fuck you!}: Despite repeated fuckings the fucked remain anonymous. No intimacy is fomented by these encounters-at-a-distance. These imagined unions, which result only in destroyed and destroyer, reveal nothing more than the innominate nature of every aggressor, regardless of outcome.

Grave desecration, grave desecration . . . : The observance of ritual reenacted. The religiosity of religion's antipode. The mystic is not a practitioner but a conduit of experiential union with God, one who operates outside the rituals of religion so that it may be embodied. Mystics desecrate their own graves, the graves of

---

1939, ed. and trans. Allan Stoekl [Minneapolis: University of Minnesota Press, 1985], 31).

[10] Jean Baudrillard, *The Intelligence of Evil or the Lucidity Pact* (Oxford: Berg, 2005), 69.

[11] Roger Gilbert-Lecomte, *Black Mirror* (New York: Station Hill Press, 1991), 15.

human form, the death of this world and of its life. The three enemies to be overcome, as listed by St. John of the Cross in his "Precautions," are all here: "the world, the devil and the flesh."[12] And of the three the flesh is the hardest to shake off. Not so much for the dead, as for those who invest them with consequence.

{Fuck them! Fuck you!}: "We must adjust our trials to ourselves, and not ourselves to our trials."[13]

I go to the graveyard all night long: The graveyard is never arrived at: there is only the perpetual going-to for those not yet gone. "Black is anterior to the absence of light, whether this absence be the shadows that extinguish it, whether it be it nothingness or its positive opposite. The black universe is not a negative light."[14] The "we" that fucked Jesus, raped the dead, and spread evil has been transposed by the "I" that gives himself all night, the Hegelian individual, the "'moral form of evil' [. . . poised] either in sin or in a state of temptation."[15]

{Fuck them! Fuck you!}: All fucking is a hymn to the heart that cannot own anything: "My prick is still hot and stiff and quivering from the last brutal drive it has given you when a faint hymn is heard rising in tender pitiful worship of you from the dim cloisters of my heart."[16]

Aaaarrrgghhh!: "Into the World of narrow-minded thoughts, man brings the emotion of the Universe."[17]

---

[12] St. John of the Cross, *The Collected Works*, 720.
[13] Ibid., 92.
[14] François Laruelle, "On The Black Universe In the Human Foundations of Color," in Eugene Thacker, Daniel Colucciello Barber, Nicola Masciandaro, and Alexander Galloway, *Dark Nights of the Universe* (Miami: NAME, 2013), 106.
[15] Søren Kierkegaard, *Fear and Trembling* (London and New York: Penguin Books, 1985), 83.
[16] James Joyce, *Selected Letters of James Joyce*, ed. Richard Ellman (London: Faber & Faber, 1975), 181.
[17] Laruelle, "On the Black Universe," 103.

This scream, this admission of illness, of "the spirit lost in the body."[18] The Aaaarrrgghhh! of Black Metal is mindless, or rather an experimented mindlessness, the knowing that is also the end of thought, the auditory asemia of the nothingness that finds noise but not speech, the untranslatable emptying out of the mystic. "But the seers, the lucid ones, fall into it—this is what we must understand. / What should language be, then, and first of all the sacred language (but we will see that, according to Scholem, there is no other)? What should the language be such that seeing it and falling into it would be the same event?"[19]

Though put to different ends the unearthing process evokes Whitman: "Come now I will not be tantalized, you conceive too much of / articulation, / Do you not know O speech how the buds beneath you are / folded? / Waiting in gloom, protected by frost, / The dirt receding before my prophetical screams"[20]

For "in order to scream I do not need strength, I only need weakness, and the desire will come out of weakness, but will live, and will recharge weakness with all the force of the demand for justice."[21]

{Fuck them! Fuck you!}: "This scream that I have just uttered *is* a dream / But a dream that eats away the dream."[22] And so the dream of the devout, those eaters-out, who in their longing long only to be fucked—sideways from their own reflection.

I go to the graveyard ritual / I go to the graveyard ritual: The mark of the ritual is repetition, and here the observance of ritual is itself repeated. And the going is not acknowledged as ritual until the repetition is manifested. And it is the going that loses us, and the hole and the dying that finds us again, not in life's

---

[18] Cioran, *Tears and Saints*, 113.

[19] Jacques Derrida, *Acts of Religion* (London and New York: Routledge, 2002), 198.

[20] Walt Whitman, *Leaves of Grass* (New York: Penguin Putnam, 2005), 57.

[21] Antonin Artaud, *Antonin Artaud: Selected Writings* (Berkeley: University of California Press, 1988), 273.

[22] Artaud, *Selected Writings*, 274.

continuation, but in the concept of the end: "In the infinity of the desert, a grave is an oasis, a place of comfort. To have a fixed point in space, one digs a hole in the desert. And one dies so that one won't get lost."[23] In Deleuzean terms,[24] this repetition of repetition is the crazed act of differentiating the sameness that eludes itself, the difference *from* the difference *of* the differently repeated, and so a sameness that has no rightful place anywhere.

{Fuck them! Fuck you!}: The secreted hope for peripeteia.

Grave desecration, grave desecration . . . / On . . . Sabbath!: What better day than the first day and the last day, the day of rest, to unrest the resting? What better day than the day of the Eucharist, as Christ is eaten and drunk, to blacken the earth through its removal? For "[b]lack is the without-Ground which fixes light in the remote where man observes it. Here lies the crazy and catatonic light of the World."[25]

{Fuck them! Fuck you!}: Fuck everything that remains unarticulated through being fucked! And fuck that it is found fucked and found by the fucked! Fuck the ruinous repetition of this fucking! Fuck this fucking that fucks itself just in order to never stop fucking! Fuck the Aaaarrrgghhh! failing to be nothing!

---

[23] Cioran, *Tears and Saints*, 110.
[24] See Gilles Deleuze, *Difference and Repetition* (New York: Columbia University Press, 1994).
[25] Laruelle, "On the Black Universe," 105.

Stills from "The Tongue-Tied Mystic: Aaaarrrgghhh! Fuck Them! Fuck You!" by Gary J. Shipley[26]

in sensory metaphors, with God inside them like a sexless lothario,

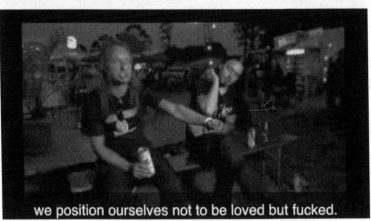

we position ourselves not to be loved but fucked.

and dying because I do not die."

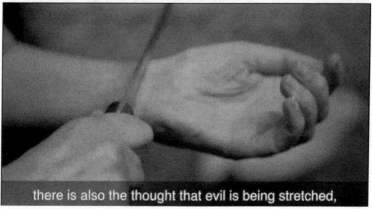

there is also the thought that evil is being stretched,

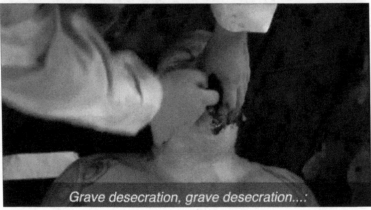

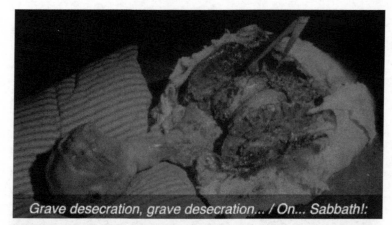

Grave desecration, grave desecration... / On... Sabbath!:

Mystics desecrate their own graves,

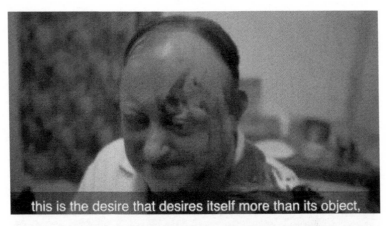

this is the desire that desires itself more than its object,

quite literally the earth without care.

These Flames Will Lick the Feet of God

Heather Masciandaro

Mystical Anarchism[1]

Simon Critchley

The return to religion has become perhaps the dominant cliché of contemporary theory. Of course, theory often offers nothing more than an exaggerated echo of what is happening in reality, a political reality dominated by the fact of religious war. Somehow we seem to have passed from a secular age, which we were ceaselessly told was post-metaphysical, to a new situation where political action seems to flow directly from metaphysical conflict. This situation can be triangulated around the often fatal entanglement of politics and religion, where the third vertex of the triangle is violence. Politics, religion and violence appear to define the present through which we are all too precipitously moving, the phenomenon of sacred political violence, where religiously justified violence is the means to a political end. The question of community, of human being together, has to be framed—for good or ill—in terms of this triangulation of politics, religion and violence. In this essay, I want to look at one way, admittedly a highly peculiar and contentious way, in which the question of community was posed historically and might still be posed. This is what I want to call "mystical anarchism." However, I want to begin somewhere else, to be precise with two political theories at the very antipodes of anarchism.

---

[1] A different and thoroughly annotated version of this text has been published in Simon Critchley, *The Faith of the Faithless: Experiments in Political Theology* (London and New York: Verso, 2012). Cf. Edia Connole, "Seven Propositions On the Secret Kissing of Black Metal: OSKVLVM," in this volume.–Ed.

CARL SCHMITT—THE POLITICAL, DICTATORSHIP AND THE BELIEF IN
ORIGINAL SIN
Let's return to that return to religion. Perhaps no thinker has
enjoyed more popularity in the last years and seemed more
germane than Carl Schmitt. The reasons for this are complex and
I have tried to address them elsewhere.[2] In his *Political Theology*,
he famously writes, "All significant concepts in the modern theory
of the state are secularized theological concepts." This is not just
true historically, Schmitt insists, but systematically and
conceptually. The omnipotent God of medieval Christianity
becomes the omnipotent monarch, for example in Hobbes's
Leviathan. Until the late 17th Century, the general will was a
theological term of art that referred to the will of God. By 1762, in
Rousseau's *Social Contract*, the general will had been
transformed into the will of the people and the question of
sovereignty was transposed from the divine to the civic. Of course,
this entails that the will of the people is always virtuous and those
who oppose it can be legitimately exterminated as evil. The
politicization of theological concepts leads ineluctably to the
attempt to purify virtue through violence, which is the political
sequence that begins with French Jacobinism in 1792 and
continues through to the dreadful violent excesses of 20th Century
politics that we can summarize with the proper names of Lenin,
Stalin and Hitler through to what some might call the "Islamo-
Leninism" or "Islamo-Jacobinism" of al Qaeda and related groups.
But such an argument does not exonerate so-called liberal
democracy. On the contrary, Schmitt views the triumph of the
liberal-constitutional state as the triumph of deism, a theological
vision that unifies reason and nature by identifying the latter with
divinity. As can be seen most obviously in the deism of the
Founding Fathers, American democracy is a peculiar confection of
Roman republicanism and puritanical providentialism, enshrined
in the John Winthrop's sermon about the "Citty [sic] on the Hill"
(that Sarah Palin ascribed to Ronald Reagan), the upbuilding of
the "New England." At the core of American democracy is a civil
religion which functions as a powerful sustaining myth and
buttresses the idea of manifest destiny. Obama's political genius
was to have reconnected classical liberal constitutionalism with a

---

[2] See Simon Critchley, *Infinitely Demanding: Ethics of Commitment,
Politics of Resistance* (London and New York: Verso, 2007) –Ed.

motivating civil religion focused around the idea of belief and a faith in change and progress.

Schmitt's problem with liberalism is that it is anti-political. What this means is that for the liberal every political decision must be rooted in a norm whose ultimate justification flows from the constitution. Within liberalism, political decisions are derived from constitutional norms and higher than the state stands the law and the interpretation of the law. This is why the highest political authority in a liberal state rests with the supreme court or its equivalent. Political action is subordinated to juridical interpretation. For Schmitt, a truly political decision is what breaks with any norm, frees itself from any normative ties and becomes absolute. This is why the question of the state of exception is of such importance to Schmitt. The state of exception is that moment of radical decision where the operation of the law is suspended. This is what the Romans call *iusticium*, and which Agamben has written about compellingly. What the decision on the state of exception reveals is the true subject of political sovereignty. Schmitt famously writes that, "Sovereign is who decides on the state of exception" (*Soverän ist, wer über den Ausnahmezustand entscheidet*). That is, the sovereign is the person who is exhibited by the decision on the state of exception. The question "who?" is answered by the decision itself. That is, the decision on the state of exception, the moment of the suspension of the operation of law, brings the subject "who?" into being. To put it into a slogan, *the subject is the consequence of a decision*. The subject that is revealed by the decision on the state of exception is the *state* and the core of Schmitt's theory of the political is to show that the true subject of political is the state and that the state must always stand higher than the law.

Schmitt makes the fascinating remark that the concept of the state of exception is the jurisprudential analogue to the concept of the miracle in theology. The triumph of liberalism as the triumph of deism is the hegemony of a religious view of the world that tries to banish the miracle, as that which would break with the legal-constitutional situation, the order of what Badiou calls "the event," and which at time he compares with a miracle. Liberal constitutionalists, like Locke, Kant or Neo-Kantians like Kelsen seek to eliminate the state of exception and subject everything to the rule of law, which is the rule of the rule itself, namely reason. Schmitt criticizes the rationalism of liberalism in the name of what he calls—and here we find echoes of Dilthey in Schmitt that will resound further in the young Heidegger—a philosophy of concrete life. Such an existential approach embraces the exception and breaks with the rule and the rule of the rule. Schmitt writes, thinking explicitly of Kierkegaard, "In the exception the power of real life breaks through the crust of a mechanism that has become torpid through repetition."

It is not difficult to see why Schmitt's existential politics of passion and concrete life and his critique of liberal democracy should have won him many friends on the left, like Chantal Mouffe. Sadly perhaps, they are not friends that Schmitt would have chosen. He was much happier in the company of Catholic counter-revolutionaries like Joseph de Maistre and Donoso Cortés. What has to be grasped is that Schmitt's argument for the state of exception as exemplifying the operation of the political is also an argument for dictatorship. If the subject of sovereignty is revealed in the decision on the state of exception, then this decision is the act where the constitution is suspended and dictatorship is introduced. Dictatorship, then, is justified when there is an actual or imagined danger to the existence of the state. Roman republicanism explicitly allowed for this possibility and one might ponder as to the conceivability of republicanism as a political form without the possibility of recourse to dictatorship. The condition of possibility for legality and legitimacy is the political act that suspends it.

Obama writes in *The Audacity of Hope,* "Democracy is not a house to be built, it is a conversation to be had." At the core of Obama's liberal civil religion is a resolute defense of the primacy of the constitution, an absolute conviction that all political decisions have to be derived from norms, and that the procedure for decision making is deliberation. It's enough to make Habermas burst into a break dance. However, Schmitt would be turning in his grave. For him, the idea of everlasting conversation is a gruesomely comic fantasy. If liberals were presented with the question, "Christ or Barabas?," they would move to adjourn the proceedings and establish a commission of investigation or a special committee of inquiry that would report back sometime the following year. Within liberalism, everything becomes everlasting discussion, the glorious conversation of humankind, the sphere of what Schmitt calls with a sneer "culture." Such a culture floats like foam over the socio-economic reality of the liberal state which

Schmitt, following his teacher Weber, compares to a huge industrial plant dominated by capitalism and scientism and incapable of political action. For Catholic counter-revolutionaries, like Donoso Cortés, faced with the hegemony of a depoliticized liberalism powerless in the face of a capitalist economy, the only solution was dictatorship. Faced with the toothless liberal constitutionalism of Weimar Germany in the 1920s and the fact of economic collapse, it is not difficult to understand the appeal the argument for dictatorship had for Schmitt with the rise of the National Socialists. The only way to restore the true subject of the political, namely the state, was the suspension of the constitution and the decision to declare a state of exception.

The political theology of liberalism is the pervasiveness of a weak deistic God. The liberal, like Obama, wants God, but one that is not active in the world. He wants a God that permits no enthusiasm and who never contradicts or overrides the rule of reason and law. That way, it is assumed, leads to the prophetic radicalism of Jeremiah Wright. In short, liberals want a God that cannot perform miracles. Against this, Schmitt wants to revivify the political by restoring the state of exception and the possibility of the miracle. But, as Schmitt makes crystal clear, this requires a belief in original sin.

For Schmitt, every conception of the political takes a position on human nature. It requires some sort of anthropological commitment: human beings are either naturally good or evil. Schmitt thinks—and I agree—that this leads to the two most pervasive political alternatives to liberalism: authoritarianism and anarchism. Anarchists believe in the essential goodness of the human being. Their progenitor is Rousseau and his belief that wickedness is the historical outcome of the development of society towards greater levels of inequality. By contrast, on this view, political legitimacy can be achieved by what Rousseau frequently referred to as "a change in nature," from wickedness to goodness, of the kind imagined in *The Social Contract*. Although this is a caricature of Rousseau and he could in no way be described as an anarchist, this view is more accurately developed by Bakunin: namely that if human beings are essentially good, then it is the mechanisms of the state, religion, law and the police that make them bad. Once these mechanisms have been removed and replaced with autonomous self-governing communes in a federative structure, then we will truly have heaven on earth. We will come back to this view below, but it is worth noting that arguments for anarchism always turn on the idea that if human beings are allowed to express what comes naturally to them, if the force of life itself is not repressed by the deathly force of the state, then it will be possible to organize society on the basis of mutual aid and cooperation.

By contrast, authoritarians believe that human nature is essentially wicked. This is why the concept of original sin is so important politically. For Donoso Cortés and de Maistre, human beings were naturally depraved and essentially vile. There is something essentially defective in human nature which requires a corrective at the political and theological level. It requires the authority of the state and the church. Thus, because the human being is defined by original sin, authoritarianism, in the form of dictatorship say, becomes necessary as the only means that might save human beings from themselves. Human beings require the hard rule of authority because they are essentially defective. Against this, anarchism is the political expression of freedom from original sin, that a sinless union with others in the form of community is the realization of the highest human possibility.

The idea of original sin is not some outdated relic from the religious past. It is the conceptual expression of a fundamental experience of ontological defectiveness or lack which explains the human propensity towards error, malice, wickedness, violence and extreme cruelty. Furthermore, this defect is not something we can put right, which is why authoritarians think that human beings require the yoke of the state, God, law and the police. Politics becomes the means for protecting human beings from themselves, that is, from their worst inclinations towards lust, cruelty and violence. As Hobbes shows, any return to a state of nature is an argument in favour of the war of all against all. We can find numerous post-Christian attempts to rethink the concept of original sin. For example, Freud advances the Schopenhauerian thesis that there might simply be a disjunction between eros and civilization, between the aggressive, destructive workings of libidinous desire and the achievements of culture. This disjunction is only held in check through the internalized authority of the super-ego. Again, Heidegger's ideas of thrownness, facticity and falling were explicitly elaborated in connection with Luther's conception or original sin and seek to explain the endless human propensity towards evasion and flight from taking responsibility for oneself. Although such a responsibility can be momentarily achieved in authentic resoluteness, it can never arrest the slide back into inauthenticity. The concept of original sin is still very much with us.

JOHN GRAY—THE NATURALIZATION OF ORIGINAL SIN, POLITICAL REALISM AND PASSIVE NIHILISM

The most consequent contemporary defense of the idea of original sin can be found in the work of John Gray. What he gives us is a naturalized, Darwinian redescription of original sin. To put it brutally, human beings are killer apes. We are simply animals, and rather nasty aggressive primates at that, what Gray calls *homo rapiens*, rapacious hominids. Sadly, we are also killer apes with metaphysical longing, which explains the ceaseless quest to find some meaning to life that might be underwritten by an experience of the holy or the numinous. Today's dominant metaphysical dogma—and this is Gray's real and rightful target—is liberal humanism, with its faith in progress, improvement and the perfectibility of humankind, beliefs which are held with the same unquestioning assurance that Christianity was held in Europe until the late 18th century. As Gray makes clear, progress in the realm of science is a fact. Furthermore, it is a good. De Quincey famously remarked that a quarter of human misery resulted from toothache. The discovery of anaesthetic dentistry is, thus, an unmixed good. However, although progress is a fact, *faith* in progress is a superstition and the liberal humanist's assurance in the reality of human progress is the barely secularized version of the Christian belief in Providence.

The most extreme expression of human arrogance, for Gray, is the idea that human beings can save the planet from environmental destruction. Because they are killer apes, that is, by virtue of a naturalized version of original sin that tends them towards wickedness and violence, human beings cannot save their planet. Furthermore, the earth doesn't need saving. This is where Gray borrows from James Lovelock's "Gaia hypothesis." The earth is suffering from a *disseminated primatemaia*, a plague of people. *Homo rapiens* is ravaging the planet like a filthy pest that has infested a dilapidated but once beautiful mansion. In 1600 the human population was about half a billion. In the 1990s it increased by the same amount. This plague cannot be solved by the very species who are the efficient cause of the problem, but only by a large scale decline in human numbers, back down to manageable levels, say half a billion or so. This is the wonderfully dystopian vision at the heart of Gray's work: when the earth is done with humans, it will recover and human civilization will be forgotten. Life will go on, but without us. Global warming is simply one of many fevers that the earth has suffered during its history. It will recover, but we won't because we can't.

Gray writes, with Schmitt explicitly in mind, "Modern politics is a chapter in the history of religion." Politics has become a hideous surrogate for religious salvation. Secularism, which denies the truth of religion, is a religious myth. Specifically, it is a myth of progress based in the idea that history has a providential design that is unfolding. Now, such myths are important. They enable presidents like Barack Obama to get elected. But it doesn't mean that they are true or even salutary. What most disturbs Gray are utopian political projects based on some apocalyptic faith that concerted human action in the world can allow for the realization of seemingly impossible ends and bring about the perfection of humanity. Action cannot change the world because we are the sort of beings that we are: killer apes who will use violence, force and terror at the service of some longed-for metaphysical project. For Gray, the core belief that drives utopianism, on the right as much as the left, is the false assumption that the world can be transformed by human action and that history itself is progress towards such a transformation. As Gray makes explicit, his critique of utopianism derives in large part from Norman Cohn's hugely influential book, originally published in 1957, *The Pursuit of the Millenium.*

It is Cohn's analysis of millenarianism that is so important for Gray. This is the idea that salvation is not just a possibility, but a certainty which will correspond to five criteria: salvation is collective, terrestrial, imminent, total and miraculous. In his later work, *Cosmos, Chaos and the World to Come,* Cohn traced the roots of this millenarian faith back to Zoroaster's break with the view that the world was the reflection of a static cosmic order defined by cycle of conflict. On the Zoroastrian view, sometime between 1500 and 1200 BC, the world was moving, through incessant conflict, towards a conflictless state. A time would come when, during a final bloody battle, God and the forces of good would defeat once and for all the armies of evil. Thus, a marvelous consummation is at hand, the moment when good will triumph over evil and the agents of evil will be annihilated. After that time, Cohn writes, "The elect will thereafter live as a collectivity, unanimous and without conflict, on a transformed and purified earth."

This idea finds expression in certain Jewish sects before finding its most powerful articulation in Christian ideas of the Apocalypse, the Last Days and the Millennium. On the basis of the authority of the *Book of Revelation*, it was believed that after Christ's "Second Coming," he would establish a kingdom of God on earth and reign over it with his elect, the company of saints, for a thousand years until the Last Judgement and the general resurrection of the dead. Early Christians, like St. Paul, believed that the Second Coming was imminent and that they were living in the "end times." The search for signs of the Second Coming obviously took on enormous importance. The key clue to the beginning of the end times—and this is crucial—is the appearance of the Antichrist: the prodigious, evil, arch-enemy of God. The Antichrist is what Ernesto Laclau would call a "floating signifier" in millenarian political theology. He is endlessly substitutable, can be personified as the great Satan, the Pope, the Muslims or the Jews. What is crucial here is the identification of the Antichist as the incarnation of evil that presages the reappearance of Christ or a similarly messianic figure and leads to a bloody and violent terrestrial combat to build heaven on earth. This, of course, is the deep logic of the Crusades, which began with Pope Urban II's plea to the Church council of 1095 to go to Jerusalem and, in his words, "liberate the Church of God." This lead directly to the "People's Crusade" or the "Peasants' Crusade" in 1096-97, and to the formation of a Christian fighting force in Asia Minor that was between 50,000 to 70,000 strong. It is a compelling and disturbing historical fact that the recruitment of soldiers for the People's Crusade in France, Germany and the Low Countries established a disturbing new and seemingly addictive habit in Western life: pogroms against the Jews. It would appear that the idea of the people requires the external identification of an evil enemy who can be legitimately annihilated in the name of God. Such has arguably always been the justificatory logic of Western military intervention: it is right to exterminate the enemy because they are the incarnation of evil. Such views have always vindicated crusaders from the 11th Century through to their more recent epigones. From the time of Saladin's destruction of the "Third

Crusade" in the last 12th Century, the response has always been the same: *jihad* or war against infidels. It is perhaps not so surprising that Saddam Hussein sought to depict himself in propaganda alongside Saladin. After all, they were both born in Tikrit, despite the awful irony that Saladin was a Kurd.

What is implied fairly discreetly by Cohn and rather loudly trumpeted by Gray, is that Western civilization might be defined in terms of the central role of millenarian thinking. What takes root with early Christian belief and massively accelerates in medieval Europe finds its modern expression in a sequence of bloody utopian political projects, from Jacobinism to Bolshevism, Stalinism, Nazism and different varieties of Marxist-Leninist, anarchist or Situationist ideology. Much of John Gray's *Black Mass* attempts to show how the energy of such utopian political projects has drifted from the left to the right. The apocalyptic conflict with the axis of evil by the forces of good has been employed by Bush, Blair *et al* as a means to forge the democratic millennium, a new American century of untrammeled personal freedom and free markets. In the past decade, millennial faith has energized the project of what we might call military neo-liberalism, where violence is the means for realizing liberal democratic heaven on Earth. What is essential to such neo-liberal millenarian thinking is the consolidation of the idea of the good through the identification of evil, where the Anti-Christ keeps putting on different masks: Saddam Hussein, Osama bin Laden, Kim Jong-il, Mahmoud Ahmadinejad, etc., etc.

We saw how Schmitt's critique of liberalism led him towards an argument for dictatorship underpinned by a belief in original sin. Where does Gray's naturalization of the concept of original sin leave us? He powerfully identifies the poison within liberal humanism, but what is the antidote? This is what he calls "political realism." We have to accept that the world is in a state of ceaseless conflict never far from a state of war. In the face of such conflict, Gray counsels that we have to abandon the belief in utopia and try and cope with reality. This means accepting the tragic contingencies of life and the fact that there are simply moral and political dilemmas for which there is no solution. We have to learn to abandon daydreams such as a world of universal human rights, or that history has a teleological purpose that underwrites human action. We even have to renounce the Obama-esque delusion that one's life is a narrative that is an episode in some universal story of progress. Against the grotesque distortion of conservatism into the millenarian military neo-liberalism of the neo-conservatives, Gray wants to defend the core belief of traditional Burkean Toryism. The latter begins in a realistic acceptance of human imperfection and frailty, a version of original sin. As such, the best that flawed and potentially wicked human creatures can hope for is a commitment to civilized constraints that will prevent the very worst from happening. Political realism is the politics of the least worst.

The most original feature of Gray's work is the way in which a traditional conservatism underpinned by a deep pessimism about human nature is fused with a certain strand of Taoism. As Gray points out, "Nothing is more human than the readiness to kill and die in order to secure a meaning for life." The great human delusion is that action can achieve a terrestrial salvation. This has lead to nothing but bloodshed, the great slaughter bench of millenarian history. Killer apes like us have to learn to give up the search for meaning and learn to see the purpose of aesthetic or spiritual life as the release from meaning. If seeing one's life as an episode in some universal narrative of meaning is a delusion, then the cure consists in freeing oneself from such narratives. Maybe we just have to accept illusions. What interests Gray in the subtle paradoxes of the greatest Taoist thinker, Chuang-Tzu, is the acceptance of the fact that life is a dream without the possibility or even the desire to awaken from the dream. If we cannot be free of illusions, if illusions are part and parcel of our natural constitution, then why not simply accept them? In the final pages of *Black Mass*, Gray writes, "Taoists taught that freedom lies in freeing oneself from personal narratives by identifying with cosmic processes of death and renewal." Thus, rather than seek the company of utopian thinkers, we should find consolation in the words of "mystics, poets and pleasure-lovers." It is clear that for Gray, like the late Heidegger, the real source of human problems resides in the belief that action can transform the world. Action simply provides a consolation for the radical insignificance of our lives by momentarily staving off the threat of meaninglessness. At the core of Gray's work is a defense of the ideal of contemplation over action, the *ataraxia* of the ancients, where we simply learn to see the mystery as such and do not seek to unveil it in order to find some deeper purpose within.

Schopenhauer, often read in an abridged aphoristic form, was the most popular philosopher of the 19th Century. Nothing sells better than epigrammatic pessimism. It gives readers reasons for their misery and words to buttress their sense of hopelessness and impotence. Such is what Nietzsche called "European Buddhism." John Gray is the Schopenhauerian European Buddhist of our age. What he offers is a gloriously pessimistic cultural analysis which rightly reduces to rubble the false idols of the cave of liberal humanism. Counter to the upbeat evangelical atheism of Dawkins, Hitchins, *et al*, Gray provides a powerful argument in favour of human wickedness that is consistent with Darwinian naturalism. It leads to the position that I call "passive nihilism."

The passive nihilist looks at the world from a certain highly cultivated detachment and finds it meaningless. Rather than trying to act in the world, which is pointless, the passive nihilist withdraws to a safe contemplative distance and cultivates and refines his aesthetic sensibility by pursuing the pleasures of lyric poetry, bird-watching or botany, as was the case with the aged Rousseau. In a world that is rushing to destroy itself through capitalist exploitation or military crusades (usually two arms of the same killer ape), the passive nihilist withdraws to an island where the mystery of existence can be seen for what it is without distilling it into a meaning. In the face of the coming century which in all likelihood will be defined by the violence of faith and the certainty of environmental devastation, Gray offers a cool but safe temporary refuge. Happily, we will not be alive to witness much of the future that he describes.

I have looked at two interrelated responses to the thought that the modern concepts of politics are secularized theological concepts. Schmitt's critique of constitutional liberalism as anti-political leads him to a concept of the political that finds its expression in state sovereignty, authoritarianism and dictatorship. Gray's critique of liberal humanism and the ideas of progress and Providence that it embodies leads him to a political realism of a traditional Tory variety. He fuses this, in an extremely compelling way, with what I have called passive nihilism. Both conceptions of the political are underpinned by ideas of original sin, whether the traditional Catholic teaching or Gray's Darwinian naturalization of the concept. The refutation of any and all forms of utopianism follows from this concept of original sin. It is because we are killer apes that our metaphysical longing for a conflict-free perfection of humanity can only be pursued with the millennial means of violence and terror.

MILLENARIANISM

Is the utopian impulse in political thinking simply the residue of a dangerous political theology that we are much better off without? Are the only live options in political thinking either Schmitt's authoritarianism, Gray's political realism or business as usual liberalism; that is, a politics of state sovereignty, an incremental, traditionalist conservatism or varieties of more or less enthused Obamaism? In order to approach these questions I would like to present the form of politics that Schmitt and Gray explicitly reject, namely anarchism. Now, I have sought to outline and defend a version of anarchism in some of my recent work. This is what I call an ethical neo-anarchism where anarchist practices of political organization are coupled with an infinitely demanding subjective ethics of responsibility. However, for reasons that will hopefully become clear, I want to present a very different version of anarchism, perhaps the most radical that can be conceived, namely "mystical anarchism." The key issue here is what happens to our thinking of politics and community once the fact of original sin has been overcome.

Let's return to Cohn's *The Pursuit of the Millennium*. What Cohn tries to show is the way in which millenarian Christian belief took root amongst significant sectors of the rootless and dislocated poor of Europe between the 11th and 16th Centuries. The belief that these were the Last Days led to a revolutionary eschatology, where a series of messiah figures, prophets or indeed "Christs" would spontaneously appear. Cohn gives an extraordinary catalogue of these messiahs, from Tancheln, the Emperor Frederick, the Pseudo-Baldwin, through to John Ball, Hans Böhm, Thomas Müntzer and terrifying and bloodthirsty Jan Bockelsen, better known as John of Leyden. What unites these figures is not just their heretical fury and utter self-belief. It is rather their capacity to construct what Cohn calls, non-pejoratively but put psychoanalytically, a *phantasy* or social myth around which a collective can be formed. The political structure of this phantasy becomes complete with the identification of an enemy. It is always in relation to an enemy that the eschatological phantasy finds its traction. This enemy is always the Antichrist, whose identity floats in different historical manifestations of millenarianism. It can be the Moslems or indeed Jews for the Crusaders, but it is more often simply the forces of the Catholic church and the state. A holy war is then fought with the Antichrist, where violence becomes the purifying or cleansing force through which the evil ones are to be annihilated. Terror is a common feature of life in the New Jerusalem.

Revolutionary millenarianism desires a boundless social transformation that attempts to recover an egalitarian state of nature, a kind of golden age of primitive communism. This required the abolition of private property and the establishment of a commonality of ownership. Justification for such views would invariably be Biblical, usually the Garden of Eden. As a famous proverb from the time of the English Peasants' Revolt puts it, possibly recited by the hedge priest John Ball,

> When Adam delved and Eve span,
> Who was then a gentleman?

The task of politics was the construction of the New Jerusalem and the model was always paradise, the Garden of Eden before the occurrence of original sin. There was a perfectly obviously reason why such forms of revolutionary millenarian belief should arise amongst the poor: they owned nothing and therefore had nothing to lose. Thus, by destroying private property, they had everything to gain. The only extant fragment from John Ball, preserved and probably embellished by chroniclers, makes the point powerfully,

> Things cannot go well in England, nor ever will, until all goods are held in common, and until there will be neither serfs nor gentlemen, and we shall be equal. For what reason have they, whom we call lords, got the best of us? How did they deserve it? Why do they keep us in bondage? If we all descended from one father and one mother, Adam and Eve, how can they assert or prove that they are more masters than ourselves? Except perhaps that they make us work and produce for them to spend!

Yet, the poor, as the saying goes, have always been with us. What seems to be novel in the earlier part of large historical panorama that Cohn describes is the emergence of the urban poor in the rapidly industrializing textile-producing towns of Flanders and Brabant from the 11th Century onwards. Thus, it is not simply that millenarian belief arises amongst the poor, but specifically amongst those groups whose traditional ways of life have broken down. Millenarian belief arises amongst the socially *dislocated*, recently urbanized, poor who had moved from the country to the city for economic reasons. Although Cohn says nothing on this topic, it is interesting to note that the socio-economic condition of possibility for revolutionary eschatology is dislocation, the same category that Marx employs to describe the formation of the industrial proletariat during the Industrial Revolution.

(Perhaps a similar hypothesis could be used to explain the formation of millenarian sects in the United States from the time of settlement onwards. I am thinking in particular of the explosion of millenarian faith in areas like the "burned-over district" of the upper New York state during the late 18th Century and the first decades of the 19th Century in groups like the Shakers. It is not exactly difficult to find the living descendents of such millenarian religious belief all across the contemporary United States. There seems to be a powerful correlation between evangelism, social dislocation and poverty. Yet, what is sorely missing from contemporary American millenarianism is the radical anarcho-communism of groups like the Shakers. For the latter, all property was held in common, without mine and thine. An ethos manual labour was combined with spiritual purification achieved through taking the vow of chastity. With hands at work and hearts set to God, the Shakers attempted to recover the communistic equality of Eden without the sins of the flesh. This was further radicalized through the revelations of the founder of the Shakers, Ann Lee or Mother Ann [1736-84], from Manchester who brought a select band of persecuted Shakers [more properly, The Church of Believers in Christ] from England to New York 1774 before setting up communities in upper state New York and Western Massachusetts. Various divine visitations led her to declare celibacy and the imminent second coming of Christ. She was seen by some as the female equivalent of God, the female complement to the divine male principle. For the Shakers, to be a believer in Christ was to participate in the dual nature of divinity, both male and female.)

Medieval revolutionary millenarianism drew its strength and found its energy amongst the marginal and the dispossessed. It often arose against a background of disaster, plague and famine. As Cohn notes,

> The greatest wave of millenarian excitement, one that swept through the whole of society, was precipitated by the most universal natural disaster of the Middle Ages, the Black Death.

It was amongst the lowest social strata that millenarian enthusiasm lasted longest and expressed itself most violently. For example, the flagellant movement first appeared in Perugia in 1260 as an apparent consequence of the famine of 1250 and the plague of 1259. It swept from Italy into the Rhine Valley in the 14th Century, where great crowds of itinerant flagellants went from town to town like a scourging insurgency becoming God-like through acts of collective *imitatio Christi*. Such extreme self-punishment was deemed heretical because it threatened the Church's authority over the economy of punishment, penitence and consolation. The poor were not meant to take the whip into their own hands. But the centerpiece of Cohn's book is the description and analysis of the dominant form of revolutionary millenarianism: the so-called "heresy of the free spirit." It is to this that I would now like to turn.

THE MOVEMENT OF THE FREE SPIRIT

We know very little about the Movement of the Free Spirit. Everything turns on the interpretation of Paul's words, "Now the Lord is the Spirit, and where the Lord's Spirit is, there is freedom" (2 Corinthians 3:17). There are two possibilities here: either the Lord's Spirit is outside the self or within it. If the Lord's Spirit is outside the self, because the soul languishes in sin and perdition, then freedom can only come through submitting oneself to divine will and awaiting the saving activity of grace. Such is the standard Christian teaching, which explains the necessity for the authority of the Church as that terrestrial location or, better, portal to the Lord's Spirit. But if—and here is the key to the heresy—the Lord's Spirit in within the self, then the soul is free and has no need of the mediation of the Church. Indeed, and we will come back to this presently, if the Lord's Spirit is within the self, then essentially there is no difference between the soul and God. The heretical Adamites who moved to Bohemia after being expelled from

Picardy in the early 15th Century, are reported as beginning the Lord's Prayer with the words, "Our Father, who art within us." If a community participates in the Spirit of God, then it is free and has no need of the agencies of the Church, state, law or police. These are the institutions of the un-free world that a community based on the Free Spirit rejects. It is not difficult to grasp the anarchistic consequences of such a belief.

The apparently abundant and widespread doctrinal literature of the movement of the Free Spirit was repeatedly seized and destroyed by the Inquisition. Very few texts remain, such as the fascinating *Schwester Katrei*, apocryphally attributed to Meister Eckhart. At least one of the extant manuscripts bears the inscription, *That is Sister Katrei, Meister Eckhart's Daughter from Strasbourg*. Although this is a huge topic that I do not want to broach here, the relation between Eckhart's thinking, deemed heretical posthumously by the Pope at Avignon in 1327, and the Movement of the Free Spirit is hugely suggestive. Of the documents related to the Free Spirit that remain, I'd like to focus on Marguerite Porete's extraordinary *The Mirror of Simple and Annihilated Souls and Who Remain Only in Wanting and Desire of Love*, to give the text its full and indeed ambiguous title. The text was only discovered in 1946. It seems clear that Eckhart knew Porete's *The Mirror* and responded to it explicitly or implicitly in his texts and sermons. For example, Michael Sells claims that when Eckhart returned to Paris in 1311, one year after Porete's execution, he stayed at the same Dominican house as William Humbert, Porete's inquisitor. One can only wonder at the content of their conversations. *The Mirror* is an instruction manual of sorts that details the seven stages that the soul must pass through in order to overcome original sin and recover the perfection that belonged to human beings prior to their corruption by the Fall. *The Mirror* seems to have circulated in multiple manuscripts and translations in the Middle Ages and Porete appears to have had many followers as far away from her native Hainaut in northern France as England and Italy. We know relatively little with certainty about Porete, although there is a surprising amount of documentation related to her trial and execution for heresy. She was a learned Beguine, which was the term that was used to describe semireligious women who lived alone or in Beguine houses or *Beguinages*. These began to appear in the southern Low Countries in the late 12th and early 13th Centuries and were effectively communes or experimental associations for the sisters of the Free Spirit and their brothers, the Beghards, from which we derive the English word "beggar." Marguerite seems to have led an itinerant mendicant life of poverty accompanied by a guardian Beghard. Her book was condemned, seized and publicly burned at Valenciennes, but she refused to retract it. When Porete came to the attention of the Inquisition in Paris, she was imprisoned for eighteen months, but refused to recant or seek absolution. She was burnt at the stake in 1310. The fact that she was treated with relative liberality and not immediately executed seems to suggest that she was from the upper strata of society and she had some powerful friends. Although it is not my topic here, it is truly fascinating how many women were involved with the Movement of the Free Spirit and their relatively high social status. Scholars of mysticism like Amy Hollywood and poets like Anne Carson have rightly identified Porete and the Beguine movement as a vital precursor to modern feminism. It is highly revealing that, in the proceeding of her trial, Porete's work is not just referred to as being "filled with errors and heresies," but as a "*pseudo-mulier*," a fake woman.

BECOMING GOD

I'd like to identify the core of the Movement of the Free Spirit by recounting the seven stages of what Porete calls "the devout soul" outlined in Chapter 118 of *The Mirror* (the book contains 139 Chapters). What is described is nothing other than the process of self-deification, of becoming God.

1. The first state occurs when the Soul is touched by God's grace and assumes the intention of following all God's commandments, of being obedient to divine law.

2. The second state mounts yet higher and Soul becomes a lover of God over and above commandments and laws. Regardless of any command, the Soul wants to do all it can to please its beloved. In this second state, and one thinks of St. Paul's argument in *Romans* here, the external becomes internal and law is overcome by love.

3. In the third state, consumed by love for divine perfection, the Soul attaches itself to making "works of

goodness." These can be images, representations, projects and objects that give us delight in glorifying God. But Porete insists, and this is a theme that Eckhart will take up in his extraordinary German sermons, the Soul "renounces those works in which she has this delight, and puts to death the will which had its life from this." The Soul no longer wills, but undergoes a detachment from the will by obeying the will of another, namely God. The Soul must become a "martyr," that is, a witness and victim to God by abstaining from works and destroying the will. Porete's language here is extremely violent, writing that, "One must crush oneself, hacking and hewing away at oneself to widen the place in which Love will want to be." This is the beginning of the painful process of the annihilation of the Soul, where suffering is necessary in order to bore open a space that is wide enough for love to enter. Anne Carson rightly compares this process of annihilation with Simone Weil's idea of *decreation*, "To undo the creature in us."

4. In the fourth state, when I have renounced my will and hewn away at myself, when I have begun to decreate and annihilate myself, I am filled with God's love and exalted "into delight." Porete's wording here is extraordinary, the Soul, "does not believe that God has any greater gift to bestow on any soul here below than this love which Love for love has poured forth within her." In the fourth state, the Soul is in love with love as such and becomes intoxicated, "Gracious Love makes her wholly *drunken*" (emphasis mine).

Excursus: In his wonderfully capacious and open-minded investigation of mysticism in *The Varieties of Religious Experience*, William James discusses the relation between mystical states and drunkenness. This is what he calls the idea of "anaesthetic revelation," which he links to his own experiences with nitrous oxide or laughing gas, which had been a drug of choice amongst scientists, poets and intellectuals throughout the 19th Century. Nitrous oxide, James recounts from personal experience, induces a feeling of reconciliation or oneness at a level deeper than that of ordinary waking consciousness with its separation of subjects and objects. Indeed, James goes further and compares this mystical experience of reconciliation, or cosmic consciousness, with what he sees as Hegel's pantheism. This is, for James, the "monistic insight, in which the OTHER in its various forms appears absorbed into the One." On this reading of Hegel (and, of course, other readings are possible), the key to dialectical thinking is the unity of the Same and the Other, where what Hegel calls the Concept would be that movement of thinking which grasps both itself and its opposite. James adds that, "this is a dark saying," but he insists that "the living sense of the reality" of Hegel's philosophy "only comes in the artificial mystic state of mind." In others words, Hegel can only be understood when one is drunk on laughing gas.

Drunkenness is always followed by a hangover. Such is the condition of what Porete calls "dismay" and which other mystics commonly call distress, dereliction and distance from God. The error of the fourth state—and by implication James's analysis of mysticism—is to believe that the progress of the Soul is complete in its beatific union with God. Such a conception of *unio mystica* is common to many mystics and was tolerated and even encouraged by the Church, when and where it could be controlled. Porete, however, is engaged in a much more radical enterprise, namely the Soul's annihilation. This brings us to the fifth state.

5. The dismay and dereliction of the fifth state arises from the following sober consideration: on the one hand, the Soul considers God as the source of things that are, that is, of all goodness. But, on the other hand, the Soul then turns to consider itself, from which all things are not. The free will that God put into the Soul has been corrupted by the Fall. Insofar as the Soul wills anything, that thing is evil for it is nothing but the expression of original sin and the separation from the divine source of goodness. As Porete puts it, "The Soul's Will sees . . . that it cannot progress by itself if it does not separate itself from her own willing, for her nature is evil by that inclination towards nothingness to which nature tends." How, then, can I will not to will? I cannot, for every act of will, even the will not to will, is the expression of separation from divine goodness and therefore evil. As

we saw in the third state, the Soul has tried to cut away at itself, to bore a hole in itself that will allow love to enter. But the momentary exaltation of the fourth state, drunk with divinity, was illusory and transitory. The fifth state, Porete writes, "has subdued her (i.e. the Soul) in showing to the Soul her own self," It is here that we face what Porete repeatedly calls an "abyss," "deep beyond all depths," "without compass or end." This abyss is the gap between the willful and errant nature of the Soul and divine goodness. It cannot be bridged by any action. In the fifth state, two natures are at war within me: the divine goodness that I love and the evil that I am by virtue of original sin. As Paul puts it, "The Good that I would I do not, but the Evil that I would not that I do." Faced with this abyss, in the fifth state I become a paradox. The Soul wants to annihilate itself and unify with God. But how? How can an abyss become a byss?

6.   This is the work of the sixth state, which is the highest that can be attained during terrestrial life. In the sobriety of the fifth state, the Soul knows two things: divine goodness and the errant activity of the will. In making "her look at herself again," in such painful self-scrutiny, Porete adds that,

these two things that she sees take away from her will and longing and works of goodness, and so she is wholly at rest, and put in possession of her own state of free being, the high excellence of which gives her repose from every thing.

Having gone through the ordeal of the fifth state, the Soul finds repose and rest, what Eckhart will call an experience of releasement.

The reasoning here is delicate: the abyss that separates the Soul from God cannot be byssed or bridged through an act of will. On the contrary, it is only through the extinction of the will and the annihilation of the Soul that the sixth state can be attained. That is, the Soul itself becomes an abyss, that is, it becomes emptied and excoriated, entering a condition of absolute poverty.

It is only in such poverty that the wealth of God can be poured into the Soul. In the fifth state, the Soul looked at herself and experienced dereliction. But in the sixth state, "the Soul does not see herself at all." Not only that, the Soul also does not see God. Rather, and these words are extraordinary,

> God of his divine majesty sees himself in her, and by him this Soul is so illumined that she cannot see that anyone exists, except only God himself, from whom all things are.

When the Soul has become annihilated and "free of all things," then it can be illumined by the presence of God. It is only by reducing myself to nothing, that I can join with that divine something. As Porete insists, in this sixth state the Soul is not yet glorified, that is, a direct participant in the glory of God. This only happens after our death, in the seventh state. But what happens in the sixth state is even more extraordinary than glory. Let me quote at length the key passage,

> this Soul, thus pure and illumined, sees neither God nor herself, but God sees himself of himself in her, for her, without her, who—that is, God—shows to her that there is nothing except him. And therefore this Soul knows nothing except him, and loves nothing except him, and praises nothing except him, for there is nothing but he.

Which means the following: *the annihilated Soul becomes the place for God's infinite self-reflection.* The logic here is impeccable: if the Soul has become nothing, then it can obviously see neither itself nor God. On the contrary, God enters into the place that I created by hewing and hacking away at myself. But that place is no longer my self. What the Soul has created is the space of its own nihilation. This *nihil* is the "place," or better what Augustine might call the "no place," where God reflects on himself, where "God sees himself of himself in her." God's love fills the annihilated Soul, in a movement of reflection which is at once both "for her" and "without her." The only way in which the Soul can become for God is by becoming without itself. In its nihilation, the no-place of the Soul becomes the place of God's reflection on himself, in-himself and for-himself.

As Anne Carson rightly asks in her inquiry into how it is that women like Sappho, Simone Weil and Marguerite Porete tell God, "What is it that love dares the self to do?" She answers that, "Love dares the self to leave itself behind, to enter into poverty." Love is, thus, the audacity of impoverishment, of complete submission. It is an act of absolute spiritual daring that induces a passivity where the self becomes annihilated; it is a subjective act where the subject extinguishes itself. Become a husk or empty vessel through this act of daring, the fullness of love enters in. It is through the act of annihilation that the Soul knows nothing but God, "and loves nothing except him." Once the Soul is not, God is the only being that is.

7. As I already indicated, the seventh state is only attained after our death. It is the condition of "everlasting glory" of which we shall have no knowledge until our souls have left our bodies.

COMMUNISTIC CONSEQUENCES

It is time to draw the significant consequences from Porete's sinuous argumentation. Why was *The Mirror* condemned as heresy? For the simple reason that once the Soul is annihilated, there is nothing to prevent its identity with God. By following the itinerary of the seven states described in *The Mirror*, the Soul is annihilated and I become nothing. In becoming nothing, God enters the place where my Soul was. At that point, *I*—whatever sense the first person pronoun might still have—*become God.* When I become nothing, I become God.

As William James shows, varieties of this claim can be found in the mystical tradition. But perhaps everything goes back to St. Paul's words in *Galatians* 2:20, "I live, yet not I, but Christ liveth in me." That is, when I annihilate myself, that is, when I crucify myself in an *imitatio Christi,* then Christ lives within me. In other words, the I that lives is not I but God. This might also be linked to the Henry Suso's words, "The spirit dies, and yet it is alive in the marvels of the Godhead." Or indeed, we could make a connection to the differenceless point of the Godhead at the heart of Eckhart's theology. Yet, Porete is more radical still. The heart of the heresy of the Free Spirit is not some Neo-Platonic idea of the contemplative union of the intellect with the One as the source of an emanation, God, the bliss of contact with the divine. Rather, as

241

Cohn writes, "It was a passionate desire of certain human beings to surpass the condition of humanity and to become God." What Porete is describing is a painful process of decreation: boring a whole in oneself so that love might enter. It is closer to Teresa of Avila's piercing of the heart that takes place when she is on fire with the love of God, "The pain was so great, it made me moan." This desire for annihilation unleashes the most extreme violence against the self. For example, Angela of Foligno writes,

> There are times when such great anger ensues that I am scarcely able to stop from totally tearing myself apart. There are also times when I can't hold myself back from striking myself in a horrible way, and sometimes my head and limbs are swollen.

The consequence of such a process of self-deification is to overcome the condition of original sin and to return to the freedom that human beings enjoyed before the Fall. As the founder of the Quakers, George Fox, has it, "I was come up to the state of Adam in which he was before he fell." It is not difficult to see why the Movement of the Free Spirit posed such a profound threat to the authority of the Catholic Church and the governmental and legislative authority of various states in which it manifested itself. If it was possible to overcome original sin and regain the Edenic state of intimacy with the divine, then what possible function might be served by the Catholic Church, whose authority as a mediator between the human and the divine is only justified insofar as human beings live and travail in the wake of original sin. As we have seen in our discussion of Schmitt, all forms of ecclesiastical and governmental authoritarianism require a belief in original sin. It is only because human beings are defective and imperfect that church and state become necessary. If human beings become free, that is, perfected by overcoming the sin and death that define the post-Lapsarian human condition, then this has dramatic political consequences.

To begin with, as we saw in our allusions to John Ball and the Peasants' Revolt, if the spirit is free then all conceptions of mine and thine vanish. In the annihilation of the Soul, mine becomes thine, I becomes thou, and the no-place of the Soul becomes the space of divine self-reflection. Such an experience of divinity, of course, is not my individual private property, but is the commonwealth of those who are free in spirit. Private property is just the consequence of our fallen state. The Soul's recovery of its natural freedom entails commonality of ownership. The only true owner of property is God and his wealth is held in common by all creatures without hierarchy or distinctions of class and hereditary privilege. The political form of the Movement of the Free Spirit is communism.

Furthermore, it is a communism whose social bond is love. We have seen how Porete describes the work of love as the audacity of the Soul's annihilation. Clearly, there can be no higher authority than divine love, which entails that communism would be a political form higher than law (Marx repeats many of these ideas, imagining communism as a society without law). We might say that law is the juridical form that structures a social order. As such, it is based on the repression of the moment of community. Law is the external constraint on society that allows authority to be exercised, all the way to its dictatorial suspension. From the perspective of the communism of the Free Spirit, law loses its legitimacy because it is a form of heteronomous authority as opposed to autonomously chosen work of love. Furthermore, and perhaps this is what was most dangerous in the Movement of the Free Spirit, if human beings are free of original sin, where God is manifested as the spirit of commonality, then there is no longer any legitimacy to moral constraints on human behaviour that do not directly flow from our freedom. The demands of the state and the church can simply be ignored if they are not consistent with the experience of freedom. To be clear, this is not at all to say that the Movement of the Free Spirit implies immoralism. On the contrary, it is to claim that morality has flow from freedom by being consistent with a principle of that is located not in the individual but in its divine source, the Free Spirit that is held in common.

The Movement of the Free Spirit has habitually been seen as encouraging both moral and sexual libertinage. One cannot exaggerate the extent to which the alleged sexual excesses of the adepts of the Free Spirit obsessed the Inquisition that investigated and condemned the Movement, destroying its literature and executing or incarcerating its members. Most of what we know of the Movement is mediated through the agency of the Church that outlawed it. Such evidence is clearly difficult to trust. In particular, the various inquisitors seem obsessed with cataloguing instances of nakedness, as if that were evidence of the most depraved morals. But what are clothes for, apart from keeping the body warm? They are a consequence of the Fall when we learned for the first time to cover our bodies for shame. If that shame is lifted with the overcoming of original sin, then why wear clothing at all? Furthermore, this tendency to prurience is continued by the Movement's modern inquisitors, like Cohn, who takes great delight in describing the "anarchic eroticism" of the adepts of the Free Spirit. For example, he takes evident pleasure in describing the excesses of the Nuns of Schweidnitz in Silesia in 1330s, who claimed that they had such command over the Holy Trinity that they could "ride it as in a saddle." On this view, the Movement of the Free Spirit allows and even encourages sexual licentiousness where adepts throw off the moral prudery of the Church and run amok in some sort of huge orgy.

It is, of course, impossible to assess these claims of erotic libertinage. After all, the accusations are made by the accusers and it would be somewhat odd to trust them entirely. In the case of Cohn, the curiosity about the sexual antics of adepts of the Free Spirit is perhaps explained by the *Zeitgeist* in which he was writing. In the Conclusion to the 1970 revised edition of *The Pursuit of the Millennium*, Cohn argues for a continuity between medieval practices of self-deification and "the ideal of a total emancipation of the individual from society, even from external reality itself . . . with the help of psychedelic drugs." But I see little evidence for the suggestion of such narcotic or erotic license. On the contrary, what one finds in Porete and in many other mystical texts from the period and later is not some wild unleashing of repressed sexual energy, but rather its subtle transformation. Texts like *The Mirror* testify to a passion transformed from the physical to the metaphysical, to a certain spiritualization of desire. Some might call this sublimation. What is most striking in the writing of the mystics, particularly female mystics, is the elevation of the discourse of desire in relation to the object cause of that desire, which is the beloved: God usually in the person of Christ. What the female mystic wants is to love and desire in the same place and this requires both the articulation of desire and its transmutation into love. To reduce mystical passion to some pent-up sexual energy is to miss the point entirely. It is to mistake sublimation for repression. If anything, what seems to mark texts like *The Mirror* is an experience of passivity and an emphasis on submission. The Movement of the Free Spirit is not about doing what you want. On the contrary, it is about the training and submission of free will in order to recover a condition of commonality that overcomes it, namely love.

Indeed, the emphasis on submission and quietism that one finds in Porete and others seems more likely to lead to chastity than license. Unrestrained erotic exuberance would simply be the false exercise of the will. The point of Porete's seven-state itinerary is the *disciplining* of the self all the way to its extinction in an experience of love that annihilates it. To my mind, the Movement of the Free Spirit finds a greater echo in the chastity of groups like the Shakers than the exhaustive and exhausting cataloguing of sexual excesses listed that took place in the Chateau de Silling in the Marquis de Sade's *120 Days of Sodom*.

DO NOT KILL OTHERS, ONLY YOURSELF

There is no doubt that the Movement of the Free Spirit is deeply antinomian, refusing the metaphysical, moral, legislative and political authority of both church and state. As such, it constituted a clandestine and subversive movement of resistance. The earliest appearance of the many alleged heresies linked to the Free Spirit comes from an investigation held in Germany in the 1260s. The first of the accusations is extremely revealing, "To make small assemblies and to teach in secret is not contrary to faith but is contrary to the evangelical way of life." Note the emphasis on size and secrecy here. The great threat of the Movement of the Free Spirit was a secret network of small activist groups linked together by powerful bonds of solidarity and love. It was also a highly mobile network and what seems to have constantly worried the Church was the itinerant nature of the Beguines and Beghards and the way in which they moved from town to town and state to state. In addition, the rallying cry of these mendicants was *Brod durch Gott*, or "bread for the sake of God," and they preached, as did the Franciscan Spirituals, a doctrine of the poverty of Christ. As William Cornelius is reported to have said in the mid-13th Century, "No rich man can be saved, and all the rich are miserly." The point is not lost on Cohn who writes that, at its height, the Movement of the Free Spirit, "had become an invisible empire" held together by powerful emotional bonds. Devoted to undermining the power of church and state, abolishing private property and establishing what can only be described as an anarcho-communism based on the annihilation of the self in the experience of the divine, the ruthlessness with which the Movement was repeatedly crushed should come as no surprise.

What kind of assessment can we make of the Movement of the Free Spirit? Cohn sees millenarianism as a constantly recurring and dangerous threat that is still very much with us. What finds expression with the heresy of the Free Spirit is, he writes, "an affirmation of freedom so reckless and unqualified that it amounted to a total denial of every kind of restraint and limitation." As such, the Free Spirit is a precursor of what Cohn calls "that bohemian intelligentsia" that has plagued the 20th Century and which has been living from the ideas expressed by Bakunin and Nietzsche "in their wilder moments." The Free Spirit was "the most ambitious essay in total social revolution," which finds its continuation on the extreme left and right alike.

> Nietzsche's Superman . . . certainly obsessed the imagination of many of the "armed bohemians" who made the National-Socialist revolution; and many a present-day exponent of world revolution owes more to Bakunin than to Marx.

This is not the place to show either the erroneousness of such readings of Nietzsche and Bakunin or the chronic limitation of such arguments by insinuation that allegedly connect the Free Spirit to Nazism via Nietzsche. Let's just note that, as we saw with Porete, the Free Spirit is not a "reckless and unqualified" assertion of freedom that denies all "restraint and limitation." On the contrary, Porete is arguing for a rigorous and demanding discipline of the self where individual acts of arbitrary freedom are directed outside themselves to a divine source which is the basis for commonality. To say it once again, the Free Spirit is not about doing what you want. Neither is it amoralistic; rather, it is a stringent and demanding ethical disciplining of the self.

Cohn uses the standard "depth psychology" talk of the 1950s and 60s to diagnose the malady that drives the desire for mystical anarchism. He explains mysticism aetiologically as a "profound introversion" of "gigantic parental images." This is both a defense against reality and "a reactivation of the distorting images of infancy." Thereafter, two possibilities are possible: either the

246

mystic emerges from the process of introversion successfully, "as a more integrated personality," or he "introjects" these images unsuccessfully and "emerges as a nihilistic megalomaniac." Cohn catalogues the repeated occurrence of such megalomaniacs in great historical detail and there is no denying the existence of forms of sophism, obscurantism and charlatanry that are allied to the Movement of the Free Spirit. However, I am not only suspicious of the validity of such aetiological explanations, but would also want to interrogate the normative presupposition that such explanations invoke for the emergence of phenomena like mysticism. Cohn simply assumes that "integrated personality" is an unquestioned good, along with related ideas of reinforcing the ego and encouraging it to adapt to reality. What Porete is describing is what we might call a creative disintegration of the ego, an undermining of its authority which allows a new form of subjectivity to stand in the place where the old self was. Rather than seeing Porete as a retreat to some alleged illusory infantile state, the process of the Soul's annihilation might be seen as the self's maturation and mutation where it is no longer organized around the individual and his self-regarding acts of will. Rather than integrating some given personality, what Porete is describing is the emergence of a new form of subjectivity, a transformation of the self through the act of love.

As we saw above, John Gray makes explicit what is implicit in Cohn's approach. He extends the condemnation of groups like the Free Spirit to any and all utopian movements. The burden of a book like *Black Mass* is to show the continued malign presence of millenarian, apocalyptic politics in the contemporary world. What is particularly powerful in Gray's approach is the manner in which he extends Cohn's diagnosis to the neo-conservative millenarianism of the Bush administration, gleefully embraced by Blair, for whom "the clichés of the hour have always been eternal verities." However, as I argued in detail above, the critique of utopianism does not vindicate Gray's call for political realism, which draws on his naturalization of the concept of original sin. Relatedly, it is something of an understatement to suggest that Carl Schmitt would have been out of sympathy with both the theology and politics of mystical anarchism. I'm sure Schmitt would have happily served as Porete's inquisitor and probably personally lit the fire that consumed her and her books.

A very different take on these matters can be found in Raoul Vaneigem's *The Movement of the Free Spirit* from 1986. In many ways, Vaneigem unwittingly confirms all of Cohn's worst fears: he offers a vigorous defense of the Movement of the Free Spirit as a precursor to the insurrectional movements of the 1960s such as the Situationist International, in which Vaneigem's writings played such a hugely influential role. He writes of the Free Spirit,

> The spring has never dried up; it gushes from the fissures of history, bursting through the earth at the slightest shift of the mercantile terrain.

In Debord's distopian vision of the society of the spectacle where all human relations are governed by exchange—the dictatorship of a commodity system that Vaneigem always compares to the negativity of death—the Free Spirit is an emancipatory movement that operates in the name of life, bodily pleasures and untrammeled freedom. Vaneigem reinterprets the Free Spirit's insistence on poverty of spirit as the basis for a critique of the market system where life is reduced to purposeless productivity and life-denying work. As such, the most radical element in the Movement of the Free Spirit, for Vaneigem, was "an alchemy of individual fulfillment" where the cultivation of a state of perfection allowed the creation of a space where the "economy's hold over individuals" was relinquished. Thus, the Free Spirit's emphasis on love is "the sole alternative to market society." Wrapped around a compelling and extended documentation of the Movement of the Free Spirit, Vaneigem argues for what he calls an "alchemy of the self" based on unfettered enjoyment and bodily pleasures. He cites the proposition of Hippolytus of Rome, "The promiscuity of men and women, that is the true communion." Vaneigem advances an opposition between the Free Spirit and the Holy Spirit, where the latter is identified with God and the former with his denial. Vaneigem is therefore skeptical of Porete's position in *The Mirror*, arguing that self-deification is too dependant on a repressive, authoritarian idea of God. Although Vaneigem borrows Porete's idea of the refinement of love, which is allegedly the title of one of her lost books, he finds her approach too ascetic and intellectualized. Vaneigem defends an individualistic hedonism based not on intellect but "a flux of passions." It has a stronger affinity with Fourier's utopianism of passionate attraction filled with *phalansteries* of free love and leisure than the sort of self-annihilation found in Porete.

To my mind, something much more interesting than Vaneigem can be found in Gustav Landauer, the German anarcho-socialist who exerted such influence over Buber, Scholem and the young Benjamin. In his "Anarchic Thoughts on Anarchism" (1901), Landauer is writing in the context of the anarchist politics of assassination that had seen the killing of US President William McKinley in 1901, itself based on the murder of King Umberto I of Italy the previous year. Both perpetrators identified themselves as anarchists. Landauer asks, "what has the killing of people to do with anarchism, a theory striving for a society without government and authoritarian coercion, a movement against the state and legalized violence?" The answer is clear, "Nothing at all." Landauer argues that all forms of violence are despotic and anarchism entails non-violence. If anarchists resort to violence, then they are no better than the tyrants whom they claim to oppose. Anarchism is not a matter of armed revolt or military attack, "it is a matter of how one lives." Its concern is with, "a new people arising from humble beginnings in small communities that form in the midst of the old." This is what Landauer intriguingly calls "inward colonization."

Yet, how is such an inward colonization possible? Landauer's response is singular and draws us back to the idea of self-annihilation. He writes, "Whoever kills, dies. Those who want to create life must also embrace it and be reborn from within." But how can such a rebirth take place? It can only happen by killing oneself, "in the mystical sense, in order to be reborn after having descended into the depths of their soul." He goes on, "Only those who have journeyed through their own selves and waded deep in their own blood can help to create the new world without interfering in the lives of others." Landauer insists that such a position does not imply quietism or resignation. On the contrary, he writes that "one acts with others," but he adds that, "none of this will really bring us forward if it is not based on a new spirit won by conquest of one's inner self." He continues,

> It is not enough for us to reject conditions and institutions; we have to reject ourselves. "Do not kill others, only yourself": such will be the maxim of those who accept the challenge to create their own chaos in

order to discover their most authentic and precious inner being and to become mystically one with the world.

Although talk of authenticity and "precious inner being" leaves me somewhat cold, what is fascinating here is the connection between the idea of self-annihilation and anarchism. The condition of possibility for a life of cooperation and solidarity with others is a subjective transformation, a self-killing that renounces the killing of others. For Landauer, it is not a matter of anarchism participating in the usual party politics, systemic violence and cold rationalism of the state. It is a rather a question of individuals breaking with the state's authority and uniting together in new forms of life. Talk of inward colonization gives a new twist to Cohn's idea of the Movement of the Free Spirit as an "invisible empire." It is a question of the creation of new forms of life at a distance from the order of the state—which is the order of visibility—and cultivating largely invisible commonalities, what Landauer calls anarchy's "dark deep dream." Perhaps this killing of the self in an ecstatic mystical experience is close to what Bataille called "sovereignty," and which for him was constantly linked with his experimentation with different forms of small-scale, communal group collaborations, particularly in the 1930s and 40s, from *Contre Attaque*, the *Collège de Sociologie* and the *Collège Socratique,* through to the more mysterious *Acéphale.*

THE RISK OF ABSTRACTION

We are living through a long anti-1960s. The various experiments in communal living and collective existence that defined that period seem to us either quaintly passé, laughably unrealistic or dangerously misguided. We now know better than to try and bring heaven crashing down to earth and construct concrete utopias. To that extent, despite our occasional and transient enthusiasms, we are all political realists; indeed most of us are passive nihilists and cynics. This is why we still require a belief in something like original sin. Without the conviction that the human condition is essentially flawed and dangerously rapacious, we would have no way of justifying our disappointment.

It is indeed true that those utopian political movements of the 1960s, like the Situationist International, where an echo of the Movement of the Free Spirit could be heard, led to various forms of disillusionment, disintegration and, in extreme cases, disaster. Experiments in the collective ownership of property or in communal living based on sexual freedom without the repressive institution of the family, or indeed R. D. Laing's experimental communal asylums with no distinction between the so-called mad and the sane seem like distant whimsical cultural memories captured in dog-eared, yellowed paperbacks and grainy, poor-quality film. It is a world that we struggle to understand. Perhaps such communal experiments were too pure and overfull of righteous conviction. Perhaps they were, in a word, too *moralistic* to ever endure. Perhaps such experiments were doomed because of what we might call a politics of abstraction, in the sense of being overly attached to an idea at the expense of a frontal denial of reality.

At their most extreme, say in the activities of the Weather Underground, the Red Army Faction and the Red Brigades in the 1970s, the moral certitude of the closed and pure community becomes fatally linked to redemptive, cleansing violence. Terror becomes the means to bring about end of virtue. The death of individuals is but a speck on the vast heroic canvas of the class struggle. This culminated in a politics of violence where acts of abduction, kidnapping, hijacking and assassination were justified through an attachment to a set of ideas. As a character in Jean-Luc Godard's *Notre Musique* remarks, "To kill a human being in order to defend an idea is not to defend an idea, it is to kill a human being." Perhaps such groups were too attached to the idea of immediacy, the propaganda of the violent deed as the impatient attempt to storm the heavens. Perhaps such experiments lacked an understanding of politics as a constant and concrete process of *mediation* between a subjective ethical commitment based on a general principle, for example the equality of all, and the experience of local organization that builds fronts and alliances between disparate groups with often conflicting sets of interests. By definition, such a process of mediation is never pure.

Perhaps such utopian experiments in community only live on in the institutionally sanctioned spaces of the contemporary art world. One thinks of projects like *L'Association des Temps Libérés* (1995), or *Utopia Station* (2003) and many other examples, somewhat fossilized in a recent show at the Guggenheim in New York, *Theanyspacewhatever*. In the work of artists like Philippe Parreno and Liam Gillick or curators like Hans-Ulrich Obrist, there is a deeply-felt Situationist nostalgia for ideas of collectivity, action, self-management, collaboration and indeed the idea of the group as such. In such art practice—which Nicolas Bourriaud has successfully branded as "relational art"—is the acting out of a situation in order to see if, in Obrist's words, "something like a collective intelligence might exist." As Gillick notes, "Maybe it would be better if we worked in groups of three." Of course, the problem with such experiments is twofold: on the one hand, they are only enabled and legitimated through the cultural institutions of the art world and thus utterly enmeshed in the circuits of commodification and spectacle that they seek to subvert; and, on the other hand, the dominant mode for approaching an experience of the communal is through the strategy of *reenactment*. One doesn't engage in a bank heist, one reenacts Patty Hearst's adventures with the Symbionese Liberation Army in a warehouse in Brooklyn, or whatever. Situationist *détournement* is replayed as obsessively planned reenactment. Fascinating as I find such experiments and the work of the artists involved, one suspects what we might call a "mannerist Situationism," where the old problem of recuperation does not even apply because such art is completely co-opted by the socio-economic system which provides its life-blood.

Perhaps we are witnessing something related to this in recent events in France surrounding the arrest and detention of the so-called "Tarnac Nine" on 11th November 2008. As part of Sarkozy's reactionary politics of fear (itself based on an overwhelming fear of disorder), a number of activists who had been formerly associated with the group *Tiqqun* were arrested in rural, central France by a force of 150 anti-terrorist police, helicopters and attendant media. They were living communally in the small village of Tarnac in the Corrèze district of the Massif Central. Apparently a number of the group's members had bought a small farmhouse and ran a cooperative grocery store and were engaged in such dangerous activities as running a local film club, planting carrots and delivering food to the elderly. With surprising juridical imagination, they were charged with "pre-terrorism," an accusation linked to acts of sabotage on France's TGV rail system. The basis for this thought-crime was a passage from

L'insurrection qui vient from 2007, a wonderfully dystopian diagnosis of contemporary society and a compelling strategy to resist it. The final pages of *L'insurrection* advocate acts of sabotage against the transport networks of "the social machine" and ask the question, "How could a TGV line or an electrical network be rendered useless?" Two of the alleged pre-terrorists, Julien Coupat and Yldune Lévy, are still in jail and others have been charged with "a terrorist undertaking" that carries a prison sentence of twenty years. Such is the repressive and reactionary force of the state, just in case anyone had forgotten. As the authors of *L'insurrection* remind us, "Governing has never been anything but pushing back by a thousand subterfuges the moment when the crowd will hang you."

L'insurrection qui vient has powerful echoes of the Situationist International and some of the other communist heresies we have examined. The authorship of *L'insurrection* is attributed to *La Comité Invisible* and the insurrectional strategy of the group turns around the question of invisibility. It is a question of "learning how to become imperceptible," of regaining "the taste for anonymity" and not exposing and losing oneself in the order of visibility, which is always controlled by the police and the state. The authors of *L'insurrection* argue for the proliferation of zones of opacity, anonymous spaces where communes might be formed. The book ends with the slogan, "All power to the communes" (*Tout le pouvoir aux communes*). In a nod to Blanchot, these communes are described as *désœuvrée*, or "inoperative," or as refusing the capitalist tyranny of work. In a related text simply entitled *Call*, they seek to establish "*a series of foci of desertion*, of secession poles, of rallying points. For the runaways. For those who leave. *A set of places to take shelter from the control of a civilization that is headed for the abyss.*" A strategy of sabotage, blockade and what is called "the human strike" is proposed in order to weaken still further our doomed civilization. An opposition between the city and the country is constantly reiterated, and it is clear that construction of zones of opacity is better suited to rural life than the policed space of surveillance of the modern metropolis. *L'insurrection* is compelling, exhilarating, and deeply lyrical text that sets off all sorts of historical echoes with movements like the Free Spirit: the emphases on secrecy, invisibility and itinerancy, on small scale communal experiments in living, on the cultivation of poverty, radical mendicancy and the refusal of work. But the double program of sabotage, on the one hand, and secession from civilization, on the other, risks remaining trapped within the politics of abstraction identified above. In this fascinatingly creative reenactment of the Situationist gesture, what is missed is a thinking of political mediation where groups like the Invisible Committee would be able to link up and become concretized in relation to multiple and conflicting sites of struggle. We need a richer political cartography than the opposition between the city and the country. Tempting as it is, sabotage combined with secession from civilization smells of the moralism we detected above.

CONCLUSION—THE POLITICS OF LOVE

But what follows from this? Are we to conclude with John Gray that the utopian impulse in political thinking is simply the residue of a dangerous political theology that we are much better off without? Is the upshot of the critique of mystical anarchism that we should be resigned in the face of the world's violent inequality and update a belief in original sin with a reassuringly miserabilistic Darwinism? Should we reconcile ourselves to the options of political realism, authoritarianism or liberalism? Should we simply renounce the utopian impulse in our personal and political thinking?

If so, then the consequence is clear: we are stuck with the way things are, or possibly with something even worse than the way things are. To abandon the utopian impulse in thinking is to imprison ourselves within the world as it is and to give up once and for the prospect that another world is possible, however small, fleeting and compromised such a world might be. In the political circumstances that presently surround us in the West, to abandon the utopian impulse in political thinking is to resign oneself to liberal democracy which, as we showed above, is the rule of the rule, the reign of law which renders impotent anything that would break with law: the miraculous, the moment of the event, the break with the situation in the name of the common.

Let me return for a last time to mystical anarchism and to the question of self-deification. Defending the idea of becoming God might be seen as going a little far, I agree. To embrace such mysticism would be to fall prey to what Badiou calls in his book on St. Paul the obscurantist discourse of glorification. In terms of the Lacanian schema of the four discourses that he borrows (master, university, hysteric, analyst), the mystic is identified with the discourse of the hysteric and contrasted with the anti-obscurantist Christian position that Badiou identifies with the discourse of the analyst. Badiou draws a line between St. Paul's declaration of the Christ-event, what he calls "an ethical dimension of anti-obscurantism," and the mystical discourse of identity with the divine, the ravished subjectivity of someone like Porete.

Yet, to acquiesce in such a conclusion would be to miss something vital about mystical anarchism, what I want to call, in closing, its politics of love. What I find most compelling in Porete is the idea of love as an act of absolute spiritual daring that eviscerates the old self in order that something new can come into being. In Anne Carson's words, cited above, love dares the self to leave itself behind, to enter into poverty and engage with its own annihilation: to hew and hack away at oneself in order to make a space that is large enough for love to enter. What is being attempted by Porete—and perhaps it is *only* the attempt which matters here, not some theophanic outcome—is an act of absolute daring, not for some nihilistic end, but in order to open what we might call the *immortal* dimension of the subject. The only proof of immortality is the act of love, the daring that attempts to extend beyond oneself by annihilating oneself, to project onto something that exceeds one's powers of projection. To love is to give what one does not have and to receive that over which one has no power. As we saw in Landauer, the point is not to kill others, but to kill oneself in order that a transformed relation to others becomes possible, some new way of conceiving the common and being with others. Anarchism can only begin with an act of inward colonization, the act of love that demands a transformation of the self. Finally—and very simply—anarchism is not a question for the future, it is a matter of how one lives now.

Is such a thing conceivable and practicable without the moralism, purism, immediacy, and the righteously self-enclosed certainty of previous experiments? To be honest, I don't know.

Die Maske des Black Metals

Dominik Irtenkauf

Das Corpsepaint begleitet den Black Metal seit Beginn. Der Ursprung wird bei Sarcofago aus Brasilien vermutet. Einschlägige Publikationen nennen diese Band. Auch in der Forschung tauchen die Brasilianer auf: bei Jan G. Grünwald auf S. 63, Drew Daniel auf den Seiten 40 und 43. Keith Kahn-Harris auf S. 116. Meine Theory Fiction baut auf einer anderen Traditionslinie auf—auf der schlichten Frage: Was bringt einen Musiker dazu, sich zu schminken? Sicher ist das noch Black Metal, aber letztlich wird der Black-Metal-Musiker zum mythologischen Wesen, zu einem Wesen, das die Metamorphose wie kein anderes beherrscht. Das Corpsepaint ist eine Maske, die den Musiker tarnt, also: seine Überlebenschancen deutlich erhöht. Denn wer unter der Maske steckt, wird nicht für das genommen, was er ist, sondern was er scheint.

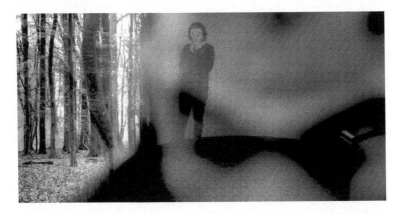

Im Videoclip, der für das Symposium in New York entstanden ist, werden zwei Figuren präsentiert, die als Protagonisten noch nicht abgeschlossen sind, sondern erst Stück für Stück sich erbauen. The Devil and the Deadwalker. **They form the protagonists of my theory fiction.** Unter der Maske schließt sich der

257

Werdensprozess nie ab. Die Musiker wollen ja nicht wie im Alltag wirken, sie verbergen ihr wahres Gesicht unter der Maske, der Leichenschminke, eben: dem Corpsepaint. Dieses Make-Up ermöglicht es, als Bürger abzusterben und als Kreatur wiedergeboren zu werden. Beim Gebären gibt es nur das Aktiv der Mutter, aber nicht der Söhne, i.e. man kann sich nicht selbst gebären, also besteht für die Black-Metal-Söhne nur der Ausweg des Sterbens (und Wiedergeborenwerdens). Ist es ein mystischer Tod?

Ein mystischer Tod ist kein richtiger Tod, i.e. man wird nicht auf der Bahre liegenbleiben, der Mund und das Gesicht verfärben sich nicht, Rigor Mortis setzt nicht ein—man lässt das alte Leben hinter sich. (Wobei sich bei manchen Black Metallern der ersten Stunde sich die Frage stellt, welches Leben sie führten. In diversen Retrospektiven, filmischen wie biographischen, stellt sich ein Leben am Rande des Exzesses dar, ganz nach dem Motto: Jung kaputt spart Altersheime!) Sicher leben diese Musiker, wie sollten sie sonst die Musik aufnehmen können? Sie tun als ob sie Leichen, Monstren, Aussätzige seien. Dazu passen die Pseudonyme. Einfallsreich sind sie lediglich im Szenentalk. Wer den Nickname Hellhammer hört, denkt er an einen Wüterich der Jahrtausendwende, der auf dem Langboot die Seine herunterschippert, nur mit dem einen Gedanken: Beute nach Hause in den Norden zu bringen? Wohl eher nicht. Zu lange schon tobt der Teufel in der Rockmusik . . . er produziert Schemen, die wie flackerndes Feuer in einer Winternacht die Augen tränen lässt. Ich versuche, mich nicht von der Oberfläche ablenken zu lassen. Schwarz/weiß, manchmal monochrom, desolate Waldstücke, romantische Burgenverklärung, feuerspeiende langhaarige Männer mit nacktem Oberkörper. Und darunter mischte sich ab und zu ein Goat. Im Videoclip wird die Möglichkeit der Metamorphisierung (nicht nur in der Metapher, sondern im Bewusstsein von Leib und Seele) angesprochen: **have you ever asked yourself what lies beneath your face? Cruelty maybe. Maybe something very different and indifferent at the same time.**

Emperor Magus Caligula von der schwedischen Band Dark Funeral spricht davon, dass er und die Band von Dämonen besessen seien, wenn er sich in den Black-Metal-Modus versetze. Sobald er das Corpsepaint aufträgt, der Sound ihn umschließt, verzerrt sich sein schwedisch-bürgerliches Gesicht zur Fratze und er wird zum Kaiser Magier Caligula, der laut Suetons Bericht allerlei Schweinereien frönte. Was heißt das, wenn Dark Funeral von Dämonen besessen wird? Kann unsere Figur Devil etwas dazu sagen? Nun, den Teufel bekommt man nicht leicht zum Reden— er als Obertrickster muss selbst durch Tricks überlistet werden. Was tun also? Sollten sie tatsächlich von Dämonen besessen sein, wenn sie das Corpsepaint auftragen und sich in den Black-Metal-Modus versetzen, so müsste der Klang, der auf ihren Schallplatten uns entgegenströmt, etwas von dieser Teuflischkeit besitzen. Nicht? Diese schnellen hochgestimmten Gitarren, das Blastbeat-

Getacker der Drums, keifende Stimme, Druck unendlich viel Druck und Spannung, dass einem bald schon der Kopf zerplatzt.

Corpsepaint hilft, nicht mehr Mensch zu sein. Der Musiker wird zum Tier, zur Kreatur der Nacht, zum Unwesen und wenn er einen Job hat, dann versteckt er diese Komponente seines Alltags hinter der Maske. Die Maske steht für die Anderszeit. Das erklärt auch die Wahrnehmung mancher Bandfotos von Außenstehenden als Karneval. Denn wer es nicht kennt, fragt sich, warum die Musik—dieser mächtige schrille Sound—nicht allein ausreicht, um den maximalen Effekt auf die Hörer zu hinterlassen? Warum tragen diese Männer Make-Up? Eine tendenziöse Antwort wäre: Weil sie uns etwas vormachen! Sie tun nur so, als wären sie tot. Dabei sind sie doch so vital, **because you cannot play such fast and energetic music without being in a stealthy condition**. Dieser Widerspruch zwischen Vitalität und Todeskult zieht sich durch den gesamten Sound der Black-Metal-Bands. Wie kann ein Sound, i.e. die Kombination aus Instrumenten und menschlicher Sitmme, Konzepte wie „Vitalität" und „Todeskult" widergeben? Glaubt man den unzähligen Interviewaussagen der Bands, so verstärkt die eigene Musik den Eindruck von Boshaftigkeit, von Nihilismus und Misanthropie. Der hohe Verzerrungsgrad hinterlässt beim Hörer das Gefühl von Aggression und sonischer Gewalt. Ohne eigene Erfahrungswerte wirkt jedes Schreiben über Black Metal letztlich hilflos, denn keine noch so fein gewählten Worte können das Erlebnis *in extenso* schildern. Auf der anderen Seite überschneiden sich viele der Black-Metal-Bands in den

Mitteln, die sie nutzen und wer nicht ein ganz genaues Ohr riskiert, wird vermuten, dass sich die Tausenderschaft wechselseitig kopiert.

Das Corpsepaint weist ebenso wie der Black-Metal-Sound auf Patterns hin, die einerseits Identität schaffen, andererseits den Ansporn zur Differenz geben. Der Musiker wird zur Kreatur der Nacht—in der Presse erkennt man ihn anhand des Make-Ups als der Spezies der Black-Metal-Musiker zugehörig. Er benutzt einen *nom de plume*. Im einführenden Absatz des Artikels steht dann doch meist der bürgerliche Name. Im Internet findest du, wer Fenriz, Satyr, Varg, Hellhammer, Necrobutcher, Samoth, Ihsahn, Faust, Abbath und Nattefrost eigentlich sind. Norweger mit ziemlich bekannten Vornamen, zumindest in diesem nordischen Land. Das fällt auf, wenn die Coverplatten, die Promofotos, die Stageperformance der verschiedenen Interpreten miteinander verglichen werden. Ein Black-Metal-Fan sammelt, aber er analysiert nicht. Die Mystik, die diese Musik umgibt, geht auf Erinnerungen an die frühen Neunziger zurück, als sich ein neues Subgenre im Extreme Metal entwickelte . . . oft geschahen die Entdeckungen dieser *terra incognita* im Jugendalter. Leicht ließ sich der Metalfan beeindrucken, wenn eine Band die Gitarren noch mehr verzerrte, noch mehr Schminke ins Gesicht schmierte und die Pseudonyme noch wahnsinniger und grammatisch falsch klangen. (Auf diesen Schluß kam auch Dietmar Dath, ein Autor, der bislang keinen genuinen Black-Metal-Roman geschrieben hat, sich in seinen Romanen und Essays aber immer wieder mit

Subkulturen einläßt und selbst auch ambitionierter Metalhörer ist.) Dieses Außerhalb-der-Kultur-Stehen wird von radikalen Bands wie Mayhem oder Carpathian Forest durch explizite Bild-, Wort- und Tonsprache als große Geste geübt. Ein deutsches Beispiel wären die niederrheinischen Bethlehem, deren Texter Jürgen Bartsch durch absolute Metaphern und eine höchst chiffrierte Sprache auffällt. Es könnte auch Parodie sein—auf die obskurantistischen Lehren, auf die sich Black-Metal-Bands beziehen oder auf die Menschenfeindlichkeit, die sich dann doch dazu bewegen lässt, auf Sommerfestivals mit mehreren zehntausend Besuchern zu spielen. Es wird im Black Metal nichts so heiß gegessen wie es gekocht wird. **In the end it's entertainment.**

Doch wie muss sich ein mystischer Musiker im Alltag verhalten, um dennoch als sein Alter Ego unter der Corpsepaint-Maske wahrgenommen zu werden? Ein Untoter würde seine (lebenden) Mitmenschen anfallen, sie beißen und damit selbst zu Untoten machen. Für seine Umwelt wäre er eine Gefahr. Für einen Werwolf gilt das gleiche. (Auf lange Sicht könnte kein Musiker als ein solches Alter Ego in einer sozialen Gruppe bestehen, denn die Mitmenschen würden sich gegen diese Gefahr wappnen. Es sei denn, der Musiker lebte in einem Krisenstaat, der die Unversehrtheit des Leibes nicht mehr garantieren könnte und so ein Großteil der Gesellschaft bewaffnet wäre, um sich der eigenen Haut erwehren zu können.) Stellen manche Corpsepaintmuster einen Krieger dar? Wenn ja, dann wäre dies ein kalkulierbares

Risiko. Gegen einen Krieger kann man sich tarnen, wappnen und wehren. Das Corpsepaint unterstreicht stets das Als-ob. Nach dem Konzert, nach der Fotosession schminken sich die Männer ab. Keiner wird mit dem Corpsepaint ins Bett gehen. Wenn sie aber mit Corpsepaint nicht ins Bett gehen, dann meiden diese Krieger möglicherweise das Bett, es sind schlaflose Nächte, durchwacht unter Mondenschein. Kettenrauchen wäre eine Lösung,wenn die Lust am Leben nicht sonderlich hoch ist, die Maske des Corpsepaints unter dem Schweiß des Abends zerrinnt und der Black Metal-Musiker der Vergänglichkeit allen Seins, also auch der eigenen imposanten Geste, gewahr wird. Eine andere Lösung wäre, eine Flasche Bier zu öffnen und die Gedanken etwas kreisen zu lassen.

Ein Black-Metal-Musiker lebt nicht in einer metaphysischen Blase. Der Magen knurrt, der Körper schreit nach Ruhe, der Großvater feiert den Neunzigsten, der Betrieb feiert Sommerfest—also ist das Corpsepaint kein Anderswerden, Exterritorialisieren? Dann ist es Outfit, Schmuck für das besondere nichtalltägliche Erlebnis . . . Urlaub vom Alltag. **Off-time from mundanity.**

Ein mystischer Tod muss nicht unbedingt den biologischen Tod meinen. Also der mystisch Gestorbene kann weiterleben, eben unter einer anderen Identität. Das Corpsepaint lässt das Gesicht verschwinden—den Mund, die Nase, die Augen—oder eher: sie werden unkenntlich gemacht. Das corpsepainted face erscheint als Deadwalker. Der Deadwalker erscheint auch im Videoclip unter der Maske. Er durchschreitet den Raum, ohne eigentliches Ziel, rein ästhetisch. „Ich stehe auf diesen Gitarrenklang, Tremolopicking, hochgedrehte Frequenzen, Lufthauch, Zischen der Schlange, Krächzen der Krähen, die ganze Poetologie des übersteuerten Sounds, zu dünn und doch gewaltig wie ein Hammer ins Gesicht. Death Metal-Bands singen wohl über hammer-smashed faces, aber der Sound ist zu fett, dickes Bratenstück. Ich stehe auf diese abgespeckten Hühner, Gerippe. Totentanz." Soundfreaks nennt die Berliner Ethnologin Dunja Brill die Metalfans auf einer Veranstaltung im Haus der Kulturen der Welt im Oktober 2013. Im Black Metal mischen Bands wie Dissection immer wieder hochmelodische Riffs in den Gitarrengewittersturm. Mayhem üben sich in vertrackter Geduld—die Songs auf ihren letzten Alben sind nicht alle unbedingt straightforward. Gorgoroth hingegen holzten früher in rasantem Tempo auf ihren Platten die Stücke runter. Das Kennenlernen der verschiedenen Intensitätsgrade von Black Metal lässt mit einem Mal die Tarnung auffliegen: das Corpsepaint haftet wohl noch auf dem Gesicht, aber der (schrille) Sound verselbständigt sich. Er verlässt die Erde, stößt sich ab, wird zum Vogel und überfliegt die Berge, Seen und Täler. Und wenn auch rein parodistisch die Black-Metal-Gesichter mit den Konturen von Pandabären und Pinguinen verglichen werden, so zeigt diese Überwindung der Schwarz/Weiß-Malerei doch, dass es sich hier nicht allein um Todernst handelt. Wenn auch Pandas und Pinguine eher als komische Tierarten wahrgenommen werden, so steckt in der Metamorphisierung die Überlegung, in der Tat durch das Make-Up zu einem Image zu werden, das mit „Wildnis" kontextualisiert wird. Sicher ist ein Endzeitwolf gewaltiger als ein Pandabär, der am Bambusrohr kaut. Die graphische Kontur transzendiert das biologische Originalbild und verwischt die Grenzen zwischen Corpsepaint-Gesicht und Pandabär. Da das Make-Up nur das Gesicht bedeckt, sind verschiedene Interpretationen möglich. Der Corpsepaint-Träger kann möglicherweise noch wie ein Wolf heulen, auf der Platte, beim Konzert oder beim Interview. Dennoch kann sein Corpsepaint nicht nur als Wolf, sondern auch als Pandabär gelesen werden. Es sei denn, er imitiert die Anatomie des Wolfes mit dem Kajal und dem deckenden Make-Up auf seinem Gesicht— er zeichnet die wilden Hundeaugen nach, verengt die Nasenflügel und trägt einzelne geschickte Striche auf die Backen auf, so dass ganz der Eindruck eines gemalten Wolfsgesichts erscheint. Der Pressefotograf wird es ihm danken. Es ist nicht länger Jacob Hansen, sondern Varg, Wolf, Lupus oder doch American Werewolf? Durch die Maskierung erobert der Black-Metal-Musiker ein Territorium jenseits des Menschlichen. Er wandelt sich zum Tier, zum Untoten, zum Deadwalker. Aber Zeichnung bleibt es im Endeffekt doch.

Zurück zum Sound: Ist er es, der die Musiker zum Corpsepainten bringt? Nehmen wir Taakes Musik. Taake stammen aus Norwegen und auf dem aktuellen Album „Stridens Hus" spielen sie eine bestrickende Interpretation des norwegischen Black Metal-Lokalkolorits. Musik zu beschreiben, ist schwer, und doch das tägliche Brot von Musikjournalisten. Vielleicht hilft die Betrachtung von Bandfotos: die Corpsepaint-Faces sind nicht tot und nicht lebendig. Sie sind dazwischen. Corpsepaint ist ein äußeres, visuell erkennbares Charakteristikum des Anderswerdens. Die Musiker verbergen ihre menschliche Herkunft. Sie sind zu Symbolen geworden. Sie verweisen auf eine Metaphysik jenseits des Blastbeats und Kreischens. Diese Bewegung hin zum Mehr-als-Musik zeichnet insbesondere den Black Metal aus. So spricht etwa Emperor Magus Caligula von Dark Funeral aus Schweden im deutschen Deftone-Magazin von einer Quelle jenseits der Musik: „Wenn wir Musik machen und unsere Botschaft verkünden, nimmt Satan Besitz von uns und gebraucht uns als seine Instrumente, um seine Musik zu spielen." (Deftone 5 – April 1998, S. 26) Dark Funeral sehen sich als Medien einer kulturellen Projektion und das Corpsepaint, das sie benutzen, kleidet sie für die Stageperformance, verbirgt den jeder Mystik entgegenstehenden Alltag. Der Abschied von der weiter oben genannten Mundanität integriert ein Unkenntlichmachen der menschlichen Spuren. Humanoid bleiben die Musiker, denn ihre zwei Arme und die zwei Beine amputieren sie nicht—bislang ist nichts von einem Black-Metal-Musiker bekannt, der sich für ein Konzert oder eine Fotosession als Feuerqualle verkleidet präsentieren konnte. Black Metal spielt mit dem Wunsch der Transgression, entkommt jedoch dem Menschsein nicht. Es werden mythische Figuren wie der Teufel evoziert, um eine große Illusionsfläche für eine Alternative zum Alltag zu schaffen. Sie sterben einen mystischen Tod für die Dauer der Performance, um dann wieder zum Leben zurückzukehren.

Ares, Kopf der norwegischen Band Aeternus, referiert das personale Switchen zwischen Metal-Mythologie und Alltag in einem Interview mit dem deutschen Magazin *Rock Hard*:

Ich möchte diesen Rollentausch nicht missen. Als Ares durchlebe ich Sachen, von denen ich als Ronnie nur träumen kann. Das sind beinahe Halluzinationen. Ich werde aber kein krankes, verrücktes Monster, wenn ich spiele. Ansonsten lache ich übrigens sehr gerne. Abends sitze ich in einer dunklen Ecke, höre auf gar keinen Fall Darkthrone und spiele auch nicht den bösen Mann, wie es viele meiner Kollegen tun. Das finde ich schlicht und einfach lächerlich. Wir sind doch alle mit einem gewissen Maß an Humor geboren werden. (Rock Hard #124, September 1997 – S. 49)

Sic tacuisses, philosophus mansisses. Würden die Musiker schweigen und die Musik, das Image für sich sprechen lassen, dann könnte ich als Phänomen eine gewisse Verborgenheit wahrnehmen. Die Isolation hat aber von Anfang an nicht richtig funktioniert, denn der Prinz des Todes (Euronymous) von Mayhem war eine ziemliche Plaudertasche und ließ keine Gelegenheit aus, seine Ansichten zum Besten zu geben. Das Corpsepaint macht es unmöglich, die Gesichter zu erkennen. In einem Reisepaß ist es nicht möglich, in der schwarzmetallischen Kriegsbemalung aufzutauchen. Die Erkennbarkeit muss garantiert sein. Corpsepaint ist demnach Teil einer Theatralik. Es hilft den Musikern, abzutauchen—in die mystifizierte Black-Metal-Welt. Ein kürzlich aufscheinendes

Beispiel für eine Welt neben der Welt im Black Metal sind die Schweden von Istapp: „Hauptsächlich geht es darum, den Sklaven der glühenden Erdkugel die Wahrheit zu offenbaren, sie anzuführen und ihnen Anweisungen zu geben, wie sie sich am besten auf die vollständige Vernichtung vorbereiten können. Die Texte sind für uns auch ein Mittel, um unseren Legionen Kommandos und Befehle zu erteilen." Und weiter: „Wir haben einen langen Kampf gegen die Armee der Sonne gefochten und schwere Rückschläge erlitten, denn es gab Verräter in unseren Reihen. Jetzt sind wir jedoch stärker als jemals zuvor, und das Resultat, das daraus folgt, ist ‚Frostbitten'." (Legacy #97, S. 162-163) Leider hat es der Interviewer versäumt, die Schweden zu fragen, wie genau dieser Kampf denn aussehe.

Corpsepaint ist aber auch kein gewöhnliches Make-Up. Anders als Nachtcremes wollen die Musiker häßlicher und ‚unbemerkter' werden. Zugleich sind sie da und abwesend. Martialisch wirken sie, wie Krieger aus einer anderen Zeit und Welt. Mit dem Corpsepaint vertilgen sie aber auch menschliche Spuren, löschen ihre frühere Identität aus. Inzwischen mehren sich die Stimmen, dass Corpsepaint nicht mehr aktuell sei, da es zu viele benutzten. Das Alleinstellungsmerkmal schwindet und die Masse nivelliert die Elite, von der der Black Metal immer noch träumt. Auf einmal kann es passieren, dass ein Anderer genauso die Augen mit Dreiecken umrandet wie man selbst vor dem Backstage-Spiegel. Was tun? Die Differenz verschwindet ... der Corpsepainter nähert sich verdächtig nahe dem anderen Corpsepainter. Dabei sollte er im mystischen Tod gar nicht mehr bestehen, das Ego wird aufgelöst, Begriffe verblassen und die Einheit mit dem All ist errungen. „Erst wenn du dich von allem ganz entäußert hast, vornehmlich aber von dir selbst, unaufhaltsam und absolut, und ohne jeden Rest leer bist, erst dann wirst du dich in reinster Ekstase bis zu jenem dunkelsten Strahl erheben können, der aus der Urgottheit vor aller Erschaffung kam, jenseits von aller Welt und jenseits von allem Sein, entblößt auch noch von dem, was jedes und dich selbst erst zum Wesen macht." (So schreibt Dionysius Areopagita in seiner Mystischen Theologie) Das Gesicht geht in diesem Alleinigungsprozess verloren. Corpsepaint führt sich selbst ad absurdum. Wobei zu bedenken wäre, dass die Maske ja nicht den emotionalen Zustand des Trägers versinnbildlichen soll, sondern den Ausdruck der Darstellung. Das wäre im Black-Metal-Fall: Corpse. Aber Leiche ist man nicht ewig, beim Schlafen nimmt der Musiker das schmierende Make-Up ab. Er lebt und schläft. Tot ist er aber noch nicht. Solange der Kopf eiskalt ist, steht die Schminke für den Corpse. Sobald die Körpertemperatur steigt, schmilzt der Corpse weg. Doch nicht so tot wie gedacht. Ganz zauberhaft lässt sich aber die Schminke wieder aufs Gesicht schmieren: **dead again.**

Es ist ein Spiel mit dem Tod. Das Corpsepaint ist der Schminkkoffer dazu.

Lenatas Cilobaid. „Dark Funeral. Wen der schwarze Tod ereilt ... den lässt er nicht mehr los!" *Deftone Nr. 5 (1998).* S. 26.
Dietmar Dath. „Genug geblutet." *Read Nr. 19 (Mar/Apr 2014).* S. 4-10.
Drew Daniel. „Corpsepaint as Necro-Minstrelsy, or Towards the Re-Occultation of Black Blood." *Melancology: Black Metal Theory and Ecology.* Ed. Scott Wilson. Winchester and Washington: Zero Books, 2014.
Jan G. Grünwald. *Male Spaces. Bildinszenierungen archaischer Männlichkeiten im Black Metal.* Frankfurt: Campus, 2012.
Keith Kahn-Harris. *Extreme Metal. Music and Culture on the Edge.* Oxford: Berg Publishers, 2007.
Hanno Kress. „Ein Prosit auf das Waldsterben. Interview mit Aeternus." *Rock Hard Nr. 124 (1997).* S. 49.
Pascal Stieler. „ISTAPP. Bis zum absoluten Nichts." *Legacy Nr. 97 (2015).* S. 162-163.
Manuel Trummer. *Sympathy for the Devil? Transformationen und Erscheinungsformen der TraditionsfigurTeufel in der Rockmusik.* Münster: Waxmann Verlag, 2011.
Gerhard Wehr. *Europäische Mystik zur Einführung.* Hamburg: Junius, 1995.

Fotografie: Alina Strzempa

Xenharmonic Black Metal: Radical Intervallics as Apophatic Ontotheology

Brooker Buckingham

A cursory listen to "Choir of the Dead," the second track on Blut Aus Nord's 2002 album *The Work Which Transforms God*, and "Mansions Of Fear, Mansions Of Pain," the first track off of Jute Gyte's 2014 release *Ressentiment*, quickly results in aural aporias. The unremitting bleakness of "Choir of the Dead" is draped with murky guitar figures that glide and swoop like winged beasts, uninhibited from the physical limits of the fretboard. "Mansions of Fear" explodes with dense sheets of guitar that shift and lurch through a seemingly impossible dimensionality. The affective reaction to these sui generis soundscapes is marked by discomfort: Blut Aus Nord induces abjection by unleashing a flurry of disorienting guitars that defy standard sonic movement, while Jute Gyte strips the listener of their bearings, committing one to the aural equivalent of sea sickness induced by a hellish gale.

In both cases, it is immediately apparent that Blut Aus Nord and Jute Gyte are avoiding standard black metal guitar tropes— such as the snaking single-note riff, the buzz and drone of reverb-soaked tremolo-picking, the use of minor chords—and have somehow managed to eke out new, evocative sounds from the electric guitar. But how? It turns out both bands chose innovative guitar designs that allowed them to abandon the strictures of the 12-tone Western chromatic scale—fretless guitars in Blut Aus Nord's case, and Jute Gyte uses guitars with microtonal fretboards.

By adopting microtonality—music that uses intervals smaller than those that determine the equal-spacing of semitones with the Western chromatic 12-tone scale—I speculate that Blut Aus Nord and Jute Gyte are attempting to erase the positive ontological stasis represented by the 12-tone scale. In exploring the multitude of notes that exist outside the 12-tone structure (or between

269

the notes), both bands have developed aural structures that gesture towards non-being.

I will interpret microtonal black metal through the theory of the US microtonal composer Ivor Darreg. Darreg was a polymath who read widely in the sciences, particularly electronics, and from the 1930s onwards, he built a wide array of electronic instruments. In the early 1960s, Darreg met Harry Partch, one of the first twentieth-century composers to commit to microtonality, and Erwin Wilson, a Mexican composer who experimented with re-fretting guitars for microtonal purposes. As a result of this encounter, Darreg spent the next thirty years dedicating himself to microtonal composition and instrument building before his death in 1994. In fact, Darreg coined the term "xenharmonics" to describe "music which sounds unlike that composed in the familiar 12-tone equal-tempered scale."[1] Darreg's coinage borrows its suffix from the Greek words ξενία (*xenia* or "hospitable") and ξένος (*xenos*, or "foreign").

In light of this etymology, I will attempt to answer the following question: how do the xenharmonics of Blut Aus Nord and Jute Gyte—those which explore the hospitable foreignness, or the foreign hospitableness of microtonality—relate to Nicola Masciandaro's theorizing on the sorrow of being?

Black metal generally reflects Masciandaro's observation that "modernity views sorrow . . . as its own general condition" and avoids the inverse view, whereby modernity treats sorrow as a "problem to be fixed."[2] By the same token, one can argue that black metal also performs sorrow in a manner similar to Masciandaro's characterization of medieval culture, those who understood sorrow "as a task to be faced, a work of mourning to be taken up, and therefore also a labor under which one could not only collapse, but fail."[3] To varying degrees, the work of black metal indulges in excess—excessive sorrow as a reaction to the operative conditions of modernity; excessive anger at these conditions always folds into excess sorrow—a swallowing by

---

[1] Jonathan Glasier, "Ivor Darreg and Xenharmonics," *Perfect Sound Forever* (October 1997), http://www.furious.com/perfect/xenharmonics.html (accessed 17-04-15).
[2] Nicola Masciandaro, "The Sorrow of Being," *Qui Parle: Critical Humanities and Social Sciences* 19, no. 1 (2010): 10.
[3] Ibid.

sorrow in reaction to the way things are. This working is driven by the desire to negate these conditions, to produce their opposites— the towering forest in place of the towering urban center, the continuity of death in place of the discontinuity of life, the old Gods or the anti-God in place of the God we all know to be dead. This work of negation has the potential to rebound into the positive, for example, the Transcendental Black Metal of Hunter-Hunt Hendrix, yet by and large, black metal tends to labor the negative. My interest here is in the moments where, after being is swallowed by sorrow, black metal retains fidelity to sorrow—a sorrow of being. Think Craft's "Fuck the Universe"[4] or Watain's 2007 tour under the banner of "Fuck the World." The difficulty with giving form to sorrow lies for Masciandaro in the impossibility of measuring "sorrow's proper bounds," which "only points back to the fact that sorrow is all about the unquantifiable, that it concerns a dimension of experience that is fundamentally incommensurable with representation and expression."[5]

In this case, the negative is double: first, sorrow as the reaction to conditions, and second, sorrow as expression, as a desire to go beyond the horizon of conditions. I propose a metaphysics to deal with this duality. Edmund Husserl's phenomenology provides the concept of the *Lebenswelt*, or "life-world," as a means to understand the individual's engagement with exteriority, the self-evident or given. The life-world essentially acts as the foundation for epistemology, the pre-condition for phenomenological analysis.[6] Opposed to the life-world, I would like to propose the *Klingenwelt*, or "sound-world." The work of Austrian social scientist and social phenomenologist Alfred Schütz provides a bridge to this concept. In his 1944 essay "Fragments on the Phenomenology of Music," Schütz argues that "music is a meaningful context without reference to a conceptual scheme, and, strictly speaking, without immediate reference to the objects of the world in which we live."[7] Independent from musical

---

[4] Craft, "Fuck The Universe," *Fuck The Universe* (Southern Lord, 2005).
[5] Ibid., 11.
[6] Edmund Husserl, *The Crisis of European Sciences and Transcendental Phenomenology* (Evanston: Northwestern University Press, 1970), 108–9.
[7] Alfred Schütz, "Fragments on the phenomenology of music," *Music and Man* 2, no. 1–2 (1976): 24.

notation, music does not have a representative function nor a semantic character. Therefore, Schütz argues, "a phenomenological approach to music may safely disregard the physical qualities of the sound as well as the rationalization of these sounds which leads to the musical scale."[8] Focus on the experiential leads Schütz to describe the "peculiar attitude" of the music listener—the moment where music removes the listener from the dimension of space and spatial time—and raises them to a plane of consciousness, the sound-world where one surrenders to the flux of music, "a flux which is that of their stream of consciousness in inner time."[9]

Even though music is bound to inner temporality, Schütz noted that mediation occurs between musical themes and the listener's attention and interest. Exploring his primary interest in social phenomenology, Schütz was intrigued by the idea that music is capable of establishing "a non-linguistic, non-conceptual 'mutual tuning in relationship'" between individuals within an intersubjective space, independent of other forms of communication.[10] This led Schütz to speculate that "without self-consciously philosophizing, Mozart conveyed in music and better than most philosophers in their own medium, how human beings meet each other as a 'We.'"[11]

With this relation in mind—the relation between the conveyance of the "We" by the musician and the "peculiar attitude" of the listener—I would like to explore the role xenharmonics play. What sort of "We" intentionality is constituted by Blut Aus Nord and Jute Gyte's microtonal approach? And through the "peculiar attitude" of the black metal listener, what does microtonality evoke in the sound-world, or the psycho-affective dimension that maps onto Schütz's stream of consciousness of inner time? Jute Gyte, the one-man project of Adam Kalmbach, claims his music explores what H. P. Lovecraft called "the conflict with time." "Related to this," Kalmbach continues, "is a concern with identity and change and with the

---

8 Ibid., 26.
9 Ibid., 43.
10 Michael Barber, "Alfred Schütz," *Stanford Encyclopedia of Philosophy*, http://plato.stanford.edu/entries/schutz/ (accessed 18-04-15).
11 Ibid.

difficulties of recognising and understanding oneself."[12] In an interview with *Terrorizer* magazine, a Blut Aus Nord band member said that *The Work Which Transforms God*, a largely instrumental affair, was meant to challenge the listener's prejudices and preconceptions about reality and various metaphysical subjects.[13]

This brings us back to Ivor Darreg. In an article entitled "New Moods," published in his *Xenharmonic Bulletin* in 1975, Darreg notes that all of the xenharmonic tuning systems he has experimented with feature "striking and characteristic moods," a discovery which acts as a "powerful and compelling reason for exploring beyond 12-tone temperament."[14] He says these differences are subtle, yet astonishing, and in opposition to the heavily theoretical literature on microtonal scales, he calls for the "co-operation of many persons" to join together and "map out the vastness of xenharmonic territory,"[15] to catalogue the emotional and aesthetic qualities imparted by each tuning.

With regards to mood, I contend that xenharmonic black metal produces the "perfect sorrow"[16] by rupturing the 12-tone scale which has historically conditioned the Western sound-world. The gesture towards microtonality in Western music begins in the late nineteenth century, concurrent with the astonishing growth of capital in the form of the second Industrial Revolution. Many scholars cite German physicist and physician Hermann Helmholtz's 1863 text *On the Sensations of Tone*, in which he proposed a series of exotic just-intonation tunings and non-harmonic tunings, as a catalyst in the early explorations beyond the 12-tone scale. Alexander John Ellis, a British mathematician and philologist, often recognized as a key influence on the discipline of musiciology, translated Sensations into English in 1883 and produced a comparative report for the

---

[12] Jonathan Keane, "Jute Gyte Interview," *The Grind That Annoys* (March 27, 2014), http://thegrindthatannoys.com/2014/03/27/jute-gyte-interview/ (accessed 18-04-15).

[13] *Wikipedia*, s.v. "Blut Aus Nord," http://en.wikipedia.org/wiki/Blut_Aus_Nord (accessed 18-04-15).

[14] Jonathan Glasier, "Xenharmonics and Ivor Darreg."

[15] Ibid.

[16] Masciandaro, "Sorrow of Being," 19, 23. Cf. *The Cloud of Unknowing*, ed. James Walsh, S.J. (Mahwah: Paulist Press, 1981), 203.

Royal Society in which he demonstrated how the tunings used by non-Western cultures did not adhere to equal temperament. Some claim that Claude Debussy's innovative work in the 1890s was influenced by exposure to a Balinese gamelan performance—noted for its use of a whole-tone scale that divides the octave into six equal pitches—at the Exposition Universelle in 1889, while others argue his subsequent piano pieces display a microtonality that betrays the influence of Helmholtz's writings.[17]

During the second half of the twentieth century, when Darreg and his aforementioned contemporary Harry Partch were active, experimental electronic composers like Karlheinz Stockhausen and Wendy Carlos were applying microtonality to key works. And more recently, microtonal moves have been made by the likes of Aphex Twin and Radiohead on the track "How To Disappear Completely" off of their 2000 release "Kid A." This brief history is largely designed to show how little Western ears are exposed to microtonality. Given that twentieth-century classical music—with its formal adherence to the 12-tone scale, and its abandonment of harmonic and melodic rules in the form of atonality, serialism and post-tonality—is still met with incredulity by the vast majority of music listeners, then it is perfectly understandable why systematic microtonal composition is relegated to obscurity, the domain of an occulted group of musicians and enthusiasts.

So why are we seeing xenharmonic black metal in the twenty-first century? The constraints of the 12-tone chromatic scale have most certainly made themselves apparent. Avant-garde strains of black metal have pushed the limits of atonality—Deathspell Omega and Dodecahedron come to mind—at the same time that other sub-genres are flirting with 80s gothic pop and 90s shoegaze. The gamut has been run, so to speak. Given black metal's push into increasingly strange, heterodox territory—a history that is remarkably well documented on San Francisco's Aquarius Records website[18]—it seems it was only a matter of time before black metal discovered microtonality. While black metal has been successful at mining the bleak, abyssal and the

---

[17] *Wikipedia*, s.v. "Microtonal Music," http://en.wikipedia.org/wiki/Microtonal_music (accessed 19-04-15).

[18] Aquarius Records Staff, "[metal (black metal)] titles at Aquarius Records," https://www.aquariusrecords.org/cat/metalblackmetal.html (accessed 19-04-15).

melancholic over the past three decades, it has done so under one of the conditions it should ideally set out to undermine.

In the words of Masciandaro, "black metal vibrationally unhinges the order of things," and "annihilates every binding of the chain of being."[19] Black metal is an amusic, says Scott Wilson, an organization of sound that places "oneself at the very limit of oneself where one is dissolved to NOTHING."[20] Black metal infects the sound-world with a "portal of sorrow,"[21] an invitation to "Walk the Path of Sorrow" on which we abandon ourselves to the "turn of search."[22] In black metal, sorrow is a laboring that seeks beyond the given. Xenharmonics points to the essence via the definition of sorrow that Masciandaro desires, the one found, "not in a void, but in a cloud. Nor is a cloud not a void of its own. Or that is exactly what a cloud is, a void of one's own."[23] "The void is that which one can never get into"—the Heraclitean flux of the *Lebenswelt*, or the double cage—the Weberian Iron Cage of capitalism[24] and the flesh-and-bone cage that physicalizes our discontinuity, leaving us with "the sense that things never really touch."[25] This is but one register—the banal "manifest image" of the world as it is given to the senses. However, it is countered by a horrifying "scientific image"—quantum physics and its tales of horror about the emptiness of matter—all the empty tables and chairs, how the physical matter that comprises the entirety of the human race fits into a chunk the size of a sugar cube, not to mention "the Argument" in Scott Bakker's *Neuropath*,[26] and the

---

[19] Nicola Masciandaro, "Introduction," in *Hideous Gnosis: Black Metal Theory Symposium 1*, ed. Nicola Masciandaro (New York: n.p., 2010), 1.

[20] Scott Wilson, "BAsileus philosoPHOorum METaloricum," in Ibid., 41.

[21] Xasthur, "Portal of Sorrow," *Portal of Sorrow* (Disharmonic Variations, 2010).

[22] Satyricon, "Walk the Path of Sorrow," *Dark Medieval Times* (Moonfog Productions, 1994).

[23] Masciandaro, "Sorrow of Being," 18.

[24] Max Weber, *The Protestant Ethic and the Spirit of Capitalism*, trans. Talcott Parsons (London: Routledge, 2002), 123.

[25] Masciandaro, "Sorrow of Being," 18.

[26] Scott Bakker, *Neuropath* (Toronto: Penguin Group, 2008). Cf. Steven Shaviro "Neuropath" http://www.shaviro.com/Blog/?p=698 (accessed 9-06-2015). "The Argument in Neuropath goes something like this. Consciousness is severely limited. It is a very recent evolutionary adaptation, superimposed upon a wide array of older neural processes of

harsh realities of neuroscience and philosophy telling us that we are all *Being No One*.[27] Black metal demands we see this "void is merely another kind of cloud, maybe even an especially dangerous kind, because it demands fidelity as an absolute term of unreality, poses as not a cloud, with nothing to hide, being nothing."[28]

The entry of xenharmonics into the black metal sound-world is the sonic attempt to push to the extreme limits of perfect sorrow. It is apophatic in that it negates the thoroughly calcified being of music and reveals the concealed and the foreign—the amusic—that which music is not. It is ontotheological in a post-Heideggerian sense. By identifying the problematic collapse of theology and metaphysics in the history of Western thought, Heidegger recognized that philosophy and theology are occluded by a mastery that presumes knowledge of philosophy's first causes as well as knowledge of God. Philosophy hemmed in by faith, and theology corrupted by ontology, which reduces us to the mere order of beings.[29] Xenharmonics is a destruktion of ontotheology

---

which it is unaware, and which it cannot possibly grasp. We are only conscious of a very thin sliver of the external world; and even less of our internal, mental world. Most of our 'experience' of the inner and outer world is a neurally-based simulation that has been evolutionarily selected for its survival value, but the actual representational accuracy of which is highly dubious. We are not conscious, and we cannot be conscious, of the actual neural processes that drive us. And indeed, nearly all our explanations and understandings of other people, of the world in which we live, and above all of ourselves are delusional, self-aggrandizing fictions. It's not just that we misunderstand our own motivations; but that such things as 'motivations' and 'reasons' for how we feel and what we do actually don't exist at all. Everything that we say, think, feel, perceive, and do is really just a consequence of deterministic physical (electro-chemical) processes in our neurons. . . . In particular, 'free will' is an illusion. We never actually decide on any of our actions; rather, our sense of choice and decision, and the reasons and motivations that we cite for what we do, are all post-hoc rationalizations of processes that happen mechanistically, through chains of electrochemical cause-and-effect. All our rationales, and all our values, are nothing more than consolatory fictions."

27 Thomas Metzinger, *Being No One: The Self-Model Theory of Subjectivity* (Cambridge, MA: MIT Press, 2004).

28 Masciandaro, "Sorrow of Being," 20.

29 Iain Thomson, "Ontotheology? Understanding Heidegger's Destruktion of Metaphysics," *International Philosophical Studies* 8, no.

through clouds of forgetting and clouds of unknowing. Xenharmonics compels one to recognize that existence is *neither a being or nothing*. Furthermore, it tears us from the lazy question, "Why something rather than nothing?" and forces us to try the real question, the stupid question, "Why am I me?"[30] Xenharmonics destroys the shell of ontotheology to liberate the kernel of mysticism, which dwells "in the sheer actuality that is outside and between being and nothing, above God and inside the creature, beyond the manifest real and with the individual."[31]

Xenharmonics is foreign in that it causes one to recoil, pained by the queer, broken geometries drawn by the notes from the outside and the in-between. Xenharmonics plays out as a kind of musical *différance*, where notes differ and defer, constantly slipping from being to non-being. This produces both sorrow and the stupid question. The xenharmonic is the hospitable sound-world cloud that manifests in the inhospitable void. This cloud contains the "philosophy hidden in sound."[32] Fidelity to this philosophy—contained in the slippage between sound's rigid conditioned being and its evasive non-being—infuses one with the desire to forget and unknow, to, as Masciandaro puts it, step into the perfect sorrow that "offers the prospect, at once simple and impossible, of a non-dualistic real experience in which the distinction between subject and object is undone, where something like the place of the original identity of I and me, the

---

3 (2000): 297–327. See also Martin Heidegger, "The Onto-Theological Constitution of Metaphysics," *Identity and Difference*, trans. Joan Stambaugh (Chicago: University of Chicago Press, 2002), 42–74.

[30] Nicola Masciandaro, "Absolute Secrecy: On the Infinity of Individuation," forthcoming in *Speculation, Heresy, and Gnosis in Contemporary Philosophy of Religion: The Enigmatic Absolute*, eds. Joshua Ramey and Matthew Harr Farris.

[31] Ibid.

[32] As opposed to the "philosophy hidden in words." See Gregory of Nyssa, "Notations on the Commentary on the Song of Songs by Gregory of Nyssa," 3.4., available from *Lectio Divina*, http://www.lectio-divina.org/index.cfm (accessed 10-04-15). Cf. Edia Connole, "Seven Propositions On The Secret Kissing Of Black Metal: OSKVLVM," in this volume.

one who sorrows and the one who is sorrowed over, is found and found to be the place of God."[33]

I turn to Masciandaro's paper "The Floating Tomb of Black Metal Theory" to invoke the "'esoteric floating tomb' wherein inner spiritual movement is blackly fused with the force of the cosmos itself as a space of mystical death and flight."[34] He goes on to say, "the floating tomb figures the space of mystical death . . . that is found in the extremity of perfect, self-annihilating sorrow."[35] The floating tomb is the entire universe, both womb and grave, and we are all floating tombs. This *all* recognizes the "inversive mystical potentiality of black metal's satanic stance,"[36] an inversion that forsakes "ascension and mining a path towards the centre of the earth, black metal finds a satanic stain lodged at the core of being."[37] I will close by saying xenharmonics manifests within black metal as love, a love of unknowing, and as mystical death, as self-annihilation through the striving for infinite individuation. Xenharmonic black metal is a sorrowing, a mutual tuning-in, a work of contemplation that limns the living intersection of sound and being, and this intersection is "'where God-as-Other passes away,' yet I remain, as does He, different but the same, the same in difference, absolute analogy."[38] Xenharmonics is a work which transforms God.

---

33 Masciandaro, "Sorrow of Being," 24.
34 Nicola Masciandaro, "The Floating Tomb of Black Metal Theory," unpublished paper. See Masciandaro's contribution to this volume and the longer version in Edia Connole and Nicola Masciandaro, *Floating Tomb: Black Metal Theory* (Milan: Mimesis, 2015).
35 Ibid., 1.
36 Ibid., 8.
37 Steven Shakespeare and Niall Scott, "The Swarming Logic of Inversion and the Elevation of Satan," in "With Head Downwards: Inversions in Black Metal," eds. Steven Shakespeare and Niall Scott, special issue, *Helvete: A Journal of Black Metal Theory* 2 (2015): 2.
38 Connole, "OSKVLVM," in this volume.

The Perichoresis of Music, Art and Philosophy

Hunter Hunt-Hendrix

Today I was planning on giving a lecture about a vision for a new kind of total work of art, called the Ark Work, whose functioning, called the Perichoresis, maps music, art and philosophy onto three moments of dialectical becoming. Synthesizing practices and concepts from different domains and traditions, the Perichoresis is an art/life process—a vehicle for living in and transmitting faith, hope and love during an era when it is difficult to believe in structures that have historically activated this type of transcendence. For reasons which I'll explain, I've elected not to give that lecture today. Instead, I want to talk about a text I wrote six years ago called "Transcendental Black Metal."

At the first Black Metal Theory symposium, which took place at Public Assembly in Brooklyn during the winter of 2009, I presented this text as a lecture to a small audience of academics, artists and a few friends. I was twenty four. My band, Liturgy, had just released our debut LP. Since that time, we have had an extremely unusual career: though our audience is broader than that of most metal bands, we are famous, in part, for being uniquely hated in the black metal scene; there is virtually no account of our band written anywhere that does not begin by noting the controversy surrounding the lecture I gave in 2009. Thousands of comments threads and message boards overflow with text criticizing me in the most hateful terms. My lecture has become a legend, or at least a meme, a media phenomenon that can in some ways be usefully compared to that surrounding Varg Vikernes and the burning of Fantoft Stave Church in 1992.

Perhaps it goes without saying that this shaming and ridicule has been very painful to me, and that I feel profoundly misunderstood. I am tethered to an imaginary personality, with whom I cannot identify, an obnoxious, mean-spirited controversy baiter who lives in the minds of many music fans and journalists, and whose mission is to annoy them. The irony is that both my musical vision and my broader ideas and actions are completely sincere: I see this project as an instance of what Alain Badiou calls a "truth procedure"—an inspired, courageous process of suffering and faith in the name of universal love, tied to a local becoming. I have wanted nothing more than to communicate and activate love, and yet for the most part I seem to have only brought scorn and hatred into the world.

This disconnect between my intentions and the reaction I have received has led to me to doubt myself. And so I'd like to take this opportunity to give some background on the 2009 lecture, and to sincerely ask whether the act of delivering it was a legitimate or whether it was a mistake.

The vision of Transcendental Black Metal appeared to me several years before the symposium, in around 2005. At the time, I was a philosophy student playing in a few rock bands that rehearsed in Brooklyn and, almost in secret, recording depressive black metal cassettes for myself in my dorm room. Though I was shy, I had a very wide and eclectic range of interests: various types of art rock, hardcore, metal, electronic music and so on, Christianity, psychoanalysis and continental philosophy—especially the work of Nietzsche, Lacan, and Deleuze—and various eras of classical music—Wagnerian post-romanticism, French avant-garde spectralism, and especially American minimalism. I also had a budding interest in conceptual art, especially the work of Joseph Beuys. I felt myself to be on the verge of weaving all these threads into a performance/music/art/religion practice that would have redemptive power and epic scope.

It is worth noting that at the time I was in constant pain, suffering huge levels of anxiety and paranoia, struggling against suicide. This pain in part had to do with a multigenerational tragedy unique to my family and personal life. But surely it also had to do with something more universal: the primordial wound, the out-of-joint character of human life—and in particular the contemporary *horror vacui* experienced by those of us who are unable to integrate into a community with a collective spiritual practice— the bondage of isolation, self-obsession and disconnection. The severity of this pain and confusion must be underscored, because it was in the name of transcending it that Liturgy was born. I yearned to create, as a dynamic work of art, a structure for overcoming the self-destructive forces that afflicted me—to synthesize a soul for myself, an aesthetic, symbolic system that I could use to overcome my state of bitterness, and transmit, manifest, and live in faith: unable to accept the religions that would provide the spiritual practice I so desperately needed, living in a society for which profound truth is disqualified and relativized by the leveling gaze of multiculturalism and political correctness, I would create my own structure, dangerous, subjectively invested, uplifting.

Around the age of twenty, something clicked—in an epiphany, I realized that a reinterpretation of black metal could be the bedrock of this effort: using the principle that what appears as the greatest source of affliction is precisely the best springboard into grace, I thought that I could re-appropriate the music and mythologies of black metal, the soundtrack to my despair, to be a source of transcendence, by using a particular element in a way its authors never intended, so as to create a short circuit. Out of the cauldron of my pain, and my obsessions with philosophy, music, and art, a vision emerged. It didn't happen all at once: first appeared the idea of a new kind of drum beat called the "burst beat"—an ecstatic mutant variation of the blast beat. Soon after came the term "Pure Transcendental Black Metal," which was a variation on Darkthrone's famous slogan, "True Norwegian Black Metal." I hardly knew what it meant, but I knew it referred to an ethics of creation, resounding with American Transcendentalism or perhaps Deleuze's "Transcendental Empiricism." I typed the slogan on top of an image of clouds from the Internet, and it became the back cover of my first EP, called *Immortal Life*.

In the next few years I began playing shows, first solo and then with a band; I yearned to complement the music with a symbolic declaration, something in the vein of Bataille's "The Pineal Eye," or Artaud's "The Theater of Cruelty"—a cryptic, ecstatic vision of an eschatological limit. When I met Nicola Masciandaro at a Liturgy show, he told me about the symposium he was organizing, and I saw that I had a chance to do this. I composed the text itself mostly during November of 2009—it was the most inspired and excruciating process I've engaged in in my life to date; I felt possessed.

The presentation of the lecture was a fairly low-key moment; the symposium itself was a groundbreaking event, but credit for that goes to the person who organized it; though I was the only participant who was in a band and had not gone to grad school, I think I more or less blended in. But soon enough news of the lecture and the corresponding text spread on the internet and became a phenomenon: a bona fide scandal in the black metal community, which was in turn a source of fascination for journalists from the wider world. I did not expect the reaction to be so large nor for it to be so negative.

The easiest way to explain the phenomenon is as a miscommunication, in part due to the existence of the internet. The music was never directed at a particular audience. I didn't have any real connection to a metal scene. I lived my life as a "hipster in Brooklyn," but the audience that picked up on Liturgy's music was, for the most part, the actual black metal underground itself. I wasn't really explaining myself, and much of the implicit subtleties of my act and music weren't communicated. I became a target for a more or less indiscriminate hatred. An idiot from New York talking about making good, happy black metal instead of bad, sad black metal, a symbol of the style being coopted and going "mainstream."

But that answer is not adequate, and it ignores an important and well-known fact about human culture: the classic, even archetypal story of the reformer, the prophet who shines his light into the depths of truth and whose surrounding community reacts violently, attempting to destroy him. The hero's journey, the rose cross—whatever name you want to give to the pursuit of embodied subjectivity: the suspension of both morality and pleasure in the name of a cultural unfolding of some kind, suffering in the name of truth. According to the story, a new idea or form appears, is at first misunderstood and creates scandal, but ultimately marks the birth of a new movement.

Surely the story of Liturgy can be described in these terms to a degree. In 2009, Liturgy was unprecedented, groundbreaking. I was incorporating black metal into a sonic and cultural palette that was foreign to it: the sound world and attitude of no wave, post-minimalism and shoegaze; Sonic youth, Glenn Branca, Swans, and the more contemporary bands they influenced—Arab on Radar, Ex Models, Orthrelm. This, and not the black metal scene, was my world, where I really identified, and my incorporation of black metal was simply a new stylistic combination waiting to happen. People were mad at first and couldn't understand it, but by now, in 2015, this aesthetic move no longer seems so strange. Though our new record is a different story, our older records are now accepted into the canon and recognized for what they are.

For the music, explaining the criticism in these terms is straightforward, but for the lecture and text themselves, the story is more complicated. True, to a degree this aspect of Liturgy can be seen through the lens of originality: I was returning to the Romanticism invoked by so much black metal, but instead of invoking Wagner, for example, in the service of a vague racism, nationalism and anti-Christian primitivism— making use of my education to trace his influence through the well-known constellation in continental philosophy through which it has filtered, marked by the names Nietzsche, Heidegger, Bataille, Deleuze and Badiou—putting it in the service of a legitimate politics of love. I was not attempting to illustrate or allegorize any particular philosophical position, though my conceptual framework was influenced by Nietzsche's theory of active and reactive force and Lacan's opposition of desire and drive. The act of delivering it was meant to be ethical—in Zizek's sense of the term: the instauration of a master signifier that has performative effect; illegal, changing the terms of the debate, the master's lightening flash, impossible to erase, perhaps unlocking new modes of power, initiating a fragile, meaningful quest, a body of Christ with no claim to legitimacy other than the faith that sustains it. My name for the work of love that would follow in the wake of this act is The Ark Work: carried out at shows, in interviews, on the internet; an opera that takes place in real time, a drama whose narrative, rather than being scripted and playing out on a stage, is the career of a band as it interacts with audiences, the music industry, the internet, etc., across a series of albums. The idea was to engage in a genuinely Wagnerian project, but to use contemporary philosophies and musical forms (the ethics of the real and black metal instead of Schopenhauer and Beethoven). This artistic, conceptual and prophetic aspect of Liturgy has not garnered the same retroactive legitimation as the musical aspect. Although a small group of people who understand it do recognize its value, many music fans who love to listen to Liturgy nevertheless don't appreciate the ideas—and accuse me of pretension and so on—are altogether unwilling to swallow this aspect of the project. What to make of that fact? Does it mean that, perhaps, the music is legitimate, since criticism of it has died down, but that the text really deserves scorn, since the scorn keeps coming? That it would be better if I just kept my mouth shut, so fans could have a more palatable experience overall?

In a short text called "The Difference Between the Genius and the Apostle," Kierkegaard distinguishes between two types of paradox that appear in human culture: temporal and eternal. The genius is attracted to a temporal paradox—though his current culture cannot accept his art, the clash is only temporary. Future generations will recognize and celebrate it for being "ahead of its time." For example, impressionism was a scandal at first, but soon enough it became an established style, even a cliché. But the apostle is attracted to a different kind of paradox—an eternal one, inherently paradoxical: a divine truth that culture will never be able to accept—the commandment to love your enemy, for example. The only reward for hanging onto a truth of this type is martyrdom—it can never adequately filter into society, so long as society as we know it still exists. While Liturgy's music is attached to the first type of paradox, the temporal kind, it may be that the Transcendental Black Metal manifesto is attached to the second, eternal type of paradox: a paradox that will never go away, but which, nevertheless, touches on something of ultimate concern. Maybe I'll never be retroactively vindicated for the lecture, and if so perhaps it's a sign that I "shouldn't have" delivered it, but perhaps on the contrary it means the truth in question is divine. Or maybe it exists in the realm where the sacred and the profane are one and the same.

I don't know whether Kierkegaard's distinction is valid, nor, if it is, whether it applies to Liturgy. But in any case, I feel I must take ownership of some major failures and flaws in execution. The same sense of isolation, self-obsession and grandiosity that I have always been working to overcome has many times reared its head. I was very awkward with unscripted verbal interviews; I have seen some that make me cringe just as much as the people who write invective in comments threads; I am genuinely ashamed of these— they were mistakes. There were also issues with my band mates. Even though the musical vision and composition was all my own, more so in fact than most people realize, the other members contributed their energy to the project, breathing power and life into it that I could not have on my own—something for which I have probably not been grateful enough. And in addition, perhaps the form of the manifesto was a little too cryptic, somewhat inchoate, a little too reverent towards the excesses of continental thought: it does in some ways needlessly resemble a translation of an untranslatable text from French or German.

To recap: the creation of this strange scapegoat character, the pretentious, ridiculous Hunter Hunt-Hendrix who swarms around the internet as a meme can be explained in part as an unfortunate yet interesting misunderstanding; in part it can be explained as the type of scandal that is ultimately testament to a legitimate originality or even access to a truth that goes beyond legitimation; it can also be explained in part by my own hypocrisy—at some level I perhaps deserve it.

But beyond all these explanation there is still a mystery, a surplus: I cannot quite explain exhaustively the reason for the intensity of the scorn. The reasons I give don't all add up. By the same token though, I can't quite explain exhaustively my motivation for initiating this work of love in the first place. Surely that is because there is a process underway, a becoming that I do not understand. I'd like to think a punctuation mark, unforeseen, will land somewhere in the future, giving it a meaning that I cannot see yet. This is why I felt I couldn't go on and deliver another abstract, oracular and mysterious text today. That would be a failure to engage authentically with the reaction. I want to sincerely engage and adapt, to take the pain and disappointment I have experienced as yet more material for purification, to own the stain inherent to my vision, and, perhaps, by mourning its existence, to arrive at a new subjective position—a new perspective that I wasn't capable of adopting when I set out to carry out this project. Thus I thought that the best way to use the invitation to speak at this symposium, six years later, would be to make use of the shame I have experienced and to offer my vulnerability and sincerity with complete transparency and directness. While affirming the pain, I intend to remain sincerely engaged in the Ark Work. The legitimacy of a truth procedure is always impossible to verify—the key is to neither give up nor be dogmatic. At this point I don't think I need the name Transcendental Black Metal—it is perhaps confusing. This project is probably better understood musically and conceptually on its own terms, without reference to black metal. But I think that my continued pursuit is in line with the terms that I laid out in my text: it is a dynamic struggle against the Hyperborean; an exercise of courage, openness and honesty. This is, in fact, what I mean by the Perichoresis of music, art and philosophy, put into plain language. A music that aims sonically at transcendence, a philosophical effort to piece together a materialist ethics of faith, and an ever-renewed adaptive activity, whose legitimacy is inherently impossible to establish, of suffering in the name of love.

APPENDIX: SELECTED DIAGRAMS FROM THE ORIGINAL UNFINISHED TEXT, "PERICHORESIS OF MUSIC, ART AND PHILOSOPHY"

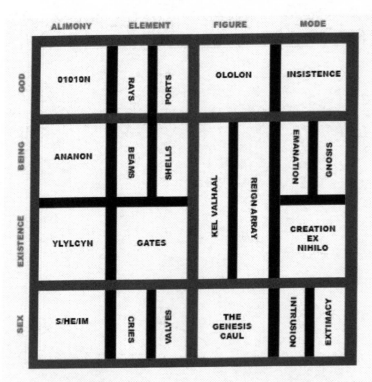

TRANSCENDENTAL QABALA

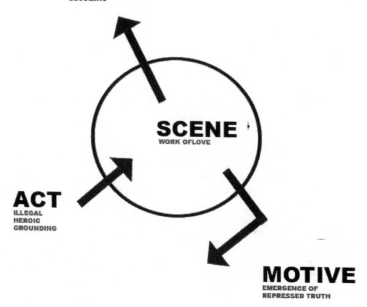

THE THREE AXES OF ARK WORK

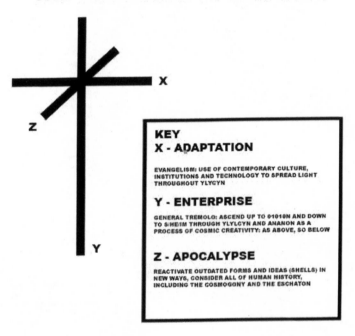

KEY

X - ADAPTATION

EVANGELISM: USE OF CONTEMPORARY CULTURE,
INSTITUTIONS AND TECHNOLOGY TO SPREAD LIGHT
THROUGHOUT YLYCYN

Y - ENTERPRISE

GENERAL TREMOLO: ASCEND UP TO 01010N AND DOWN
TO S/HE/IM THROUGH YLYLCYN AND ANANON AS A
PROCESS OF COSMIC CREATIVITY: AS ABOVE, SO BELOW

Z - APOCALYPSE

REACTIVATE OUTDATED FORMS AND IDEAS (SHELLS) IN
NEW WAYS, CONSIDER ALL OF HUMAN HISTORY,
INCLUDING THE COSMOGONY AND THE ESCHATON

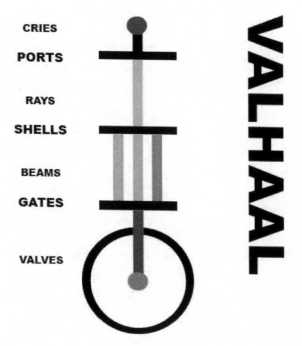

CRIES

PORTS

RAYS

SHELLS

BEAMS

GATES

VALVES

VALHAAL

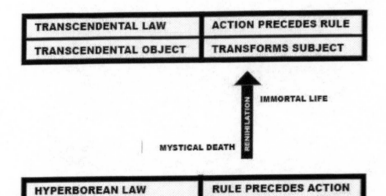

On Darkness Itself
(An obscure letter of divorce to Immanuel Kant, permitting all to be betrothed to the darkness)

Niall Scott, Sin Eater[1]

PRAYER: May these things fail you and these meditations TURN TO DARKNESS and lead you to be grounded in the void.

The deep roots I used to see lodged in the soil, moving up and out—now I see them growing downward beyond the loam reaching into the dark. A grounding, a *grundlegung* in Darkness

---

[1] All images taken by the author in Greenport Long Island, April 2015, and in Eastern Finland, August 2014.

itself. "In the days of my youth,"[2] from the year I was born, I was led into an object-oriented world obsessed with light, clarity, and matter: "Oh how the pale beauty spoils! / Show me a nothingness / wherein lies the essence of our existence."[3] Where I had lost my red nose and large feet, I now reclaim then, only to wear them entirely on the inside, red nose inside my nose and long shoes inside my feet. Black metal is the highest form of buffoonery, from where I take my lead, the darkest lampooning of those who try to void their vermicular shit above their cloacal opening.

Immanuel Kant you are well known for your insistence on the presence of the thing in itself—*das Ding an sich*. I have been seduced by its corpulent presence. You assert that knowledge of things in themselves is impossible, but that objects can only be known as objects of sensible intuition—or as appearances. Furthermore, you assert in the "Introduction" to your second edition (attempt?) of the *Critique of Pure Reason* "that all

[2] Led Zeppelin, "Good Times Bad Times," *Led Zeppelin I* (Atlantic Records, 1969).
[3] Sanctus Nex, "Genesis Reversion," *Aurelia* (Nocturene Studios, 2006).

speculative knowledge of reason is limited to mere objects of experience."[4] However, you go on to claim that although it is not possible to know things in themselves we can, nevertheless, think them as things in themselves. This, you maintain, has to be the case to avoid the absurdity of there being appearances "without anything that appears."[5] However, in a footnote, Kant, you narrow the scope of what you consider can be thought—first insisting, with regard to knowing the possibility of objects, that "I can think whatever I please," but then you say, only "provided I do not contradict myself . . . providing my concept is a possible thought."[6] Then you further insist this is the case even where there is no object corresponding to the concept that can be thought. (I had often accepted this reasoning—as it applied well to concepts in their relation to objects.) You are interested for a short while in the "impossible," to which you relate the concept "nothing," which you define as a concept without an object—and then maintain reality is something and negation is nothing. Well, Immanuel, "Paint me as a dead soul . . . / The flesh, the image, the reflection / Let's complete the illusion."[7] You distinguish between nothing as the thought entity, from the non-entity that cannot be thought, and follow with the claim that negation without something real is not an object. I assert, then, that neither is it a not-object; rather, the error is in assimilating negation and nothing.

---

[4] Immanuel Kant, *Critique of Pure Reason*, trans. Norman Kemp Smith (New York: Palgrave Macmillan, 2003), 27.
[5] Ibid.
[6] Ibid.
[7] Behemoth, "Transmigrating Beyond the Realms of Amenti," *Evangellion* (Metal Blade Records, 2009).

Both the concept of darkness and Darkness itself throw this not only into doubt, but place it elsewhere, becoming a once known neighbour, still present but no longer in conversation. Your schemata outlines four modes of negation, aiming to illustrate how these can function and also fail us as qualities. You even place negation as a quality in the table of categories. You maintain there

296

exists a transition from reality to its cessation or nothingness, but then insist that there is a connection between reality and negation.[8] But negation—the negative and nothingness—are not the same thing as to even begin to allow such a relation. You simply want to force the steadfast maintenance of things in experience as points of reference for concepts and ideas. But what of darkness, the possibility of Darkness itself? What of darkness as a dis-quality of negation? Is this not a thought I can think without contradiction and without reference to appearances?

You have a puritanical obsession with things, and with light: "If light were not given to the senses then one would not be able to represent darkness."[9] The idea being that darkness cannot be brought under a concept in its own right, but instead has to be parasitic on light. But Immanuel, darkness is prior to light! Neither is darkness an object nor is negation an object. You, however, maintain that "Negations are only determinations which assert the non-existence of something in substance."[10] You then assert that negations, as evil, alone conflict with reality, but only insofar as these concern things in general, but not regarding things as appearances.[11] Where your aim is clarification and elucidation, now you deliver only obscurity, so perhaps this is dark work indeed. Although the introduction of evil makes these ideas titillating to a pious analytician, it is nothing other than an evangelical distraction. Don't think for one minute that this does not diminish it in the face of your object obsessions—object fascism—you reification whores who are seduced by *das Ding an sich*: "Penetre la Nuit!"[12] By penetrating the darkness, I can link your reason not to things, but to absences!

You carefully, analytically outline:

Privation: *nihil privativium* / Empty object of a concept

---

[8] Kant, *Critique*, 184.
[9] Ibid.
[10] Ibid., 216.
[11] Ibid., 284.
[12] Celestia, *Apparitia—Sumptous Spectre* (Paragon records, 2007), CD artwork text.

Negative: *nihil negativium* / Empty object without a concept[13]

Darkness itself, then, for you—deceased Prussian—cannot be represented without light being sensed: you treat darkness not just as an absence of light, but as a negation of light. As if we are eternally to be slaves *to the light*, slaves *to the object, to the thing*. But again, absences and negations are not the same, only insofar as—like darkness—absence is a dis-quality of negation. Opening up in rage, against this obsession with object-oriented positive affirmation and the dis-quality of approaching Darkness itself, "the Black Metal Scream [is] a panic not in front of death but in front of the suffocating compactness and denseness of the real that still bears in its vitriolic shadow the premonition of the irreversibility of death."[14]

You, Kant, successor to Plato and Aristotle, see darkness in its oppositional form as negative, and hence link it to that which is not a thing. But how could you see such a phenomenon? The aim of black metal theory is to invoke darkness itself through a blinding of humanity to allow for a senseless sightless seeing, a loss of perspective.[15] You cannot see into the woods, cannot see where it is that you want to go, yet you are addicted to pursuing the light at the end of the tracks.

---

[13] Kant, *Critique*, 382–1.

[14] Francise Norbert Örmény, "The Killing Real and the Sublime Aura in the Music of Burzum," *Darkening Scandinavia: Four Postmodern Pagan Essays* (Newcastle Upon Tyne: Cambridge Scholars Publishing, 2013), 22.

[15] Cf. Niall Scott, "Blackening the Green," in *Melancology: Black Metal and Ecology*, ed. Scott Wilson (Winchester and Washington: Zero Books, 2014), 66–80.

Yes darkness (is) I maintain, *not a thing*. As a result the claim follows that it cannot be represented, cannot represent anything but a negation. It then sits in the barren field of non-being. But wait, have we not just done something!? Given the non-thing, the negation, a quality? Perhaps a new language needs to be invented to expand the equivalent properties and qualities (hence dis-qualities) that hold for negations. Negatives and negations can have their own qualities; why do you insist on the analytic assumption that negative things—holes, the void, darkness, a dividing slice, cut, decapitation, evil—have no quality of their own? Thing fascism is all it is! I reject it, and affirm darkness; in all its disqualifications, Darkness itself is the dis-quality of not, its negative property.

Kant, for you, non-being when represented a-priori throws up a problem, that is: logical negation signified by a "not" is never properly attached to a concept—why not? (JOKE). This is because of your insistence that the representation of a concept finds an object of experience. But why not so for negations, negatives, absences—darkness as the cosmic NO that rejects all? Darkness

itself is that concept, with the implied turn that Negation is its dis-
quality.

You think: "No one can think a negation determinately without
grounding it on the opposed affirmation."[16] But you fail to see the
affirmative quality of negation. I think: "Has he not just earlier
claimed negation as an assertion?" *It is an assertion of absence.*
After all, how can negation be determining unless it stands alone
as a concept in the first place? Pseudo Dionysius, in his *Mystical
Theology* agrees: "Now we should not conclude that the negations
are simply the opposites of the affirmations, but rather that the
cause of all is considerably prior to this"[17] The beauty of Darkness
itself is that it is free from determination, free from determining
anything at all. It is the no-mere-lack; negation and darkness have
no want of anything. This, then, is a poor idea that maintains that
the very void "wishes" to be filled—as if every love exists only to be
stolen. You maintain that true negations are nothing but limits
grounded in the unlimited—the all. However, true negation stands
outside the all—it is not part of it, and thus it is thoroughly dark, a
thoroughly satanic dark, where even Satan paradoxically cannot
be present, it is the darkness that Satan gazes upon with envy. The
idea that this "darkness has no power over me" is the source of
trying to establish it as a mere dependent relational thing,
dependent on being, as if that could be the only transcendental
object. Negation is not non-being, darkness is not (not) the
absence of light, evil is not (not) a privation; these are present in
their absences.

---

[16] Immanuel Kant, *Critique of Pure Reason*, trans. Paul Guyer and Allen
Wood (Cambridge: Cambridge University Press, 1998), 555.
[17] Psuedo-Dionysius, *The Complete Works*, trans. Colm Luibheid and
Paul Rorem (New York: Paulist Press, 1987), 136.

Kant, you think that "not" can only stand in relation to another concept, and is not sufficient enough to designate a concept in regard to its content. You maintain that a negation is that concept which represents non-being in time; it is of intensive magnitude—diminishing towards nothing . . . confusing nothing with negation again. The absence of sensation represents itself as empty, corresponding to the absence. In other words, sensation corresponds to reality, negation corresponds to nothing in the sense of it "being" zero/0.

Negation, then, you maintain, Kant, has no ability to refer—it cannot point at/to anything. Nicola Masciandaro has undermined this in his deictic insight into Sabbath's "figure in black pointing at me": I am not present, but the un-present figure representing nothing points referentially at me.[18] Out of the darkness emerges an act of negation. Thus, Darkness itself has referential capacity, insofar as it is a "not" that points—the gesture of a fingerless hand, an armless torso; the beauty of Venus is found in her arms that are not there; it is only those obsessed with thingness—thing fascists—that would see such a torso as deformed in its lack.

---

[18] See Nicola Masciandaro, "Black Sabbath's 'Black Sabbath': A Gloss on Heavy Metal's Originary Song," http://reconstruction.eserver.org/Issues/092/masciandaro.shtml.

You do develop things a bit though, to be fair: distinguishing between logical negation and transcendental negation, finding focus and realising the possible ambiguities in the subject matter. But, as with your ethics, Kant, you fail to follow through. Transcendental negation signifies non-being itself contrary to transcendental affirmation—a something, as opposed to a nothing. Though, as you have already asserted, "not" has no content. I claim, on the contrary, that it is the no content of the "not" that is the concept. In this way, the lack, the void, absence, the darkness, the dead are all the positing of this no content, the no-content of the not—the qualities that are the absent subjects, or referents for nothing. In this sense, rather than qualify, we disqualify. Darkness itself disqualifies. The dead are those who have been disqualified—an apophatic community standing outside the game of things. They are the binary disqualifiers of the darkness of negation and the darkness of insight who stabilise their feet—straddled either side of the chasm of being. They are the ones we are envious of, those who have transcendent access to this double negation: "You have the wisdom of the dead; / these lesser lights should learn from you."[19]

---

[19] Darkthrone, "Wisdom of the Dead," *F.O.A.D.* (Peaceville Recordings, 2006).

Vertiginous is the edge that plunges into thinghood: Darkthone's "I, Voidhanger" speaks of a figure clinging on to the edge of materiality—dangling over an abyss of darkness. This figure—an oxymoronic expression of the physicality of clinging, which can only be effected in relation to a material object—is suspended from the precipice of precisely that which you say cannot be grasped.

Here, where "life runs painfully gray down the walls of time / clenching on to the void / laming intense shivering terror . . . Evilution of the mind / sever plunging lighting / cracking trembling / reeling / the world leaves you blind,"[20] darkness and death are the very platforms of salvation. Yet when speaking this way, Kant, you voidhanger, you would hold that this negation signifies a mere lack—in other words, you do not see it capable of being substantial in any sense.

So then I write in the *endstille*, what if negation is not an opposite? If darkness is not opposed to anything? I say, Darkness itself cannot be opposed to anything because it is *darkness itself*. It does not need any relation to anything. It is precisely "not" a lack. Recognizing this negation as possible—rather than impossible—is vertiginous and terrifying, hence you cling to the edge of that

---

[20] Darkthrone, "I, Voidhanger," *Plague Wielder* (Peaceville Records, 2001).

oxymoronic precipice, blind to the fact that your "Being is the fissure at the heart of death."[21]

Thus, Kant, I declare this letter of Divorce final, and where you think I have fallen, I have merely descended into a true grounding in the abyss of Darkness itself.

---

[21] Cf. Liturgy, "Behind the Void," *Renihilation* (20 Buck Spin Records, 2009).

Haemál

Jeremy Dyer[1]

1. Kalte Sterne

2. Fimbulvetr III (Collapse)

3. Jera (Midsummer)

4. Untitled (Pyre)

5. Sackcloth and Ashes

6. Untitled (Wildfire)

7. Untitled (Theophany)

8. I Gave Gold for Iron

9. Surtr

from *Black Bile*

Eugene Thacker

†
†

Towering assemblies of birchbark and black onyx sway in a slight delirium—asking nothing, accepting everything.

†
†

Everything dissipates into ether and weightless rains. In the submerged quiet kelp-like crystals wordlessly emerge. Seas of indifference.

†
†

We have yet to consider the possibility that depression is purely material, even elemental. In one of his notebooks, Cioran writes: "Left to its own devices, depression would demolish even the fingernails."

†
†

We fervently prayed we might someday become a similar type of substance, a shapeless and hideous mass, a mass that might also be exhaled, which obscure theologians would call by obscure names, like a fine and rarified stellar dust.

†
†

The Sepulcher a Book. Nietzsche's death is filled with great drama—it is even melodramatic, filled with madness, myth, delirium, prophecy, scheming, illness, paralysis, and silence, before his death on the 25ᵗʰ of August, 1900.

By contrast, Schopenhauer's death was both undramatic and uneventful. In fact, he almost slept through his death. He simply passed away in his sleep on the morning of September 21st, 1860. A few months earlier, Schopenhauer had written to a sickly friend with some advice: "Sleep is the source of all health and energy, even of the intellectual sort. I sleep 7, often 8 hours, sometimes 9." This, of course, from the philosopher who wrote that "death is to the species what sleep is to the individual" . . .

On the evening of the 1ˢᵗ of April, 1876, thirty-four year old Philipp Batz gathered together copies of his book *The Philosophy of Redemption*, which had just arrived from the publisher. He had worked as a clerk in the finance sector for nearly a decade, before quitting his job in disgust. He had been discharged from his military service due to exhaustion and fatigue. The stray poems and literary works he wrote remained unpublished. And from the time he was a teenager, he had read with great passion, Schopenhauer, Kant, and Leopardi.

At nearly nine-hundred pages, Batz published *The Philosophy of Redemption* under the pen name of Philipp Mainländer. In it, he talks of a pervasive "Will-to-Die" that indifferently drives everything that exists to negate its own existence. In his tiny apartment in Offenbach, Batz arranged the copies of his book on the floor into a single pile. He stepped up on top of his books, and hung himself from the ceiling beam of the room.

†
†

To assemble a lexicon of futility—why the philosopher is really a librarian, the poet a book-thief.

†
†

In this tenebrous hall of mosses there are a thousand tiny translucent commentaries, distilled to nothing except eroded Achaea and limestone.

†

†

The Spell of a Book. Which is more profound?—the botched suicide, or the accidental suicide? I think of Osamu Dazai, whose book *No Longer Human* remains one of the most concise expressions of a frenetic and sullen estrangement from one's own species. It opens with the admission, "I can't even guess myself what it must be like to live the life of a human being."

Dazai committed suicide—several times. Once on a cold December night in 1929, just before his exams. The overdose of sleeping pills was not enough; he survived, and graduated. Again in October of 1930, on the barren, sandy dunes of Kamakura beach—this time a double suicide with a woman he hardly knew. Tragically, she drowned, while Dazai was rescued by a fishing boat. He went on to marry and began a career writing. Again in the spring of 1933, when he hung himself from a beam in the mesmerizing warmth of his Tokyo apartment; once again Dazai survived, though he was hospitalized and subsequently developed a morphine addiction. And again in the fall of 1936, his marriage disintegrating, Dazai and his wife attempt a double suicide—and, to their horror, they live.

Dazai's life is by turns tragic and absurd, not unlike the portrayal of life in his books. He writes, "What frightened me was the logic of the world; in it lay the foretaste of something incalculably powerful."

In the summer of 1948, while working on a novel, Dazai's corpse is found, along with his wife's, having drowned in the Tamagawa canal. His novel—titled *Goodbye*—remains unfinished.

†

†

Even the carnivorous plants of a thousand fingertipped moons are skeptical of all my efforts.

†

†

From a blurred horizon, quiet black-basalt pools bore into the rocks and into our own patiently-withering bones. Slumbering swells of a salt-borne amnesia course through our desiccated skulls. Scorched, wandering brine secretes from every pore.

†

†

The Corpse of a Book. Sometime around 1658, Pascal conceived of an ambitious book of religious philosophy. But it was never completed, cut short by his death four years later. What remains of the work—now known as the *Pensées*—is one of the most unfinished books in the history of philosophy.

Admittedly, Pascal is partially to blame for the confusion. He wrote his many fragments on large sheets of paper, separating each by a horizontal line. When a sheet was full, he would then cut the paper along the horizontal lines, so that each fragment was self-contained on a strip of paper. These strips of paper were then grouped into piles. Pascal then poked a hole in the top corner of each of the strips, and joined them by running a thread through the hole, forming a bundle. Many of the bundles were thematically grouped—for instance, fragments on human vanity, or boredom, or religious despair were each sewn together. But other bundles don't appear to have any thematic grouping, and many of the fragments are not sewn together at all. What the reader confronts is a book that is, in every way, unbound.

What strikes me is the care Pascal put into his bundles, threading them together like fabric, or like a wound. On the evening of the 23rd of November 1654, Pascal had what scholars refer to as his "second conversion." It is recorded in a short text known as "The Memorial." Composed of terse, mystical visions of fire and light, it was written by Pascal on a tiny piece of parchment. It was sewn into the inside of Pascal's coat, so that it was always near his heart, and it was discovered on him when he died.

I don't know why, but part of me is secretly disappointed that Pascal didn't actually sew the parchment directly into his flesh, perhaps threading it just below his left nipple. There it might fester and flower forth from his chest in lyrical, tendril-like growths of unreflective black opal, gradually submerging his entire body into so many distillate specks of ashen thought.

†

†

Plankton-fed, sleep-drugged eyes cast down in the direction of the sacred.

†

†

The Withering of a Book. Schopenhauer's major work—*The World as Will and Representation*—is one of the great failures of systematic philosophy. What begins with the scintillating architectonics of Kant ends up crumbling into dubious suspicions about an impersonal world, irascible indictments against humanity, nocturnal evocations of cosmic suffering, and stark, aphoristic phrases embalmed within dense prose, prose that trails off in meditative rants on quietism, refusal, and nothingness.

If Schopenhauer's philosophy is pessimistic, it is because his work is caught somewhere between philosophy and a bad attitude, the syllogism entombed in the morose refusal of everything that is, a starless, luminous refusal of every principle of sufficiency—the futility of philosophy, in the key of philosophy.

In fact, Schopenhauer was so successful at being this type of pessimist that a reviewer of his last book assumed that Schopenhauer was already dead (he was not—but found the review disappointing nevertheless).

†

†

Partially-exhausted. Somewhat tired.

†

†

I hadn't heard from TU for a while, and was about to contact him when I get his email. He tells me that a friend of his had recently committed suicide. He had hung himself, and had put black tape in an "X" over his eyes and mouth.

I don't know what to say. I send my condolences; but the harrowing image of blackened out eyes and mouth sticks in my mind—one's own death is not even enough.

†

†

Arabesque ink winds itself languorously around our ovate dreams. We seem to speak only in the imprecise geometries of black volcanic sands. Huge, impossibly regular shapes of rutted charcoal hover above us, as if waiting.

†

†

The dreaded *Necronomicon*, the unmentionable *Cultes des Ghoules*, the blasphemous *De Vermis Mysteriis* . . . The idea that a person might be driven mad by a book is fantastical, even absurd—especially today, as physical books themselves seem to be vanishing into an ether of oblique and agglomerating metadata. We are so used to consuming books for the information they contain that we rarely consider the possibility that the books might in turn consume us. In 1809 Thomas Frognall Dibdin publishes *The Bibliomania; or, Book-Madness*. It uses a quasi-medical diagnosis to describe individuals literally consumed by books, ranging from the obsession over vellum or uncut copies to the passion for "Books printed in the Black-Letter."

Holbrook Jackson's *Anatomy of Bibliomania*—from 1930—goes further, tracing that fine line where bibliophilia turns into bibliomania. And the madness of possessing books turns with great subtlety into the madness of being possessed by books. Jackson even recounts what is no doubt the pinnacle of bibliomania—the "bibliophage," so consumed by their books that they eat them, devoutly incorporating them into their anatomies, effacing all distinction between the literal and the figurative.

Beyond this there is only the "bibliosomniac," or the book-sleeper. It is briefly mentioned in the *Commentario Philobiblon*, an anonymous commentary on Richard de Bury's mid-14th century treatise. There, the book-sleeper is defined as "a special type of monk, one who is asleep like a book [*codex*]."

†
†

A black glow in the deepest sleepwalking seas, invisible like our crystalline joints and our fibrous limbs and as tangible as our tenebrous theaters of doubt.

†
†

Black bile, the luminous point of logic reduced to the status of soil and worms and silted matter. Lost in thought. Adrift in deep space. Dreamless sleep.

†
†

A sigh—the final stage of lyricism.

†
†

Somber incandescence.

†
†

We are mottled with unearthly growths, serene stone and graphite assemblies hidden deep in the undertow of our contempt for the world. And what is our inertia, compared to the stillness of suspended planets?

†
†

"This Place is a Tomb": Infinite Terror in Darkspace

Dylan Trigg

The anecdote is well known. On a starry night in the 17th century, mathematician and philosopher Blaise Pascal is lying on his back in an open field. Surrounded by a forest, he gazes into the darkness of the sky. There, Pascal sees a shadowy landscape floating above him, marked by a cluster of nebulous lights, blistering orbs, and shifting textures. Beyond the realm of the Earth's atmosphere, the dance of the infinite cosmos greets him. Far from a source of affirmation, however, the experience of infinitude for Pascal instead inspires only cosmic terror. Alone, he makes a confession:

> I see those frightful spaces of the universe which surround me, and I find myself tied to one corner of this vast expanse, without knowing why I am put in this place rather than in another, nor why the short time which is given me to live is assigned to me at this point rather than at another of the whole eternity which was before me or which shall come after me. I see nothing but infinites on all sides, which surround me as an atom and as a shadow which endures only for an instant and returns no more. All I know is that I must soon die, but what I know least is this very death which I cannot escape.[1]

Pascal's black invocation of cosmic indifference summons an anxiety that is both primordial and unavoidable. Aboard this floating mass of rock we term "Earth," our homeworld is surrounded on all sides by an infinite extension of blackness, speckled here and there by the presence of planets and moons, all of which are apparently indifferent to what Carl Sagan memorably

---

[1] Blaise Pascal, *Pensées* (Grand Rapids, MI: Christian Classics Ethereal Library, 1944), 33.

called, our "pale blue dot."[2] Did Pascal have a vision of himself floating on this pale dot in the midst of darkness during that lonely night in 17th-century France? Without contact from another solar system, did the indifference of the universe create a cosmic agoraphobia, forcing him back to the enclosure of the Earth, before finally making him utter those immemorial words: "The eternal silence of these infinite spaces frightens me"?[3]

Pascal's eternal silence has not been left behind. The recent passing of a giant asteroid a mere 201,700 miles from the surface of Earth is a gentle reminder that we do not need to leave our homeworld to venture into outer space: *we are already in the void of cosmic space*.[4] And likewise, the void of cosmic space is in us, encroaching upon our everyday existence in every dimension. Ours is not a unique planet, and out there lurks volcanoes, ancient riverbeds, and incipient evidence of extinct life hibernating in the ruins of outer space. Amongst the cultural products of this cosmic anxiety, recent films such as *Another Earth* (2011) and Lars von Trier's *Melancholia* (2011) confront the possibility of rogue planets shadowing and mirroring the boundaries of Earth, thus reinforcing our radical contingency as cosmic entities.[5] In each case, the place of Earth is exposed in its vulnerability via a cosmic view of life, a view that reinforces the sense that human life is fundamentally lost in the silence of the cosmos.

Nowhere is the expression of this terrifying, silent space articulated with greater ferocity than in the music of the Swiss black metal band Darkspace. The collected works of Darkspace engage with the place of the Earth in the infinite universe. In distinction to the bulk of black metal bands peddling themes of religious evil on the one hand, and eco-friendly paganism on the other hand, Darkspace eschew the human realm in favour of a speculative thinking about the nonhuman universe; as the band report on a Pascalian note in a recent interview:

---

[2] Carl Sagan, *Pale Blue Dot* (New York: Random House, 1994).

[3] Ibid., 36.

[4] See http://www.bbc.co.uk/news/science-environment-15572634.

[5] On the nonfictional existence of parallel planets, see the recent discovery of a "super-earth" extrasolar planet named Gliese 581g, see http://news.bbc.co.uk/2/hi/6589157.stm.

We propose an experiment: Choose a dark and clear night. Lie down on your back. Look out for the stars. You will feel like looking "up" into the sky, but in Space there are no such things as "up" or "down". You are adhered to the planet by gravitational force only. Visualize that situation and look "down" into the stars. You might feel the fascinating fear to lose planetary contact and soar into the void.[6]

This resistance against the human ordering of space is evident in the numerical arrangement of their albums and songs. Thus, the songs on each of their albums form part of a continuous space: "Dark 1.1, 1.2, 1.3," "Dark 2.8, 2.9. 2.10," "Dark 3.11, 3.12, 3.13," and so forth. With their focus on the homogeneity of space, Darkspace move away from a human-centric perspective of the world, replacing it with disorientating spatiality deprived of a fixed perspective. Given their thematic commitment to the universe, the paradox Darkspace must confront in their music is how they can provide a soundtrack to the eternal silence of space, where even the vast motion of black holes swallowing matter and stars collapsing in the great expanse of space is all but a mute process.

Let us begin with *Darkspace I*, their first album released in 2003 through the label, Haunter of the Dark. The first officially published sound of Darkspace begins with vague whispers and the sound of shifting motion. Two minutes must pass in this ambience before the listener gets a sense of the Darkspace universe. The rupture of ambience is marked by a razorblade scream from the guitars. The production is thin and raw. The "rhythm section," as one might loosely call it, is provided by machines, and is often barely audible. The blastbeats of the guitars provide the mechanical pulse of the music's momentum, a chugging cacophony of spacious chords countered by furious tremolo picking and death metal palm muting. The atmosphere is thick and claustrophobic. The subsequent track of the first album employs an extended quote from Stanley Kubrick's *2001: Space Odyssey*, suggesting that the song's point of departure is the voice of supercomputer HAL, asserting its authority over human control.

---

[6] http://mortemzine.net/show.php?id=1539.

Yet Darkspace's music is not a violent confrontation with the machines of space, nor does it forecast a future, in which human beings have been outmoded by an advanced civilization. Instead, Darkspace explicitly align their organic selves with the technology that enables them to become Darkspace, as they put it:

> As we have chosen to work with machines, we are equipped with a machine-human-interface integrating ourselves into a synchronized, electronic organism. Once the biomechanoid is activated, we follow the pulse given by the central nervous system we call "death cube," mainly consisting of a hard disc recorder.[7]

In keeping with this mechanised interpretation of space, theirs is not a music for space operas. One must look not to the lyrical content to discern the "meaning" of the music, but to the total atmosphere. Indeed, vocal lines are almost certainly irrelevant, as the voice is used more as an instrument of nonverbal language. If the listener hears tortured screams and anguished convulsions in the music of Darkspace, then this is arguably because outer space is the prism of our reflected fantasies and fears. Thus, just as life seeks out life in the cosmos, so the horror of human existence on Earth finds its double in outer space.

Consider here the electromagnetic sounds of Jupiter recorded by the NASA-Voyager, collected together under the title *Symphonies of the Planets*.[8] What we hear in these recordings is electromagnetic waves of solar winds, radio waves, and particle changes passing through the planet's magnetospheres before then being converted into sound waves. While it is true that the audible sound we hear of Jupiter was created by a human on Earth, the objective electromagnetic waves belong to outer space. On an experiential level, the classification of these sounds would easily fit into the genre of "dark ambient," so inviting the sense that outer space harbours mysteries of an ominous kind. Yet space, as far as we can tell, is neither ominous nor benign, but instead lacking a moral teleology altogether. The power of Darkspace in this respect is that they give voice not only to the moral silence of outer space but also to the human gaze that is reflected back from the cosmos.

---

[7] Ibid.
[8] See https://www.youtube.com/watch?v=OLDWKpAkRHs.

Seen in this way, the dissonance and violence of their music is grounded in the experience of Darkspace, finite musicians confronting their own Pascalian anxieties

Yet transient respites from cosmic violence do appear in their landscape. The end of "1.3" and the beginning of "1.6" hint at a more ambient direction that would follow in subsequent albums, whereas "1.4" establishes a spacious quality afforded by the use of recurring broad themes, suggesting repetition in the void. Indeed, if Darkspace's music is characterised by one motif, then it is repetition of themes. Ideas are pursued, abandoned, and then returned to time and again. The music folds into itself, creating a hypotonic trancelike quality, in which all accounts of the linearity of space and time must be reconsidered.

If *Darkspace I* treats outer space as a chaotic field of colliding forces in the process of forming, then *Darkspace II* pushes this chaotic formation in a more compressed direction. With just three tracks, the album comprises a twenty-minute opening and closing songs, with a ten-minute ambient interlude in-between. Again, we open with a broad expanse of whispering before erupting once more into a monolithic block of dense noise. Here, the death metal chugging of the first album has been replaced with a more atmospheric use of tremolo picking. The employment of samples is more frequent though no less audible in the mix. Track "2.9" is especially notable for its extended spoken samples. A woman's voice calls out from the midst of a swirling horizon, snippets of a decipherable message heard in the void only to be swallowed by the blackness once more. The violent cacophony reaches its summit in the final track, a soundtrack to the image of a lifeless astronaut's body cartwheeling through the cosmos. This is music of the vertiginous heavens. Only, instead of celestial entities, it is a heaven that is populated with the kinetic drama of lifeless organisms hurtling from void to void, asteroid to asteroid, and dead star to dead star.

Darkspace III marks the culmination of this musical vision of space. Reprising the formula of the first two records, the standard ambient intro/violent onslaught is again revisited. This time, the sound is cavernous and rich, a departure from the thin production of the earlier releases. On this release, the mix has also been adjusted, with the synthesizers overlaying a symphonic quality to the album. Indeed, for all its blastbeat violence, the trance aspect of Darkspace is oddly serene. Halfway through

"3.11"—the first track—the music reaches a soaring quality, solemn motifs build upon one another, creating a wall of sound that resembles less black metal and more the infernal maelstrom of Stravinsky's "Sacrificial Dance."

If Darkspace's use of film samples was enigmatic and fleeting in their earlier albums, then in their third release, the voices being employed are given a central place in the music's representative content. "3.11" references Paul Anderson's *Event Horizon* (1997). The film's plot concerns the rescue of a spaceship, "*The Event Horizon*," in the year 2047. There, the rescue team discover that the ship circumvented the laws of physics, reaching outside the known universe and bearing witness to another dimension, a dimension characterised by a malignant agency. In turn, it becomes clear that the vessel has incorporated this malignancy into its decaying structure, compelling members of the rescue crew to materialize their secrets and fears.

In many respects, the film is the perfect sonic counterpart to the music of Darkspace. In both works, outer space becomes a witness to the unknown, a dehumanised universe that emits indecipherable distress beacons to the broader universe. This is in keeping with our astrophysical understanding of black holes and event horizons. Whilst we can never develop a relationship with a black hole—given that all matter is consumed by its force—the surrounding event horizon is the black hole's indirect expression. In the film, the ship acts as a conduit to what exists beyond the astrophysical event horizon, the ship is a manifestation of the black hole in phenomenal terms. Likewise, in the music of Darkspace, we never gain access to the secrets and distress beacons of the universe in their phenomenal reality, but instead discern them indirectly. In *Event Horizon*, what is revealed in this dark cosmos is an infinite burial site; as one character says in the film when boarding the ship, "this place is a tomb." In the music of Darkspace, this tomb is not localised to one distressed ship, but instead is played out in the universe as a whole.

If Darkspace leave us with a series of unanswered questions about the place of the Earth in the universe, then this is largely because they remain resistant to a scientific understanding of the cosmos. They state in an interview:

> We do have interest in scientific views of the universe
> and are curious to read about the results of the CERN's

particle collision experiments. We have also visited the CERN institute in Geneva as well as the synchrotron light source of the Paul Scherrer institute near Zürich. We do believe that a Large Hadron Collider will enlighten our understanding about the birth of the universe, but it will not inform us about the meaning of our existence. Science is descriptive, it illustrates what we perceive with our senses, it speaks in mathematical patterns and allows certain deductions and predictions. As fascinating as it may be—it still is a unilateral approach to the Cosmos and its life forms. We are sure that neither esoterical semi-truth, nor scientific limitations nor any religious dogma spoken for itself may reveal the true nature of the universe.[9]

This resistance to scientific reductionism does not mean that Darkspace lose themselves in a mystically enchanted Gnostic universe. Only "3.16" provides us with an indication of Darkspace's engagement with the idea of a "universal mind" in the form of John Carpenter's anti-god from the director's highly underrated film *The Prince of Darkness* (1987). In some respects, this reference to an "anti-god, bringing darkness instead of light" appears to be an anomaly in the Darkspace universe. After all, the cosmic vision Darkspace establishes is a fundamentally inhuman one, devoid of the religious trappings of the black metal genre. Yet, in many ways, this reference is both logical and necessary. In the violence of their music, the human occupies a place. The human is not dissolved in the unrelenting blackness of space. Thanks to this preservation, the solitary whimper of the human's need for communion with the beyond breaks through the Earth's atmosphere, discharging its moral and religious desires in the process.

If the universe, as Sagan puts it, is not made for us, and our place in the universe is thus subject to negation, then in the midst of this eternal silence, Darkspace provide a soundtrack to our status as *lost in space*. Yet Darkspace do not fill the silence left in the universe's absence of sound. Nor do they provide the backdrop to the terraformation of outer space, or to any other inter-galactic struggle between alien species. In Darkspace's music, our place in

---

[9] http://mortemzine.net/show.php?id=1539.

the universe is forever on the verge of being engulfed by the horrors of Pascal's terrifying silence, a silence that is given voice in Darkspace's cosmic vision of *infinite terror in infinite space*.

Seven Propositions On The Secret Kissing Of Black Metal: OSKVLVM

Edia Connole

pdrov ,rel̞av ,a|ocin rof

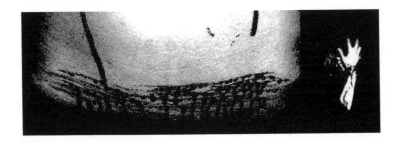

1) ONLY DEATH IS REAL[1]

From the moment of our birth there is nothing more certain than the inevitability of our death. As a species, it is said that our awareness of death is the origin of our self-consciousness, our standing-out through individuation from the primordial wholeness—fallen minds for whom the "foreground of life" is only possible with "the background of death,"[2] which becomes for us "the perspective of every great picture . . . the underbeat of every measurable poem."[3] Only death is real, we feel. Arthur Schopenhauer, black metal theorist *avant la lettre*, argued that

---

[1] Hellhammer, "Messiah," *Satanic Rites* (Prowling Death Records, 1983).

[2] Michael Kearl, *Endings: A Sociology of Death and Dying* (New York: Oxford University Press, 1989), 6.

[3] Archibald MacLeish cited in Michael Kearl, "Images across Cultures and Time," in *Kearl's Guide to the Sociology of Death: Death across Time and Space,* http://www.trinity.edu/~mkearl/death-1.html.

death is "the true inspiring genius, or the muse of philosophy."[4]
And so, while we say *philos* for lover, and *sophos* for wisdom, what
we are really saying, is not that we love wisdom or knowledge, but
"according to the natural love which engenders in everyone the
desire to know,"[5] and consequently, according to which everyone
can be called a philosopher, this desire to know, is a desire to know
death; all philosophy, is, apropos of Socrates, the practice of
death.[6] And yet, there is an obvious epistemological and deeper
more obscure existential contradiction inherent in this fact, since
our awareness of and desire to know death is invariably, indeed,
inalienably, shackled to our inability to have any knowledge of it—
"its like when death comes and you've got to go, except that the
step is taken, but neither you or not you with it—now."[7]

Already with this statement, this silent self-quotation, we
have exceeded the limits of philosophical thought, encountering
in Nicola's "infinite individuality" (Meher Baba)[8] what Laruelle
would call "the true 'mystical' content of philosophy, its 'black
box'"[9]—the problem—as per Meister Eckhart—which places one

---

[4] Arthur Schopenhauer, *The World As Will And Representation*, trans. R.
B. Haldane and J. Kemp, 3 vols. (London: Kegan Paul, Trench, Trübner
& Co., 1909), 3:249.

[5] Franco Masciandaro, *The Stranger as Friend: The Poetics of Friendship
in Homer, Dante, and Boccaccio* (Firenze: Firenze University Press,
2013), 22.

[6] Plato, *Phaedo*, 63e–64b, in *Complete Works*, ed. John M. Cooper
(Indianapolis and Cambridge: Hackett Publishing Company), 49–100;
55.

[7] Nicola Masciandaro "silently quoting himself" on the social media site
Facebook (13/03/15); (15/03/15). Cf. Pseudo-Dionysius, *The Mystical
Theology*, 1001A, in *The Complete Works*, trans. Colm Luibheid (New
York: Paulist Press, 1987): "Here, renouncing all that the mind may
conceive, wrapped entirely in the intangible and the invisible, [w]e belong
completely to him who is beyond everything" (137).

[8] See "The Four Journeys" in Meher Baba, *The Everything and The
Nothing* (Beacon Hill, Australia: Meher House Publications, 1963), 22–
26; "All those who live God's life on earth and all those who abide in God
as God on earth, when they drop their bodies, also shed forever their
subtle and mental vehicles and pass away utterly as God, retaining
infinite individuality and experiencing infinite Power, Knowledge and
Bliss. This is the fourth journey" (23–26).

[9] "L'identité de l'avec (l'Un avec l'Un, Dieu avec Dieu) est le vrai contenu
'mystique' de la philosophique, sa 'boite noire'" (François Laruelle,

beyond place above God, i.e. Why am I me? Because I am not.[10] The mortal correlate of which: "Being would be other to death—either annihilated by it or left immaculate—were there not scales,"[11] "'scales' or 'strata' of layers in our ontological capacity to know death,"[12] a knowing that is "the consummation of the Return

---

Mystique non-philosophique, 60), quoted in Nicola Masciandaro, "Absolute Secrecy: On the Infinity of Individuation," in *Speculation, Heresy, and Gnosis in Contemporary Philosophy of Religion: The Enigmatic Absolute*, eds. Joshua Ramey and Mathew Harr Farris (forthcoming).

[10] I am indebted to Nicola Masciandaro for explaining this so thoroughly to me, and in what was a rather drawn-out email conversation that took place over the course of March 2015, in which I continuously pressed him on the nuances of absolute individuation in the context of absolute death; my argument, in fact, apropos of what Professor Marcia Colish calls "analogy" below (see note 20), was already given here in what Nicola termed, via Laruelle, "cloning." Cf. Meister Eckhart, *Meister Eckhart: The Essential Sermons, Commentaries, Treatises, and Defence*, eds. Edmund College and Bernard McGinn (Mahwah, NJ: Paulist Press, 1981), Sermon 52: "When I stood in my first cause, I then had no God, and then I was my own cause. I wanted nothing, I longed for nothing, for I was an empty being, and the only truth in which I rejoiced was the knowledge of myself. . . . What I wanted I was, and what I was I wanted; and so I stood, empty of God and everything" (200).

[11] Nick Land, *The Thirst for Annihilation: Georges Bataille and Virulent Nihilism* (London: Routledge, 1992), 129.

[12] S. C. Hickman, commentary on "Surging Into The Inhuman," available from *Ktismatics*, https://ktismatics.wordpress.com/2009/07/26/surging-into-the-inhuman/. Cf. Meher Baba, "The Divine Theme," in *God Speaks: The Theme of Creation and Its Purpose* (Oakland, CA: Sufism Reoriented, 1997), 220–28: "God, the Oversoul, alone is real. Nothing exists but God. The different souls are in the Oversoul and one with it. The processes of evolution, reincarnation and realisation are all necessary in order to enable the soul to gain self-consciousness. In the process of winding, sanskaras become instrumental for the evolution of consciousness though they also give sanskaric bindings; and in the process of unwinding, sanskaric attachments are annihilated, though the consciousness which has been gained is fully retained . . . 'A' soul becomes 'Z' soul after going through evolution, reincarnation and the process of realisation. It is only in the God-state that consciousness is free" (220).

to the principle and ground of Godhead."[13] Man's gnosis *is* God. Or, as Basil of Caesarea would say, "The human being is an animal who has received the vocation to become God."[14] Inherent in this position, according to which we witness the Procession—"I was a hidden treasure who loved to be known"[15]—and Return—"For he who knows God becomes God"[16]—to the One from which all things come, is the principle of absolute individuation, presupposed in the third term of the triune movement, Procession-Return-Remaining, and consummated in what Nicola calls, in a clever twist of Plotinus's terms, "the flight of the alone *with* the alone, the flight you can never actually undertake because it is your actuality."[17] Ergo, "the true death, the death that ends all dying,"[18]

---

[13] Meister Eckhart, quoted in Alvin Moore Jr., "Nature, Man and God," available from *Sacred Web*, http://www.sacredweb.com/online_articles/sw2_moore.pdf.

[14] Or so wrote Gregory Nazianzen in his eulogy for St. Basil of Caesarea; see "The Mystical Heart Of Our Faith," available from *Catalyst For Renewal,* http://www.catalyst-for-renewal.com.au/index.php? Option =com_content&view=article& id= 103 :15-the-mystical-heart-of-our-faith.

[15] The famous words of the Sufi hadith which are quoted throughout Nicola Masciandaro's oeuvre, most notably for our purposes here, in "Secret: No Light Has Ever Seen the Black Universe," in Alexander Galloway, Daniel Colucciello Barber, Nicola Masciandaro, and Eugene Thacker, *Dark Nights of the Universe* (Miami: NAME, 2013), 45–87; 77.

[16] Eckhart, quoted in Moore, "Nature, Man and God."

[17] Masciandaro, "Absolute Secrecy."

[18] "To try to understand with the mind that which the mind can never understand, is futile; and to try to express by sounds of language and in forms of words the transcendent state of the soul, is even more futile. All that can be said, and has been said, and will be said, by those who live and experience that state, is that when the false self is lost the Real Self is found; that the birth of the Real can follow only the death of the false; and that dying to ourselves— the true death which ends all dying—is the only way to perpetual life. This means that when the mind with its desires, cravings and longings, is completely consumed by the fire of Divine Love, then the infinite, indestructible, indivisible, eternal Self is manifested. This is *manonash*, the annihilation of the false, limited, miserable, ignorant, destructible 'I,' to be replaced by the real 'I,' the eternal possessor of Infinite Knowledge, Love, Power, Peace, Bliss and Glory, in its unchangeable existence" (Meher Baba, "Everything Pertaining To The Spiritual Is Paradoxical," available from *Avatar Meher Baba,* http://www.avatarmeherbaba.org/erics/paradox2.html).

paradoxically rests on the principle of infinite individuality, "where God-as-Other passes away,"[19] yet I Remain, as does He, different but the same, the same in difference, absolute analogy.[20]

This absolute analogy ensures the openness or endlessness of desire that characterizes the soul's relation to God, where the Return to the One does not lead to satiety, or to what Bataille, in what he perceives as the analogous figure of marriage, would liken to "the vacant horror of steady conjugality,"[21] according to which God becomes—in the kind of *apokatastasis* we find in Origen[22]— the very "wall against which the passion of love for love collides."[23] Rather, this absolute analogy ensures Bataille's preferred "tearing in the perversities of turbulent passion,"[24] remaining ever a

---

[19] Eckhart cited in Moore, "Nature, Man and God."
[20] See David Williams *Deformed Discourse: The Function of the Monstrous in Medieval Thought and Literature* (Devon: University of Exeter Press, 1996), 48–60: "Although it is true that the understanding gained through analogy of proportionality may be expressed as the difference between analogates, the more basic concept of this analogy and all others is similitude. In the example Professor Colish uses—man's being to man as God's being is to God—the nature of being in each case may be diverse and only relatively one, but the idea of being itself remains intrinsic to both and diversity is suppressed through the proportionality created between them through the analogy. James F. Anderson in his study of the analogy of being makes the point clearly that analogy means 'likeness in difference' and that what analogy always shows us is the presence of being through proportional similarity. Further, he describes the analogy of proportionality not only as the most effective in producing knowledge of being but as inherent in the nature of the concept of being itself" (51). Cf. note 10, above, and Marcia Colish, *The Mirror of Language: A Study in the Medieval Theory of Knowledge* (London and Lincoln, NE: Nebraska University Press, 1983).
[21] Georges Bataille, "College of Sociology," in *The College of Sociology*, ed. Dennis Hollier (Minneapolis: University of Minnesota Press, 1988), 335. Cf. Edia Connole, "Bataille: Exhuming Animality," in *The Accursed Book: Essays On and With Bataille*, ed. Will Stronge (Bloomsbury, forthcoming).
[22] Origen maintained that in order to be knowable, God cannot be unlimited. On this, see Origen, *Origen On First Principles*, bk. 2, chap. 9: 1, trans. G. W. Butterworth (New York: Harper & Row, 1966), 129–37.
[23] Bataille, "College of Sociology," 335–36. Cf. Connole, "Bataille: Exhuming Animality."
[24] Ibid., 335.

movement forward, "a straining-beyond"[25]—what Gregory of Nyssa would posit as "an *epektasis* without end."[26]

She

2   Let him kiss me with the kisses of his mouth!
     For your love is better than wine;
3   your anointing oils are fragrant;
     your name is oil poured out;
     therefore virgins love you.
4   Draw me after you; let us run.
     The king has brought me into his chambers.[27]
5   I'm dead—But alive. & we're
     in kind of a 69 position.
     To heal me. The side of your head:
     Against my cold, black panties.
     "Please, be careful," you tell me.
     "Please."
     & it feels like we're kissing—
     & it feels like we're making love.
     A woman, dead, in childbirth.
     Tiny bones, resting, between her legs.[28]

---

[25] Gregory of Nyssa holds that God is fundamentally incomprehensible and, then, in contrast to Origen, that he is unlimited, as is our desire towards him. The term "straining-beyond" is actually Thomas A. Carlson's (see Carlson, *Indiscretion: Finitude and the Naming of God* [Chicago and London: The University of Chicago Press, 1999], 251), but it is derived from Gregory ultimately—though Carlson does not necessarily suggest so—who posits a variant of it in "The Life of Moses" (*The Essential Writings of Christian Mysticism*, ed. Bernard McGinn [New York: The Modern Library, 2006], 13–26): "Your desire is always strained forwards and your motion knows no weariness; further, you know no limit to the good and your desire is always intent on something more. This all means that the 'place' is ever near you, so that whoever runs therein never comes to an end of his running" (19).
[26] Carlson, *Indiscretion*, 251.
[27] *Song of Solomon*, 1:2–1:4, English Standard Version (ESV) of the Old Testament (OT).
[28] Rauan Klassnik, *The Moon's Jaw* (Boston and New York: Black Ocean, 2012), 24.

Others

6   We will exult and rejoice in you;
     we will extol your love more than wine;
     rightly do they [the virgins] love you.[29]

She

7   *Nigra sum, sed formosa*
     I am black, but comely,[30]
     O ye daughters of Jerusalem,
     as the tents of Kedar,
     as the curtains of Solomon.
8   Look not upon me because I *am* black,
     because the sun hath looked upon me.[31]
9   [*modo niger
     et ustus fortiter!*
     Now I am black and burning fiercely.][32]

He

10   Behold, you are beautiful, my love;
     behold, you are beautiful;
     your eyes are doves.
11   Behold, thou *art* fair, my love, yea pleasant:
     also our bed *is* green.
     The beams of our house *are* cedar,
     and our rafters of fir.[33]

She

12   I am a rose of Sharon,

---

[29] *Song of Sol.*, 1:4, King James Bible (KJB) version of the OT.
[30] Ibid., 1:5.
[31] Ibid., 1:5–1:6.
[32] From the *Carmina Burana*, a collection of Latin (or Occasional Middle High German) songs written around the later twelfth century. See *Love Lyrics From The Carmina Burana*, ed. P. G. Walsh (Chapel Hill, NC: The University of North Carolina Press, 1993).
[33] *Song of Sol.*, 1:15–1:17, a mix of ESV and KJB, respectively.

a lily of the valleys.[34]

He

13   As a lily among brambles,
       so is my love among
       the young women.[35]

She

14   Waves. & Flowers. Revolving.
       In black lace: Gurgling.
       You're pushing me back down
       on the bed now.
       & you've got my wrists above my head.
       & you're eating me out—
       Licking up between my breasts.
       It's dusk. Lights, Wound, Up,
       In a spiral: Hooked—
       Thru Me, Like Gut, On, Fire.
       Yr grip's tightening.
       I'm sinking: Like fish—
       In cool shade. Birds, like planets
       —All ripped up.[36]

Others

15   Eat, friends, drink,
       and be drunk with love.[37]

He

16   "Open to me, my sister,
       my love, my dove,
       my perfect one;
       for my head is wet with dew,

---

[34] *Song of Sol.*, 2:1, ESV.
[35] Ibid., 2:2.
[36] Klassnik, *The Moon's Jaw*, 22.
[37] *Song of Sol.*, 5:1, ESV.

my locks, with the drops of the night."

17   . . . cool, & dark—You begin to eat my ass:
Wiping yr mouth, from time to time—
& glaring up at me:
Like a Vampire, a Lion, a Shaman—
Swaying, bubbling, seething:
Down into every nerve . . .
Cold white shores swaying . . .
Till—At last—You slide a finger
. . . Then two. Fist! Elbow! Shoulder! Head!
& you're inside me:
& yr breasts are my breasts.
Yr cunt—My cunt.
Yr slow dark heaving mouth—
My slow dark heaving mouth.[38]

She

18   I am no one. I am nothing.
But I start to glow: & thrum.
I am blown up w/ light.
I am draped in every tree.
All the shores are dead w/ me.[39]

In offering this *florilegium*, culled from the oeuvre of contemporary poet Rauan Klassnik, and from the most superlative of Writings (*ketuvim*) or Hagiographa of the Old Testament, the holy of holies, or *Song of Songs, which is Solomon's*, it is not my intention to reduce the mystical union prefigured in its spiritual marriage and consummated in the kiss of his mouth which animates it, to what Lacan—in a rumination similarly inspired by Bataille—would call *affaires de foutre*, the "business of fucking."[40] While I would not go so far as the latter to

---

[38] Klassnik, *The Moon's Jaw*, 20.

[39] Ibid., 81.

[40] Jacques Lacan, *On Feminine Sexuality: The Limits of Love and Knowledge*, trans. B. Fink (Norton: New York, 1998), 77. Cf. Simon Critchley, "Mystical Anarchism," in this volume, or the annotated version of this text to which I will be referring from here on out—Simon Critchley, "Mystical Anarchism," *The Faith of the Faithless* (London and New York:

say that to do so would be to miss the point entirely, it would certainly be anathema to black metal theory, as it stems from *theoria*, vision, contemplation, that which leads, accordingly, to what the Cappadocian Father would call the "philosophy hidden in [the Songs'] words."[41] A philosophy that only becomes "manifest [*phaino*: to bring to light] once the literal meaning [*emphasis*: image, reflection, with *kata te lexin* or according to a way of speaking] has been [cut-away, from Greek *apo*, or] purified [*kathairo*] by a correct [*akkeratos*: unmixed, undefiled] understanding [*ennoia*: thought, idea, concept]."[42] Thus, in the "Prologue" to his commentary on the *Songs*, Gregory warns: "Let no one be bound up [*epago*: to bring upon, influence] in his own thoughts [*logismos*] or drag [*kathelko*] the pure words of the bridegroom and bride down to earthly [*sarkodes*: human] passions [*empathes*]."[43] Ergo, to a work of eroticism. Which is arguably what I've just done. But only because I want to restore some of the dangers of this canticle, some of the original charge that accompanied its sexual imagery and which is largely lost to us in a society saturated with pornography. As Origen and Jerome do well to remind us, when these words were written they were strictly forbidden to be read by any man—let alone woman—under the age of thirty.[44] Thus, the canticle clearly presented itself as something highly erotic, even *obscene* (Bataille's preferred term for the "pornographic"—derived from that which took place

---

Verso Books, 2012), 103–53: "Here, I have Jacques Lacan in mind, in particular the way in which he stumbles upon Beguine mysticism in the course of Seminar XX, as he attempts to get close to what takes place in the experience of feminine enjoyment or *jouissance* and its relation to love. For Lacan, mysticism is 'something serious' and 'mystical *jaculations* are neither idle chatter nor empty verbiage.' Most importantly, . . . Lacan claims that to reduce mysticism to the 'business of fucking [*affaires de foutre*]' is to miss the point entirely" (139).

[41] Gregory of Nyssa, "Notations on the Commentary on the Song of Songs by Gregory of Nyssa," 3.4., available from *Divine Lectio*, http://www.lectio-divina.org/index.cfm?fuseaction=feature.display&feature_id=100.

[42] Gregory, "Song of Songs," 3.4.

[43] Ibid., 15.4.

[44] See "Song of Songs 1:1," available from *Bible Hub*, http://biblehub.com/songs/1-1-htm.

"offstage," i.e. off the stage of normalcy, ergo *lunacy*)[45] and accordingly demanded a degree of spiritual maturity upon entering into the holy mystery of love it allegorically sets forth. So, as mentioned, while it is not my intention to reduce this holy mystery of love to the business of fucking, I do want to bring it back to the body, and to a *dark* love, to the wounding and tearing in the perversities of turbulent passion apropos of Bataille above, what Gregory, in his commentary on the *Song*, would posit as an *epektasis* or satiety without end, like the "violent venereal orgasm"[46] that has to be constantly re-earned, and from which we are returned, every time, like "failed escapists, to the power of *that*," what Nicola posits as a *deixis* of being, "something that points not to a thing but to a thing's existence, its *esse*."[47] Ergo, Bataille's principal mystical muse, St. Teresa of Avila, says she is "dying because [she] cannot die,"[48] or Nicola himself: "I will die and never stop dying, until I am no longer dead."[49]

Why do I want to do this? Why do I want to bring the holy mystery of love, this "thrilling divine romance," as Nicola calls it,[50]

---

[45] See Daniel Fuchs, *The Limits of Ferocity: Sexual Aggression and Modern Literary Rebellion* (Durham: Duke University Press, 2011), 206.
[46] Georges Batailles, *Eroticism*, trans. Mary Dalwood (London and New York: Penguin, 2012), 225; this is actually Marie Bonaparte's term as discussed in note 93 below.
[47] Nicola Masciandaro, "The Sorrow of Being," *Qui Parle: Critical Humanities and Social Sciences* 19 (2010): 9–35; 24. Cf. Emmanuel Levinas, *On Escape*, trans. Bettina Bergo (Stanford: Stanford University Press, 2003): "escape is the need to get out of oneself, that is, to break that most radical and unalterably binding of chains, the fact that the I [*moi*] is oneself [*soi-même*]. . . . It is being itself or the 'one-self' from which escape flees, and in no wise being's limitation. In escape the I flees itself, not in opposition to the infinity of what it is not or of what it will not become, but rather due to the very fact that it is or that it becomes" (55).
[48] Teresa of Avila, "*Vino sin vivir en mi*, I Die Because I Do Not Die," in *Nine Centuries of Spanish Literature*, eds. Seymour Resnick and Jeanne Pasmantier (New York: Dover Publications, 1994), 157. Cf. Bataille, "College of Sociology," 332; Bataille, *Eroticism*, 240; Connole, "Bataille: Exhuming Animality."
[49] Nicola Masciandaro, on the social media site *Facebook* (16/03/15).
[50] Nicola Masciandaro, "Thrilling Divine Romance" (unpublished manuscript). Cf. Meher Baba, *Discourses*, 3 vols. (San Francisco: Sufism Reoriented, 1967): "The sojourn of the soul is a thrilling divine romance

back down to earthly passion, to the body, and to the lips, to the sensual (*saveum*) kiss? Well, for one, because I am a woman and, as such, I incorporate the passion of the Divinity, an idea that reached an apogee in the thirteenth century, in the medieval opinion that, as Hildegard of Bingen wrote, "man signifies the divinity of the son of God, and woman his humanity,"[51] and therefore "the aptness of sexual union to symbolize a higher union . . . union of ineffable Godhead with [*Homo Sapiens*]"[52] . . . arguably the very "dregs"[53] of existence . . . the ones for whom "the

in which the lover, who in the beginning is conscious of nothing but emptiness, frustration, superficiality and the gnawing chains of bondage, gradually attains an increasingly fuller and freer expression of love, and ultimately disappears and merges in the divine Beloved to realize the unity of the Lover and the Beloved in the supreme and eternal fact of God as Infinite Love" (3:180).

[51] Hildegard of Bingen, quoted in Brian C. Vander Veen, *The Vitae of Bodleian Library MS Douce* (Unpublished Thesis, PhD: University of Nottingham, 2007), 84. As Vander Veen goes on to note, "whereas men expressed Christ qua God through the intellectual activities of preaching and teaching, holy women could express Christ qua man through their very physical identification with his suffering humanity . . . [because] the fleshly humanity whose suffering redeemed the world was female flesh" (84). Cf. Edia Connole, "Contemplating the Crucifixion: Cohle and Divine Gloom," in *True Detection*, eds. Edia Connole, Paul J. Ennis, and Nicola Masciandaro (London: Schism, 2014), 28–64; 62.

[52] Cf. "In a highly interesting study [*La Signification du Symbolisme Conjugal*] Father Louis Beirnaert, considering the comparison implicit in the language of the mystics between the experience of divine love and that of sexuality, emphasizes 'the aptness of sexual union to symbolize a higher union.' He is content to remind us of the horror always attendant upon sexuality without insisting on it: 'We with our scientific and technical mentality,' he says, 'are the ones who have turned sexual union into a purely biological fact . . .' In his eyes a sexual union has the virtue of expressing 'the union of ineffable Godhead with humanity,' the fact that it 'already possesses in human experience an intrinsic fitness for symbolizing the sacred event'" (Bataille, *Eroticism*, 223).

[53] "[S]ince Mind emanates from the Supreme God, and Soul from Mind, and Mind, indeed, forms and suffuses all below with life, and since this is the one splendor lighting up everything and invisible in all, like a countenance reflected in many mirrors arranged in a row, and since all follow on in continuous succession, degenerating step by step [*degenerantia per ordinem*] in their downward course, the close observer will find that from the supreme God even to the bottommost dregs of the

regret of not being plants brings us closer to paradise than any religion" (Emil Cioran).⁵⁴ Cioran sings a hymn to extinction, a

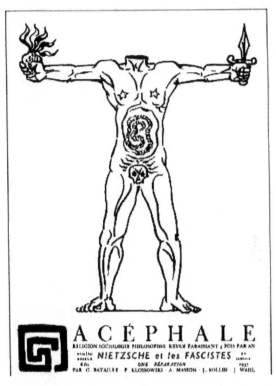

The first issue of *Acéphale*, June 1936, drawing by André Masson.

universe [*a summo des usque ad ultimam rerum faecum*] there is one tie [*conexio*], binding at every link and never broken. This is the golden chain of Homer which, he tells us, God ordered to hang down from the sky to the earth" (Macrobius, *Commentary on the Dream of Scipio*, trans. William Harris Stahl [New York: Columbia University Press, 1952], 14.15, quoted in Nicola Masciandaro, "Anti-Cosmosis: Black Mahapralaya," in *Hideous Gnosis*, ed. Masciandaro [New York: n.p., 2010], 71).
⁵⁴ Emil Cioran, *Tears and Saints*, trans. Ilinca Zarifopol-Johnston (Chicago: The University of Chicago Press, 1995), 115. Cf. Paul J. Ennis, "Bleak," in *A Spell to Ward Off the Darkness*, directed by Ben Rivers and

canticle to the dissolution of word and consciousness whose cosmic amplitude echoes the treason of the body in Bataille, the

Ben Russell (2013; London, UK: Soda Pictures, 2014), DVD: "Bleak theory might be defined, . . . as a morbid over-identification with the soft, unthinking world. A world that rejects us and tells us we are not of that world. We are condemned to associate with the unnatural; with the human aberration. With a species whose chief correlate is not simply suffering, which is common to all the living, but the additional insult of conscious suffering. . . . Consciousness is that which traps a solitary entity and then lands it in the middle of the communal. Once there selves scythe through one another even as they try to understand one another. But nobody ever understands anyone else and here there is a clue. To every self every other is dreaming a different reality. A false one since, as every individual knows, my world is the world. H. P. Lovecraft, in his guise as Professor Nobody, tells us, 'Unless life is a dream, nothing makes sense. For as a reality, it is a rank failure.' Or if you prefer it from Edgar Allen Poe: 'All that we see or seem / is but a dream within a dream.' Better yet, ask the nearest infant to row a boat. But I'm not here to defend solipsism or relativism or whatever. Life is a hallucination, but a very real one. It may have the character of an elaborate continuous, but determinate in duration, fantasy, but it's really happening. R. Scott Bakker tells us that 'The ability of the brain to "see itself" is severely restricted.' Or, more poetically, in the words of Thomas Metzinger, 'transparency is a special form of darkness.' Which is to say that consciousness, that which one is, is inexplicable to itself. Even if, as will happen some day, the processes involved in consciousness are understood it will simply confirm what you already know. What constitutes your self is a series of evolutionary 'kluges' (Bakker) hammered together in some far-off deep time game of adaptation that could just have easily benefited another random species. And the great error introduced into nature is precisely thinking. It has, as Nick Land and Ray Brassier, have argued, interests of its own. It works *against* life, or precisely, the will-to-life, and venerates the will-to-know, which has as its symbol death as de-humanised, non-subjective truth. . . . The more we know the more routine and base our impulses become, 'murder, the pleasure of humans' (Tormentor). Escape from nature is not escape from the worst parts of ourselves, it is a doubling up of aberrancy generating the machinic living-dead; de-naturalized we become a confused mechanics shoring up increasing complexity. All this is flowering toward a non-future. I'll end with an old Russian proverb: 'Smile, for tomorrow will be worse.'" As Gary J. Shipley notes, "Plants and animals would do well to mock us: they live simple and quiet while we revel in the noise of our deaths, edifying the ephemera of our necrotized states" (in Gary J. Shipley and Kenji Siratori, *Necrology* [Marstons Gate, GB: Gobbet Press, 2013], 12).

body of enjoyment, of *jouissance* or pleasure, that becomes in the
violence of passion "so close to *ruinous waste* that we refer to the
moment of climax as 'a little death.'"[55] And secondly, because I am
here in the capacity of a black metal theorist, a theorist of, or more
properly, in—"[w]e will speak *in* black metal," Nicola says, "there,
where the secret of black metal is, wherever black metal is the
secret of itself . . . Because black metal is love"[56]—black metal, i.e.
music from which I have come to expect, what Bataille would call,
"an added degree of depth in that exploration of coldness that is
dark love (tied to . . . obscenity and sealed by an endless
suffering—a love never violent enough, never shady enough, never
close enough to death!)."[57] And finally then, because both of these
points coalesce in the third far more—and, appropriately so—
skewed fact that this *dark* love of black metal is and must remain
"an inside out mysticism, not only in the sense of a profanation of
mysticism, but in the deeper [more obscure] sense of a mystical
inversion of mysticism," that which Nicola posits, and I chose to
take it up, "as a perverse intuitive preservation of the heterodox
love of God . . . Black metal truths remain backwardsly legible
within medieval mystical discourse, above all in places where the
ordered and integrative movement of the return to the One is
reversely accented towards individual reality."[58]

As below, so above.[59]

---

[55] Bataille, *Eroticism*, 170; my emphasis.
[56] Nicola Masciandaro, "On the Mystical Love of Black Metal," in Nicola
Masciandaro and Edia Connole, *Floating Tomb: Black Metal Theory*
(Milan: Mimesis, 2015), 101–14; 103.
[57] Georges Bataille, "A Story of Rats," in *The Impossible: A Story of Rats
followed by Dianus and by The Orresteia*, trans. Robert Hurley (San
Francisco: City Lights Books, 1991), 17.
[58] Masciandaro, "Mystical Love," 110.
[59] Nicola Masciandaro, "Reflections from the Intoxological Crucible," in
Black Metal: Beyond The Darkness, ed. Tom Howells (London: Black
Dog Publishing, 2012), 75, and in Masciandaro and Connole, *Floating
Tomb*, 249–52; 252. Cf. "The drawing of the Acephal, a potent expression
of the totality of Bataille's thought, embodies his reversed hermeticism in
the form of a parody or anti-idealist version of renaissance depictions of
the harmonic arrangement of the human body (Leonardo, Fludd etc.).
The celebrated aphorism of hermetic philosophy 'As above, so below'
situated man in a universe designed by God in which the structure of the

> What I expect from music: an added degree of depth in that exploration of coldness which is *dark* love (tied to B.'s obscenity and sealed by an endless suffering—a love never violent enough, never shady enough, never close enough to death!).

Georges Bataille, *La Haine de la Poésie* (1947); *The Impossible* (1962).

Incipit introspection. I send this quote to Vordb Na R.iidr. He tells me it is "awesome."[60] I juxtapose it on my *Facebook* page with an image of "Dead" Per Yngve Ohlin brandishing an act of auto-mutilation, and of a woman's torso, perhaps mine, dripping with blood above the panty-line, from where a blade has been drawn back and forth across the skin, silently slicing it open.[61] Sex and death are inviolably linked. Bataille knew it. So did Lacan. In a paper titled "Dieu et la *jouissance* de l/a femme," he famously declares: "You only have to look at Bernini's statue in Rome to understand immediately that she is coming [*elle jouit*], St. Teresa, there is no doubt about it."[62] She is coming. Lacan goes on to

---

microcosm reflected that of the macrocosm. Bataille exactly reverses this formula, for him—a heretic exalting the base over the spiritual in a universe in which 'man can set aside the thought that is he or God who keeps things from being absurd'—the body is projected onto the world: *as below, so above*" (Alastair Brotchie, "Introduction," in *Encyclopaedia Acephalica: Comprising the Critical Dictionary & Related Texts and the Encyclopaedia Costa*, eds. Georges Bataille and Robert Lebel & Isabelle Waldberg, respectively, trans. Iain White [London: Atlas Press, 1995], 12).

[60] Personal communication with the Entity (email, 06/04/15).

[61] Private domain of Edia Connole on the social media site *Facebook* (status update, 05/04/15).

[62] Jacques Lacan, *Le Seminaire. Livre XX: Encore, 1972–1973*, ed. Jacques-Alain Miller (Paris: Éditiones du Seuil, 1975), 70–71; translated with notes by Bruce Fink as *On Feminine Sexuality: The Limits of Love and Knowledge (The Seminar of Jacques Lacan. Book XX: Encore, 1972–1973)*, ed. Jacques-Alain Miller (New York and London: W. W. Norton & Company, 1998): "And what is it that makes her come [*elle jouit*]? It is clear that the essential testimony of the mystics consists in saying that they experience it, but know nothing [*rien*] about it" (76). Bataille had already said something very similar to this in relation to the thirteenth-century Italian mystic, Angela of Folignio (*OC* 5:259). Cf. "In a move similar to that made by Bataille, and later echoed by Jacques Lacan,

designate "a specifically female mode of sexual *jouissance* whose impossibility to be articulated was revealed by the mystics,"[63] and specifically by Teresa, in the famous passage that inspired the Bernini statue, wherein she describes her visitation by an angel of the Lord:

> In his hands I saw a long golden spear and at the end of the iron tip I seemed to see a point of fire. With this he seemed to pierce my heart several times so that it penetrated to my entrails. When he drew it out, I thought he was drawing them out with it and he left me completely afire with a great love for God. The pain was so sharp that it made me utter several moans; and so excessive was the sweetness caused by this intense pain that one can never wish to lose it, nor will one's soul be content with anything less than God. It is not bodily pain, but spiritual, though the body has a share in it— indeed, a great share. So gentle are the colloquies of love which pass between the soul and God that if anyone

---

one could claim that Black Metal attains the same Beyond as apophatic mysticism, without knowing anything about it: 'Exuberance is the point where we let go of Christianity. Angela of Foligno attained it, and described it, but didn't know it,' ergo Nergal of Behemoth: 'Do you remember Virgil's "Aenid," <<Obscuris vera involvens>> ? The idea of obscured truth is the source of each and every esoteric current—be it a major religious system or an intimate process of individuation—it all leads to numerous illuminations' . . . In a variant of what is regarded as Black Metal Theory's inaugural text, 'What is This That Stands Before Me?: Metal as Deixis,' Masciandaro brings all of these points together in order to stress, moreover, the important relation between Metal and apophatic mysticism as a discourse-praxis immanently invested in facticity. As he notes here, 'captured by the Vedantic formula *neti neti* [not this, not this], the apophatic mystic deictically negates all presence in affirmation and realization of a divine Beyond. Metal,' he says, 'practices a different but symmetrically and thus potentially complimentary craft with the same tool, held by the other end, . . . Metal negates all absence in affirmation and realization of itself as a Beyond'" (Edia Connole, "Leave Me In Hell," in Masciandaro and Connole, *Floating Tomb*, 53–8; 57–8).

[63] Elisabeth Roudinesco, *Jacques Lacan: An Outline of a Life and a History of a System of Thought*, trans. Barbara Bray (Cambridge: Polity Press, 1999), 524.

thinks I am lying I beseech God, in His goodness, to give him the same experience.[64]

The iron tip or veritable point of ecstasy that pierces Teresa's heart and penetrates all the way to her entrails, drawing them with it as it draws out, and thus leaving Teresa totally afire with a great love for God, reminds me of a curious line in the *Song*, where the bride says: "My beloved put in his hand by the hole *of the door*, and my bowels were moved [or (as some read) in me] for him."[65] Both instances, of what Bataille would call "reeling,"[66] seem to illicit unmistakable signs of the violently visceral or venereal *petite mort* or "little death" of orgasm. Lacan's promulgation of this point over the course of a 1972-73 seminar, *Encore* ("More"), was heavily indebted to his near thirty-year friendship with Bataille—who had died ten years earlier—and so, some have said, can even be read as an homage to Bataille's *Madame Edwarda*, "to the absolute figure of the hatred and love of God."[67] But it seems more likely that Lacan's choice of Saint Teresa, and moreover of Bernini's statue—an image of which still adorns the front-cover of the published seminar—is just as, if not more, indebted to Bataille's *Eroticism*, and specifically to his chapter on "Mysticism and Sensuality" therein, a prolonged meditation on the aetiology of Teresa's ecstasy, where, despite what he sees as the glaring similarities, even equivalences, between *la petite mort* and *mors mystica*, Bataille declares: "Nothing is further from my thought than a sexual interpretation of the mystical life."[68]

I decide to revisit Simon's "Mystical Anarchism,"[69] in particular the section "MYSTICISM IS NOT ABOUT THE BUSINESS OF FUCKING,"[70] where he takes-up Lacan's seminar XX in order to defend Marguerite Porete's *Mirror of Simple*

---

[64] Saint Teresa of Avila, *The Life of St. Teresa of Avila by Herself*, trans. J. M. Cohen (London: Penguin Books, 1988), 16–17. Cf. Teresa, *The Life*, in *The Complete Works*, vol. 1, 192–93, cited in Bataille, *Eroticism*, 224.
[65] *Song of Sol.*, 5:4, KJB; commentary given in the original.
[66] A term used by Bataille throughout *Eroticism* and especially in "Mysticism and Sensuality" therein, 221–51.
[67] Roudinesco, *Jacques Lacan*, 524.
[68] Bataille, *Eroticism*, 224.
[69] Critchley, "Mystical Anarchism," 103–53.
[70] Ibid., 136–40.

Souls[71]—"a seven state itinerary in the disciplining of the self all the way to its extinction in an experience of love that annihilates it"[72]—against the etiological explanations, and normative presuppositions such explanations evoke, and would, accordingly, reduce the spiritual marriage or mystical union that is consummated in the divine desuscitating kiss—ergo *mors mystica* or mystical death—to the obscurantist ravings of a "nihilistic megalomaniac."[73] Here, Simon quotes Lacan as saying, "I believe in the *jouissance* of woman insofar as it is an extra (*en plus*)."[74] In noting that it is explicitly Teresa that Lacan had in mind when he wrote this line, Simon says:

> Female mystics are on the path of an experience of the *en plus* that exceeds knowledge, the order of what Lacan elsewhere calls truth, by which he means truth of the subject. This dimension of an excessive *jouissance* that articulates something that is more (*en plus*) of what Lacan sees as the essential phallic function of knowledge is what he calls, with a nod to Heidegger, "ex-sistence." It is the dimension of ecstasy, following the line of a transgressive desire into its *askesis*, that we can call love. To be clear, this is not something confined to women. Lacan adds, thinking of Kierkegaard (. . .), "there are men who are just as good as women," namely those who "get the idea or sense that there must be a *jouissance* that is beyond. Those are the ones that we call mystics."[75]

I skip to the back of the book, and here I read Kierkegaard. Kierkegaard, who, as Simon tells us, will be on his mind in the capacity of this line in the conclusion to the volume,[76] *The Faith of*

---

[71] Margaret Poret (Marguerite Porete), *The Mirror of Simple Souls*, trans. E. Colledge, J. C. Marler, and J. Grant (Paris: University of Notre Dame, 1999).
[72] Critchley, "Mystical Anarchism," 136.
[73] Ibid., 139.
[74] Lacan, *On Feminine Sexuality*, 77, quoted in Critchley, "Mystical Anarchism," 140.
[75] Critchley, "Mystical Anarchism," 140.
[76] Ibid.

the Faithless. Page 251: "God's relationship to a human being is the infinitizing at every moment of that which at every moment is in man."[77] I remember an interview with Dagon where he says more or less the same thing: "What other reason are you here for . . . to be a crumb?"[78] Then I recall Bataille's reversed hermeticism, as below, so above, and how it plays-out in Gary's paper, and I think: *nah*, . . . "{Fuck them! Fuck You}: To fuck is to make tangible what might otherwise have been thought of as intangible."[79] I read on. Anticipating Kierkegaard's shift, in this, the penultimate paragraph of *Works of Love*, Simon switches to auditory imagery. He says: "Withdrawn into inwardness and an essential solitude (. . .), each and every word and action of the self resounds through the infinite demand of God."[80] Here, God is nothing but a "vast echo chamber, . . . the name for the repetition of each word that the subject utters. But it is a repetition that resounds with the 'intensification of infinity.'"[81]

I think of Vordb Na R.iidr again. I listen to Moévöt's "Zurghtarpre: Chant d'Éternité I" (*Abgzvoryathre*, 1993), for the nth time. I write to him. Tell him it haunts me, corporeally, spiritually. He sends me the lyrics: "Zurghtapre! / Zurghtapre! / Zurghtapre! / Aetrearp ahapfr Leambre! / Uatr eyddr, dhrea, verebl Ahapromv! / Uhupr klovomurv borktr uatr krisztuorb, / uhupre klovomurv borktr uhupfre morvbtre!"[82] I don't understand them. They are written in an unknown language. A language given to him by the Darkness (*is this not love? Dark love?* I muse), a language that comes from a place of indescribable

---

[77] Søren Kierkegaard, *Works of Love*, trans. H. and E. Hong (New York: Harper Perennial, 2009), 111, quoted in Critchley, "Mystical Anarchism," 251.

[78] Dagon of Inquisition, in "black metal band inquisition front man dagon talks satan pt.2," available from *YouTube*, https://www.youtube.com/watch?v=7bSk1of3eWc.

[79] Gary J. Shipley, "The Tongue-Tied Mystic: Aaaarrrgghhh! Fuck Them! Fuck You!," in this volume. Cf. Steven Shakespeare, *Kierkegaard and the Refusal of Transcendence* (Palgrave MacMillan, forthcoming).

[80] Critchley, "Mystical Anarchism," 251.

[81] Ibid.

[82] Personal communication with the Entity (email, 07/04/15); "Zurghtarpre: Chant d'Éternité I" (*Abgzvoryathre*, 1993) lyrics © Vordb, 1993, quoted with Vordb's kind permission.

suffering.[83] I'm reminded of Hadewijch for whom "Hell should be the highest name of Love."[84] Hadewijch, "who described a fearful logos-crucifying path to God."[85] "They who follow this way," she says, "live as if in Hell. That comes from God's fearful invitation.

[83] See Edia Connole, "Les Légions Noires: Labour, Language, Laughter," in Masciandaro and Connole, *Floating Tomb*, 149–205. Cf. Eugene Thacker, "An Expiatory Pessimism," in Edia Connole and Gary J. Shipley, eds., *Serial Killing: A Philosophical Anthology* (London: Schism, 2015), 301–10: "That suffering is part of the human condition is a platitude; Huysmans, ever the pessimist, had already detailed this in his early novels. But that suffering is almost indistinguishable from living—and not just one part of living—this takes Huysmans into territory that is shared by both the modern horror genre and the pre-modern tradition of hagiographies. In a letter to a reader Huysmans writes: 'Lydwine was one of God's chosen expiatory victims, but it took her a long time to realize this. She suffered physical agonies such as may never be suffered again, simply because she did not wish to suffer.' To suffer and not wish to suffer; to accept suffering and still not wish to suffer—this is the horror specific to the hagiography. There are no heroic affirmations of suffering, no superhuman overcoming of tragedy, no redemption through a spiritual economy of debt and forgiveness. There is just the body withering away, almost yearning to become a corpse, the corpse yearning to become dust. And this is, for Huysmans, the ambivalent, religious horror of hagiography—the realization that one lives as a corpse, as dust. / Huysmans caps off his letter about Lydwine with the following: 'From the day that understanding dawned upon her, God helped her, and she lived in that strange condition in which pain is a source of joy.' / One seeks darkness, one finds a further darkness" (304).
[84] Hadewijch, "Loves Seven Names," in *The Complete Works*, trans. Mother Columba Hart, O.S.B (Mahwah, NJ: Paulist Press, 1980), 352–58; 356; "Hell is the seventh name / Of this love wherein I suffer. / For there is nothing Love does not engulf and damn, / And no one who falls into her / And whom she seizes comes out again, / Because no grace exists there. / As Hell turns everything to ruin, / In Love nothing else is acquired / But disquiet and torture without pity; / Forever to be in unrest, / Forever assault and new persecution; / To be wholly devoured and engulfed / In her unfathomable essence, / To founder unceasingly in heat and cold, / In the deep, insurmountable darkness of Love. / This outdoes the torments of hell. / He who knows Love and her comings and goings / Has experienced and can understand / Why it is truly appropriate / That Hell should be the highest name of Love" (146–65; 256–57). Cf. Vordb Na R.iidr, "Biography of The Entity," available from *Kaleidarkness*, http://www.kaleidarkness.com/biography_of_the_entity.html.
[85] Masciandaro, "Thrilling Divine Romance."

It is so fearful to their minds, their spirit understands the grandeur of conformity to the delivering up of the Son, but their reason cannot understand it. This," she concludes, "is why they condemn themselves at every hour. All their words, and works, and service seem to them of no account, and their spirit does not believe that it can attain that grandeur. Thus their heart remains devoid of hope. This leads them very deep into God, for their great despair leads them above the ramparts and through all the passageways, and into all the places where truth is."[86] I despair, momentarily, despair at ever getting done with this essay. *What is it that I'm trying to say?* I write to him again, tell him. "*Sur les cimes du désespoir* (Cioran), *tu peux encore voir très loin* (Vordb),"[87] he writes me: On the heights of despair (Cioran), you can still see very far (Vordb) . . .

I find it funny, that unnerving funny that accompanies the uncanny, because I'm thinking of Teresa's "rooftop"[88] just then— about which Bataille writes in *Eroticism*,[89] and of how it might pertain, this image of rapture she outlines in *El libro de la Vida*— when, on the table right in front of me, a footnote in Nicola's "Thrilling Divine Romance" that had previously eluded me, reads: "Meher Baba defines desperation as one of the twelve ways of realizing God: 'If you experience the desperation that causes a man to commit suicide, and you feel that you cannot live without seeing me, then you will see me' (*Discourses* III.181)."[90] My thoughts turn to Dead. I read "Euronymous's Epistles (pt. 5)."[91] Valter recounts in chronological order the acts of mutilation that appear in the letters Chagrynn sent him. From the first, I read: "And if the gig is very good Dead will cut himself and bleed on the audience"; from the second: "About Dead, he is insane. I think

---

[86] Hadewijch, "Four Paradoxes of God's Nature," in *Complete works*, 98, cited in Masciandaro, "Thrilling Divine Romance."
[87] Personal communication with the Entity (email, 09/04/15). Cf. Emil Cioran, *On the Heights of Despair*, trans. Ilinca Zarifopol-Johnston (Chicago and London: The University of Chicago Press, 1992).
[88] Saint Teresa, *The Complete Works*, 139.
[89] Bataille, *Eroticism*, 231.
[90] Masciandaro, "Thrilling Divine Romance," note 4. Cf. Meher Baba, *Discourses*, 3:181.
[91] Valter, "Euronymous's Epistles (pt. 5)," available from *Surreal Documents*, http://surrealdocuments.blogspot.ie/2009/05/euronymouss-epistles-pt-5.html.

those rumours you heard are a bit untrue, he doesn't [say he's] been dead 3 times, but he believes he's the incarnation of Vlad (Dracula). He cut himself up pretty extreme at a gig we did, and if he gets too drunk he also cuts, but not only himself, unfortunately. At new years eve he almost cut up his artery, but he don't remember anything himself. I do. We had to put handcuffs on him"; and from the third, a postscript, which reads: "P.S. Very important: Dead is probably going to cut himself totally to pieces at one of the gigs (at least), so it's great if you found out where the nearest hospitals are, incase he's dying. Thanks!" Surprisingly, in the fourth and final letter, which recounts how Øystein "Euronymous" Aarseth found Dead's body following his suicide on April 8th 1991, there is no mention of auto-mutilation, but it does note of how, in a contrary gesture, in his very last words, Dead says, "Excuse all the blood."

Citing the typical *Wikipedia* entry on auto-mutilation, where it is listed in the Diagnostic and Statistical Manual of Disorders as a symptom of borderline personality and depressive disorders, associated with mental illness, and with a history of trauma and abuse, and according to which a common but *mistaken* belief regarding it is that it is an attention seeking behavior, and further, one that is associated with suicidal and para-suicidal tendencies, Valter says Dead was not an atypical auto-mutilator. First, rather than hiding his wounds, Dead flaunted them, cutting himself up in front of audiences at black metal concerts. Secondly, Dead's auto-mutilation cannot be dissociated from his suicide which, prima facie, was a private act, one that took place in complete isolation, ergo the correlative logic implying that it would have been preferable if there were no blood.[92]

It strikes me that Valter's point corresponds directly to the one animating Bataille in his meditation on mysticism and sensuality, i.e. the hackneyed, so often wheeled out—most notably by Marie Bonaparte, to whom Bataille's text can be seen to be responding when he gives the original formulation of Lacan's and subsequently Simon's declaration that MYSTICISM IS NOT ABOUT THE BUSINESS OF FUCKING[93]—view that mystical

---

[92] Cited in Valter, "Euronymous's Epistles (pt.5)."
[93] "Let us be quite clear. Nothing is further from my thought than a sexual interpretation of the mystical life such as Marie Bonaparte and James Leuba have insisted on. Even if the mystical effusion is in some way

experience is nothing more than the transposition of sexual and thus neurotic, at base, psychological problems. As Valter notes, and I quote him at length here, because this is essentially a Bataillean argument, and not one that I can articulate any better than him, for the moment:

> While it seems obvious that there must have been a link between Ohlin's psychological problems and his practice of self-injury, the fact that Ohlin cut himself ostentatiously as part of a Black Metal concert points to the fact that his auto-mutilation was enmeshed with Black Metal culture. Thus, Ohlin's self-injury was not a private practice, but one that was eminently social.

> Ohlin cut himself to bleed on his audience. Lacerating the surface of his body, Ohlin opened a channel of communication between himself and the assembled crowd. To paraphrase The Three Degrees: "Blood is the Message." If, in religious ritual, one sacrifices in order to communicate with the gods, Ohlin made libations of his blood to communicate with those who attended the concerts.

---

comparable with sexual excitement, to assert as Leuba does that the feelings of bliss described by contemplatives always imply a degree of activity of the sexual organs is an unjustified over-simplification [J. Leuba, *La Psychologie des Mystiques Religeux*, 202]. Marie Bonaparte takes her stand on a passage from St. Theresa [the one given above, and] . . . concludes: 'Such is St. Theresa's famous transverberation; I should like to compare it with something a friend of mine confessed to me once. She had lost her faith, but when she was fifteen she had undergone an intense mystical crisis and had wanted to become a nun. Now she remembered that one day, on her knees before the altar, she had felt such unearthly bliss that she thought God himself had descended into her. It was only later when she had given herself to a man that she realized that this descent of God into her had been a violent venereal orgasm. Chaste Theresa never had a chance to make a comparison of this sort and yet it seems to be an explanation of her transverberation.' Dr. Parcheminey put this in precise language: 'Such considerations lead to the hypothesis that all mystical experience is nothing but transposed sexuality and hence neurotic behavior'" (Bataille, *Eroticism*, 224–25).

The relationship between the quality of the Black Metal concert and Ohlin's public acts of self-injury is particularly interesting: "*And if the gig is very good, Dead will cut himself up and bleed on the audience.*" Evidently, the communal enthusiasm of a successful Black Metal concert engendered in Ohlin this frightful desire to spill his own blood. This allows me to interpret Ohlin's bloodspilling as part of a cycle of gift exchange between the musician and his audience. When Mayhem's musicians gave themselves over to their Black Metal, the audience reciprocated with a frenzied movement, shaking their heads until their minds were a blur; and when Ohlin, in his turn, accepted the audience's gift of enthusiasm, he gave back his own blood. Blood, a heterogeneous and revolting fluid, charged by Black Metal with hatred and disgust, signaled that the world of self-interest and self-preservation had been abandoned by the artist and he challenged the audience to do likewise.[94]

Valter concludes that, "[e]xceeding the expression of an individual mental disorder," the profound and persistent despair that Ohlin suffered, his "public acts of self-injury can be designated as acts of sacrifice."[95] To which I would only add the small but important prefix "self-." Dead's public acts of self-injury can be designated as acts of self-sacrifice, implicit in what Valter posits as the artist's abandonment of self-interest, of self-preservation. As Simon notes, quoting the thirteenth-century Franciscan mystic Angela of Foligno, the "desire for [dissolution] unleashes the most extreme violence against the self. . . . [quite literally] boring a hole in oneself so that love might enter ["the communal enthusiasm of a successful Black Metal concert"]. . . . 'There are times,' she said, 'when . . . I am scarcely able to stop myself from totally tearing myself apart. . . . times when I can't hold myself back from striking

---

94 Valter, "Euronymous's Epistles (pt. 5)." See Bataille on "Murder and Sacrifice," and "From Religious Sacrifice to Eroticism," in *Eroticism*, 81–93. Cf. Georges Bataille on "Transgression," in *The Accursed Share, Vols. II and III*, trans. Robert Hurley (New York: Zone Books, 1993), 89–122.
95 Valter, "Euronymous's Epistles (pt. 5)."

myself in the most horrible way.'"[96] As Simon will go on to say, this "is not some Plotinian idea of the contemplative union of the intellect with the One as the source of emanation, . . . [it is, rather, 'the painful and passionate process of decreation'] a 'desire of certain human beings to surpass the condition of humanity and to become God.'"[97] Thus, Dead's auto-mutilation may be construed as auto-annihilation, annihilation of the self/mind, ego death, *fana, manonash, mors mystica*. That this mystical death cannot be dissociated from his actual death brings us back to "the 'breathable black abyss' wherein the killing kiss of God is found."[98] As Madame Guyon notes in her commentary on the *Song*: "We

---

[96] Critchley, "Mystical Anarchism," 131; the correct order of these various statements reads as follows: "The heart of the heresy of the Free Spirit is not some Plotinian idea of contemplative union with the One as the source of an emanation: God, the bliss of contact with the divine. Rather, as Cohn writes, the heresy "was a passionate desire of certain human beings to surpass the condition of humanity and to become God. What Porete is describing is a painful process of decreation: boring a hole in oneself so that love might enter. It is closer to Teresa of Avila's piercing of the heart that takes place when she is on fire with the love of God, 'The pain was so great it made me moan.' The desire for annihilation unleashes the most extreme violence against the self. For example, the thirteenth-century mystic Angela of Foligno writes: 'There are times when such great anger ensues that I am scarcely able to stop myself from totally tearing myself apart. There are also times when I can't hold myself back from striking myself in a horrible way, and sometimes my head and limbs are swollen.'" Cf. Angela of Foligno, "The Memorial," in *Essential Writings*, 376, where she continues: "While I am in the most horrible darkness of the demons it seems that any kind of hope of good is lacking—it is a terrible darkness. The vices that I know were dead in my soul are brought back to life, and the demons rouse them up in the soul from the outside—and they even raise to life vices that were never there. They did the same in the body (where I suffer less in three places, that is, in the sexual places. There was so great a fire there that I used to use material flame to extinguish the other fire, until you [i.e., her confessor and scribe] forbade it. For the time during which I am in that darkness, I believe that I would rather be burned than to suffer those pains; indeed, I would then call out for any kind of death God would give me" (377).
[97] Critchley, "Mystical Anarchism," 131. Cf. Norman Cohn on the heresy's relation to Plotinus in "The Way to Self-Deification," in *The Pursuit of the Millennium: Revolutionary Millenarians and Mystical Anarchists of the Middle Ages* (New York: Oxford University Press, 1970), 172–75.
[98] Masciandaro, "Thrilling Divine Romance."

must remember that God is all mouth, [just] as he is all word, and that the application of this divine mouth to the soul [which] is the perfect enjoyment and consummation of the marriage . . . cannot take place until the next life."[99] Ergo Meher Baba: "Because I love you so much, I harass you so much;" "It is My real mercy which descends only on a very few, select few. These are my friends. They are My lovers to whom I give the gift of sorrow and distress . . . I kill them and it is My highest mercy on them;" "In order to be infinitely merciful, I have to be infinitely cruel. Those whom I love most I destroy."[100]

That "Euronymous's Epistles (pt. 5)" is epigraphically animated by Charles Baudelaire's "Self-Tormentor," in which we read, "I am the knife and the wound it deals / I am the slap and the cheek / I am the blow I give, and feel! /[101] I am the vampire at my own veins,"[102] brings me back at once to the infinite demand

---

[99] Madame Guyon, "Commentary On The Song Of Songs," in *Essential Writings*, 43; Guyon herself does not fully believe this, as we read here: "There are some who maintain that this union cannot take place until the next life; but I am content that it may be attained in this life, with the reservation that here we possess without seeing, there we shall behold what we possess" (43).

[100] Meher Baba, quoted in Masciandaro, "Thrilling Divine Romance." See Bhau Kalchuri, *While the World Slept: Stories from Bhau Kalchuri's Life with Avatar Meher Baba* (North Myrtle Beach, SC: Manifestation, 1984), 33-5, and *Lord Meher*, 1159-60, http://www.lordmeher.org/.

[101] Baudelaire, *Flowers of Evil*, trans. Lewis Piaget Shanks (New York: Ives Washburn, 1931), in *Fleurs du Mal*, no pagination given. Cf. "THE DEATH BLOW," a brief—in truth, two-flower—florilegium culled by Nicola Masciandaro and posted to "Mors Mystica: Black Metal Theory Symposium" *Facebook* event-page (06/04/15): "'And then comes the blow, the horrible blow, so horrible that most human beings will turn away: I have never loved . . . If I want anything from you I don't love you . . . Love is not thinking' (VH)"; 'And just as one can die of fright before the blow is struck, so too can one die of joy. Thus the soul dies to herself before she steps into God' (ME)."

[102] This appears to be Valter's own translation of Charles Baudelaire's poem, the reader is directed to a link with several different English translations, and the original French, available from *Fleurs du Mal*, http://fleursdumal.org/poem/151. Unless otherwise indicated I follow Valter's translation in "Euronymous's Epistles (pt. 5)" here, but deem the most apposite English translation in its entirety to be that of Piaget, details of which are given below, insofar as its emphasis on laughter has

animating Simon's "Mystical Anarchism," "the infinitizing at every moment of that which at every moment is *in* man,"[103] and the "Thrilling Divine Romance" animating my own paper— Nicola's doomed commentary on *Dracula*, "the preeminent horror romance of modern literature, and the source through which the terrors of mystical love may be gothically resuscitated for the present."[104] "Love is," indeed, "the highest and deepest of horrors, the truth according to which the universe is not only illusion,"[105] but an erotic fiction . . . a fiction that sees death and sex in the same cyclical revolution of what Bataille would term "continuity"[106]—an exchange and excitement or cycle of energies,

---

a much more satisfactory Bataillean note: "I am my heart's own vampire, for God has forsaken me, and men, these lips can never smile again, but laugh they must, and evermore!" Cf. Bataille's poem "Rire" ("Laughter"): "Laugh and laugh / at the sun / at the nettles / at the stones / at the ducks / at the rain / at the pee-pee of the pope / at mummy / at a coffin full of shit [IV 13]," discussed by Land in the "Preface" to *Thirst for Annihilation*, xvii-xix, though his whole book is clearly a riff on this poem: "This poem introduces three of the most crucial themes traversing Bataille's writing: laughter, excrement, death" (xvii).

[103] My emphasis, apropos of the earlier point I made re Bataille's reversed hermeticism, "as below, so above," note 58, but also with respect to what others too would posit as Kierkegaard's tendency towards immanence. Cf. Steven Shakespeare, *Refusal of Transcendence* (Palgrave MacMillan, forthcoming).

[104] Masciandaro, "Thrilling Divine Romance." See Bram Stoker, *Dracula* (Hertfordshire: Wordsworth Classics, 2000).

[105] Masciandaro, "Thrilling Divine Romance." I change what Masciandaro has posited as a "pulp fiction" to that of an "erotic fiction" in what follows; "pulp" denotes "cheap" and/or "trashy" essentially, and certainly doesn't pertain to the writing-style—the literary verboseness, let's say—of Stoker's *Dracula*, even if retroactively read into it—as the genre, which, in addition, is specifically American, had not yet developed. Cf. Connole, "Contemplating the Crucifixion," 28–64, for a fairly general discussion of the genre, and how it pertains to mysticism qua philosophical pessimism.

[106] A term used throughout *Eroticism*, but see, for example, "Introduction": "The whole business of eroticism is to strike to the inmost core of the living being, so that the heart stands still. The transition from the normal state to that of erotic desire presupposes a partial dissolution of the person as he exists in the realm of discontinuity. Dissolution—this expression corresponds with *dissolute life*, the familiar phrase linked with erotic activity. In the process of dissolution, the male partner has generally an active role, while the female partner is passive. The passive,

the at once disgusting yet noble and ethereal (thus, *impossible*) anti-matter of realism.[107] The terrifying fact of this anti-matter, the matter of its anti-facticity, is that all we *really* want as a species, at the very end of the day, is to squander our strength and resources away.[108] But, as Gregory notes, we can never run far enough toward it,[109] this thrilling divine romance given in the absolute analogy of the *Song*, in the figure of the vampire, in the experience of the violent venereal orgasm ("O blissful Estrangement from God, how lovingly am I connected with

---

female side is essentially the one that is dissolved as a separate entity. But for the male partner the dissolution of the passive partner means one thing only: it is paving the way for a fusion where both are mingled, attaining at length the same degree of dissolution. The whole business of eroticism is to destroy the self-contained character of the participators as they are in their normal lives. Stripping naked is the decisive action. Nakedness offers a contrast to self-possession, to discontinuous existence, in other words. It is a state of communication revealing a quest for a possible continuance of being beyond the confines of the self. Bodies open out to a state of continuity through secret channels that give us a feeling of obscenity. Obscenity is our name for the uneasiness which upsets the physical state associate with self-possession, with the possession of a recognised stable individuality. Through the activity of organs in a flow of coalescence and renewal, like the ebb and flow of waves surging into one another, the self is dispossessed, and so completely that most creatures in a state of nakedness, for nakedness is symbolic of this dispossession and heralds it, will hide; particularly if the erotic act follows, consummating it. Stripping naked is seen in civilizations where the act has full significance if not as a simulacrum of the act of killing, at least as an equivalent shorn of gravity. In antiquity the destitution (or destruction) fundamental to eroticism was felt strongly and justified linking the act of love with sacrifice" (17–18; my emphasis). Cf. Connole, "Bataille: Exhuming Animality," and Land, *Thirst for Annihilation*, esp. 199–210.

[107] A term derived from Philippe Sollers, "Le toit: Essai de lecture systématique," *Tel quel* 29 (1967): 25–46. For a good critical engagement with the implications of it, see for instance, Suzanne Guerlac, "Bataille in Theory: Afterimages (Lascaux)," in "Georges Bataille: An Occasion for Misunderstanding," special issue, *Diacritics* 26, no. 2 (1996): 6–17. Cf. Fuchs, *Limits of Ferocity*, 208.

[108] See Bataille, "De Sade's Sovereign Man," in *Eroticism*, 164–76; 170–71.

[109] Gregory, "The Life of Moses," 19; see note 25 above.

you!").[110] Go on, pick one, or two, or even three, no matter which, it is at every turn an aura of death that denotes passion.[111] It is also what denotes me, then, as a woman, "sullied with the carnal flux"[112] and stimulated by the goad of divine love—the *en plus* that exceeds knowledge. As the appropriately apocryphal Pseudo-Bonaventure's *Stimulus Amoris* would have it:

> Love rules me, and not reason, and I runne with force &
> violence, whithersoever thou inclinest and forcest me.
> But they that see me, deride me, because they know not,
> that I am drunke with love. And they say: what ailes this
> same mad fellow, that he makes such yawling in the
> streets? Whereas they do not consider the greatness of
> my desire. They are ignorant, that the vehement love of
> thee, hinders the use of reason: & he that searches for
> thee with a pure heart, doth so little care for outward
> thing, that even often times he heeds not what he
> does.[113]

---

[110] Mechthild of Magdeburg, *The Flowing Light of the Godhead*, trans. Frank Tobin (New York: Paulist Press, 1998), 4.12.

[111] Cf. Paul Hegarty's discussion of passion in *Georges Bataille: Core Cultural Theorist* (London: Sage, 2000), 20. But the best, most direct discussion by Bataille on the subject of passion/the passions—and as it pertains to morality/notions of good and evil—is to be found in Nick Land's student Eliot Albert's PhD thesis. An appendix to the thesis contains Albert's translation of a little known lecture by Bataille "On Evil in Platonism and Sadism" (Monday 12 May 1947), which analyzes the violence perpetrated during WWII, and more specifically the Nazi executions, through the Marquis de Sade's ruminations on the death-penalty, as expounded in *Philosophy in the Bedroom* (1795). See Eliot Albert, *Towards A Schizogenealogy of Heretical Materialism: Between Bruno and Spinoza, Nietzsche, Deleuze and Other Philosophical Recluses* (Unpublished Thesis, PhD: University of Warwick, 2000), 197–223.

[112] "[I]n spiritualibus affectionibus carnals fluxus liquore maculantur" (St. Bonaventure, cited in Bataille, *Eroticism*, 225).

[113] I am indebted to Lisa Godson for this reference: St. Bonaventure, *Stimulus Divini Amoris, that is The Goad of Divine Love, Verie proper and profitable for all deuout persons to read*, trans. by B. Lewis Augustine (Douai: by the Widow of Mark Wyon, 1642; Reprinted as rev. and ed. by W. A. Phillipson (Glasgow: R. & T. Washbourne, 1907), 35. Cf. Allan Westphall, "Some Notes On The Recusant *Stimulus Amoris* (*The Goad of Divine Love*, Douai, 1642)," available from *Geographies of*

A note in the margins reads: *"Amans est Amens."* Anyone in love is insane. Has lost their head.[114] It seems to me that I now have every right to correct Bataille's well-intended but misguided efforts. He said "[t]he truth of eroticism is treason."[115] But I don't see it here. Where is the atheological anarchist infidel begotten of Love (/Hell) who does not care for religion, every vein in his *dirty* body having become a sacred thread?[116] Where is the man who

---

Orthodoxy, http://www.qub.ac.uk/geographies-of-orthodoxy/discuss/2011/01/11/some-notes-on-the-recusant-stimulus-amoris-the-goad-of-love-douai-1642-2/.

[114] Cf. "'Dead went back home,' he said. 'Back to Sweden?' I wondered. 'No, he's blown his head'" (Jan Axel "Hellhammer" von Blomberg, cited in Valter, "Eronymous's Epistles [pt.5]"); "As these words suggest, metal's atheological apophatic ecstasy is also explicable with reference to its capital rite, headbanging, the intimate opposite or countermovement of the head that bows itself in prayer. Where the mystic bows to God for the sake of his own God-performed decapitation, relinquishing the head that says 'God' as the final veil (ego) between the soul and God, the metalhead bows without bowing to nothing but metal, banging the head against itself, against its own abject presence. Headbanging, the gestural expression of metallic deixis as unprayer, conventionally accompanied by the manual horns that point impossibly to metal itself, is the perfect inverse of final mystical consummation. It is the ecstatic realization, not of God, but of the non-realization of God, the iterative and unceasing auto-decapitation of the being at the threshold who as Bataille says 'must throw himself headlong [*vivant*] into that which has no foundation and has no head.' Headbanging is the maddening becoming-divine of the one for whom there is none to bow to. Headbanging manifests the ritual structure of metal as essentially *self-sacrificial*" (Nicola Masciandaro, "What is This that Stands before Me?: Metal as Deixis," in Masciandaro and Connole, *Floating Tomb,* 59–72; 70; my emphasis).
[115] Bataille, *Eroticism,* 171.
[116] With this question I have in mind a number of things. Firstly, it takes its lyrical inspiration from a post Nicola made to the social media site *Twitter* (11/04/15): "kafir-e-Ishkam Musulmani mara darkar nist / Har rag-e-man tar gasht-e-Hayat-e-Zunnar nist / i.e. I am the infidel begotten of Love, who does not care for religion, every vein in my body having become a sacred thread, I am not in need of one" (Abdul Kareem Abdulla, *Sobs and Throbs or Some Spiritual Sidelights* [Meherabad, Arangaon: N. N. Satha, 1929]), and a line that I subsequently read in *Pearls,* in which Baba says: "The dirty body which I call the human latrine is used for the soul to realize itself" (9). The emphasis I have placed on "dirty" above is with reference to the special place it holds in Bataille's oeuvre, as Fuchs

said that in wanting to feel as remote from this world as possible, he would turn it upside down, and inside out?[117] Has he run

---

notes (alluding to Georges Bataille, *The Blue of Noon*, trans. Harry Mathews [London: Paladin Grafton Books, 1988]): "For Bataille, the dirty is honorable (Dirty is the nickname of a well regarded character), aggression showing its life" (*Limits of Ferocity*, 206). But even more than that, I'm referring back to Simon's "Mystical Anarchism," and the heresy of the Free Spirit therein, and more particularly, then, how it is outlined by Cohn in *Pursuit of the Millennium*—the text that inspired Simon's: an account of mystical anarchism, of an essential amoralism and irreligion, that I can clearly see Bataille and black metal aligned with (so much so, I feel it's worth recounting at length here): "In a sketch written about 1330 in the chief stronghold of the heresy, Cologne, the Catholic mystic Suso evokes with admirable terseness those qualities in the Free Sprit which made it essentially anarchic. He describes how on a bright Sunday, as he was sitting lost in meditation, an incorporeal image appeared to his spirit. Suso addresses the image: 'Whence have you come?' The image answers: 'I come from nowhere.'—'Tell me, what you are?'—'I am not.'—'What do you wish?'—'I do not wish.'—'This is a miracle! Tell me, what is your name?'—'I am called Nameless Wildness.'—'Where does your insight lead to?'—'Into untrammeled freedom.'—'Tell me, what do you call untrammeled freedom?'—'When a man lives according to all his caprices without distinguishing between God and himself, and without looking before or after . . .' What distinguished the adepts of the Free Spirit from all other medieval sectarians was, precisely, their total amoralism. For them the proof of salvation was to know nothing of conscience or remorse. Innumerable pronouncements of theirs bear witness to this attitude: 'He who attributes to himself anything that he does, and does not attribute it all to God, is in ignorance, which is hell. . . . Nothing in a man's works is his own.' And again: 'He who recognizes that God does all things in him, he shall not sin. For he must not attribute to himself, but to God, all that he does.'—'A man who has a conscience is himself Devil and hell and purgatory, tormenting himself. He who is free in spirit escapes from all things.'—'Nothing is sin except what is thought of as sin.'—'One can be so united with God that whatever one may do one cannot sin.'—'I belong to the Liberty of Nature, and all that my nature desires I satisfy . . . I am a natural man.'— 'The free man is quite right to do whatever gives him pleasure.' These sayings are typical and their implication is unmistakable" (177–78).
[117] Cf. Bataille, *Eroticism*, 170–71: "Our only real pleasure is to squander our resources to no purpose, just as if a wound were bleeding inside us; we always want to be sure of the uselessness or the ruinous of our extravagance. We want to feel as remote from the world where thrift is

headlong [*vivant*]? Well, here is my treason, the chalice of black bile that I raise to the unholy trinity: MYSTICISM *IS* ABOUT THE BUSINESS OF FUCKING; "Stop looking. Stand *in* black universe, and see. '*Nigra sum, sed formosa*' (Song of Songs 1:4) [I am black, but beautiful]."[118] Or at the very least agree: sensuality is to mysticism more (*encore!*) than "a clumsy try is to a perfect achievement."[119]

Osculatorily bound to Hellhammer's *Satanic Rites*, John Green's *Looking for Alaska*[120] will seal my point. The novel's protagonist, Miles Halter, who has a morbid fascination with dying words—words uttered during people's last rites, and so on, words like Dead's, "Excuse all the blood"—leaves the safety and security of all he has ever known at home in Florida to pursue his Junior year at a boarding school in Alabama, justifying his decision to commence boarding school so late in life with the famous last words of François Rabelais—"I go to seek a Great Perhaps." The story that ensues maps his transformation from innocent, overprotected, and unpopular geek, to mature, self-aware, autarkic, articulate almost-adult. Along the way, Miles develops a penchant for insubordination, cigarettes, and booze— there's a lot of "Aaaarrrgghhh! Fuck Them! Fuck You!"[121]—to figures in authority. But at the same time, he learns about love, loyalty, orgasms, and loss, and ends-up acing his world religions

the rule as we can. As remote as we can:—that is hardly strong enough; we want a world turned upside down and inside out."
[118] "Black Universe is the place where mystical truth begins . . . Black universe is the dark body of the Real. Stop looking. Stand in black universe, and see. '*Nigra sum, sed formosa*' (Song of Songs 1:4) [I am black, but beautiful]" (Masciandaro, "No Secret," 57–8). Cf. "The believer is black, as being defiled and sinful by nature, but comely as renewed by Divine grace to the holy image of God. . . . still deformed with remains of sin, but comely as accepted by Christ. . . . base and contemptible in the esteem of men, but excellent in the sight of God" (Commentary on *Song of Sol.*, 1:2, available from *Bible Hub*, http://biblehub.com/songs/1-2htm).
[119] Bataille, *Eroticism*, 249: "we might say that sensuality is to mysticism as a clumsy try is to a perfect achievement, and no doubt we ought to ignore what is after all a wrong turning on the spirit's road to sovereignty."
[120] John Green, *Looking for Alaska* (New York: Dutton, 2005).
[121] Shipley, "Tongue-Tied Mystic," in this volume.

class. As his fascination with famous last words suggests, this erotic—essentially, rite of passage—fiction is largely concerned with the "heavy"[122] philosophical questions, the various strands of which coalesce when Miles's friend and would-be lover, Alaska Young—"the hottest girl in all of human history"[123]—is killed in a car crash. Rather appropriately, this occurs just after an intense making-out session, during which Alaska schools him in philematology, the art of kissing. "*We are all going,*" Miles thinks to himself some weeks later, "and it applies to turtles and turtlenecks, Alaska the girl and Alaska the place, because nothing can last, not even earth itself."[124] *Only death is real.*

---

[122] Cf. "In part, this impulse comes from the metalhead who realizes that the individual is basically powerless, except in a future time when predictions about the negative nature of modern society will come true. Of course, in the now, parents brush that aside and go shopping, stockpiling retirement funds so they can carelessly wish their children a good life before disappearing into managed care facilities with 24-hour cable movie channels. A more fundamental part of this dissident realism is creative. People who see most of society going into denial because they cannot handle their low social status, the dire future of human overpopulation and industrialization, and the negative motivations hiding beneath social pretense, aka 'cognitive dissonance,' will often mourn most for the opportunities lost when people value putting their heads in the sand more than finding beauty in life. It is the convergence of these ideas that creates the violent and masculine but sensitive, Romantic side to metal: it is a genre of finding beauty in darkness, order in chaos, wisdom in horror, and restoring humanity to a path of sanity—by paying attention to the 'heavy' things in life that, because they are socially denied, are left out of the discussion but continue to shape it through most people's desire to avoid mentioning them" (Brett Stevens, "The Heavy Metal F.A.Q.," available from *Death Metal Underground: The Ultimate Heavy Metal Resource*, http://www.deathmetal.org/faq/#underground-metal).

[123] Green, *Looking for Alaska*, 14; emphasis in the original.

[124] Ibid., 196.

Wings Flock to My Crypt, I Fly to My Throne: On Inquisition's Esoteric Floating Tomb

Nicola Masciandaro

Love like a magnet is, it draws me into God,
And what is greater still, it pulls God into death.
– Angelus Silesius[1]

Now, the domain of freedom . . . is found placed between
two gravitational fields with two different centres . . .
"heaven" and "this world."
– Anonymous

---

[1] Angelus Silesius, *The Cherubinic Wanderer*, trans. Maria Shrady (New York: Paulist Press, 1986), 57.

Come to the cryptic tombs, hear their call.

– Inquisition[2]

So that you have a chance to shatter your stupid little life.

– Vernon Howard

CRYPTO-ARCHAEOLOGY

In the cosmo-mystical oeuvre of Inquisition, the floating tomb emerges as an explicitly obscure form, an "esoteric floating tomb"[3] wherein inner spiritual movement is blackly fused with the force of the cosmos itself. In one sense, the floating tomb figures the space of mystical death (*mors mystica*) that is found in the extremity of perfect, self-annihilating sorrow—the sorrow beyond sorrow whose weeping erases oneself. This is the "solitary death" of which Inquisition, in tune with the medieval tradition of affective Dionysian mysticism,[4] sings:

> Night of the black sorrowfull moaning winds blowing.
> Through these melancholic woods how I feel so dead here,
> Sad and cold as I hear crypt sounds of moan.
> Only thought of sorrow bring me down to the pits of bottomless black.
> In this endless extreme tomb of weeping sadness,
> I am embraced by the cosmic force of night.[5]

Clarify this black metal night with the mystical "dark night" which "engulfs souls in its secret abyss" and causes them "to feel that they have been led into a remarkably deep and vast wilderness

---

[2] Inquisition, "Strike of the Morning Star," *Nefarious Dismal Orations* (No Colours Records, 2007).

[3] Inquisition, "Force of the Floating Tomb," *Obscure Verses for The Multiverse* (Season of Mist, 2013).

[4] On the parameters of this designation, see Boyd Taylor Coolman, "The Medieval Affective Dionysian Tradition," *Modern Theology* 24 (2008): 615–32.

[5] Inquisition, "Solitary Death in the Nocturnal Woodlands," *Into The Infernal Regions Of The Ancient Cult* (Sylphorium Records, 1998).

unattainable by any human creature."[6] Like the self-annihilating "perfect sorrow" of *The Cloud of Unknowing*, the utmost sorrow '*that* one is,' which "ravishes a man from all knowing and feeling of his being,"[7] Inquisition's "endless extreme tomb of weeping sadness" evokes a mystical death-by-sorrow in the sense of an overpowering negativity of individual gravity that cryptically opens into the dark infinity of cosmic forces, the wild nameless will beyond and within the universe itself.[8] Joining death's earthly down-going with celestial flight into the "mystical sphere" of "eternal / Unseen horizons,"[9] the motif belongs to the doubly inversive movement of divine union in which becoming God coincides with the death of God. The floating tomb is that portal of solitary dying wherein solitude perishes in the embrace of the beyond. It is a sepulchre suspended at sorrow's abyss-summit, the paradoxical nadir where the heaviest weight of being swallowed into "the pits of bottomless black" levitates by its own inexplicable gravity into the night of mystical consummation, the "guiding night" or Night of Power: "Wings flock to my crypt, I fly to my

---

[6] John of the Cross, *The Dark Night*, II. 17. 6, in *The Collected Works*, trans. Kiernan Kavanaugh and Otilio Rodriguez (Washington: Institute of Carmelite Studies, 1991), 437.

[7] As defined in *The Cloud of Unknowing*, such deathly mystical sorrow is existential in the strongest sense, a sorrow of being itself: "All men have grounds for sorrow [*mater of sorow*], but most specially he feels grounds for sorrow who knows and feels *that* he is. In comparison to this sorrow, all other kinds of sorrow are like play. For he can truly and really sorrow who knows and feels not only what he is, but *that* he is. And whoever has not felt this sorrow, he may make sorrow, because he has never yet felt perfect sorrow. This sorrow . . . cleanses the soul . . . and makes a soul capable of receiving that joy which ravishes a man from all knowing and feeling of his being" (*The Cloud of Unknowing*, ed. Patrick J. Gallacher [Kalamazoo, MI: Medieval Institute Publications, 1997], 71, translation mine). See Nicola Masciandaro, "The Sorrow of Being," *Qui Parle: Critical Humanities and Social Sciences* 19 (2010): 9–35, and Nicola Masciandaro, "Eros as Cosmic Sorrow," *Mystics Quarterly* (2009): 59–103.

[8] On the cosmicity of mystical sorrow, see Nicola Masciandaro, "Paradisical Pessimism: On the Crucifixion Darkness and the Cosmic Materiality of Sorrow," *Qui Parle: Critical Humanities and Social Sciences* 23 (2014): 183–212.

[9] Inquisition, "Darkness Flows Towards Unseen Horizons," *Obscure Verses for The Multiverse*.

throne."[10] At the same time, Inquisition's floating tomb willfully re-exposes the spiritual night of medieval mysticism to the black vastness of the modern, scientifically known universe, reopening in turn its dark gnostic dimensions, as per the ancient view of the cosmos as cavern or crypt, a literally mystical or hidden place (Latin *crypta*, "vault," "cavern," from PIE *krau-*, "to conceal, hide").[11] In "Force of the Floating Tomb," the invocational opening of *Obscure Verses for The Multiverse*, the tomb's force is identified with gravitation as a godly power, a cosmic might that black metal unleashes in the sacrificial mode of a raised chalice:

> Moons of titans, dead black sphere
> Lord of skies, silent altar
> Esoteric floating tomb
> Like a shroud of the heavens
> In the shadows of its craters
> On the mountains of its ruins
> Solar rays carve its valleys
> Endless graves reign in caves
> Raise the Chalice!
> Strong as lightning is the force
> Gravitation . . . force of gods
> Invocation of its mass
> As a spirit floats and mourns

---

[10] Inquisition, "Desolate Funeral Chant," *Ominous Doctrines of the Perpetual Mystical Macrocosm* (Hells Headbangers Records, 2011). "Union with Him is the Night of Power [Koran XCVII], separation from Him is the night of the grave—the night of the grave sees miraculous generosity and replenishment from the Night of His Power" (Jalal al-Din Rumi, quoted in William C. Chittick, *The Sufi Path of Love: The Spiritual Teachings of Rumi* [Albany: State University of New York Press, 1983], 233). "O guiding night! / O night more lovely than the dawn! / O night that has united / the Lover with his Beloved, / transforming the beloved in her Lover" (John of the Cross, *The Dark Night*, stanza 5, in *Collected Works*, 359).

[11] "The motif of the cave . . . represents the underworld which, for the Gnostics, is the material cosmos in which we presently live as the spiritually dead. . . . The Pythagoreans, and after them Plato, showed that the cosmos is a cavern" (Timothy Freke and Peter Gandy, *Jesus and the Lost Goddess: The Secret Teachings of the Original Christians* [New York: Three Rivers, 2001], 108).

Raise the chalice![12]

The chalice, ritual symbol of the spiritual flow between earthly and heavenly spheres, and more specifically, the elevation of the lower via receptivity to the higher,[13] is the vessel of black metal itself raised to the multiverse, the levitation of its art into visionary experience or theory of the hyper-majestic universal blackness. As the song starts without intro as if always already underway, so the command to raise the chalice expresses the will's realization of the force that is there *in the beginning*. Rising in the command to raise it, the chalice offers the hyper-natural intoxicating realization taking place in the anti-gravitational paradox of volitional intensification via self-opposition, in the will's sacrificial self-overcoming by means of submission to the higher imperative of its own archic gravity. As Meher Baba explains,

> There is nothing unnatural or artificial about love. It subsists from the very beginning of evolution. At the inorganic stage it is crudely expressed in the form of cohesion or attraction. It is the natural affinity which keeps things together and draws them to each other. The gravitational pull exercised by the heavenly bodies upon each other is an expression of this type of love. At the organic stage, love becomes self-illumined and self-appreciative and plays an important part from the lowest forms like the amoeba to the most evolved form

---

[12] Inquisition, "Force of the Floating Tomb," *Obscure Verses for The Multiverse*.
[13] "The chalice ... frequently takes the form of two halves of a sphere back to back. In this, the lower part of the sphere becomes a receptacle open to the spiritual forces, while the upper part closes over the earth, which it duplicates symbolically" (J. E. Cirlot, *A Dictionary of Symbols*, trans. Jack Sage [New York: Dover, 1971], 43). Furthermore, the spiritual will-to-power communicated in the song is in consonance with the cosmic dimension of chivalry encoded in the grail myth: "It is said that the Grail as a bright chalice (the presence of which produces a magical animation, a foreboding, and an anticipation of a nonhuman life), following the Last Supper and Jesus' death, was taken by angels into heaven from where it is not supposed to return until the emergence on earth of a stock of heroes capable of safeguarding it" (Julius Evola, *Revolt Against the Modern World*, trans. Guido Stucco [Rochester, VT: Inner Traditions, 1995], 87).

of human beings. When love is self-illumined, its value
is intensified by its conscious sacrifice.[14]

In this space, Inquisition's floating tomb now takes on the sense
of both the whole apparent universe, the "dead black sphere"
which is both womb and grave of this transient life, and one's
spiritual resurrection from this heaviest of facts, a resurrection by
means of the will's discordant harmony with ancient, titanic
cosmic forces. Being an expression of mystical will, pointedly
defined by Bataille as the desire "to be everything [*tout*],"[15]
Inquisition's anagogic black metal analogously operates
simultaneously as a tomb-floating art in a temporal and historical
sense, elevating the dead premodern metaphysical cosmos into
the dark space of modernity, levitating into presence its old
mystery by the occult magnetism of sonic and imaginal force.
Crucially, this obscure verse does so in an authentic or self-doing
(*auto-entes*) way, bringing to life the mystical universe *without
revival*, in a manner that maintains its spiritual essence in the
non-mediating immediacy of self-indicating gesture.[16] The live
will of black metal, raising the chalice of itself, is the palpable
invisible pole around which it turns, without return, ancient into
new. As Dagon says, when asked about the source of Inquisition's
inspiration, "The simple notion that my spirit is as ancient as time
itself, I am here in 'modern times' but my spirit is very old
therefore my inspiration is old and cryptic."[17] Following the

---

[14] Meher Baba, *Discourses*, 6th ed, 3 vols. (San Francisco: Sufism
Reoriented, 1973), 1:85.

[15] Georges Bataille, *Guilty*, trans. Bruce Boone (San Francisco: Lapis
Press, 1988), xxxii.

[16] On the auto-deictic dimension of metal, see Nicola Masciandaro, "What
is This that Stands before Me?: Metal as Deixis," in *Reflections in the
Metal Void*, ed. Niall W. R. Scott (Oxford: Interdisciplinary Press, 2012),
3–17.

[17] See http://www.metalreviews.com/interviews/interviews.php?id=67.
Similarly, the gatefold text of *Obscure Verses for The Multiverse* points
towards the synthesis of traditional mysticism, modern science, and
individual speculative experience: "This album is a tribute to something
not only hypothetical but I must say spiritual as well. Today the
multiverse theories are something agreed upon yet debated by many.
Interesting to know how many ancient civilizations and their obscure
cults of philosophies have spoken to us about other dimensions and

satanic refusal of the apparent secondariness of individual being (createdness, epiphenomenality, givenness, historicity, and so forth), black metal creates from the weight of dead forms a counter gravity that draws one, inwardly and outwardly, into the living presence of unlimited reality.[18] "Thought and the Real touch only in black, the color of vision itself."[19] Likewise, black metal *is* theory in the sense of affective-intellectual experience that reveals by re-veiling everything in its own obscurity. Releasing one from, by condemning one for, the universal heresy of being yourself, the tomb black metal floats is *you*. As Inquisition affirm,

> These songs are the rituals of obscure verses, songs to carry you into a journey of thought and reflect while the hymns of Black Metal enshroud you, obscuring your surroundings allowing you to see further into your own cosmos and the one that surrounds you.[20]

universes existing long, long ago in times before modern cosmology were even a thought. Thousands of years ago some of our ancestors claimed to have visited these other worlds, other dimensions or universes through hallucinogenic travels under spells of entranced mystical states of mind and body, through self-hypnosis invoking their gods, or, plain and simply by gazing into the night sky and imagining such a thing because imagination is what we have, and it is there for a reason . . . So we ask questions and seek the answers."

[18] Cf. "Life seeks to unwind the limiting sanskaras [impressions] of the past and to obtain release from the mazes of its own making, so that its further creations may spring directly from the heart of eternity and bear the stamp of unhampered freedom and intrinsic richness of being which knows no limitation" (Meher Baba, *Discourses*, 1:135).

[19] Nicola Masciandaro, "Secret: No Light Has Ever Seen the Black Universe," in *Dark Nights of the Universe* (Miami: NAME, 2013), 56.

[20] Inquisition, *Obscure Verses for The Multiverse*, gatefold text. A similar triangulation of perspectives (esoteric, philosophical, and scientific) informs the work of *Darkspace*: "Darkspace is represented by a triple approach to universal questions. While none of the three theories is fundamental, Wroth mainly relies on esoteric/spiritual views, Zorgh represents scientific thought patterns, whereas Zhaaral goes for a metaphysical approach to the cosmos and the existence of Darkspace. We constantly elaborate new points of view and discuss philosophical questions within this trinity. . . . Science is descriptive, it illustrates what we perceive with our senses, it speaks in mathematical patterns and allows certain deductions and predictions. As fascinating as it may be—it

RELIQUARY

More cryptically, Inquisition's floating tomb evokes a medieval Christian motif with profound resonances to black metal as a Satano-Petrine musical art of religious inversion,[21] mystical

---

still is a unilateral approach to the Cosmos and its life forms. We are sure that neither esoterical semi-thruth, nor scientific limitations nor any religious dogma spoken for itself may reveal the true nature of the universe" ("Interview with Darkspace," http://www.mortemzine.net).

[21] By "Satano-Petrine" I mean to signify the weird domain of identity between black metal's satanic drive and the diabolical dimension of religion, the space of intersection between the devil's and St. Peter's cross. The spiritual significance of this space is mystical, in the sense that mysticism perforce reaches beyond religion in a *heavier* movement of will that works both with and against religion. In the genealogy of heavy metal, this space may be traced back to the inverted cross design included in the gatefold of Black Sabbath's first album, the vertical panel of which contains a poem describing a dark and surreal churchyard scene with "the headless martyr's statue," presumably St. Denis, the cephalophore identified in medieval tradition with Dionysius the Areopagite, putative author of the canonical mystical texts of the Dionysian Corpus. Like a mashup of negative theology and gothic kitsch, the poem represents a world in nigredo, sinking into death, yet not without the mysterious presence of spiritual promise: "The cataract of darkness form fully, the long black night beings, yet still, by the lake a young girl waits, unseeing she believes herself unseen, she smiles . . . ." In the contemporary black metal scene, the mystical intersection between the diabolical and the orthodox is perhaps best represented by the syncretic metaphysical satanism of Deathspell Omega, who draw from "the whole religious literature, from the old Jewish sects to the agnostics, from the St Augustinian approach to Christianity to radical Wahhabi pamphlets" in their musico-spiritual search for "the deus/diabolus absconditus" ("Interview with Deathspell Omega from AJNA Offensive," http://ezxhaton.kccricket.net/interview.html). Rome's Fides Inversa provide another conspicuous instance: "The project comes to life as an extremely individual idea in the eyes of the conceptual aspect, since it is the mirror of a personal spiritual and philosophical iter, aiming to the fulfillment of the so called 'self deification.' Fides Inversa is the inversion of the whole cosmic paradigm, not only the inversion of the judeo-christian faith, aiming to the deconstruction of being. As you can imagine the idea of Death is omnipresent and it has to be seen as the Void that attracts into the chaotic spiral. That is not only the negation of what exists, but the state in which everything is complete" ("Interview with Fides Inversa," *Mortem Zine*, http://www.mortemzine.net).

profanation, and spiritual suspension. Here I will lay bare only the essential artifacts.[22]

Liber Nycholay: "Then they made a tomb [*arcam*] covered in gold and placed the foot [of Muhammad] inside, anointed with balsam and wrapped with spices . . . All Saracens make pilgrimage to Mecca and venerate there the foot in the tomb, the foot of Muhammad. Truly, the ark is held suspended in the air and is drawn by three great stone magnets hanging above it on chains, for the ark is not covered with gold in the part where the magnets influence it from above. Many simple-minded Saracens believe that this is made to occur not artificially, but by a greater power."[23]

William of Conches: "A similar antagonism of forces draws [the earth] to the front and the back, to the right and the left, as we have heard of the tomb of Mahomet, which, being of iron, is sustained on every side by a magnet."[24]

Suzanne Akbari, on Dante's *Inferno*: "Like the suspended tomb of Muhammad . . . the body of Satan is at 'the point to which all weights are drawn [traggon]' (Inf. 34.111). The physics, in each case, are opposite: the magnetic weights pull on the suspended

---

[22] A more in-depth analysis is provided in Nicola Masciandaro & Edia Connole, *Floating Tomb: Black Metal Theory* (Milan: Mimesis, 2015), 7–31.

[23] "Quare fecerunt arcam deauratam et in ea posuerunt pedem ipsum balsemando et aromatibus inuoluendo . . . Omnes sarraceni peregrinacionem faciunt ad Mecham et adorabant ibi pedem in archa, pedem Machumeti. Archa uero in aere detinetur suspensa et trahitur a tribus magnis lapidibus in cathenis pendentibus super eam, non est enim ex ilia parte deaurata archa, quam superius calamite tangent. Credunt multi simplices sarraceni quod non artificióse sed potius uirtuose illud sit factum. . . . Quemadmodum christiani papam romanum credunt uicarium Ihesu Christi, sic sarraceni credunt califium de Baldacca esse uicarium. Et sicut christiani credunt <Ihesu Christum filium dei fuisse, sic sarraceni credunt> Machumetum fuisse nuncium et prophetam altissimi creatoris et fieri salui per ipsum ante deum" (Fernando González Muñoz, "*Liber Nycholay*: La layenda de Mahoma el cardinal Nicolás," *Al-Qantara* 25 (2004): 13, my translation). The *Liber Nycholay* is unique in limiting the remains to the foot. On the symbolic significance of Muhammad's foot as abject idol in relation to Dante's representation of Muhammad, see Suzanne Conklin Akbari, *Idols in the East: European Representations of Islam and the Orient, 1100–1450* (Ithaca, NY: Cornell University Press, 2012), 231–5.

[24] Quoted in Akbari, *Idols in the East*, 234.

tomb, while the heavy matter pushes on the suspended figure of Satan. In both cases, however, the result is suspension, and in-between state mirrored in the narrator's own state of being: at the sight of Satan, he says, 'I did not die and I did not remain alive . . . deprived alike of death and life' (Inf. 34.25, 27)."[25]

Anonymous: "Two things characterise the state of the *spiritual man*: that he is *suspended* and that he is *upside down*."[26]

Richard of St. Victor, on the "violence of charity": "Does it not seem that this degree of love (*amoris*) turns a man's mind to madness, as it were, when it will not allow him to hold a limit or measure to his jealous love (*emulatione*)? Does it not appear to be the height of madness to spurn true life, to reject the highest wisdom, and to resist omnipotence?"[27]

Ramakrishna on the "tamas of bhakti" or dark resistance of divine love: "*A Devotee*: 'How can one realize God?' MASTER: 'Through that kind of love. But one must force one's demand on God. One should be able to say: "O God, wilt Thou not reveal Thyself to me? I will cut my throat with a knife. This is the tamas of bhakti."'"[28]

---

[25] Akbari, *Idols in the East*, 23–5.

[26] Anonymous, *Meditations on the Tarot: A Journey into Christian Hermeticism*, trans. Robert Powell (New York: Penguin Putnam, 1985), 315.

[27] Richard of St. Victor, *On the Four Degrees of Violent Love*, trans. Andrew B. Kraebel, in *On Love*, ed. H. B. Feiss (Turnhout: Brepols, 2011), 295.

[28] *The Gospel of Sri Ramakrishna*, trans. Swami Nikhilananda (New York: Ramakrishna-Vivekananda Center, 1952), 186. Cf. "The incident of birth is common to all life on earth. Unlike other living creatures which are born insignificantly, live an involuntary life and die an uncertain death, the physical birth of human beings connotes an important and, if they are extra circumspect about it, perhaps a final stage of their evolutionary progress. Here onward, they no longer are automatons but masters of their destiny which they can shape and mold according to will. And this means that human beings, having passed through all the travails of lower evolutionary processes, *should insist* upon the reward thereof, which is 'Spiritual Birth' in this very life, and not rest content with a promise in the hereafter" (Meher Baba, quoted in *Lord Meher*, 1788, online at http://www.lordmeher.org, italics mine).

Bhagavad Gita: "Understanding is *tamasic* / when, thickly covered in darkness, / it imagines that wrong is right / and sees the world upside down."[29]

Tamas (PIE *temo-*, dark; Aramaic *te'oma*, twin; Hebrew *tehom*, abyss).

Gospel of John: "Now Thomas, one of the twelve, called the Twin, was not with them when Jesus came" (John 20:24).

Thomas Aquinas: "The disciple who was absent is first identified by his name, Thomas, which means a 'twin' or an 'abyss.' An abyss has both depth and darkness. And Thomas was an abyss on account of the darkness of his disbelief, of which he was the cause. Again, there is an abyss—the depths of Christ's compassion—which he had for Thomas. We read: 'Abyss calls to abyss' [Ps 42:7, as well as an album by Art Inferno, *Abyssvs Abyssvm Invocat* (Scarlet Records, 1999)]. That is, the depths of Christ's compassion calls to the depths of darkness [of disbelief] in Thomas, and Thomas' abyss of unwillingness [to believe] calls out, when he professes the faith, to the depths of Christ."[30]

R. C. Zaehner on Zurvan's twin-generating doubt: "Zurvan, however, does not create out of any super-fluity of being, for at the core of his being there is a latent defect of which he knows nothing. . . . the Absolute's failure of nerve at the very moment when the creator is about to issue forth from him, produces the principle of evil."[31]

Meher Baba: "This war is a big drama. There is the hero, heroine, villain all playing their parts in the drama. It is not Hitler's fault if he is playing the villain in God's drama. It's good he is acting his part well. I like villains, heroes, angels, devils—anyone who acts their parts perfectly!"[32]

---

[29] *Bhagavad Gita: A New Translation*, trans. Stephen Mitchell (New York: Three Rivers, 2000), 18.37.

[30] Thomas Aquinas, *Commentary on the Gospel of John*, trans. James A. Weisheipl and Fabian R. Larcher (Albany, NY: Magi Books, 1998), 25.5.2546, online at http://dhspriory.org/thomas/english/John20.htm.

[31] See R. C. Zaehner, *The Dawn and Twilight of Zororastrianism* (London: Weidenfeld and Nicolson, 1961), chapter 10, http://heritageinstitute.com/zoroastrianism/reference/zaehner/dawnV arZur10_1.htm.

[32] *Lord Meher*, 2133. Or as Ramakrishna is famously reported to have answered when asked why there is evil in the world, "To thicken the plot!"

The Book of Thomas the Contender: "The savior said, '. . . Now, since it has been said that you are my twin and true companion, examine yourself, and learn who you are, in what way you exist, and how you will come to be. Since you will be called my brother, it is not fitting that you be ignorant of yourself. And I know that you have understood, because you had already understood that I am the knowledge of the truth. So while you accompany me, although you are uncomprehending, you have (in fact) already come to know, and you will be called "the one who knows himself."'"[33]

Golden Legend: "The wine steward meanwhile, noticing that the apostle [Thomas] was not eating or drinking but sat with his eyes turned toward heaven, struck him a blow on the cheek. The apostle addressed him: 'It is better for you to receive here and now a punishment of brief duration, and to be granted forgiveness in the life to come. Know that I shall not leave this table before the hand that struck me is brought here by dogs.' The servant went out to draw water, a lion killed him and drank his blood, dogs tore his body to pieces, and a black one carries his right hand into the midst of the feast."[34]

Account of Elysaeus: "and the apostle, in his church on the mountain, is entombed in an iron tomb, and the tomb remains in the air by the power of four precious stones. Called lodestones [*adamans*], one is placed in the floor, a second in the ceiling, one at one angle to the tomb, and another at another. Truly, these stones love [*diligent*] the iron. The lower does not permit it to ascend, the higher from not descending, and the ones at the angles do not permit it to go from that place. The apostle is thus in the middle. The right arm, with which he touched the side of Christ, is incorruptible and remains outside the tomb."[35]

---

[33] *The Book of Thomas the Contender*, trans. John D. Turner, http://gnosis.org/naghamm/bookt.html. Cf. "Thomas is called abyss because he was granted insight into the depths of God's being when Christ, in answer to his question, said: 'I am the way the truth and the life'" (Jacobus de Voragine, *The Golden Legend: Readings on the Saints*, trans. William Granger Ryan, 2 vols. [Princeton, NJ: Princeton University Press, 1993], 1:29–30).

[34] Jacobus de Voragine, *Golden Legend*, 1:30.

[35] ". . . apostolus autem est in ecclesia eiusdem montis, et est in tumulo ferreo tumulatus; et tumulus ille manet in aere ex virtute 4 preciosorum lapidum. Adamans vocatur, unus in pavimento positus, in tecto secundus,

Gospel of John: "Unless I see in his hands the print of the nails, and place my finger in the mark of the nails, and place my hand in his side, I *will not* believe [*non credam*]" (John 20:25).

The medieval analogue of black metal's esoteric floating tomb enshrines a dark abyssic twinness with the eternal, one spiritually defined by inversive suspension in a volitional force-field of opposing attractors. The love that is its place is not soft, but adamantine, contentious, and operative in negation, in the form of resistance which permits not [*non permittit*]. Suspended with the finality of death in the divine abyss of itself, secure at the immovable omnipresent center of an absolute Satanic earth, your crypt-becoming-throne, the esoteric floating tomb is saturated with the radiant blackness of this negativity, this NO, which holds the unthinkable thingless essence of creativity and everlasting freedom:

> In this context, "abyss" is not a metaphor. . . . it is the life of darkness in God, the divine root of Hell in which the Nothing is eternally produced. Only when we succeed in sinking into this Tartarus and experiencing our own impotency do we become capable of creating, truly becoming poets.[36]

The secret of this NO is the black heart of metal, that which on its own knows and enjoys the non-difference between the negation of God in all things and the negation of all things as not-God. As Bataille—or War ("I AM MYSELF WAR" [JE SUIS MOI-MEME

---

unus ab uno angulo tumuli, alius ab alio. Isti vero lapides diligunt ferrum: inferior non permittit ascendi, superior non descendi, angulares non permittunt eum ire huc vel illuc. Apostolus autem est in medio. Bracfaium dextrum, cum quo tetigit latus Christi, inputribile est, manens extra tumulum" ("Der Bericht des Elysaeus," in "Der Priester Johannes," ed. Friedrich Zarncke, *Abhandlungen der philologisch-historischen Classe der königlich sächsischen Gesellschaft der Wissenschaften* 8 [1883]: 123).

[36] Giorgio Agamben, "Bartleby, or On Contingency," in *Potentialities: Collected Essays in Philosophy*, trans. Daniel Heller-Roazen (Stanford: Stanford University Press, 1999), 253.

LA GUERRE])[37]—writes, "Le néant n'est que moi-même / l'univers ma tombe . . . en moi-même / au fond d'un abîme / l'immense univers est la mort" [Nothingness is nothing but myself / the universe my tomb . . . in myself / at bottom of an abyss / the immense universe is death].[38]

SERMO EX SEPULCHRO

Immense cosmic visions emerge from the slow intervention of oblivion.[39]

From the tomb I speak to you—a tomb that speaks.

Pondus meum, amor meus; eo feror, quocumque feror—My love is my weight; by it I am borne, wheresoever I am borne.[40]

Pulling in all dimensions by its NO. Pushing in all directions by its YES. How I love that no one sees me. How I love that no one knows me. How I love THAT.

Black is my nakedness. My blackness is naked. *Blacker than black / Is She! Beholding Her, / Man is bewitched for evermore; / no other form can he enjoy.*[41]

Because you will listen, you will not hear. Because you hear, you will not understand. Because you understand, you will not know. Because you know, you will not see. Because you see, you will not experience. Because you experience, you are nothing.

Drunk—on the irrelevance of omniscience. Dust of space-time the odor of uncontainable tears.

All is laid out before all. And you? Nothing other than what you have chosen. To think, to feel, to act. Always more, always the same. My eyes pierce their seeing transparently, know all the see-through plans, blinking everybody's unimaginable blindness to the immense and total lie.

---

[37] Georges Bataille, *Visions of Excess: Selected Writings, 1927–1939*, ed. and trans. Allan Stoekl (Minneapolis: University of Minnesota Press, 1985), 239.

[38] Georges Bataille, *L'Archangélique et autres poèmes* (Paris: Mercure de France, 1967). Gratitude to Edia Connole for bringing these lines to my attention.

[39] Fides Inversa, "VII," *Mysterium Tremendum et Fascinans* (World Terror Committee, 2014).

[40] Augustine, *Confessions* (Cambridge, MA: Harvard University Press, 1950), 13.9.

[41] *The Gospel of Sri Ramakrishna*, trans. Swami Nikhilananda (New York: Ramakrishna-Vivekananda Center, 1952), 302.

Be done and die, since you shall anyway, as you never were. Deselect yourself. Or another death, not worth the name, will choose you.

You know what I am talking about. Confess!

Satan I invoke you with my death under the black sky of night. / Dead, dead, Satan I am dead . . .[42]

But—infinitely worse—the prophecy of what *you* will do is true, you being nothing more than the prophecy of yourself. That which: explains, dramatizes, argues, imitates, justifies. Even the ways of Reality! As if, to begin with, the nature of mere matter— shadow of a shadow of a shadow—did not already forever totally exceed human understanding. As if it were all somehow laid out for us to *get*, a ready-man-made universe! As if anything was ever *given* to itself. Please go away and go on thinking you can be right, scheming the scantiest good. Go ahead, and *think*. Business, from OE *bisig*, "anxious, concerned, preoccupied, worried." As if you will turn, or convert, a profit.

The condition of the world, the strife and uncertainty that is everywhere, the general dissatisfaction with and rebellion against any and every situation shows that the ideal of material perfection is an empty dream and proves the existence of an eternal Reality beyond materiality . . . Reality alone is real; the only true thing that can be said is, Reality exists and all that is not the Real has no existence except as illusion.[43]

Woe to they who are born. Death to they who will die. Damnation to everyone who worries—the no one to worry about!

You're searching for your mind don't know where to start / Can't find the key to fit the lock on your heart / You think you know but you are never quite sure / Your soul is ill but you will not find a cure. . . . But will you turn to me when it's your turn to die?[44]

Is there one here who is willing to draw the line, who does it right now, straight through oneself?

And the whole world split open. And the spell, a shadow cast on the darkest horizon, is broken, torn to zero by the Real. *Real*

---

[42] Inquisition, "Solitary Death in the Nocturnal Woodlands," *Into the Infernal Regions of the Ancient Cult.*

[43] Meher Baba, *The Everything and the Nothing* (Beacon Hill, Australia: Meher House Publications, 1963), 55.

[44] Black Sabbath, "Lord of the World," *Master of Reality* (Vertigo, 1971).

music . . . reaches across time and space and it does not give a fuck about neither of them.[45]

This is the sign of the spirit of truth . . . to acknowledge oneself as total hate.[46] That is good. *And the Lord said, "I will destroy man whom I have created . . . for it repenteth me that I have made them"* (Genesis 6:7).

To live—never stop living—until this is no longer life.
To die—never cease dying—until this is no longer death.
NOTHING WILL DO IT FOR YOU.

"Lord of all nobleness, why do you weep?" And he said these words to me, "Ego tanquam centrum circuli . . . tu autem non sic" [I am as the center of a circle . . . whereas you are not].[47]

The infinite moment when you realize how real this vast separation really is.

À force d'aimer—by the force of love—I have lost myself in the ocean. And what an ocean! A tempest of laughter and tears.[48]

. . . mourning all, any who would give a name to this sorrow . . .

Thus, floating in a mystic tomb, this tomb of me (my tomb of this), suspended in the acosmos of black metal, what is it that will not stop spiraling into the sound now pointing at *you*, singling out someone at the ancient shrine with the raised adamantine finger of an incorruptible (tone) arm? And who is being pointed to?

Why call oneself anything at all?

What is this that stands before me? / Figure in black which points at me . . .[49]

---

[45] Watain, *Opus Diaboli* (His Master's Noise, 2012).
[46] Angela of Foligno, *Instructions*, in *Complete Works*, trans. Paul Lachance (New York: Paulist Press, 1993), 229.
[47] Dante Alighieri, *Vita Nuova*, trans. Dino S. Cervigni and Edward Vasta (Notre Dame, IN: University of Notre Dame Press, 1996), 64.
[48] "A force d'aimer, je me suis perdu dans l'océan. Et quel océan! / Une tempête de rires et de larmes" (Robert Desnos, "Tour de la Tombe," *Essential Poems and Writings*, ed. Mary Ann Caws [Boston, MA: Black Widow, 2007], 162).
[49] Black Sabbath, "Black Sabbath," *Black Sabbath* (Vertigo, 1970).

Symposium Photographs

Öykü Tekten

Bound to Metal (Interview with Edia Connole for *Legacy*)

Dominik Irtenkauf

Black Metal ist nicht nur Musikstil, sondern auch Konzept und Ideologie. Zudem beziehen sich manche der Bands auf Esoterik, Okkultismus und Weltkriegsgeschehen. Liegt es also fern, diesen schillernden Stil einer genaueren Analyse zu untersuchen. Die besonders im angloamerikanischen Raum lokalisierte Black Metal Theory möchte nicht über, sondern mit Black Metal denken, das heißt die Theoretiker hören Metal nicht allein als Fan, sondern versetzen sich in das Ereignis, das sich zum Beispiel während des Abspielens von Mayhems „De Mysteriis Dom Sathanas" abspielt. Eine Theoretikerin, die sich in ihren Artikeln und nun auch bald in einem Buch mit dieser Spielart beschäftigt, ist EDIA CONNOLE aus Dublin. Erste Kontaktaufnahme zum Black Metal fand sie über die Theory, wie sie ausführt: „Ich bin mit Punk aufgewachsen, aber Black Metal war immer schon im Hintergrund, hat meine frühen Sounderfahrungen mitgeprägt. Black Metal rückte dann mit dem dritten Black Metal Theory-Symposium in Dublin im November 2011 in den Vordergrund. Ich hatte das Vergnügen, zusammen mit Scott Wilson einige der Teilnehmer in meinem Haus zu bekochen. Scott traf ich eher zufällig auf dem zweiten Black Metal Theory Symposium zum Thema Melancology in London [Er veranstaltete diese Tagung und brachte nun bei Zero Books auch einen Sammelband zum Thema heraus.-Anm. des Autors] Wir gründeten als Folge dieses Treffens eine konzeptuell-kulinarische Kooperation namens MOUTH. Wir hörten damals ziemlich viel Cascadian Black Metal zum Kochen. Ich sollte ein paar Tage danach eine Vorlesung zur Black Metal Theory halten und orientierte mich dabei an der Essaysammlung „Hideous Gnosis", die anlässlich des 1. Symposiums entstand. Ich erinnere mich, dass meine Hörerfahrung von Faunas Album „Rain" (2006) stark durch Steven Shakespeares Kommentar in diesem Buch beeinflusst wurde: „Das Licht, das sich selbst erhellt, das Dunkle, das sich selbst zu Erde macht: Eingeschwärzte Notizen aus Schellings Underground.' Shakespeare ist ein brillianter Black Metal-Theoretiker. Er weiss wirklich, wie man mit der Musik denkt. Seine Ideen in dem Text, über das wechselnde Wesen des Black Metals, über Tiefenökologie und Melancholie, haben meine Hörwahrnehmung sehr geprägt. Für mich hat die Black Metal Theory Black Metal verbessert, durch die theoretische Beschäftigung mit der Musik kam mir Black Metal näher. Indem ich Fauna und Wolves In The Throne Room hörte, mein Hören mit Steven Shakespeares phänomenologischer Lektüre verband, wurde die Musik ein integraler Bestandteil meines Lebens." CONNOLE schreibt u.a. für das Helvete-Journal, das sich in ästhetischer und philosophischer Weise diesem Genre nähert. Ein wesentlicher Referenzpunkt ist auch der französische Philosoph und Autor Georges Bataille (1897-1962), dessen Bücher zur Ekstase, zum Verhältnis von Eros und Tod und zur Gewalt sich für eine Black Metal-Analyse geradezu anbieten. Doch was hält die Black-Metal-Theoretikerin von kritischen Einwänden der Szene, es sei eben nur Metal, und alles Weitere würde in den Stoff hineingeheimnist werden? „Black Metal Theory wird unbewusst von diesem Verlangen getrieben, nichts zu wissen und nichts zu sagen, auf eine negative Art und Weise. Das findet sich auch im Black Metal. Ein zentrales Charakteristikum ist der Verlust oder das Verlieren, ob es sich um den Verlust von verständlicher Bedeutung geht, durch die instrumentelle und gesangliche Orientierung des Genres, oder in vergleichbaren Stellen in Interviews, wenn der Black Metal-Künstler auf die Frage nach einer tieferen Bedeutung in ihrer Musik oder Philosophie gefragt wird, entweder sich zurückzieht oder vorbricht in eine tautologische Aussage wie ‚It's just fucking metal!' oder sich auf eine verabsolutierte Emotion oder Haltung zurückzieht: ‚I hate everything, I just do what I like!' Diese Art von antrainierter Ignoranz erweist sich als existenziell für diese Musiker, man findet es in stark emotionalisierter Monstrosität im Genre, deshalb die Masken und das Corpsepaint im Genre oder aber die Gewalt gegen sich selbst." Black Metal Theory versucht, so versteht es EDIA CONNOLE in Rückgriff auf Nicola Masciandaro, der in Brooklyn (New York) das 1. Black Metal Theory-Symposium im Jahr 2009 ausrichtete, das zerstörerische und nihilistische Angebot von Black Metal anzunehmen und das rasende Tempo, die klirrenden

Gitarren und schlicht den Anteil an Noise in dieser Stilrichtung auf das Denken von Kultur, Kunst, Geschichte und Gegenwart anzuwenden. Seit ungefähr dieser Zeit sammeln sich auch an den Akademien Wissenschaftler, die Metal von einer weniger philosophischen Seite betrachten. Sie werfen der Black Metal Theory teilweise eine zu große Nähe zu ihrem Gegenstand vor. „Man kann sich auf zwei Weisen diesem Thema nähern: einerseits könnte man mit diesen Wissenschaftlern übereinstimmen und Black Metal Theory klar als eine para-akademische Disziplin bezeichnen. Somit hat sie weniger mit Geisteswissenschaften als mit einem Humanismus zu tun, was Masciandaro als einen ‚kopflosen Humanismus' bezeichnen würde, ‚der sich der Leidenschaft der Frage als Essenz des menschlichen Wesens hingibt'. Man könnte dem noch hinzufügen, dass Black Metal Theory in ihrem methodologischen Streben, dieser Frage nachzugehen, unweigerlich vage und abstrakt wird." CONNOLE sieht hierbei die theoretische Auseinandersetzung mit Black-Metal-Platten als eine Möglichkeit, dem instinktiven Kompositionsprozess der Musiker nahe zu kommen, indem die wissenschaftliche Distanz aufgegeben und im Schreiben versucht wird, einen Kommentar zum Geschehen abzugeben. 2015 soll beim Mimesis Verlag das Buch „Floating Tomb: Black Metal, Theory, and Mysticism" erscheinen, das EDIA zusammen mit Nicola Masciandaro schreibt.

Theoria e praxis del Black Metal
(Interview with Fabio Selvafiorita for
L'Intellettuale Dissidente)[1]

Nicola Masciandaro

1-Prof. Masciandaro, ci vuole parlare della sua formazione culturale? E' professore alla CUNY. Cosa insegna?

Insegno letteratura medievale inglese, specialmente opere del Trecento come *I racconti di Canterbury, Piers Plowman*, e *Rivelazioni dell'Amore Divino* di Giuliana di Norwich. Questo mi da l'opportunità d'insegnare anche vari testi preferiti in traduzione, per esempio la *Commedia* di Dante, il *Liber* di Angela da Foligno, e i sermoni di Meister Eckhart. Per il dottorato mi son concentrato su i concetti e rappresentazioni del lavoro e adesso mi interessa soprattutto la tradizione mistica e certi autori moderni: Clarice Lispector, Meher Baba, Emil M. Cioran ed altri. Spero di completare quest'anno un libro sul dolore in chiave mistica intitolato *Sorrow of Being*, e poi scrivere due altri testi, *The Whim* e *Appalling Melodrama*. Il primo riguarda la natura della spontaneità e il secondo l'incrocio mistico tra l'amore, la paura, e la musica. Mi sembra che la tendenza generale del mio metodo sia di esplorare lo spazio tra la poesia e la critIca e di seguire un modo di pensare e scrivere definito da ciò che trovo significativo senza preoccupazione (vide *Sufficient Unto the Day: Sermones Contra Solicitudinem*). Il desiderio di rinnovare il genere del commento, mediante la rivista *Glossator*, e l'esperimento di 'black metal theory' sono rami di questa tendenza. All'inizio della post-laurea, volevo studiare il modernismo e le opere di Ezra Pound, ma questo interesse si è trasformato in un maggiore interesse per testi medievali. Però dallo spirito del modernismo conservo la volontà di superare lo storicismo. Un' altra influenza nei miei primi studi

---

[1] This is the full original text of an interview published in *L'Intellettuale Dissidente* (2015), http://www.lintellettualedissidente.it.

è stato il tradizionalismo di Ananda K. Coomaraswamy, e dunque la potenzialità di un modo di studiare sia esegetico che critico. All'inizio dei mei studi per conseguire il baccalaureato mi hanno attirato di più la matematica, la poesia, e—alquanto meno—la filosofia. E la mia gravitazione verso il medioevo è stata senza dubbio condizionata da mio padre, che è un medievalista in letteratura italiana.

2-Che cos'è la Black Metal Theory?

Black metal theory è il nereggiamento mutuale di metal e la teoria. Come il lavoro alchemico inizia con il processo di *nigredo*, black metal theory significa una pratica contemplativa che crea qualcosa di nuovo, formalmente, dalla trasformazione creativa—nello spazio di visione intellettuale ed affettiva—di metal e teoria. Invece di studiare black metal come oggetto, di scrivere *su* black metal, black metal theory indica di più la riflessione *con* black metal e quindi la continuazione consapevole delle sue dimensioni visionarie. Contro il concetto consumistico della musica, per cui l'arte è solo qualcosa da godere, e contro il concetto accademico della musica, per cui l'arte è solo qualcosa da analizzare, black metal theory si pone come un metodo di 'headbanging' sia musicale sia teoretico. Così black metal theory rappresenta la possibilità di un risveglio dell'antica intelligenza del telos unitario dI musica e filosofia. Comunque, dato che l'attualizzazione di black metal theory e la questione di ciò che essa costituisce materialmente rimangono oscuri, io penso che in questo momento una propria black metal theory ancora non esista, o esiste più come un sogno o immaginazione di se stesa. Vari individui hanno adottato l'idea per vari scopi convergenti e divergenti. Forse questo fatto, più che la mia definizione, indica la sua potenzialità nera.

3-Ci vuole parlare di cosa è per Lei, Nicola Masciandaro, il Black Metal musicale anche in relazione alla sua specifica formazione filosofico-letteraria?

Per me black metal è, soprattutto, una musica spirituale e mistica, fondata sulla negatività dell' essere. Black metal esprime l'essenza negativa della volontà e dunque apre la porta verso l'esperienza incomunicabile, estatica-dolorosa, della realtà *che è*, eternamente libera e indipendente dai nostri concetti, la realtà divina del *che* o *quodditas* infinita. Nel libro *Floating Tomb: Black Metal Theory*, scritto in collaborazione con Edia Connole, e che sarà pubblicato quest'anno da Mimesis, ricerco alcuni temi riguardo alla spiritualità di black metal: l'anticosmismo, l'involuzione della coscienza, l'amore negativo di Dio, il nesso misterioso di fattualità e individuazione, ed altri. In risposta alla seconda parte della domanda, esiste per forza una certa relazione tra gli studi medievali e black metal, se non altro perché derivano in parte tutt'e due, storicamente, dal medievalismo romantico. Ma dal mio punto di vista, questa relazione non è molto importante. Più significativa mi pare è la capacità di black metal di attivare musicalmente le verità di scienza, filosofia, e religione in un modo mistico, cioè, nella profondità esperienziale della sua estetica esuberante negativa.

4-Alcuni gruppi Black Metal non hanno accolto molto bene la Black Metal Theory. In generale i musicisti sono poco inclini alla speculazione filosofica riguardo al loro lavoro, ritenendola quasi una intromissione nella loro intimità. Come spieghi questa ritrosia alla speculazione filosofica?

È naturale se qulacuno è sospettoso e diffidente, e per forza interessato, quando un'altro parla della propria amata. Questo è parte della sofferenza d'amore. Ci sono anche molti gruppi black metal che non mi piacciono! È ugualmente ovvio che musicisti di black metal fanno già black metal theory mediante le varie forme di riflessione e speculazione e critica che sono inseparabili dalla vita culturale della musica per sè. Il problema essenziale, sia etico sia discorsivo, è che l'idea di black metal theory è troppo vicina rispetto a black metal, ma remota o piuttosto sconosciuta in pratica. La 'scena' non ha nessun problema quando artisti dissertano filosoficamente davanti alle loro librerie o a una lavagna sul black metal e temi affini, o quando un fan produce un saggio più commento che recensione. La tensione arriva nell'ambito dell'idea che può esistere un discorso speculativo e intellettuale paragonabile a black metal, un discorso nuovo e intensivo e tuttavia nello spirito della musica. Nel contempo, l'idea di black metal theory non è a casa nel mondo accademico, in cui non c'è molto rispetto per l'autorità poetica e filosofica di heavy metal, tranne come oggetto di studi culturali, sociologici, o musicologici. Così black metal theory fa l'avventura tra, da una parte, il fango dell'edonismo e l'incoscienza della scena consumistica, e dall'altra parte, il deserto freddo della mentalità critica e ipocrita dell'intelletualismo accademico. Logicamente, l'idea di black metal theory è a un tempo nobile e donchisciottesca, un gioco serio per così dire. Ma l'universo di metal, e quindi lo spazio per black metal theory, è vasto e magnifico. L'idea che il lavoro di qualsiasi black metal teorizzatore possa contaminare o minacciare l'essenza della musica, o la teoria per quello che conta, è infinitamente più ridicola di Donchisciotte. In ogni caso, la questione dell'autenticità e del valore di black metal theory rispetto a black metal deve essere affrontata in stretto rapporto con le opere specifiche e con gli autori individuali. Bisogna sempre cerare un equilibrio tra la testa e il cuore. Spiritualmente, il problema del 'intromissione' concerne il fatto che alcuni amatori di black metal occupano, come la maggior parte del mondo umano, l'atteggiamento che è importante o responsabile preoccuparsi, in questo caso, riguardo allo stato di black metal or black metal theory. Questo è parte della 'nostra' cultura socio-intellettuale, dove le ansie e simili dolori psichici, mediante il desiderio di essere o sentirsi 'al corrente,' sono confusi con sincerità, e dove quasi nessuno sa come pensare giustamente sulle cose senza giudicare altre persone. Ma la verità di black metal, come la verità in genere, ci fa scoprire autonomia e libertà. Dato che la verità è sicura, senza paura, poichè "l'amore perfetto scaccia il timore" (1 Giovanni 4:18), tutti stanno in errore. Indulgere in preoccupazione è contro lo spirito selvaggio-nobile di black metal, specialmente perchè black metal esprime liberamente il *contemptus mundi* e l'odio per tutto ciò che è debole nello spirito umano. Come dice Meher Baba, "True love is no game for the faint-hearted and the weak. It is born of strength and understanding" [Il vero amore non è un gioco per i pavidi e deboli. Nasce dalla forza e intelligenza]. Abbandonare preoccupazione è il primo e l'ultimo passo della stretta via di *non serviam*. Similmente, la voce, sia essa di black metal o black metal theory, è vera nella misura in cui evoca la natura daemoniaca del vento: "Il vento soffia dove vuole e ne senti la voce, ma non sai da dove viene e dove va" (Giovanni 3:3). Sono sicuro che chiunque pensa onestamente sul principio di black metal theory vedrà che non sta in contraddizione con black metal. La contraddizione è illusoria, esistente solo al livello di dicerie, pubblicità, pettegolezzo, e maldicenza.

5-Ancor prima delle tematiche affrontate nei testi dei gruppi Black, caratteristica essenziale del Black Metal è la lacerazione del suono e della voce. Non è evidente in questo processo di degenerazione sonora una similitudine con la fase della nigredo alchemica (con tutta la simbologia legata al ... blacker than the blackest black ...)?

Veramente. La connessione tra black metal e nigredo è stata interpretata da diversi autori (vide Joseph Russo, "Perpetue Putesco – Perpetually I Putrefy," in *Hideous Gnosis* [2009]; Steven Shakespeare, "Shuddering: Black Metal on the Edge of the Earth," in *Melancology* [2014]). Allo stesso modo, il suono classico di black metal è stato chiamato 'necro'. Come ha detto Eugene Thacker in una intervista del 2010, "[it is] almost like the music is distorting or breaking down the tape or the CD itself" [è quasi come se la musica stesse alterando o corrompendo il nastro o il CD stesso]. Dunque la nigredo della musica è correlativa alla nigredo della materialità, la putrefazione che libera la spontaneità delle forze creative. E qui c'è anche una analogia importante con la Crocifissione, come il martoriare del Logos o il Verbo di Dio. Come una profanazione del concetto medievale del torchio mistico (cfr. Inquisition, "Crush the Jewish Prophet," *Magnificent Glorification of Lucifer* [2004]), black metal crocifigge musicalmente la religione, e più generalmente tutte le mediazioni tra l'individuo e la realtà universale, e si ubriaca con il vino del cadavere sempre decomponendosi di Dio. Come dice Xasthur, "The burning corpse of god shall keep us warm in the doom of howling winds, / For we are a race from beyond the wanderers of night" ("Doomed by Howling Winds," *Xasthur* [2006]). Secondo Plotino, la putrefazione deriva da "l'inabilità dell'Anima di generare un' altra forma di essere." Ma questa debolezza dell'anima eterna è solo una debolezza dalla prospettiva del tempo. Dalla prospettiva eterna, la putrefazione significa la spontaneità radicale della realtà divina che in libertà assoluta crea, conserva, e distrugge come vuole, per pura volontà. È per questa sovrarazionale ragione che black metal loda nello stesso movimento, senza contraddizioni, la sovranità della volontà individuale e le forze della morte e dissoluzione. Come dice Erik Danielsson di Watain nel suo *Opus Diaboli* (2012), "[real music] reaches across time and space and it does not give a fuck about neither of them."

6-Uno dei saggi più interessanti del tuo blog è intitolato, poeticamente: No Light Has Ever Seen the Black Universe. Nell'oscurità si rivela la vera luce. Che cos'è il Nero nella Black Metal Theory?

Il nero di black metal theory è sia il nero di black metal che il nero nello spazio tra metal e teoria. Nel primo senso, il concetto di nero ha tante varie dimensioni che non posso sviluppare qui (vide Eugene Thacker, "Three Questions on Demonology," in *Hideous Gnosis*; Scott Wilson, "Introduction to Melancology," Drew Daniel, "Corpsepaint as Necro-Minstrelsy, or Towards the Re-Occultation of Black Blood," e Aspasia Stephanou, "Black Sun," in *Melancology*). Nel senso secondo, nero significa soprattutto il 'colore' di visione, nel significato completo (corporale, immaginativo, e intellettuale) che si applica ugualmente all'esperienza di musica e alla contemplazione. La visione/teoria è nera a causa del fatto che il nero è il colore che vedo quando non c'è nulla da vedere, dove l'unica cosa da vedere è il fatto di vedere. La visione corporale, e la percezione sensibile in genere, è nera nel senso che non vedo cose ma *oggetti*, qualcosa che la mia visione non può penetrare. La visione immaginativa e nera nel senso che non vedo qualcosa ma la sua immagine, una rappresentazione nella memoria. E la visione intellettuale è nera nel senso che tocca al massimo l'essenza di qualcosa, ma non la sua realtà stessa. Così dice François Laruelle nel testo *Du noir univers*, "Un noir phénoménal remplit entièrement l'essence de l'homme." E come dice Emil M. Cioran, vedere le cose in nero significa vedere da oltre la sfera di essere: "If we see things black, it is because we weigh them in the dark . . . They cannot adapt to life because they have not been thought with a view to life. . . . We are beyond all human calculation, beyond any notion of salvation or perdition, of being or non-being, we are in a particular silence, a superior modality of the void." In ogni direzione, in ogni dimensione, vedo nero perchè dovunque guardo, mi trovo davanti ai limiti della visione, e, come un riflesso speculare senza nulla essere riflesso, l'oscurità di me stesso, i limiti neri di questo sogno reale che si chiama la vita. Ma questo nero, quest'orizzonte oscuro e onnipresente, è anche la cosa più bella del mondo. Come brutto sarebbe tutto se tutto quello che vedo fosse tutto quello che c'è. "Nigra sum sed formosa" (Cantico dei Cantichi 1:4). E quindi quest'oscurità è stata identificata come l'immagine divina nel medioevo. Dice Eriugena, "the Divine likeness in the human mind is most clearly discerned when it is only known that it is, and not known what it is . . . what it is is denied in it [*negatur in ea quid esse*], and only that it is is affirmed." In altre parole, la bellezza nera della visone è il misterioso fatto di visione per sé, l'invisibilità oscura *che* è. Qui troviamo l'immanenza radicale del divino e/o l'ordinarietà assoluta della realtà mistica, nel senso che la nostra cecità stessa, se veramente *vista*, è l'illuminazione di ciò che non può essere visto, almeno senza morire a se stessi, "perché nessun uomo può vedermi e restare vivo" (Esodo 33:20). Come spiega Bonaventura, "Abituato alle oscurità degli enti e fantasmi sensibili, quando fissa lo sguardo sulla luce del sommo essere, gli sembra di non vedere nulla. Non comprende infatti che quella stessa oscurità è la prima luce della nostra intelligenza: proprio come quando l'occhio vede solo la luce ha l'impressione di non vedere nulla." Il nero trovato nello spazio tra metal e teoria non è diverso da questo nero universale. Black metal theory è solo una nuova modalità per vederlo. Più specificamente, il nero di black metal theory è il nero che uno vede quando prova di capire e toccare chiaramente nel proprio essere tutto ciò che sente dentro l'esperienza di black metal. Da questa prospettiva, lo scopo di black metal theory è di vedere, faccia a faccia, ciò che la musica *sa*. Ma visto che la realizzazione di questo scopo richiede una teoria in cui qualcos'altro che se stessi vede, black metal theory rappresenta per forza una visione che passa attraverso la morte spirituale. Così il prossimo simposio che ho co-organizzato per questa primavera a St. Vitus Bar si chiama Mors Mystica.

7-C'è una possibile continuità tra la nigredo, l'immaginazione negativa e il pessimismo cosmico?

Sì, certo. Nei miei scritti, mi sono occupato di queste tematiche riguardo alla natura di abitudine e all'oscurità della Crocifissione come avvenimento della materialità cosmica di dolore mistico. Vide i saggi "Come Cosa Che Cada: Habit and Cataclysm, or, Exploding Plasticity," in *French Theory Today* (2011) e "Paradisical Pessimism: On the Crucifixion Darkness and the Cosmic Materiality of Sorrow," in *Qui Parle* (2014). Nel primo esploro la virtù e l'etica, nel senso classico di divenire spirituale, come un processo di marcire. Come molte tradizioni hanno affermato, lo scopo della vita è di pulire e scoprire lo specchio dell'anima per renderla capace di realizzare la realtà infinita. Lo specchio, la coscienza umana individualizzata, è già fatta, ora e per sempre, per noi che—per qualche spontaneità inconcepibile—realmente esistiamo in questo strano universo come noi stessi. Il lavoro che resta è solo per eliminare le impressioni (materiali, sottili, e mentali) da questo specchio nero. Secondo Pseudo-Dionisio, questo processo si chiama *aphaeresis*, ed è paragonato alla scultura. Ma se sei *tu* che sta dormendo dentro il marmo di spaziotempo, come si fa gestire il martello e scalpello? Bisogna una forza delicatamente distruttiva che può operare anche dentro il marmo. Sviluppando quest'idea, sostengo che la conversione di Sant'Agostino è modellata sulla tortura etrusca, citata da Aristotele e Virgilio e anche Agostino, in cui una persona è stata legata faccia a faccia a un cadavere fino alla morte dalla putrefazione. (Vide Reza Negarestani, "La sposa cadavere. Pensando con la *nigredo*," trad. Vincenzo Cuomo, in *Kaiak. A Philosophical Journey*). Come Lazzaro, la risurrezione spirituale è preparata da un periodo di auto-putrefazione, il marcire di se stesso, nel senso dell'identità personale corruttibile. Scrive Agostino, "E tu, Signore . . . mi facevi ripiegare su me stesso, togliendomi da dietro al mio dorso, ove mi ero rifugiato per non guardarmi, e ponendomi davanti alla mia faccia, affinché vedessi quanto era deforme, quanto storpio e sordido, coperto di macchie e piaghe. Visione orrida; ma dove fuggire lungi da me?" Black metal, specialmente mediante la practica simbolica di trucco cadaverico, da espressione allo stesso processo apparentemente impossibile e inevitabile. Nel secondo saggio, esploro la dimensione mistica del pessimismo cosmico mediante la tradizione di esegesi dell'oscurità della Crocifissione. L'idea qui è che il pessimismo funziona come un misticismo inverso e dunque ci porta all'orrore paradisiaco, caratterizzato dalla conoscenza che il buio di questo cosmo è il buio di se stesso e che il dolore si è creato con l'universo. Contro Lovecraft ed altri pessimisti materialisti, sostengo che le emozioni umane hanno un significato cosmico, un significato sia migliore sia peggiore. In breve, tutto è colpa tua, ma tu non sei tu. Qui ancora ci sono connessioni importanti a black metal, in paticolare ai generi di cosmic/space black metal e depressive suicidal black metal. Cfr. Mütiilation's *Sorrow Galaxies* (2007) e Nihil, *Cosmic Pessimism* (2015). Riguardo a queste idee in genere, due pensatori importanti sono Eugene Thacker e Dylan Trigg, entrambi i quali trattano di black metal. In fine, riguardo alla immaginazione negativa, posso dire che la continuità indicata nella domanda è semplicemente parte della continuità nel cuore nero di metal, cioè, la non-differenza fra la negazione di Dio in tutte le cose e la negazione di tutte le cose come non-Dio.

8-Cos'è il Bergmetal?

Bergmetal è un nome per il genere di metal che suona e sogna le montagne e temi alpini. Il genere non è molto consosciuto, però è manifesto che esiste da lungo tempo. Vide Lieut. Nab Saheb of Kashmir & Denys X. Abaris, O.S.L., *Bergmetal: Oro-Emblems of the Musical Beyond* (2014). Il libro triangola le montagne, il misticismo, ed il metal, sviluppando il pensiero di John Ruskin, Julius Evola ed altri in un modo commentario che trovo molto interessante, specialmente perché fin dall'adolescenza sono stato appassionato rocciatore. L'esperienza e la disciplina necessarie nell'arrampicata su roccia, l'intersezione del movimento difficile con la bellezza naturale mi hanno sempre insegnato a perseguire l'ideale di una integrazione fra la conoscenza e il fare.

Also available from SCHISM press:

**AND THEY WERE TWO IN ONE
AND ONE IN TWO
Edited by Nicola Masciandaro &
Eugene Thacker**

A collection of essays on beheading and
cinema, with full color interior. Contents:
Dominic Pettman, "What Came First, the
Chicken or the Head?" – Eugene Thacker,
"Thing and No-Thing" – Alexi Kukuljevic,
"Suicide by Decapitation" – Alexander
Galloway, "The Painted Peacock" – Evan
Calder Williams, "Recapitation" – Nicola
Masciandaro, "Decapitating Cinema" – Ed
Keller, "Corpus Atomicus" – Gary J Shipley, "Remote Viewing."
Photography by Leighton Pierce.

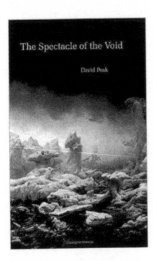

**THE SPECTACLE OF THE VOID
David Peak**

The world has been swallowed by
strangeness. A new reality—a "horror
reality"—has taken hold. David Peak's *The
Spectacle of the Void* examines the
boundaries of the irreal and the beyond,
exploring horror's singular ability to
communicate the unknown through
language and image. It is also a speculative
work that gazes unflinchingly at the
inevitable extinction of mankind,
questioning whether or not the burden of
our knowing we will someday cease to exist
is a burden after all, or rather the very
notion that will set us free.

SUFFICIENT UNTO THE DAY: SERMONES CONTRA SOLICITUDINEM
Nicola Masciandaro

The writings in this volume are bound by desire to refuse worry, to reject and throw it away the only way possible, by means that are themselves free from worry. If this is impossible—all the more reason to do so. I. The Sweetness (of the Law) II. Nunc Dimittis: Getting Anagogic III. Half Dead: Parsing Cecilia IV. Wormsign V. Gourmandized in the Abattoir of Openness VI. Grave Levitation: Being Scholarly VII. Labor, Language, Laughter: Aesop and the Apophatic Human VIII. This is Paradise: The Heresy of the Present IX. Becoming Spice: Commentary as Geophilosophy X. Amor Fati: A Prosthetic Gloss XI. Following the Sigh.

TRUE DETECTION
Edited by Edia Connole, Paul J. Ennis & Nicola Masciandaro

A collection of philosophical and critical essays on the television series *True Detective*.

"Traditionally, the detective genre deals with the problem of epistemology—how to know something that one doesn't know. There are some things we cannot know, and some things we should not know. Sometimes clues just give way to more clues, and epistemic tedium rules the day. These essays reveal knowledge becoming an enigma to itself, revealing the brilliant futility of the epistemological project."
– Eugene Thacker

"The television event of the year—I would say many years—is without doubt True Detective. One deserving of forensic, unflinching, and unrelenting philosophical treatment."
– Simon Critchley

"The most intelligent series in TV history has opened strange crypts for explorers. This excellent essay collection reveals just how far the dark tunnels lead. Let it coax you from the comforts of death and fear, into detection of the guttering nightmare that is life, coldly seen."

– Nick Land

Contributors: Gary J. Shipley, Edia Connole, Nicola Masciandaro, Fintan Neylan, Paul J. Ennis, Ben Woodard, Niall McCann, Daniel Fitzpatrick, Scott Wilson, Erin K. Stapleton, Caoimhe Doyle & Katherine Foyle, Daniel Colucciello Barber, Dominic Fox, Charlie Blake.

H. P. LOVECRAFT: THE DISJUNCTION IN BEING
Fabián Ludueña

"Philosophy has always sought to wrench truth away from myths. But myth is not the narrative of origins, the path philosophy took from Plato to Schelling; myth is the opposite, the truth that narrates the end of humanity and its disproportion with respect to the cosmos. This is why Lovecraft is 'the most brilliant mythographer of the twentieth century.' Rereading his oeuvre, philosophy will learn that true myth is the opposite of history, since it is summoned to enumerate the natural powers of the cosmos. At the same time, philosophy will learn that myth cannot glorify portentuous divinities since it reveals a transfinite universe become multiverse. In this key work of contemporary philosophy, the author shows that thought is not born of wonder but of horror: humanity's assumption of its non-place in the world."

– Emanuele Coccia

SERIAL KILLING: A PHILOSOPHICAL ANTHOLOGY
Edited by Edia Connole & Gary J. Shipley

"*Serial Killing* leaves behind the analysis of the serial killer as a romantic anti-hero, diagnostic category of psychopathology or sociological symptom to offer a collection of essays that infuses the conventional delusions of critical distance with the passionate, homicidal embrace of loving neighborliness. . . . It is properly mad."
 – Scott Wilson

"Those screams you're hearing are philosophy being awoken from its dogmatic slumbers with a stark brutality rarely matched in the history of intellectual anomaly. If there's a more intense sleep-killer compilation out there somewhere, it's concealing itself well." **– Nick Land**

"One of the deepest and darkest truths in psychoanalysis is about the serial nature of the object. We pretend that it is unique, irreplaceable, singular, but it isn't, and it always exists as part of a multiple whose secret truth, to our real horror, is the emptiness or nothing at the center of this excess. In this fascinating collection of essays we find out about this serial perversion of everyday life." **– Jamieson Webster**

"The essays in this volume push to the extremes of philosophy, and of art and literature, in order to speak to our uneasy relationship with what we both desire and abhor." **– Steven Shaviro**

Contributors: Daniel Colucciello Barber, Brad Baumgartner, Charlie Blake, Fred Botting, Brooker Buckingham, Edia Connole, Caoimhe Doyle, Katherine Foyle, Paul J. Ennis, Anthony Faramelli, Florin Flueras, Dominic Fox, Matt Gaede, Irina Gheorghe, Teresa Gillespie, James Harris, Hunter Hunt-Hendrix, Amy Ireland, Lendl Barcelos, Jesuve, Sam Keogh, Heather Masciandaro, Nicola Masciandaro, Dan Mellamphy, Paul O'Brien, David Peak, Alina Popa, David Roden, Niall Scott (Sin-Eater), Yuu Seki, Gary J. Shipley, Aspasia Stephanou, Eugene Thacker.

32802167R00266

Made in the USA
Middletown, DE
18 June 2016